# VOCATIONAL SPECIAL NEEDS

## PREPARING
## T & I TEACHERS

MICHELLE DONNELLY SARKEES
JOHN L. SCOTT

AMERICAN TECHNICAL PUBLISHERS, INC.
ALSIP, ILLINOIS 60658

# CONTENTS

## ACKNOWLEDGMENT

The authors wish to express their gratitude to Dr. Calfrey C. Calhoun of the Business Education Department at the University of Georgia for his expert editing and suggestions, to Douglas H. Gill of the Vocational Special Needs Department at the University of Georgia for his help in developing the timely module concerning curriculum modification, and to Betsy A. Willis for typing the manuscript.

This book is dedicated to Bob, Erin and Sarah Sarkees and Janice, Marci and Ashley Scott.

# HOW TO USE THIS BOOK

This book is divided into ten modules, each covering a specific area of vocational special needs education. Each is self-contained and can be studied independently of the other modules. All modules have the same organizational structure, featuring the following components:

*Introductory Statement:* provides an overview of the module content.

*Module Objectives:* inform readers of the areas they should be familiar with when the module is completed.

*Content:* provides information about a specific area relating to special needs learners in T & I programs. The body of the module is divided into subsections for easy location of pertinent information. Many modules also contain illustrations that can be useful to T & I personnel working with special needs learners.

*Summary Statement:* provides a synopsis of the information covered in the module.

*References:* provide sources of further information related to the module content.

*Self-Assessment Questions:* provide readers with a means of reviewing what they have learned from the module.

*Associated Activities:* provide ideas for activities that can be useful in working with special needs learners enrolled in T & I programs.

*Case Histories:* provide an example of a handicapped or disadvantaged learner who has successfully been integrated into a T & I program. The specific support services, instructional techniques and resources used by the T & I teacher to assist the learner are described. A *Case History Activity* follows in which a similar situation is presented for the reader to complete. Information used in completing the exercise should relate specifically to the situation of the reader. A special profile worksheet is provided for the reader to identify specific personnel, support services, architectural changes, adaptive equipment, curriculum modification, instructional materials/supplies, teaching techniques, agency involvement and job placement assistance which may be necessary.

In addition to the modules, this book contains appendices:

*Appendix A:* provides the names and addresses of professional associations, agencies, and organizations that can assist in developing and implementing vocational special needs programs.

*Appendix B:* provides three easy-to-use readability formulas to determine the reading level of books and materials used in T & I programs.

*Appendix C:* presents an architectural accessibility checklist for identifying possible barriers for handicapped individuals that may exist in vocational facilities.

A glossary is also provided of terms used in this book.

The authors hope that the information presented in this book will help make it possible for handicapped and disadvantaged learners to participate in and benefit from trade and industrial programs.

# MODULE 1

## Justification for Integrating Special Needs Learners into Trade and Industrial Programs

Handicapped and disadvantaged students now have the right to enter vocational programs in order to develop salable skills. Handicapped and disadvantaged students have special needs, but as human beings they have the same needs and desires as anyone else to develop a salable skill, enter the labor force, and become contributing members of society.

Rather than looking for pity and depending on charity, these individuals have expressed a preference for the independence and self sufficiency that can be gained through employment. Trade and industrial (T & I) programs are an excellent source of job preparation for this population. Trade and industrial teachers who have worked with special needs students have found that they have greater ability than was expected. Teachers have expressed amazement at the quality and quantity of specific skills that these students have developed. Successful experience with students who have special needs has led teachers to have more confidence and less anxiety.

There are important reasons for revising attitudes toward special needs learners. Some of the reasons are legal. Other reasons have come from a greater feeling of moral responsibility for the less fortunate in society. However, regardless of the motive for changing attitudes, accommodation to these students must be made. Special needs students are already joining regular classrooms through the process of *mainstreaming*.

It should be noted that the concept of mainstreaming is often misunderstood. Mainstreaming is not a matter of dumping all special needs students back into regular programs. The true meaning of mainstreaming is to place these students in regular programs whenever possible along with the support services that are necessary to help them succeed. In other words, it is a cooperative effort among educational personnel to provide services that will best meet the needs of these learners.

This module contains a rationale for integrating handicapped and disadvantaged students into T & I programs. The rationale is presented in four sections including: (a) Individual Rights and Considerations, (b) Economic Considerations, (c) Legal Considerations, and (d) Commitment of Trade and Industrial Teachers toward Serving Special Needs Students. The goal of this module is to encourage the formation of positive attitudes toward special needs learners.

## MODULE OBJECTIVES

After you have read and reviewed this module, studied the case history, reviewed the self assessment questions, and completed some of the associated activities, you should be able to:

1. Discuss the educational rights of handicapped and disadvantaged persons, as human beings, to develop their vocational potential in T & I programs:

2. List the positive contributions to our economic system of providing special needs individuals with vocational education and employment opportunities;

3. Describe the effect that individuals who are dependent on society have on our economy;

4. List the specific laws related to vocational education for special needs learners and explain the major provisions of each act;

5. Discuss the implications of the legislation for special needs learners for T & I programs;

6. Discuss how the commitment of T & I teachers toward serving special needs students is changing today; and

7. Explain why it is critical for T & I teachers to be committed to serving special needs students in their regular vocational classes.

## RIGHTS AND INDIVIDUAL CONSIDERATIONS

For most people, work is an important part of life; it is more than a way to make a living. Work provides a sense of recognition and self-respect. Many people feel that their work is a part of their identity, and many develop close friendships through work. People who are handicapped or disadvantaged need work and the advantages of work just as other people do; however, prejudices often directed toward special needs persons have caused them to be treated as surplus citizens who are incapable of becoming contributing and productive members of society.

During the past several decades, the rights of handicapped and disadvantaged individuals has been a strong public issue. Although traditionally they have been overlooked and denied the rights that are taken for granted by the rest of us, public schools have been trying to remove the barriers that confront special needs learners. These barriers include attitudinal, educational, and physical obstacles that prevent full participation in regular public school programs. Efforts to provide equal educational rights include access to regular vocational programs.

### The Value of Human Potential

The importance of vocational education for handicapped youth can be seen in a position paper released by the United States Office of Education on June 10, 1978. A summary of important points includes the following:

> It is the position of the U.S. Office of Education that an appropriate comprehensive vocational educa-

tion will be available and accessible to every handicapped person.... Vocational education must provide the education and training to develop occupational competencies .... Appropriate comprehensive vocational education for handicapped persons will provide sequential educational instruction and training appropriate to the needs and progress of each handicapped individual. (National Association of State Boards of Education, 1979).

As educators, we must extend our professional commitment to all students. The worth and dignity of each human being must be recognized. The potential of each individual learner must be assessed and developed to the fullest. The responsibility of each T & I teacher is to help all learners, including special needs students, become productive members of the labor force.

Special needs students should be able to participate in any T & I program. In other words, the standards for T & I programs must be established with the needs of special needs students in mind. Standards should not be used to exclude students. All students deserve the advantage of having a salable skill.

To develop such standards, we must first accept these learners as capable human beings. It may be necessary to revise attitudes about the capabilities required for vocational programs. Certainly, we should not conclude that having one handicap means that a person is handicapped in every way. Such a conclusion has resulted in the denial of opportunities to develop skills. Consequently, the rate of unemployment is usually high for persons with any handicap.

### Why Vocational Education Opportunities Are Necessary

Large numbers of special needs individuals have left our public schools without the salable skills needed to secure a job. They often face unemployment and under-employment. Many remain dependent on society. This causes a drain on our economy as well as a great loss of undeveloped potential.

Participation in T & I programs can provide the first real feeling of accomplishment that these students experience. School has given many of them a sense of frustration and failure. The opportunity to enroll in vocational programs promises them a chance to develop their aptitudes and abilities. Perhaps for the first time, these students can achieve success and develop a sense of self-worth and independence.

## The Mainstreaming Effort

Enrollment in T & I classes generally will be accomplished through mainstreaming. However, mainstreaming does not mean that every handicapped or disadvantaged student will be integrated into regular programs. It does mean that each learner, as an individual, must be given the chance to develop his or her vocational potential to the maximum degree.

Mainstreaming also means that proper support services and resources necessary for each special needs learner must be provided. This will make the task of providing appropriate training for these students much easier for T & I teachers. Therefore, the total responsibility for preparing these students with a salable skill will be shared. The technical knowledge and skills represented in T & I departments must be combined with the expertise of special education teachers, the support of agencies, and the aid of resource personnel if the mainstreaming process is to be successful. Through coordination and cooperation, it will be possible to plan so that the special needs learners can experience success in regular programs.

## ECONOMIC CONSIDERATIONS

There are important economic reasons for providing vocational education opportunities for special needs learners. Recent statistics support the need to expand vocational training opportunities for special needs learners.

## Economic Facts

Consider the following economic facts:

1. Of all families on welfare in this country, 20 percent have disabled people as the head of the household. (Bowe,1978)

2. Men who are disabled earn an average weekly salary that is twenty-two percent lower than the weekly salary earned by men who are not disabled. (Levitan and Taggart, 1977).

3. During an average year, approximately three-quarters of all non-disabled adults hold jobs. Of all disabled adults, only about two-fifths hold jobs. (Levitan and Taggart, 1977).

4. The average yearly income for totally disabled individuals who are married was approximately $6,000. Among those who are not married the average yearly income was about $1,600. (Social Security Administration, 1972).

5. Educating the handicapped is cost beneficial. The total cost of caring for a handicapped individual for 60 years, given the estimated figure for the care of an institutionalized person of $2,500 per year, would be $250,000. If the same person is given an appropriate education and is ultimately employed, there would be a positive contribution of $60,000 rather than a cost of $250,000. (Meetings and debates of the 90th Congress, U.S. Congressional Record, CXIV, No. 150).

6. Estimates for support individuals on welfare or related public assistance program now average over $10,000 per year per client. Contrast this to the study conducted in 1974 by the Olympus Corporation which found that average cost per completer in vocational education programs on a national scale was approximately $2,400. Even if the excess cost of educating special needs learners in vocational education is more than the average cost, it would not exceed the cost of providing them with public assistance.

3

7. The cost to society of taking care of a disabled person in an institution exceeds $250,000 over the lifespan of each person. (United States Office of Education, 1974).

8. It costs over $12 billion each year to supply 2.8 million disabled people with monthly social security disability insurance (SSDI) benefits. (Social Security Administration, 1978).

9. The cost of providing assistance to disabled individuals who are dependent on society because they are not employed exceeds $100 billion each year. (American Coalition of Citizens with Disabilities, Inc., 1979).

10. In 1975 nine percent of the gross national product was spent on dependent living programs. (Bowe, 1978). Dependent living programs are those which pay for the support of individuals who are not able to take care of themselves (e.g., programs for the severely disabled).

11. It is predicted that if disadvantaged and minority youth are not aided in developing their vocational and employment opportunities in the future, the unemployment rate for this group could be 13 times greater than for the general population by 1990. (Pinn, 1979).

## Educational Facts

The following educational facts indicate that economic conditions may not change for some time:

1. Of those individuals judged totally disabled, 44 percent were reported to have an elementary school education or less, 33 percent had a high school education or less, and only 9 percent had any college education. (Social Security Administration, 1972).

2. The Bureau of Education for the Handicapped estimated in 1976 that less than 25 percent of the handicapped students leaving school were pursuing post education or were fully employed. At that time it was predicted that two-thirds of the handicapped population leaving school were either unemployed or underemployed. (Bureau of Education for the Handicapped, 1976).

3. The Bureau of Education for the handicapped estimates that, with vocational education services, 75 percent of the physically handicapped and 90 percent of the mentally handicapped could work either in a sheltered environment or in the competitive labor market. Without these services, however, millions of handicapped youth will be unemployed, underemployed, on public assistance or totally dependent on society. (Comptroller General of the United States, 1976).

4. In 1976 only four percent of all the individuals registered in Title I programs of the Comprehensive Employment and Training Act (CETA) were identified as handicapped. (Department of Labor, 1977).

5. A recent study revealed that only two percent of the total enrollment of students in vocational education programs was identified as handicapped learners. This figure is surprising considering that the Education Amendments of 1976 provided a fund for vocational education opportunities for these students. (United States Office of Education, 1978).

6. In 1975 over five million secondary level disadvantaged students in our nation's schools were not given an opportunity to develop their vocational potential through enrollment in vocational education programs. (United States Office of Education, 1975).

7. In 1975 over four and a half million disadvantaged youth who were identified as drop-outs left school without a skill to help them find a job. (United States Office of Education, 1975).

These facts present a clear picture of the implications to our economy. Unless a strong commitment is made on the part of educators to provide these learners with the knowledge and skills needed to secure employment, the burden of providing for them will rest with the taxpayers of this country. The cost of dependent living programs such as unemployment, social security disability insurance, and welfare payments runs high.

The cost of providing vocational preparation for special needs learners in regular T & I programs may exceed the cost of preparing other students. These excess costs provide the support personnel, facilities modifications, adaptive equipment and aids, instructional materials, and curriculum alternatives necessary for these students to successfully acquire a vocational skill. It may be argued that education cannot afford these extra costs. However, the statistics reveal what it will mean to these students, to our economy, and to our society if these learners are allowed to leave school without a salable skill. Also, it must be emphasized that not all special needs students mainstreamed into regular programs will require these resources and modifications, and those who do may not need them continuously.

It is far more cost effective to educate special needs learners for competitive employment while they are in school than to train them through other programs. Vocational education programs represent the most practical way of providing opportunities for these individuals. Trade and industrial teachers can contribute by joining the effort to match student abilities to specific vocational skills and provide the labor force with a source of capable workers who will add to our economic system rather than deplete it.

## LEGAL CONSIDERATIONS

### Background for Legislation

Recent legislation has been passed to ensure the educational rights of special needs individuals in this country. Before these laws existed, handicapped and disadvantaged people were ignored by society and were not considered to have the same rights as other citizens. Pressure from lobby and parent groups began to mount. These groups asserted that all human beings, as individuals, deserve to share the same rights. A great number of lawsuits were filed across the country demanding equal educational opportunities for all people. As a result, laws were passed to protect the rights of handicapped individuals.

Vocational education is recognized as the most realistic method of assisting individuals to bridge the gap between education and employment. Therefore, the same rights to vocational training should be available to all students in our secondary and post-secondary schools. The legislation described in the following text guarantees these rights.

*The Vocational Education Act of 1963* (Public Law 88–210). This law was based on the recognition that individuals with special needs require assistance in order to achieve success in regular vocational programs. This was the beginning of a movement to provide opportunities to develop vocational potential in the form of salable skills for the competitive labor market.

The Act stated that vocational education services should be available to "persons who have academic, socioeconomic, or other handicaps that prevent them from succeeding in the regular vocational education program." It provided for access to vocational training and retraining for all people according to interests, needs, and abilities.

However, few vocational education resources were made available to special needs students as a result of this law. A national survey, conducted three years after this law went into effect, identified only 79 programs in 12 states that were preparing these students with vocational skills. In reality, the law had served primarily to focus attention on the need to provide vocational education opportunities for this population.

*The Vocational Education Amendments of 1968 (Public Law 90–576).* This legislation further emphasized the need to provide vocational education skills for special needs learners. It separated this population into two distinct categories—disadvantaged individuals and handicapped individuals. Separate vocational programs were discouraged except when they were in the best interest of these students. Otherwise, students were expected to be integrated into regular programs and provided with appropriate support services and resources.

In order to aid states in providing these services, the law allocated federal funds such that, for any fiscal year, a state must use at least 10 percent of its basic vocational funds to provide programs for the handicapped and 15 percent of the basic vocational funds to provide programs for the disadvantaged.

These funds can be used only to provide services over and above those available to all students in regular vocational programs. For example, the funds can be used to provide many services that would be helpful to the vocational teacher in working with special needs learners. Some of the resources that could be provided by these funds include: (a) staff development, (b) flexible scheduling, (c) recruitment activities to reach potential employers, (d) curriculum modifications, (e) equipment modifications, (f) development of appropriate instructional materials, (g) specific educational services to assist special needs students to succeed in vocational programs, and (h) additional staff to coordinate and supervise work-study programs.

*The Education for All Handicapped Children Act of 1975 (Public Law 94–142).* This law, considered to be a civil rights bill for the handicapped, expresses a national commitment to provide a free and appropriate public education for every handicapped person between the ages of three and twenty-one. It assures more than eight million handicapped students in this country the right to develop their potential to the maximum. States and local school systems are required to provide all identified handicapped students with an education designed to meet their needs and abilities as well as related services necessary to aid them in school.

This far-reaching law contains six general themes for the handicapped: (1) a free, appropriate public education; (2) an individual education program; (3) access to records; (4) the right of due process; (5) placement in the least restrictive environment; and (6) nondiscriminatory testing. Each of these provisions has implications for T & I teachers who are working with handicapped students in their programs.

1. A free, appropriate public education assures that a special education program with appropriate related services will be developed for each identified handicapped student. These students must be provided with the same educational opportunities that all other students enjoy, including access to vocational education programs that are realistic in light of their abilities and interests.

2. An individual education program (IEP) is mandated for every handicapped student each year. This plan specifies long-range and short-term goals developed especially for the student as well as the support services that are required to meet those goals. Evaluation criteria are included in the IEP so that progress can be determined.

The IEP is developed by the teachers responsible for providing educational services to the student. If a handicapped student is enrolled in a vocational program, the vocational teacher should be involved in developing, implementing and evaluating this plan. A meeting is held with teachers, parents, and an administrator to discuss and approve the IEP. It is evaluated at least once a year and revised to meet the changing needs of the student.

Trade and industrial teachers who have handicapped students in their programs should combine efforts with special education personnel and become involved in developing specific program objectives, participating in the IEP conference, and helping to evaluate the progress of the student. This topic is discussed in detail in Module 4.

3. The provision of access to records gives parents of handicapped students the right to view all records that are on file for their son or daughter. The parents

also may ask to have changes made in the records if they believe the information is incorrect or misleading. Individuals 18 years or older have the right of access to their own records.

4. The right of due process guarantees that a specific procedure must be followed in thoroughly evaluating a student thought to be handicapped so that the decision regarding the proper educational placement is in the best interest of the student. Parents are involved at all steps of this evaluation and decision-making process. This guarantee prevents schools from placing students in special education programs who do not really belong there. This process is discussed in detail in Module 3.

5. Placement in the "least restrictive environment" gives handicapped students the right to be placed in regular education programs whenever possible. They are assured of being placed in classrooms and programs that do not restrict their abilities.

Handicapped students can only be placed in separate classes or programs when it can be shown that the student cannot succeed in the regular program even with the aid of appropriate support services. This provision means that more and more handicapped students will be mainstreamed into regular vocational programs where they can learn to function in a normal environment rather than in isolated classrooms. Support services will help the vocational teacher work with these students.

6. The guarantee of nondiscriminatory testing means that the tests used to evaluate handicapped students cannot be racially or culturally biased and must be administered in the language spoken in the student's home. This provision also states that the results of only one test cannot be used to make a decision about placing the student. A variety of test results must be considered before a decision can be made.

*The Rehabilitation Act of 1973 (Public*

*Law 93–112): Sections 503 and 504.* In the past, employers were encouraged to hire handicapped persons by telling them that it was good for business. It was presented as an economic issue. However, even though employer studies have shown that handicapped workers perform as well on the job as nonhandicapped workers, affirmative action hiring was not taking place.

Section 503 of this Act represents an historic step to provide employment opportunities for handicapped individuals. Any employer receiving federal assistance in the form of contracts for $2,500 or more is required to develop an affirmative action plan to recruit, hire, train and advance in employment handicapped individuals. Employers receiving federal contracts for $50,000 or more and having 50 or more employees must develop and implement an affirmative action program within 120 days that outlines specific policies and procedures regarding handicapped individuals. This program must be reviewed and updated once a year.

Section 503 also requires that employers make a "reasonable accommodation" for handicapped workers. This means that specific changes must be made to the work environment to meet the needs of the handicapped worker. These changes may require, for instance, that a work table be raised or lowered to accommodate a handicapped employee or that a blind employee be provided with a tape recorder. This requirement does not mean that an employer must assume a huge financial hardship, as in totally rebuilding or renovating a facility, in order to make the work environment accessible. Funds are available to help employers make appropriate changes to the work site.

This move to regulate the hiring, training and promoting of qualified handicapped persons represents a positive step in providing this population with employment opportunities to help them achieve economic independence. As federal contractors and subcontractors begin to actively recruit handicapped individuals for available positions they will look to existing vocational programs for assistance in identifying and attracting qualified handicapped persons who have the requisite skills for employment.

Section 504 of this law, passed in 1977, guarantees basic civil rights for handicapped individuals. This means that qualified handicapped individuals cannot be denied access to private or public programs and activities that receive HEW funds solely because of their disability. This includes all public secondary and post-secondary facilities.

According to the 504 regulations, the term "handicapped" includes those individuals who have impairments or conditions such as "speech, hearing, visual and orthopedic impairments, cerebral palsy, epilepsy, muscular dystrophy, multiple sclerosis, cancer, diabetes, heart disease, mental retardation, emotional illness, and specific learning disabilities." In addition, alcohol and drug addicts are also considered to be handicapped individuals. Clearly, this will include a great many more people than were previously considered to be handicapped.

Discrimination is no longer allowed in educating handicapped individuals, in admitting them to vocation programs or in providing them with equal employment opportunities. Fair treatment of the disabled in each of these areas is now the rule. Section 504 assures a free, appropriate public education for the handicapped with any necessary related services. Handicapped students must be placed in regular programs to the maximum extent possible with supplementary aids and services to help them succeed. This includes access to vocational education programs. Specific modifications may have to be made to vocational facilities and programs in order to make them accessible to this population.

Specific requirements are set forth for secondary and adult education programs, post-secondary education programs and employers. Public elementary or secondary programs must provide handicapped students the opportunity to participate in existing services such as: regular program options, nonacademic services, extracurricular activities, school-sponsored interest groups and clubs, and counseling services. Evaluation procedures used to assess the aptitude or achievement level of the learner must be appropriate and must be administered periodically. An Individualized Education Program (IEP) must be developed and implemented for each handicapped individual according to the guidelines set forth in Public Law 94-142 (Education for All Handicapped Children Act). In addition, reasonable accommodation must be made to assure that programs, services, and facilities are accessible to the handicapped.

Post-secondary programs cannot discriminate against handicapped individuals in recruitment or admissions. Admission quotas cannot be used. Any admission tests, including standardized tests, must be selected and administered so that the test records the aptitude or achievement level of the student rather than the disability. Reasonable modifications must be made to insure accessibility to programs, services and facilities. Modifications, such as extended time for completing course or degree requirements and adapting the manner in which the course is taught, must be made according to the specific needs of the individual. In addition, auxiliary or support aids must be provided as necessary. These aids might include special equipment or classroom aids for physically handicapped learners, interpreters, library readers, cassette recorders and taped text information. Often these aids can be provided by outside agencies or organizations.

Employers may not discriminate against qualified handicapped persons in recruitment, hiring or promotion on the basis of their disability. Employers are required to make facilities accessible, to modify work schedules, to restructure jobs and to provide for the modification of necessary equipment or devices. However, the extent or cost of these accommodations cannot create an undue hardship on the employer. Pre-employment medical examinations or specific questions regarding the handicapping condition are not allowed under the 504 regulations.

*The Education Amendments of 1976, Title II (Public Law 94-482).* Public Law 94-482 should be understood in relationship to the regulations stated in Public Law 94-142 and Sections 503 and 504 of the Rehabilitation Act of 1973. The content of these Acts is similar. They complement one another and should be implemented cooperatively.

This law emphasizes the need to prepare all students for employment. It therefore attempts to assure that handicapped and disadvantaged individuals will be granted equal access to programs and services that have often been denied to them. This legislation requires states wishing to receive federal vocational education monies to meet certain requirements.

States must expend 10 percent of the funds from their basic state grants to provide vocational education opportunities for handicapped students and 20 percent for disadvantaged students. Set-aside funds allotted for vocational education for disadvantaged persons must be used primarily in areas of high youth unemployment or school dropouts.

These federal funds are to be matched on a fifty-fifty basis with state and local funds. All money spent must be used to assist special needs learners in regular existing vocational education programs whenever possible.

Federal set-aside funds for vocational education for handicapped persons must be used for purposes that match the goals stated in Public Law 94-142. As a result, handicapped students must be educated and enrolled in regular vocational programs to the greatest extent possible in order to satisfy the requirement for the least restrictive environment. The specific nature of the vocational education program goals and objectives for each handicapped student must be planned and implemented according to the contents of the IEP.

The state plan for vocational education must parallel with the state plan for the education of handicapped students. Specific provisions for providing programs and services for special needs learners must be included in annual and five-year state plans developed for vocational education.

National and state advisory councils for vocational education must include one or more persons who have special knowledge, experience or qualifications relating to the specific educational needs of physically or mentally handicapped individuals. These councils must also insure representation by one or more persons who have knowledge about the needs of poor and disadvantaged individuals. The input from these members of the advisory councils is essential because it can affect decisions made about vocational education opportunities for special needs individuals.

*The Comprehensive Employment and Training Act, Amendments of 1978 (Public Law 95-524).* The Comprehensive Employment and Training Act (CETA) was passed in 1973 to provide services for unemployed, underemployed and economically disadvantaged individuals. Criteria for eligibility also includes in-school youth who fall into one of these categories. These services are provided in the form of training and employment opportunities. They can be provided through such vehicles as public service employment positions, classroom and laboratory training, work experience programs, and on-the-job training experiences. The overall objective of CETA is to assure that job training and other related services lead to self-sufficiency through employment.

Under the new CETA regulations, handicapped individuals are designated as a "special emphasis group." They are considered to be eligible for participation

9

in CETA programs, regardless of their income levels, because their disabilities may cause substantial barriers to employment.

Other provisions for handicapped individuals included in the amended CETA act are: (a) handicapped representatives must be represented on each government agency planning council, (b) handicapped membership must be included on each state employment and training council, (c) efforts to remove architectural barriers must be undertaken by participating government agencies, and (d) public information programs must be developed to provide job training and employment opportunities for disabled veterans.

The objective of the CETA legislation is to provide local communities with funds to develop and administer manpower training programs that will train individuals in areas which are identified as local employment problems. Each local labor market has specific labor needs, degrees of unemployment, and target population groups.

Areas with a population of more than 100,000 people which are awarded funds through CETA are called prime sponsors. To apply for funds under this Act, a unit of local government with a population of 100,000 or more should contact the Department of Labor. Examples of units of local governments which may apply as prime sponsors for CETA funds include large cities, counties, or consortiums. Units of government with smaller populations can be covered by "balance-of-state prime sponsors" usually coordinated through the governor's manpower office.

Each prime sponsor must develop a comprehensive employment and training plan consisting of a long-range plan and an annual plan. These plans must provide information regarding: (a) plans to involve educational agencies in cooperative planning, (b) plans for the use of public vocational education facilities, (c) a description of services and facilities that are available, and (d) the methods utilized in determining how services will be delivered. The training programs offered by prime sponsors are developed in response to specific local needs.

Prime sponsors are encouraged by CETA regulations to coordinate with existing secondary and post-secondary vocational programs involved in developing and implementing the necessary training programs for CETA participants. Prime sponsors often contract with secondary and post-secondary vocational education institutions to provide the training necessary for their CETA participants. This format will help to establish articulation and cooperative planning between vocational education and CETA.

Prime sponsors are also required by CETA legislation to develop an individualized employment plan for each participant in a Title II program. This plan is essentially a detailed description and evaluation of training and support services provided for the individual. These services include counseling, preplacement assessment, skill training, remedial and basic instruction, personal development skills, job exploration, placement assistance, financial allowances, and retraining and upgrading services. In the case of handicapped participants, this individualized employment plan can be coordinated with the learner's individualized education program (IEP).

The title most likely to affect vocational education programs is Title IV, Youth Programs. The programs funded under this section were originally authorized by the Youth Employment and Demonstration Projects Act of 1977 (YEDPA). These programs include: (a) Youth Incentive Entitlement Pilot Projects (YIEPP), (b) Youth Community Conservation and Improvement Projects (YCCIP), and (c) Youth Employment and Training Programs. The final program originally authorized by YEDPA is the Youth Adult Conservation Corps, now covered by Title VIII of the CETA amendments of 1978.

The primary objective of Title IV is to present options which may be helpful in solving problems associated with youth unemployment. Local prime sponsors receiving funds under this section are responsible for administering programs which provide training and support services for youth to make them more employable, assist them in finding employment, and help to ease the transition from school to work.

In the future, it is expected that more vocational education programs will be incorporated into this process in coordination with CETA prime sponsors. Disadvantaged and handicapped individuals will most certainly be target populations for training programs established under these regulations.

Throughout the provisions in this Act is an emphasis on developing linkages and promoting cooperative efforts between CETA (prime sponsors) and vocational education programs (educational/agencies/institutions). It is hoped that this proposed cooperation will decrease the number of duplicated services and increase the training and services provided for eligible individuals. Open communication between vocational educators and CETA prime sponsors is important if these two program areas are to complement each other with parallel goals, objectives and implementation strategies.

CETA programs can be a source of assistance to vocational programs by providing eligible students with wages or allowances while they attend school to develop the skills necessary to succeed in the competitive labor market as well as supplementing the vocational training that they receive in the vocational programs.

### Implications for Trade and Industrial Programs

The past several decades have been years of action. Several laws have been passed to protect the civil rights of handicapped and disadvantaged people in our society. Because of this legislation, equal educational and employment benefits are available to all citizens.

One of the educational rights guaranteed to special needs learners through these laws is access to vocational programs through which salable skills can be developed. Hopefully, preparation for employment will make it possible for these individuals to contribute to the economy rather than becoming dependent on society.

There is a great challenge facing T & I teachers as a result of the equal rights legislation for special needs individuals. Handicapped and disadvantaged students will be mainstreamed into T & I programs. However, laws also require that teachers be assisted through appropriate resources and support services.

The funds made available through the legislation will benefit the special needs cause. This money can be spent in a number of ways to help these students to succeed in T & I programs. For instance, program and curriculum modifications, special materials, and equipment and facilities modifications can be provided from federal and state set-aside funds.

The laws granting equal rights to special needs people are here to stay. Rather than offering these people pity, educators must begin to provide them with opportunities to develop their vocational potential. The time for action has come. With in-service training and cooperative planning among professional personnel, preparing these learners for competitive employment can be a shared task.

## COMMITMENT OF TRADE AND INDUSTRIAL TEACHERS TOWARD SERVING SPECIAL NEEDS STUDENTS

The commitment of T & I teachers and other school personnel toward serving special needs students is critical. Only with commitment will the promises of equality of opportunity for all students become a reality. This section of the module presents the story of the commitment of T & I teachers toward serving special needs students in existing T & I programs.

## Past Commitment Lacking

In the past, the commitment of T & I teachers toward serving special needs students in regular vocational programs has been lukewarm at best. There have been many reasons for reluctance to work with these students. One of these is that negative attitudes, stereotypical thinking and misconceptions have run wild. For instance, one T & I teacher expressed the belief that special needs students prefer dull, repetitive work. This teacher said that these students have no need of the extensive vocational training offered in T & I programs.

Another reason has been the local practice of placing students into existing vocational classes without adequately preparing students and teachers. Appropriate support services have been lacking. The problems associated with placing students in appropriate employment situations after they have received training has been a frustrating experience for teachers. This frustration has contributed to a negative attitude toward serving special needs students in vocational programs.

## The Key to Increased Commitment

Addressing the issues related to vocational education for special needs students is an enormous task. The task calls for an increased commitment to serve these students as well as a new openness accompanied by fresh approaches. The key to increased commitment is adequate preparation for the task.

Today, the level of commitment of T & I teachers toward serving special needs students is rapidly increasing. T & I teachers, special education teachers, special needs support personnel, counselors, school administrators, and interested members of the community at the local school level are learning how to work together effectively to meet the challenge of educating special needs students.

## Teacher Preparation

Within the past several years, the preparation of school personnel, including vocational teachers, has emerged as a top priority. Many states and local school systems have recognized the need for teacher education for those who work with or will be working with special needs students. Programs at the state and local levels have been conducted to assist educators to understand the need for their participation in this task. Training programs have focused on the development of teacher competence. Effective curriculum materials have been developed. A number of states have gone so far as to make course work in the area of special needs a certification requirement.

As local schools respond to the mandates of equal rights legislation, mainstreaming efforts are increasing. More special needs students are being placed in regular vocational classes and more support services are being provided to help these students succeed.

## Attitudinal Barriers

Attitudinal barriers are beginning to dissolve. The negative attitudes held by T & I teachers in the past toward serving special needs students are beginning to crumble. Many of these teachers are now actively involved in mainstreaming efforts. They are learning that special needs students can be successful in T & I programs when necessary support services are available. As these students succeed, T & I teachers should feel an increased sense of confidence in their effectiveness as teachers of special needs students.

## Alternative to Trade and Industrial Teacher Commitment

Without the continuous commitment of all educators, as well as the provision of appropriate educational opportunities and support services, special needs students will continue to experience great difficulty in becoming self-sufficient, productive workers. Moreover, trade and industrial teachers will be deprived of the opportunity to share their knowledge and skills with these students. The dwindling number of young men and women who want to prepare for a trade or occupation will become even smaller. The end result of the lack of commitment of T & I teachers will be the unacceptable, age-old problem of waste, idleness, and dependency.

## SUMMARY

Every handicapped and disadvantaged student deserves the same educational opportunities that are available to other students enrolled in public schools. This right includes access to regular vocational programs where they can develop salable skills. Such skills will enable them to become contributing members of the labor force.

Special needs learners, by public demand and by recent legislation, must be given the right to develop a productive skill. In order to assure this right, educators must begin to change the negative image they hold of these individuals. This means forming new impressions of the abilities of these learners and the types of skills they can develop. It means reconsidering the range of jobs in which they can function.

In order for equal educational opportunities to be made available to special needs learners, there is a great need for all educators, including T & I personnel, to assume more responsibilty in working with them in existing programs. This will mean pooling the skills, resources, and knowledge of teachers. If these students are allowed to leave school without a salable skill, a great percentage of them will remain dependent on society through unemployment and public assistance. This causes a heavy drain on the economic system of our country. It also wastes the vocational potential that could be developed and put to constructive use in the labor market. Therefore, it is necessary that local school systems accept the responsibility to provide special needs students with appropriate vocational opportunities by providing them with access to vocational education programs.

## REFERENCES

Bowe, F. *Handicapping America.* New York: Harper and Row, 1978.

Disability statistics. *American Coalition of Citizens with Disabilities Newsletter,* 1979, *2* (1), 5.

Jensen, R. Equal access for the disadvantaged: the need to break some barriers. *American Vocational Journal,* 1977, *52* (6), 28–30.

Levitan, S. and Taggart, R. *Jobs for the disabled.* Washington, D.C.: George Washington University, Center for Manpower Policy Studies, 1976.

Mainstreaming and the law. *Exceptional Parent,* 1978, *8* (4), L1–L2.

National Association of State Boards of Education. *Vocational education of handicapped youth—state of the art.* Washington, D.C.: Author, 1979.

Phelps, A., and Halloran, W. Assurance for handicapped learners. *American Vocational Journal,* 1976, *5*(8), 36–37.

Pinn, J. Reaching our forgotten inner-city youth. *American Vocational Journal,* 1979, *54* (5), 33–35.

Schools and employers have major responsibilities under new 504 regulations. *Manpower and Vocational Education Weekly,* May 5, 1977, 6–8.

Social Security Administration. *Work disability in the United States.* Washington, D.C.: Author, 1978.

Tindall, L. Breaking down the barriers for disabled learners. *American Vocational Journal,* 1975, *50* (8), 47–49.

Tomlinson, R., and Albright, L. Public Law 94-142 is coming! Are you ready? *School Shop,* 1977, *36* (6), 28–31.

Weintraub, F., Abeson, A., Ballard, J., LaVor, M. (Ed.). *Public policy and the education of exceptional children.* Reston, Virginia: The Council for Exceptional Children, 1976.

# SELF ASSESSMENT: JUSTIFICATION FOR INTEGRATING SPECIAL NEEDS LEARNERS INTO TRADE AND INDUSTRIAL PROGRAMS

1. Why should handicapped and disadvantaged individuals be given the opportunity to develop their vocational potential?
2. What role does work play in the lives of special needs people?
3. Why have special needs individuals been excluded by society from education and employment?
4. What are a few things that T & I teachers will have to consider when special needs students enter their programs?
5. Why has the rate of unemployment been so high among handicapped and disadvantaged persons? What can be done about this situation?
6. Explain why participation in trade and industrial programs can be the first successful experience that special needs learners have ever had in school.
7. What effect will the mainstreaming movement have on trade and industrial programs?
8. What effect will integrating special needs students into trade and industrial programs have on our economy?
9. If the cost of providing education for special needs students exceeds the cost of preparing other students, why should extra funds be spent for this purpose?
10. Name several things that can be provided with funds that are set aside for special needs students that will benefit them in trade and industrial programs.
11. Why has legislation been passed to guarantee special needs individuals equal access to vocational education and employment opportunities?
12. Name the specific laws passed that relate to vocational education for people with special needs and the important provisions of each.
13. What effect will this legislation have on trade and industrial programs?
14. Why have T & I teachers been reluctant to work with special needs students in the past?

# ASSOCIATED ACTIVITIES

1. Your administrator has asked you to talk to the other teachers in the T & I department of your school at a special meeting because you have been working with several handicapped and disadvantaged students in your program. You are to address the issue of integrating these students into T & I programs. In outline form, prepare the notes that you will use for your presentation.

2. List the barriers that can face special needs learners when they attempt to enroll in vocational programs. Next, examine your own program and list the specific barriers that would make it difficult for these students to enter and/or succeed. Prepare a plan to eliminate or modify these barriers so that learners with special needs could succeed in your program.

3. You have decided to submit a paper to your State T & I Journal. The topic you have chosen is "Mainstreaming: A Reality for T & I Programs." Prepare a two-to-three-page paper containing all the important points of this topic for possible publication.

4. Special state funds have been set aside to provide support services and aids for handicapped and disadvantaged students in vocational programs. Because you are working with special needs students, your supervisor has asked you to identify what you need in order to help them succeed in your program. First, list the resources that can be purchased with special set-aside funds. Next, identify the specific items that would help the special needs learners in your program. Give a reason for including each item on your list.

5. Schedule an appointment with your school administrator to look into the possibility of obtaining some of the special set-aside funds for special needs learners. If a formal proposal is required, ask the special education teacher and the administrator to help you prepare it for funding consideration.

## CASE HISTORY: KARYN'S STORY

Karyn is a mildly handicapped learner enrolled in a nurse's aide program. She has been in a special education program for educable mentally retarded students since the fifth grade. Her records show that she reads at the fourth grade level with little difficulty and can independently perform math problems at the fifth grade level.

Karyn has participated in several regular classes during the last three years. She has received passing grades in these classes with the help of the special education teacher.

Karyn has wanted to be a nurse's aide since she read about this area in her career education class. She is cheerful, cooperative, friendly and gets along well with others in the class. She always tries her best on class and laboratory assignments, and she takes unfinished work back to the special education class with her. Her determination and dedication have made her progress much faster in the nurse's aide program than would be expected.

When Karyn was first enrolled in the nurse's aide program, the instructor had some concerns about her ability to develop marketable skills that would lead to employment. However, the special education teacher has involved the instructor in the development of Karyn's IEP (individual education program). The IEP includes long-range goals for Karyn to work toward during the coming year, short-term instructional objectives that will help the instructor in planning for Karyn, and the support services that will be provided to help her proceed. By using the IEP as a management tool, the program instructor feels confident that Karyn will be able to realize her career goal, though it may take her a longer period of time to successfully complete the program requirements.

The special education teacher has been an important support to both Karyn and the instructor. Karyn spends several hours a day in the special classroom. The teacher helps her by reviewing what is covered in the nurse's aide class as well as covering technical vocabulary terms, written assignments and handouts on an appropriate reading level, working on related math, rewriting and administering tests orally.

For example, Karyn has mastered such procedures as bed making, general comfort measures, and taking blood pressure and pulse recordings. She is currently having problems taking temperatures. The instructor and the special education teacher are using cooperative planning measures to work with Karyn in this area.

## CASE HISTORY ACTIVITY

Joe has just enrolled in your program. He has been diagnosed as mildly mentally retarded and is enrolled in a special education program in your school. Joe seems to be shy and insecure about his ability to succeed in the program, though he expresses an interest in being there. He presents no behavior problems. He has not made any friends in the classroom yet.

The special education teacher has contacted you to provide you with some initial information about Joe. You know that his reading level is 3.8 and his math level is 4.1.

Based on this information, complete the case history profile worksheet for Joe's participation in your program.

# CASE HISTORY PROFILE WORKSHEET

Student: _____ Page: _____

Handicapping Condition(s): _____

T & I Program: _____ Academic Levels: _____

Career Goal/Occupational Interest: _____

Considerations (e.g., medication, behavior): _____

_____

| Adaptation | Specific Services Needed | Where to Obtain Service |
|---|---|---|
| Cooperative Planning (School Personnel) | | |
| Support Services | | |
| Architectural Changes | | |
| Adaptive Equipment | | |
| Curriculum Modification | | |
| Instructional Materials/ Supplies | | |
| Teaching Techniques | | |
| Agency Involvement | | |
| Possible Job Placement | | |

# MODULE 2

## Identifying Special Needs Learners and Helping Them Succeed in Your Program

In order for T & I teachers to work more effectively with special needs students, they should become familiar with the general characteristics associated with each group. Ten special needs groups are described in this module: (1) mentally handicapped learners, (2) learners with emotional problems, (3) visually handicapped learners, (4) hearing impaired learners, (5) learning disabled learners, (6) speech impaired learners, (7) health impaired learners, (8) physically handicapped learners, (9) multi-handicapped learners, and (10) disadvantaged learners. Although general characteristics are given in this module for each category, keep in mind that individual differences will be seen in each learner.

Each special needs learner is unique and has a learning capacity rate and style that differs from other students in the same category. Therefore, each student will progress at a rate based on individual abilities and interests, regardless of the characteristics that are associated with the category to which he/she has been assigned.

This module presents an overview of the nature and needs of handicapped and disadvantaged students. Hopefully, the information will help T & I teachers to better understand the learning problems of these students so that they can adapt their programs to provide appropriate vocational education opportunities.

## MODULE OBJECTIVES

After you have read and reviewed this module, studied the case histories, reviewed the self assessment questions, and completed the associated activities, you should be able to:

1. Differentiate between (a) handicapped learners, (b) disadvantaged learners, and (c) special needs learners;

2. Identify the specific categories of handicapped learners;

3. List the general characteristics associated with each category of handicapped learners;

4. Identify the specific categories of disadvantaged learners;

5. List the general characteristics associated with each category of disadvantaged learners.

## SPECIAL NEEDS LEARNERS— GENERAL DEFINITIONS

### Definitions

It is important for T & I teachers to know who special needs learners are and what their needs are in order to provide appropriate vocational education opportunities. Learners with special needs are generally divided into two major categories—handicapped and disadvantaged:

1. "Handicapped individuals" are those who are mentally retarded, hard-of-hearing, deaf, speech impaired, visually handicapped, seriously emotionally disturbed, crippled, or health impaired in other ways that require special education and related services. Because of their handicapping condition, these people cannot succeed in the regular vocational education program without special education assistance. They may require a modified vocational education program (Education Amendments of 1976, Public Law 94–482, Section 195).

Many handicapped individuals can be productive if they are given appropriate vocational education opportunities. Educators estimate that 75 percent of physically handicapped and 90 percent of mentally handicapped individuals can be employable either in the competitive labor market or in more highly supervised work settings such as sheltered workshops and work activity centers. The skills and expertise of T & I personnel can be significant in providing opportunities for these individuals to become independent and self-sufficient (Comptroller General of the United States, 1976).

2. "Disadvantaged individuals" are those (other than handicapped persons) who have academic or economic handicaps and who require special services and assistance in order to enable them to succeed in vocational education programs (Education Amendments of 1976, Public Law 94–482, Section 195).

3. "Special needs individuals" are those persons who need special assistance or services in order to enter a regular vocational education program and successfully complete the requirements.

This population includes both handicapped and disadvantaged individuals as well as other groups such as minority or racial group members, persons with limited English-speaking ability, persons in correctional institutes, migrant workers, and persons who are gifted and talented (National Center for Research in Vocational Education, 1979).

These individuals will have difficulty succeeding in vocational education programs without assistance in the form of support services, different teaching techniques and/or specific modifications in vocational programs and facilities.

## MENTALLY HANDICAPPED LEARNERS

"Mentally retarded" means significantly subaverage general intellectual functioning existing concurrently with deficits in adaptive behavior and manifested during the developmental period, which adversely affects (an individual's) educational performance (Public Law 94–142, 121 a. 5).

Illustration 2.1 provides an overview of general characteristics often associated with mentally retarded learners. If you have a student in your program who frequently exhibits a number of these characteristics and is not receiving special education services, refer the individual for appropriate assessment and diagnosis.

Mentally retarded learners have below-average general intellectual functioning abilities. This means that they perform poorly on achievement tests and score below average on individual standardized intelligence tests. It is important to note that the results of intelligence tests, or I.Q. scores, cannot alone accurately predict the social and vocational potential of a person. The I.Q. score merely predicts the potential academic ability level of the individual. Many people with low I.Q. scores can be successful at developing a vocational skill and finding employment. Other factors such as performance skills, verbal ability, problem-solving skills, perceptual ability and mechanical aptitude also affect the intelligence level (Brolin, 1977, p. 7). Mentally retarded individuals frequently have below-average functioning levels in these areas.

Mentally retarded individuals also have deficits in adaptive behavior. This means that, in addition to performing below average on achievement tests, intelligence tests, and academic areas, they also have problems meeting or coping with the standards that are expected of others in the same peer and cultural group. Examples of these standards include appropriate personal-social behavior, adequate daily living skills, minimal basic academics, independent problem-solving abilities, and appropriate manipulative skills.

Learners who are classified as mentally retarded are usually placed in a special education class and/or resource room where they are assisted in developing academic, social, prevocational and/or self-care skills. The development of these areas is important if they are to be successfully mainstreamed into T & I programs.

## Illustration 2.1

### OVERVIEW OF GENERAL CHARACTERISTICS
### OF MENTALLY HANDICAPPED LEARNERS

Some of the general characteristics that mentally handicapped learners *may* exhibit are shown in this illustration. Remember that not every mentally handicapped learner will display all of these characteristics.

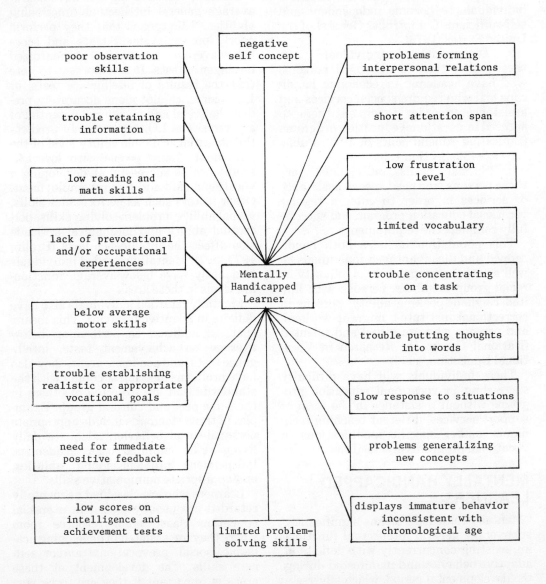

Mentally retarded learners have a learning capacity that is less than "average." At the maximum, they can be expected to reach a sixth-grade level in reading and math. These learners often have difficulty in analyzing situations or tasks. Their skills in logical reasoning are limited or have not been fully developed. In some cases this may be due to the limited number of appropriate experiences to which they have been exposed.

A short attention span is often exhibited by these learners. However, when appropriate instructional materials and teaching techniques are used, many of them are able to concentrate on tasks for longer periods of time. A low "frustration tolerance" is frequently associated with this population. These learners become easily frustrated when assignments or tasks are not appropriate for their ability level or when too much new material is presented at one time.

Many mentally retarded learners have problems expressing themselves verbally to others and/or in understanding what is being said to them. Their vocabulary is not as advanced as their peer group. Recall is another problem associated with these learners. New concepts must be reinforced systematically so that they can remember important points.

In the past many individuals who are classified as mentally retarded came from low socioeconomic or minority group backgrounds. Factors such as poor health conditions, poor dietary habits, inadequate medical care, lack of exposure to common everyday experiences, cultural differences and language barriers can contribute greatly to low scores on standardized intelligence tests. Therefore, caution must be observed when testing these individuals so that they are not unfairly labeled as mentally retarded.

Many individuals who are classified as mentally retarded can be trained for competitive employment and are able to lead independent lives. In the past, the lack of vocational competence of this group could be attributed, in part, to lack of experience and inadequate training of teachers. Therefore, opportunities for these students to enter vocational programs have been few and far between. Trade and industrial teachers can be instrumental in providing realistic vocational education opportunities for this population. Utilizing appropriate instructional materials and techniques, they can help many of these individuals to develop realistic skills that will help them to become economically independent upon leaving school. Support personnel and resources will help in this quest.

## Levels of Mental Retardation

The American Association on Mental Deficiency (AAMD) identifies four levels of mental retardation. These levels classify retardation according to severity. The four levels are listed along with the range of I.Q. scores associated with each level. The two most widely used individual standardized intelligence tests are given as indicators.

| Levels | Stanford-Binet Intelligence Test —I.Q. Scores | Wechsler Intelligence test —I.Q. Scores |
|---|---|---|
| Mild (EMR) | 68–52 | 69–55 |
| Moderate (TMR) | 51–36 | 54–40 |
| Severe | 35–20 | 39–25 |
| Profound | 19 and below | 24 and below |

(Haring, 1978, p. 104).

*Mildly Retarded.* Mildly retarded learners are known as "educable mentally retarded" (EMR) students. They usually receive some career education and/or pre-vocational experiences in the lower grades or in junior high school to prepare them with skills that will help them to become independent. Practical academics are emphasized in their instructional program so that they will be able to be mainstreamed into regular programs and classrooms.

Many mildly retarded learners are capable of being successfully mainstreamed at the secondary level. Trade and industrial teachers will undoubtedly work with this population in existing programs. They usually receive assistance from special education personnel in the form of related academics, remedial help and work study opportunities.

These individuals will be able to function at a maximum of sixth grade in reading and math. Their self-help skills are generally well developed. They are able to communicate with others and act independently in most situations. They can usually be prepared for semi-skilled or unskilled jobs through appropriate vocational education opportunities.

*Moderately Retarded.* Moderately retarded learners are known as "trainable mentally retarded" (TMR) students. These individuals will generally be able to recognize survival words and functional vocabulary but will not have extensive formal reading skills. Major objectives of their instructional program include developing self-help skills and basic social skills.

Many trainable individuals can develop skills that will enable them to perform subcontracting parts assembly work or production items in sheltered workshop facilities. Some TMR individuals can be trained for unskilled jobs in the competitive employment sector and can perform tasks with few or no errors with a minimum of supervision. Productivity rates generally increase the longer the individual performs the same task.

These learners were formerly placed in separate facilities. Today, many of them are being moved back into classes in public schools. They will generally remain in segregated, self-contained classes for the majority of the school day. Specialized programs are developed to emphasize socialization and self-care skills.

By using appropriate tasks and instructional techniques, T & I teachers can help TMR students develop skills so that they can be at least partially self-sufficient.

*Severely and Profoundly Retarded.* In the past vocational opportunities have been practically non-existent for individuals in this category. Severely and profoundly retarded learners are usually found in segregated facilities or institutional settings. As a result of recent legislation for the handicapped, appropriate programs are now being developed for these individuals so that they may function in the least restrictive environment.

Severely retarded learners do not develop academic skills. The emphasis in their instructional program is on developing basic self-care, socialization, communication and leisure skills. They are usually at least semi-dependent on others.

Profoundly retarded individuals are often totally dependent on others and require almost total supervision. They generally are not able to protect or care for themselves and will not be able to function in regular classroom situations.

Trade and industrial personnel will not be working with severely and profoundly retarded individuals in regular programs. However, T & I personnel may be called upon as consultants if specific training activities are being established.

## Mental Age

When working with mentally handicapped students, it is important to keep in mind that their mental age (MA) differs markedly from their chronological age (CA). Physically, these students may not appear different from others in their age group. However, their mental development will be much slower.

The mental age of individuals is determined by comparing their I.Q. score with their chronological age. The lower the I.Q. level, the lower the mental age level will be. The mental age is indicative of the student's ability to learn. The lower the mental age, the slower the rate at which the student will learn. A quick formula can be used to determine the MA of a learner. The general formula is as follows:

$$MA = \frac{I.Q. \times CA}{100}$$

That is, mental age is equal to the I.Q. score multiplied by the chronological age divided by 100. If the learner is 16 years or older, the CA in the formula is always 15.

For example, a mentally retarded student who is 16 years old with an I.Q. of 60 will have a mental age of 9. This is calculated by using the formula presented in the former paragraph.

$$MA = \frac{(60) \times (15)}{100}$$

$$MA = 9$$

This learner will learn at about the rate of a 9-year-old child rather than at the rate demonstrated by other average 16-year-old students. The T & I teacher needs to consider the mental age of students when developing and implementing realistic program objectives.

## Working with Mentally Handicapped Learners in Trade and Industrial Programs

Some general suggestions for T & I teachers who work with mentally retarded learners follow:

1. A step-by-step approach to instruction can help eliminate frustration in these students. Introduce new material in small amounts and check to make sure that the student understands each step before continuing to the next step.

2. Consider the reading level of the student before assigning a textbook, workbook or handout.

3. Use the demonstration approach whenever possible so that students can see an illustration of what you are talking about.

4. Allow these learners to take tests orally. In many cases they will be able to correctly answer questions verbally when they are read aloud. If they had to read the same questions and write the correct responses, their academic deficiencies would result in frustration and failure. If special education personnel are orally administering the test, they may tape-record the responses. One can then listen to the recording and evaluate the student according to the responses.

5. Develop task analysis procedures. In this way, students can display competence on step one before having to go on to step two. This approach will also allow them to progress at their own learning pace while allowing them to feel successful. The task analysis can be broken down into smaller steps depending on the rate at which students progress.

6. Establish instructional objectives that parallel the abilities of the students.

7. Provide for repetition and review. These students have trouble developing a clear understanding of new material the first time it is introduced.

8. Allow extended time for students to complete assignments and tasks.

9. Provide positive reinforcement when students successfully complete a task. This will help them to develop a feeling of accomplishment and thus motivate them to continue.

10. Individualized instruction and programmed learning materials are very successful methods to use when working with these students.

11. Overlearning is very important for these learners. Do not rush them into new material until they have had sufficient time to grasp what has already been presented. Check their comprehension by asking them to explain and/or demonstrate. Allow sufficient time for overlearning.

## LEARNERS WITH EMOTIONAL OR BEHAVIORAL PROBLEMS

"Seriously emotionally disturbed" means a condition exhibiting one or more of the following characteristics over a long period of time and to a marked degree, which adversely affects educational performance:

1. An inability to learn which cannot be explained by intellectual, sensory, or health factors.

Sarah is a 17-year-old girl enrolled in a high school welding program. Her records reveal that she has average intelligence but her grades in school show that she is failing in most classes. She displays frequent mood changes during the day. One minute her behavior is aggressive, and the next minute she becomes withdrawn and will not respond to others around her. When assigned a task in the welding class or laboratory, she is sometimes uncooperative and defiant. Sarah is reluctant to participate in any group activities because she is generally not accepted by her peers. Her continual demand for attention in class is beginning to irritate Mr. Jones, the welding teacher. When he approached the guidance counselor to complain about the situation he was told that Sarah has been experiencing some problems in the home. Her father is an alcoholic and frequently is out of work. She spent several years in a foster home. Recently, her mother was involved in a serious car accident. Sarah is now responsible for managing the household as well as caring for seven brothers and sisters. Mr. Jones and the guidance counselor feel that Sarah can be helped through cooperation with the special education teacher and some behavior modification techniques.

2. An inability to build or maintain satisfactory interpersonal relationships with peers and teachers.

3. Inappropriate types of behavior or feelings under normal circumstances.

4. A general pervasive mood of unhappiness or depression.

5. A tendency to develop physical symptoms or fears associated with personal or school problems.

The term includes (individuals) who are schizophrenic or autistic. The term does not include (individuals) who are socially maladjusted, unless it is determined that they are seriously emotionally disturbed. (Public Law 94–142, 121 a. 5).

Illustration 2.2 provides an overview of general characteristics often associated with learners who have emotional or behavioral problems. If you have a student in your program who frequently exhibits a number of these characteristics and is not receiving special education services, refer the individual for appropriate assessment and diagnosis.

Emotional or behavioral problems often affect the student's ability to learn. This handicap can have a number of causes, including the inability of the student to cope with psychological stress, problems in the central nervous system, injury to the brain, social and economic factors of the home environment, or a chemical imbalance within the body.

Many students in the public schools today have minor behavioral problems. Individuals classified in this category usually have long-standing problems. Their behavior is frequently inappropriate for the time and place in which it occurs. Another important distinction is that the rate of inappropriate behavior differs significantly from average learners. Students with emotional or behavioral problems display disruptive or withdrawn behavior more frequently than their peers.

Although the behaviors exhibited by these learners vary from student to student, there are some general characteristics. Generally they lack the ability to control their own behavior. When they react to anxiety situations, their behavior is frequently inappropriate and not accepted by either peers or adults. Behaviors often associated with this category include strange mannerisms, uncooperative attitudes, frequent mood changes, and severe depression. Other common characteristics include defiance, short attention span, and demands for constant attention. Many individuals in this category have at least average intelligence. However, they are easily frustrated. They often resist authority and tend to ignore discipline attempts. Many display immature behavior and can sometimes be destructive to others or to themselves. When new tasks are assigned, many of

**Illustration 2.2**

## OVERVIEW OF GENERAL CHARACTERISTICS OF LEARNERS WITH EMNOTIONAL OR BEHAVIORAL PROBLEMS

Some of the general characteristics that learners with emotional or behavioral problems *may* exhibit are shown in this illustration. Remember that not every emotionally disturbed or behavior disordered learner will display all of these characteristics.

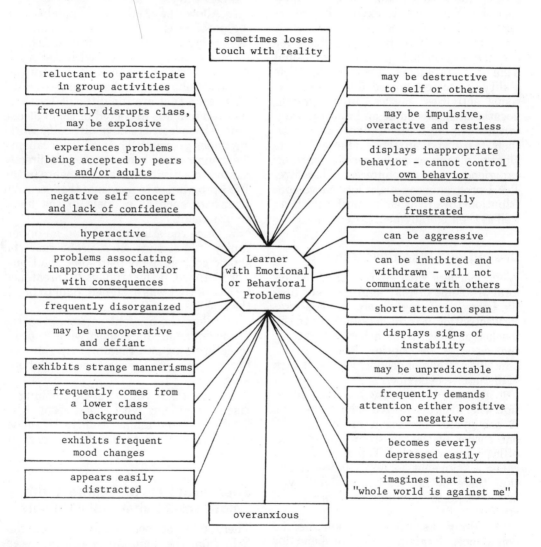

these individuals exhibit extreme anxiety and fears. Still others are shy and reclusive. When attention is drawn to them, they may appear not to hear or see others and often will not communicate with others around them.

Hyperactivity is another sign of an emotional or behavioral problem. Students who are hyperactive are described as impulsive, overactive and restless. They have a difficult time staying in one place and are continually on the go. They have trouble concentrating on one task for an extended period of time and are easily distracted. Some of these learners may be on medication or specially prescribed diets to control their excitable behavior. Structure is extremely important in their educational programs.

Lack of self-confidence is a problem for the majority of learners with emotional behavioral problems. They doubt their ability to succeed in academic, motor and social activities. Success in developing vocational skills can be an important key toward helping these students cope with their fears and anxieties about failure. Doubts disappear as successful learning experiences are encountered. Therefore, T & I programs can make a positive contribution toward their mental health as well as their employment potential.

## Dealing with Disruptive Behavior

When learners with emotional or behavioral problems display aggressive or hostile behavior during classroom or laboratory activities, it is often disruptive to the teacher as well as the other students in the class. A description follows of an effective method of dealing with outbursts of disruptive behavior.

1. Remove the student from the situation where the disruptive behavior occurs. A one-on-one discussion in the hall, in one corner of the classroom, or in your office is recommended. This is sometimes called a "time-out zone." It is important that there be no "audience" while you are trying to communicate with the student.

2. Calmly discuss the reason for the conference. Explain that the behavior was inappropriate for the classroom or laboratory and that it disrupted everyone in the class. Do not yell. If you show anger or hostility, the student will become excited and difficult to manage. If you

are calm, the student should begin to calm down also.

3. Let the student know that you are concerned about the situtation and would like to help with any problem that exists. If the student feels that you care about him/her, it will create a feeling of security that will foster communication rather than hostility.

4. Allow the student to explain what the problem is. Give him/her a chance to release any frustrations and insecurities. In many cases, students with emotional or behavioral problems will display disruptive behavior if they are presented with tasks that are too difficult for them or if too much is expected of them at one time. These learners have difficulty working under pressure. The problems causing the inappropriate behavior may be directly related to activities or assignments in the T & I program or to incidents that occurred elsewhere such as a crisis in the home environment.

5. Once the student has had an opportunity to discuss any problems, you should cooperatively plan some solutions. For instance, if the student is threatened by a task that was assigned, plan to break the task into small steps.

6. Allow the student to remain in the "time-out zone" for a short while in order to calm down and regain composure before returning to the classroom or laboratory.

7. Stress that you are always willing to discuss problems with the student. This will help to minimize feelings of inadequacy as well as to develop a sense of rapport.

## Sources of Help for Learners with Emotional or Behavioral Problems

There may be occasions when outside help from the community will be necessary to assist learners with emotional or behavioral problems. Special education personnel can be very helpful in identifying these sources and making arrangements for services to be provided.

These sources may include community mental health centers, counseling centers associated with local colleges or universities, psychiatric units located in local hospitals or clinics, and crisis centers. There may be additional sources available in the local community. Advocacy groups and professional organizations can also be helpful in suggesting techniques to use with these students. Again, special education personnel can contact these groups and then work cooperatively with the T & I teacher.

## Working with Learners with Emotional or Behavioral Problems in Trade and Industrial Programs

Some general suggestions for T & I teachers who work with learners with emotional or behavioral problems follow:

1. The key to working with students in this category is to be consistent in your standards and expectations regarding their participation in the T & I program. When they first enter the program, firmly establish any rules, regulations or program standards as well as the consequences if they are not met. Be firm and consistent. Follow through with any consequences as they become necessary.

2. Contact the special education teacher in your school or district. Cooperatively plan some behavior modification techniques that can be implemented while students participate in T & I program activities. These techniques can also be reinforced by special education personnel during the time when students are outside class.

3. Offer positive reinforcement for desirable behavior. Praise will help students feel confident and successful.

4. Provide a structured program with tasks and activities that do not require a great deal of decision-making. These students need to know boundaries and limitations as well as exactly what is expected of them. Routine gives them a feeling of security.

5. Provide examples and tasks that are as concrete and meaningful as possible. The procedures to follow should be demonstrated before an assignment is made so that students know exactly what to do. Abstract concepts can cause them to become frustrated.

6. The contract system is a very effective method to use with these learners. The contract specifies the tasks that the student will complete or the behavior that the student will change. Rewards and consequences are agreed upon between the teacher and the student. A time limit is usually established. Both the teacher and the student can then monitor the contract.

7. Instruction should contain only a few new steps so that students do not feel overwhelmed with new material. Always build on previously mastered tasks. As nearly as possible, maintain a success-oriented environment.

8. Hyperactive students should be given opportunities to move around. This movement can be incorporated into the task or activity. The teacher can also ask the student to help organize the tool room, help supervise clean-up activities, or take a message to the main office.

9. Programmed learning materials and individualized instruction are excellent methods to use with these learners. They can work successfully at their own pace without feeling threatened or pressured.

## VISUALLY HANDICAPPED LEARNERS

"Visually handicapped" means a visual impairment that, even with correction, adversely affects (an individual's) educational performance. The term includes both partially sighted and blind (individuals). (Public Law 94–142, 121 a. 5).

Illustration 2.3 provides an overview of general characteristics often associated with visually handicapped learners. If you have a student in your program who frequently exhibits a number of these characteristics and is not receiving special education services, refer the indi-

Scott is 24 years old and is enrolled in a post-secondary auto mechanics program. During the time he was in high school, he received help from itinerant teachers in mobility training. Scott was enrolled in the transportation cluster program during his last two years of high school. His instructor reports that he did very well in the program.

After graduation, he worked for several years at a service station as a general attendant. Not satisfied with this job as a final career choice, Scott contacted the State Office of Vocational Rehabilitation. Scott completed a number of vocational assessment activities to further explore his aptitudes and interests. As a result of several counseling sessions it was recommended that Scott enroll in the auto mechanics program. Vocational Rehabilitation has supplied Scott with a number of specially designed tools that are helpful to him. Upon completion of the program, Scott will also receive job placement from his rehabilitation counselor, who is working cooperatively with the auto mechanics instructor.

vidual for appropriate assessment and diagnosis.

Learners who are visually handicapped may have problems achieving success in school. They require learning experiences and materials adapted to meet their needs. Individuals classified as visually handicapped are divided into two groups according to their ability to see printed material and other objects around them.

Many visually handicapped learners have difficulties in motor coordination, mobility, speech and language development and interpersonal relationships.

## Blind Individuals

Individuals who are classified as blind have a visual disability so severe that they must depend to a great extent on the sense of hearing and touch rather than on the sense of sight. There are state laws that define the guidelines for legal blindness. These guidelines differentiate between individuals classified as blind and those classified as partially sighted.

Blind individuals become aware of their environment through the senses of smell, touch and hearing. The age at which individuals become blind greatly affects their specific educational needs. Those who have been blind since birth have difficulty understanding concepts such as depth, space and relationship of one object to another. A person who becomes blind later in life will have problems adapting to blindness but can rely on experiences from the past. This memory of visual experiences will be helpful in adjusting to educational experiences.

The development of reading skills is one area that will be difficult for blind students. Some blind individuals know how to read braille. Braille is a system of reading that involves touching rather than seeing. Characters have been developed by introducing combinations of six raised dots. By running their fingers over the characters, blind individuals learn to read the characters just as sighted people learn to recognize and read letters and words. However, reading braille is more time-consuming than reading regular print. Visually handicapped individuals who use this method will read at a slower rate than sighted students who read regular print (about 70 words per minute as opposed to about 245 words). A print-scanning device called an Optacon has been developed to allow blind individuals to read printed words. This reading machine translates printed letters into vibrations. By feeling these vibrations, blind people can put the letters together to form words and as a result can read without ever actually seeing the words.

## Partially Sighted Individuals

State laws define guidelines for classifying individuals as partially sighted. Generally, such individuals have limited vision even with corrections such as heavy lenses or surgery. Modifications will have to be made to vocational educa-

## Illustration 2.3

### OVERVIEW OF GENERAL CHARACTERISTICS
### OF VISUALLY HANDICAPPED LEARNERS

Some of the general characteristics that visually handicapped learners *may* exhibit are shown in this illustration. Remember that not every visually handicapped learner will display all of these characteristics.

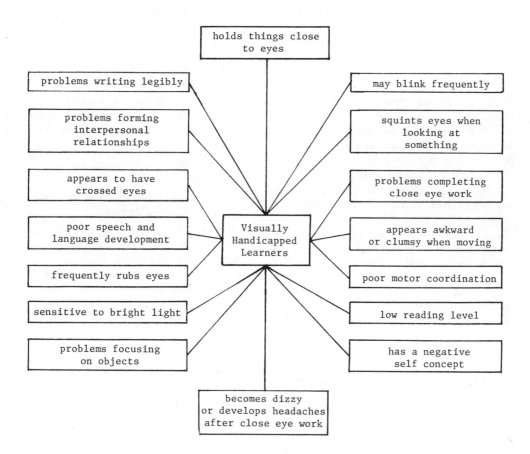

tion materials, equipment or facilities in order for them to succeed. These learners, though they have some degree of sight, will rely heavily on tactile experiences and materials that enable them to learn through the sense of touch.

Partially sighted students exhibit a variety of visual problems. They differ from blind individuals in that they have limited ability to see print. Some will have problems seeing clearly; some may not be able to tell the difference between colors. Some will be very sensitive to light while others may have a narrow field of vision that will limit their ability to see. However, it is generally accepted that these students should apply whatever visual ability they have to assigned tasks.

Optical aids, such as enlarged print and magnifiers, can be extremely useful in working with these students. In addition, special lighting and prescription lenses can help to make the learning process more meaningful.

## Specialized Equipment, Materials and Aids

*Equipment.*

1. The Optacon is a machine that allows visually handicapped individuals to "read" printed material. The scanner converts printed words into a tactile pattern that can be felt.

2. The Stereotoner is a machine that converts printed words into auditory tones.

3. The Kurzweil reading machine takes the words on a printed page and converts them on a computer into words so that even a blind individual can "read."

4. A braillewriter is a machine similar to a typewriter. It has six keys and converts writing into braille.

5. Desks or tables with adjustable tops can help partially sighted students to focus materials in the best light.

6. Overhead projectors will produce a larger image on a screen than information written on a chalkboard.

7. Talking Book machines are specially adapted record players for visually handicapped individuals. Talking Books are recordings of books and other printed materials made for use with this machine.

8. Talking calculators can help these learners to succeed in calculating.

*Materials.*

1. Books and other printed material with large type. Many materials are available from the American Printing House for the Blind, 1839 Frankfort Avenue, Louisville, Kentucky 40206. A catalog is published each year to describe aids and appliances for visually handicapped individuals. A section is devoted to vocational aids. The catalog can be obtained from the American Foundation for the Blind.

A list of specialized aids follows.

1. Magnifiers for partially sighted learners.

2. Peer or volunteer readers from the school and/or community.

3. An organization called Recording for the Blind has locations across the country. This organization provides recording services through trained volunteers who record books on open reel tapes or cassettes and provide accompanying raised line drawings. These recordings are then made available to visually handicapped individuals. Services are provided for elementary and high school students, undergraduates and graduate students, and professional and business adults requiring material essential to their occupations.

4. A slate and stylus to punch out braille notes.

5. Special contact lenses or glasses for partially sighted learners.

6. Braille devices, tools and instruments such as braille rulers, micrometers, feed indicators and control dials all have raised markings to assist visually handicapped learners.

7. Specially designed guards and templates designed for laboratory equipment and machinery.

8. Attachments or auditory warning signals for machinery that will produce an audible sound when a machine is on.

9. Partially sighted learners may require special lighting to allow them to use their vision to the maximum capacity.

10. Control dials and switches on machines and equipment that are easily accessible to these students will be hlepful.

11. Teachers can make their own raised dots to form braille labels and instructions by using dots of glue.

12. Diagrams using raised lines and models which are three-dimensional can help these students to form a "mental blueprint" of what the instructor is explaining.

## Working with Visually Handicapped Learners in Trade and Industrial Programs

Some general suggestions for T & I teachers who work with visually handicapped learners follow:

1. As soon as visually handicapped students are enrolled in your program, orient them to the classroom and laboratory environment so they can develop appropriate mobility, safety and motor skills. It is crucial that they become familiar with the layout of the rooms as well as the specific tools, equipment and materials that will be used. A guided tour of the room is excellent, allowing them to feel where everything is located as you describe the surroundings verbally. They can then form a "mental blueprint." Do not rearrange the rooms without informing them.

2. Do not become overprotective or try to restrict learners from moving around the classroom or laboratory. A wide variety of experiences is important for them to become familiar with their surroundings.

3. When addressing students, specifically call them by their names so they know to whom you are speaking.

4. Read words and figures aloud as you write them on the chalkboard. Students can then keep up with the content of the instruction.

5. Allow learners to use cassette recorders during class discussions and lectures.

6. Establish raised lines around safety areas in the laboratory so that students can avoid accidents.

7. When demonstrating a new task, procedure, piece of equipment or tool, allow students to actively use their sense of touch so they will be able to understand the process. For example, take their hand and follow through with the process as you explain it verbally. This method is far more effective than merely telling them to "insert this part into this opening."

8. Peer tutors can be very helpful when laboratory assignments are made. Tutors should help these students to succeed as opposed to completing the assignment for them.

9. Have printed material converted to enlarged print, thermoform print or braille.

10. Tape-record lectures and demonstrations. Students can then borrow the tapes to review material covered in class.

11. Student notetakers are helpful. Special pads are available that slip under a notebook page and will record a carbon copy of notes taken. In this manner visually handicapped students can either use a magnifier to read notes, or have them transcribed on a cassette or typed on a braille typewriter.

12. When making decisions about class seating arrangements, allow these students to sit where they can hear and where the glare of the lights or sunlight will not bother them.

13. Allow students to type assignments, reports, tests, etc. Many of them can type much faster than they can write or transcribe in braille.

14. Allow students to tape-record answers to tests or lengthy written assignments.

## HEARING IMPAIRED LEARNERS

The Bureau of Education for the Handicapped defines hearing impaired learners as "individuals who have a sense of hearing inadequate for success in learning situations."

Illustration 2.4 provides an overview of general characteristics often associated with visually handicapped learners. If you have a student in your program who frequently exhibits a number of these characteristics and is not receiving special education services, refer the individual for appropriate assessment and diagnosis.

MEET RICK, A HEARING IMPAIRED
LEARNER . . .

Rick is a 17-year-old boy enrolled in a cosmetology program. Rick has been deaf since he was five years old. He attended the state school for deaf students until he was 15 years old. He developed lipreading and sign language skills in his communication classes at the state school.

This is the second year that Rick has been enrolled in the cosmetology program. Mrs. Jones, his teacher, reports that Rick has been doing very well in the program. His reading level is low and he requires some assistance from the resource room teacher several times a week to assist him in reading required course material. In addition, Rick works with the district speech therapist and the itinerant teacher.

Mrs. Jones and the other students in the class have learned to face Rick when they are speaking to him so that he can read their lips. Mrs. Jones has also modified her classroom instruction to meet Rick's needs with the help of the itinerant teacher for the hearing impaired. When the time arrives for Rick to review for and take the state board examinations, an interpreter will be provided for him.

Individuals who are hearing impaired do not have the ability to adequately develop speech, language and communication skills through the regular hearing process. They are usually regular in their physical, emotional and intellectual development. Their problem lies in the area of mastering appropriate speech and language skills. Individuals classified as hearing impaired are divided into two groups: deaf or hard-of-hearing. Hearing impaired students, including both deaf and hard-of-hearing learners, need special education services, special training techniques, appropriate learning materials or supplementary aids in order to learn effectively.

Classification in one of these categories is determined primarily by the type and degree of the hearing loss. The degree of the hearing loss is determined by measuring the intensity of sound needed for the person to be able to hear. These tone and frequency levels are measured by an audiometer. Depending on the degree of impairment, students may have problems learning the skills necessary to speak, read and write in a regular fashion.

The age at which an individual suffered a hearing loss is important. Those who were born deaf or with a hearing loss will have difficulty in developing regular speech patterns. They may also have problems developing reading skills. Individuals who had the benefit of verbal instruction before suffering a hearing loss will be able to rely on their auditory memory as an aid to learning. These people will display better speech and language skills and may have higher reading levels as a result of previous learning.

## Deaf Individuals

"Deaf" means a hearing impairment so severe that the individual is impaired in processing linguistic information through hearing, with or without amplification, which adversely affects (the individual's) educational performance. (Public Law 94–142, 121 a. 5).

Individuals who are deaf have extreme or severe hearing losses and must use the senses of touch, smell and sight in the learning process. The education of deaf individuals has improved greatly in recent years, in large part because of the advances made in technology. This population was formerly educated in separate, local or regional facilities. This situation is changing as a result of legislation mandating that these learners be educated in the "least restrictive environment." Many of them are now being transferred from separate facilities back to regular programs in local districts.

School districts are now experimenting with various delivery systems to provide these learners with appropriate services and resource assistance from trained specialists.

## Illustration 2.4

### OVERVIEW OF GENERAL CHARACTERISTICS
### OF HEARING IMPAIRED LEARNERS

Some of the general characteristics that hearing impaired learners *may* exhibit are shown in this illustration. Remember that not every hearing impaired learner will display all of these characteristics.

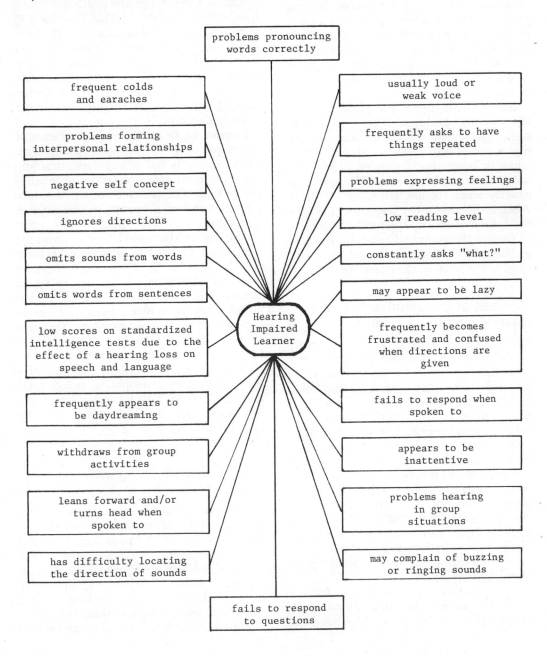

## Hard of Hearing Individuals

"Hard of hearing" means a hearing impairment, whether permanent or fluctuating, that adversely affects (an individual's) educational performance but which is not included under the definition of "deaf" in this section. (Public Law 94–142, 121 a. 5).

Individuals who are hard of hearing cannot hear the spoken word as clearly as someone with regular hearing. However, with a hearing aid or other supplemental aids, they can use their sense of hearing to some degree in the learning process.

Hearing aids do not completely correct the hearing problem. There is always some distortion. These devices do not make words any clearer but only make what is being heard louder. Therefore, hard-of-hearing students will never hear exactly what regular students will hear. Also, the farther away the student is from the source of sound, the harder it will be to receive the sound adequately. Because of this, these students should be seated close to the front of the classroom.

## Methods of Communicating with Hearing Impaired Learners

Hearing impaired individuals use a variety of methods in communicating with others, including: (a) the manual alphabet, (b) a sign language system, (c) lipreading and (d) total communication. Each separate method or combination of methods helps hearing impaired persons to understand what others are saying and to express their own ideas.

The manual alphabet is a procedure by which an individual uses different finger positions on one hand to represent the 26 letters of the alphabet. Also called fingerspelling, this technique enables the hearing impaired person to substitute the words formed by these visual letters for spoken language.

The *American sign language* (AMESLAN) is a manual language system consisting of signs formed by the hands to represent concepts. This system is a shortcut to having each word presented completely. There are gaps that the hearing impaired person fills in. For instance, a student using this system would sign "Not understand" to mean "I do not understand."

Another sign language system is called *signed English* (SIGLIGH). This form of sign language presents each and every word that is being said. It does not leave any gaps to be filled in. Using the previous example, the student would sign the complete thought ("I do not understand") rather than an incomplete thought ("not understand").

Lipreading, or speechreading, is another technique used by the hearing impaired. This system is not always accurate and the individual gets only some of what is being said. The problem occurs because a great number of sounds in the English language looks like other sounds when lipreading is attempted. For instance, it is difficult to tell the difference between an "h" and a "k." Therefore, hearing impaired individuals must try to fill in the sounds they cannot see or understand. They often pick up clues by watching the face of the speaker. Teachers should remember to face students and to enunciate clearly when talking.

A third method of communication for hearing impaired people is called total communication. This represents a combination of finger-spelling, lipreading and speaking out loud.

## Cooperative Planning with Interpreters

An interpreter is sometimes provided for hearing impaired students who are not totally proficient at lipreading. This person will interpret what you are saying in class to the hearing impaired student through signing. This process will involve a combination of finger-spelling, American sign language and mouthing the words.

The interpreter will usually stand within

several feet of the teacher during a lecture or demonstration so that hearing impaired students can keep both interpreter and teacher within eyesight. Students should be seated away from any glaring light in a spot that will enable them to clearly see. Teachers should check with the interpreter to determine whether they are talking too fast, especially when technical terms are being used. These terms will have to be completely spelled out by the interpreter and will take longer to interpret. There may also be times when the interpreter will ask to have information repeated.

It is often helpful for the interpreter to have a copy of lecture or class notes prior to the class session. This material will then be more familiar to the interpreter. Key concepts can be introduced to hearing impaired students by the interpreter before they are presented in class. A list of relevant vocabulary and technical terms should also be provided for the interpreter. Otherwise these students can easily become confused and frustrated when new material and/or unfamiliar terms are used in class.

The T & I teacher should establish a positive working relationship with the interpreter. Cooperative planning will help to provide hearing impaired students with the best possible means of communication in the T & I program. Both the interpreter and the hearing impaired students should take part in the cooperative planning process so that realistic goals can be established and implemented.

## Specialized Equipment and Materials

*Equipment.*

1. Visual signals can be installed on machinery and equipment to indicate when they are on (e.g., red lights).

2. Visible warning signals can be attached to warning bells to ensure proper safety (e.g., flashing lights).

3. Amplifiers and headphones can be helpful with hard-of-hearing students.

*Materials.*

1. Visual materials such as transparencies, films with captions, slides, and charts will be helpful in illustrating a point.

## Working with Hearing Impaired Learners in Trade and Industrial Programs

Some general suggestions for T & I teachers who work with hearing impaired learners follow:

1. Seat students near the front of the room to make lipreading easier.

2. Seat students with their backs to any glaring lights. The lights in the room may also have to be adjusted accordingly.

3. Select hearing volunteers from the class to take notes using carbon paper so that hearing impaired students can concentrate on the teacher.

4. Present students and/or their interpreters with a copy of your class outline or notes before you begin teaching. They can then familiarize themselves with the content of the instruction and will be better prepared to keep up in class.

5. Provide students and/or interpreters with related vocabulary words and technical terms and their definitions so they may develop a basic understanding.

6. Do not wander around the room when talking. Face students when you are talking. Make certain you have their attention before speaking. For instance, if you are writing on the chalkboard and talking at the same time, they will not know what you are saying. Instead, write on the board, face the class again, and begin speaking. Maintaining eye contact is very important.

7. Utilize visual techniques whenever possible, including demonstrations, hands-on experiences, charts and diagrams, as opposed to the lecture approach.

8. Speak at a normal pace and at your usual volume. Students who lipread learn to do so with normal speech patterns and volumes. However, if your normal rate of speaking is very fast, try to slow down a bit.

9. Peer tutors can be very effective in helping these students review class notes and complete student laboratory assignments.

10. When hearing impaired students work in noisy areas, such as a laboratory, advise them to turn the volume on their hearing aids down.

11. The reading level of materials should be considered when assigning work. These students often have reading levels below grade level.

12. Use concrete examples whenever possible.

13. Ask students to explain new material to you after you have introduced it. This will allow you to judge whether or not students comprehend material you have presented to them.

## LEARNING DISABLED LEARNERS

"Specific learning disability" means a disorder in one or more of the basic psychological processes involved in understanding or in using language, spoken or written, which may manifest itself in an imperfect ability to listen, think, speak, read, write, spell, or to do mathematical calculations. The term includes such conditions as perceptual handicaps, brain injury, minimal brain disfunction, dyslexia, and developmental aphasia. The term does not include (individuals) who have learning problems that are primarily the result of visual, hearing, or motor handicaps; or of mental retardation; or of environmental, cultural, or economic disadvantage. (Public Law 94–142, 121 a. 5).

Illustration 2.5 provides an overview of general characteristics often associated with learning disabled students. If you have a student in your program who frequently exhibits a number of these characteristics and is not receiving special education services, refer the individual for appropriate assessment and diagnosis.

The area of learning disabilities is the most recent category of handicapped

---

MEET TOM, A LEARNING DISABLED STUDENT . . .

Tom is 16 years old and is enrolled in a high school machine shop program. Mr. Grange, the teacher, noticed that Tom appears to perform inconsistently in class. Some days he will be inattentive and appear uninterested in what is happening in class. On these days Tom does not listen to directions and is very unorganized when working on assignments. Other days are completely different and Tom seems like another person. He asks frequent questions during class demonstrations and discussions and even shows leadership abilities during small group activities.

Tom is reading several grade levels below average. His spelling is poor and his handwriting is hard to read. He also has problems reading, comprehending, and completing math problems. However, he easily grasps concepts when they are presented verbally in class.

Recently, Mr. Grange has had an opportunity to work with Mr. Powell, the resource room teacher, who works with learning disabled students. Mr. Grange learned that Tom has above average intelligence but his problem lies in the fact that he has a visual perceptual problem. His most effective mode of learning is through auditory methods.

Mr. Grange and Mr. Powell are now cooperatively planning Tom's program. Mr. Grange is using appropriate teaching techniques to meet Tom's needs. Mr. Powell is working with him in the resource room one period per day to help with related academics. Tom is now showing remarkable progress in the machine shop with this support help.

---

learners to be established. In the past, problems arose over an accepted definition for this group of individuals. Until the 1960s many learning disabled students were often mislabeled and placed in special education programs designed for mentally retarded or emotionally disturbed students. Today, however, we realize that these individuals have unique learning problems.

Learning disabilities are usually caused by (a) an emotional or behavioral disturbance or (b) a weakness or injury to the brain area. As a result, these individuals may have difficulty using certain muscles, remembering facts, seeing, hearing, comprehending, or controlling their behavior in a given situation.

This handicapping condition affects more males than females. Emotional and behavioral problems are almost always associated with these individuals because they have so much potential and yet have suffered so many failures and frustrations in school. These learners appear normal physically.

Generally students with learning disabilities have average or above average intelligence. They are usually quite capable of performing well, yet their school records will usually be poor. Many times their grades in one class differ greatly from their grades in another. They are sometimes described as having "hidden" handicaps, because they may be able to cover up their weakness by emphasizing their strong points. They learn in different ways from their peers. Their main problem can be described as a great discrepancy between the ability level and the performance level. Weaknesses are usually most evident in reading and math. Such students often have low motivation and a general lack of interest in schoolwork. Problems associated with learning disabilities are found in the areas of behavior, perception, motor activities and language development.

## Behavioral or Emotional Problems

Learning disabled individuals often have behavioral or emotional problems and are frustrated because their disability makes it difficult for them to succeed in school. They may exhibit the following characteristics:
1. Inappropriate reactions to frustrating situations.
2. Inability to stick to one task or activity.
3. Inability to develop positive peer relationships.

4. Hyperactive behavior.
5. Inability to shift from one task to another with ease.
6. Difficulty developing appropriate problem-solving skills.
7. Lack of emotional stability.
8. Short attention span.
9. Low self-concept.
10. Insecurity.
11. Over-dependence on others.

## Perceptual Problems

Learning disabled individuals may have perceptual problems. Their central nervous system is affected, which results in learning and behavior problems. They will have problems identifying, discriminating and interpreting information. They will also have definite weak and strong learning modes (i.e., visual, auditory, tactile) and must be taught through their strong learning modes in order to profit from instruction.

Problems in perception are usually visual and/or auditory. These individuals see and hear things in a distorted manner because their brain does not accurately perceive what is being presented. However, their sight and vision is normal. These learners may exhibit the following characteristics:

*Visual Perception.*
1. Difficulty recognizing letters and figures.
2. Problems with left-to-right progression.
3. Reversing letters in words (*was* for *saw, b* for *d*).
4. Difficulty reading and comprehending written directions.
5. Difficulty interpreting words (for example, the word *engine* might appear to be *ncinc).
6. Difficulty remembering what was read.
7. Difficulty judging distance or size.

*Auditory Perception.*
1. Difficulty recognizing sounds.

**Illustration 2.5**

## OVERVIEW OF GENERAL CHARACTERISTICS
## OF LEARNING DISABLED LEARNERS

Some of the general characteristics that learning disabled learners *may* exhibit are shown in this illustration. Remember that not every learning disabled learner will display all of these characteristics.

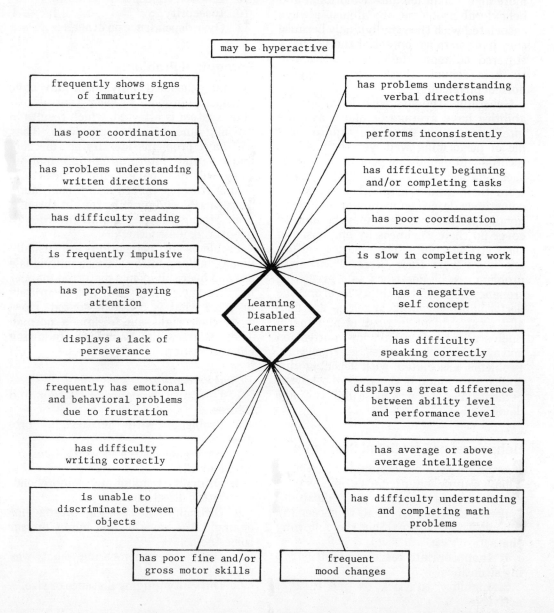

2. Difficulty understanding verbal directions.

3. Difficulty remembering what was heard.

4. Difficulty comprehending a series of directions.

## Motor Activity Problems

Learning disabled individuals may have problems with motor activities. They may exhibit the following characteristics:

1. Lack of balance.

2. Awkwardness when completing tasks.

3. Lack of coordination.

4. Poor gross and/or fine motor abilities.

5. Difficulty telling the difference between left and right.

6. Saying or writing the same thing repeatedly.

## Language Development Problems

Learning disabled individuals may have problems in language development. They may exhibit the following characteristics:

1. Limited verbal speech patterns.

2. Poor grammar.

3. Poor sentence structure.

4. Difficulty understanding the concept of time (today, yesterday, tomorrow).

5. Difficulty understanding the concept of direction (around, above, under).

6. Difficulty putting concepts or thoughts into words.

## Learning Modes

Learning disabled students must be taught through their strongest learning modes. Although these individuals are quite capable of learning, many have difficulty learning when traditional teaching methods are used. It is important to identify the proper learning mode or style for each learning disabled student. For example, some students learn best using a visual approach, others should have auditory training, and still others benefit most from hands-on experiences. When an appropriate learning style is used with these learners, they develop vocational skills that will enable them to enter and contribute to the labor force.

Most learning disabled students are served in regular education programs. They usually receive their primary support services in a resource room. Resource room personnel can be very helpful to T & I teachers in planning an appropriate program for these students as well as helping them with related academic work.

## Working with Learning Disabled Learners in Trade and Industrial Programs

Some general suggestions for T & I teachers who work with learning disabled students follow:

1. Identify the strong learning mode for each student. Special education personnel can tell you whether students learn better visually, auditorily or through hands-on experiences. Appropriate program planning should then be developed accordingly.

2. Tape record lessons, directions and assignments for students who are auditory learners. This method will allow them to learn through the auditory channel and provide them with an ample opportunity to review.

3. Use visuals and demonstrations as often as possible when explaining new concepts. This will especially help students who are visual learners. Provide actual hands-on activities to reinforce classroom instruction and discussions.

4. Use concrete examples whenever possible. Abstract concepts confuse and frustrate these students.

5. Allow students to use a typewriter in preparing assignments and tests so that they do not have to worry about how to make letters. This method also helps them to put letters and words in proper sequence.

6. It is helpful to provide students with an outline of what you will be covering in class. They can then review this material

before and after it is presented. It can also be an aid to the resource teacher who will be reinforcing what you are teaching in your program.

7. Make sure all printed materials are clear and readable. If printing is faded this will only add to the problems these students have in reading and comprehending written language.

8. Allow students to tape-record assignments if they have visual perception problems.

9. Allow students to take tests orally. Having special education personnel or a teacher's aide read test questions aloud and taping the responses is a highly successful technique.

10. Present new information in small amounts. Students will become confused and frustrated if confronted with too much new material at one time. Make sure that they have overlearned one concept before going on to the next.

11. Make sure that writing assignments are relevant to the content of the program. Writing is often difficult for these students and "busy work" will cause them to feel overwhelmed and react inappropriately.

12. Allow students a longer period of time to complete assignments if necessary.

13. List assignments in steps. These students have a difficult time remembering a series of directions. They can more easily follow directions given one at a time.

14. Task analysis is an excellent technique to use with these learners. It lowers the frustration level, allows them to progress at their own pace, and offers immediate feedback after each step.

15. Student-teacher contracts work very well with these students. Specific tasks or assignments can be identified along with corresponding time limitations. In this manner, students know exactly what is expected of them and how long they have to complete assigned work.

16. Programmed instruction materials and individualized instruction techniques are both very effective with these learners.

## SPEECH IMPAIRED LEARNERS

MEET CHARLES, A SPEECH IMPAIRED LEARNER . . .

Charles is 17 years old and is enrolled in a heating, air conditioning and refrigeration program. Charles was very shy and withdrawn when he first entered the program. Mr. Porter, the teacher, learned that Charles has a problem with stuttering and delayed speech. Because of his speech problem, Charles is hesitant to talk to anyone in the class or to participate in group laboratory activities.

Miss Larsen, the district communication specialist, works closely with Charles and Mr. Porter to help make the placement in the program a successful one. She spends several hours a week with Charles, both in individual speech therapy sessions and in the T & I classroom. Miss Larsen also works with Mr. Porter to help him develop appropriate techniques to use with Charles. Mr. Porter now feels much more comfortable communicating with Charles. Gradually, Charles is gaining confidence in himself due to successful completion of various assignments. This has helped his stuttering and delayed speech and prompted him to participate in several small group activities. Mr. Porter is very pleased with the progress Charles has made.

"Speech impaired" means a communication disorder such as stuttering, impaired articulation, a language impairment, or a voice impairment, which adversely affects (an individual's) educational performance. (Public Law 94–142, 121 a. 5).

Illustration 2.6 provides an overview of general characteristics often associated with speech impaired learners. If you have a student in your program who frequently exhibits a number of these characteristics and is not receiving special education services, refer the individual for appropriate assessment and diagnosis.

Individuals are classified as speech impaired when their speech patterns differ from the normal. These speech disorders can interfere with their ability to communicate with others and cause them to be maladjusted. They are not recognized as being handicapped until they speak. Therefore, they are often withdrawn and have problems developing interpersonal relationships.

Speech handicaps are very common in individuals who have cerebral palsy, brain damage, hearing loss or cleft palate. However, most people who have a speech impairment have normal intelligence and motor abilities.

Speech impaired individuals may exhibit problems such as (a) pronouncing words incorrectly, (b) lisping, (c) stuttering, (d) volume that is too loud or too weak, (e) delayed speech, (f) leaving sounds out of words, (g) adding sounds to words and (h) uneven rhythm of words. Speech impaired students usually have limited vocabulary and many have low reading levels.

Individuals are identified as speech impaired through diagnostic testing by speech clinicians. After the evaluation, the speech specialist will develop a plan for correction of the specific problem areas. Speech therapists and communications specialists are professionals trained to help remediate speech impairments. In many school districts, itinerant speech therapists will travel to several schools to serve all students with speech impairments. These personnel are available to work with regular classroom teachers who have speech impaired students in their classrooms. Speech and hearing clinics are also available in many communities. They are found in hospitals, clinics and universities.

Resource rooms are often available in schools to help students with academic problems associated with a communication handicap. These support people can help speech impaired learners with related academic work necessary for success in the vocational program.

Individuals with speech impairments are found in all areas of the work force. They have no problems developing the specific skills necessary for employment.

They may, however, need some accompanying help in personal adjustment to learn to cope with their handicap.

## Working with Speech Impaired Learners in Trade and Industrial Programs

Some general suggestions for T & I teachers who work with speech impaired learners follow:

1. Always maintain eye contact with students when they are having difficulty communicating (e.g., stuttering, delayed speech). This will give them the confidence to complete their message.

2. Work cooperatively with the speech therapist and/or communication specialist to determine which technique will be most helpful in assisting students to communicate effectively.

3. Encourage peer tutoring and small group activities that will help to promote positive interpersonal relationships with other students in the class. Acceptance and improved self-concept can help them to improve their speech patterns. Likewise, nervousness and uneasiness can make the speech impairment worse.

4. Develop a list of technical terms and vocabulary frequently used in the program. This list should be shared with the speech therapist or communication specialist to help these students become familiar with the terms and feel more comfortable pronouncing them aloud.

5. Always allow students sufficient time to complete their sentences. Do not try to finish their thoughts for them when they have difficulty talking. Nodding your head while they are talking often gives them the confidence to finish. It lets them know that you are interested in what they have to say and are willing to wait for them to complete expressing their thoughts.

6. Speech impairments are often associated with a hearing impairment. Refer individuals who display the characteristics of having a speech impairment for a hearing test.

## Illustration 2.6

### OVERVIEW OF GENERAL CHARACTERISTICS
### OF SPEECH IMPAIRED LEARNERS

Some of the general characteristics that speech impaired learners *may* exhibit are shown in this illustration. Remember that not every speech impaired learner will display all of these characteristics.

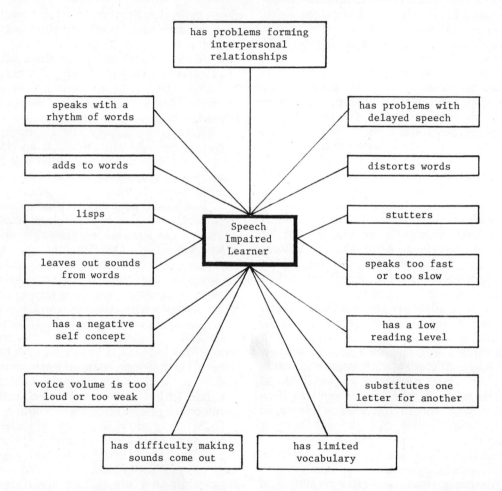

7. Speech impairments can often be the result of dental problems. The school clinic should be able to assist in setting up a dental appointment. An examination can determine whether a condition such as an extreme overbite is the cause of the speech impairment.

8. Try not to act uncomfortable when these students are communicating with you. If you appear to be embarrassed it will make students uncomfortable and the abnormal speech patterns may increase.

9. Do not force students to prepare oral presentations or reports for the rest of the class until they are established and feel comfortable in the classroom environment. As speech impaired students begin

to feel accepted in the class and experience success, they will be able to assume more responsibilities. This will encourage them to speak more openly in class.

10. Check the reading level of the students. Many speech impaired individuals have low reading levels as a result of their disability. Revise your course materials accordingly.

# HEALTH IMPAIRED LEARNERS

MEET MARIA, A HEALTH IMPAIRED LEARNER . . .

Maria is 40 years old and is enrolled in a health occupations program at the post-secondary level. Maria has a heart condition. In addition, she has severe problems with allergies. She stayed at home until her children were well established in school before deciding to return to school to become a dental hygienist. Maria discussed her health related problems with Mrs. Desmond, the health occupations teacher, after enrolling in the program. Mrs. Desmond's primary concern was what she could do to modify the program, if necessary, to meet Maria's special needs.

After discussing the program requirements and specific job entry level requirements, it was determined that substantial program modifications would not be necessary. Maria is under the supervision of her family physician. She takes medication each day for her heart condition and receives frequent allergy shots. She has lived with her health impairment long enough to realize her own limitations.

Maria must be careful to watch her diet, eliminating those things she is allergic to. She must also be careful not to overtax her strength. Keeping these limitations in mind, Maria should have no problem completing the course or in finding employment in her chosen area.

"Other health impaired" means limited strength, vitality or alertness, caused by chronic or acute health problems such as heart condition, tuberculosis, rheumatic fever, nephritis, asthma, sickle cell anemia, hemophilia, epilepsy, lead poisoning, leukemia, or diabetes, which adversely affects (an individual's) educational performance. (Public Law 94–142, 121 a. 5).

Illustration 2.7 provides an overview of general characteristics often associated with health impaired learners. If you have a student in your program who frequently exhibits a number of these characteristics and is not receiving special education services, refer the individual for appropriate assessment and diagnosis.

Individuals who are classified as health impaired have chronic health problems that will affect their strength and vitality. These conditions will also affect their ability to participate in regular classes without some special consideration. These learners tire easily and may need an opportunity to rest during the school day. They may also appear to be frail. Often they are described as being inattentive.

Students who are health impaired frequently miss school because of health problems. In many districts they are eligible for home instruction. Home instruction teachers act as a liaison between the home and the school. These personnel can be helpful to the regular classroom teachers in transferring work from the school to the student and in providing remedial instruction. Many districts have one or more itinerant home instruction teachers who provide services to hospital/home-bound students in all the schools.

## Working with Health Impaired Learners in Trade and Industrial Programs

Some general suggestions for T & I teachers who work with health impaired learners follow:

1. Use available resource personnel such as social workers and itinerant teachers for homebound students as a liaison between the T & I program and the home. These resource people can deliver materials, assignments and handouts to health impaired students and often provide remedial instruction.

2. Allow students to work on program requirements at their own pace.

3. Individualized instruction and pro-

**Illustration 2.7**

## OVERVIEW OF GENERAL CHARACTERISTICS
## OF HEALTH IMPAIRED LEARNERS

Some of the general characteristics that health impaired learners *may* exhibit are shown in this illustration. Remember that not every health impaired learner will display all of these characteristics.

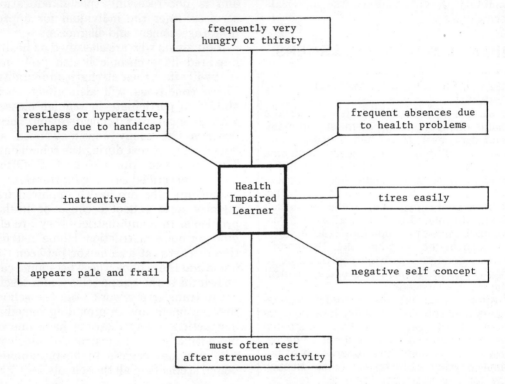

grammed instruction materials will be very helpful in planning for these students.

4. Tape lectures so that these students can listen to them at home. This will help them to keep up with the instructional content of the program.

5. When students do attend school, allow them sufficient time to rest during the day. Cooperative plans can be made with school health personnel. For exam-

ple, arrangements can be made with the school nurse to allow these students to use the clinic facilities during their study periods to rest.

6. Cooperatively assess the stamina and strength requirements involved in your program with support personnel to determine whether the limitations of the students are too great to allow them to succeed.

## ORTHOPEDICALLY OR PHYSICALLY HANDICAPPED LEARNERS

MEET MATT, A PHYSICALLY HANDICAPPED LEARNER . . .

Matt is 30 years old and is enrolled in a drafting program at the post-secondary level. Matt had polio as a child. As a result, he has to wear braces and use crutches to walk. Matt had a brief exploratory experience in drafting during high school. He has now decided to return to school to become a draftsman.

Matt has been faced with few difficulties since he entered the program. Mr. Lane, the teacher, checked to make sure that the classroom was accessible. A few desks were rearranged to make the aisles wider. He also made a convenient space available where Matt can store his crutches. A drafting table was adapted with an adjustable top so that Matt can use it in a sitting position or when he stands. Matt often prefers to work in a standing position because his legs become cramped when he sits too long.

Mr. Lane feels that Matt is performing very well in the program and has assured him that he should have no trouble finding a job when he completes the program.

"Orthopedically impaired" means a severe orthopedic impairment which adversely affects (an individual's) educational performance. The term includes impairments caused by congenital anomaly (e.g., clubfoot, absence of some member, etc.), impairments caused by disease (e.g., poliomyelitis, bone tuberculosis, etc.), and impairments from other causes (e.g., cerebral palsy, amputations, and fractures or burns which cause contractures). (Public Law 94–142, 121 a. 5).

Illustration 2.8 provides an overview of general characteristics often associated with physically handicapped learners. If you have a student in your program who frequently exhibits a number of these characteristics and is not receiving special education services, refer the individual for appropriate assessment and diagnosis.

Learners in this category possess a wide variety of unique characteristics. They differ as much from one another as nonhandicapped people do. Often the specific statements made about them refer to the degree of the disability rather than to the disability itself. Examples of physical disabilities include individuals who have: (a) amputations, (b) cerebral palsy, (c) multiple sclerosis, (d) muscular dystrophy, (e) back or spinal injuries, (f) polio (poliomyelitis), and (g) cystic fibrosis.

Learners who are physically disabled represent a wide range of performance and ability levels. Some individuals have only mobility problems while others have trouble developing appropriate work tolerance levels. Therefore, such factors as physical strength, motor ability, muscular control and coordination must be considered for each individual when developing and/or modifying vocational instruction.

The first and foremost objective in planning for these students is to provide access to the classroom, laboratory, machinery, equipment and tools. Common architectural barriers that prevent physically handicapped students from participating in regular programs include doorways and aisles that are too narrow, worktables that are too high or too low, slippery floors, the absence of ramps and handrails, inadequate restroom facilities, lack of elevators, and height and placement of controls on machinery and equipment.

Architectural accessibility is crucial if physically disabled students are to gain access to and succeed in T & I programs. According to Section 504 of the Rehabilitation Act of 1973, adaptations must be made to facilities, instructional procedures and materials for handicapped individuals as the need arises. Special funds are available to make public facilities accessible to the handicapped.

In many cases existing facilities are adequate with slight modifications. For example, one student may require a change in the way the classroom is ar-

Illustration 2.8

## OVERVIEW OF GENERAL CHARACTERISTICS
## OF PHYSICALLY HANDICAPPED LEARNERS

Some of the general characteristics that physically handicapped learners *may* exhibit are shown in this illustration. Remember that not every physically handicapped learner will display all of these characteristics.

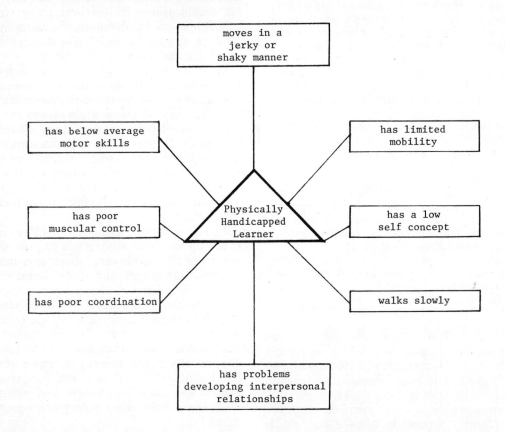

ranged in order to maneuver a wheelchair around freely. Another student with braces may require that the work bench be raised so that he/she may stand while working. Still another student may require a nonskid floor surface for safe walking with crutches. Many physically disabled students will require specific adaptive devices, such as wrist hold-downs for those with poor hand coordination and special pedals or hand controls for operating machinery.

Several sources of support are available to T & I teachers. Vocational rehabilitation departments can often provide these learners with the adaptive devices necessary for their success in vocational training programs. Physical therapists and occupational therapists work with physically handicapped individuals to strengthen their physical capacity to perform tasks. They can also offer recommendations concerning program modifications that would help these learners to be more successful in developing their vocational potential.

## Accessibility to the School

Before programs can be made accessible to physically handicapped individuals, the building that houses the program must itself be made accessible. Therefore, the following modifications should be provided as necessary:

1. Adequate parking spaces available.
2. Curbcuts to the sidewalk.
3. Walkways that have an appropriate slope and width.
4. Appropriate ramps leading to the building entrance.
5. Guide-rails in the hallways.
6. Ramps or elevators leading from one floor to another.
7. Doorways that are at least 32" wide.
8. Accessible lavatory facilities (i.e., stalls, mirrors, sinks and towel dispensers).
9. Nonskid floor surfaces.

## Accessibility in the Trade and Industrial Classroom/Laboratory

Before physically handicapped students can succeed in T & I programs, they must have access to the classroom and laboratory facilities. Therefore, the following modifications should be provided as necessary:

1. Doorways at least 32" wide.
2. Aisle width sufficient for wheelchairs or individuals with crutches.
3. Accessible work stations (i.e., enough room between stations for wheelchairs).
4. Worktables at appropriate height (i.e., for wheelchairs or individuals on crutches who may prefer to stand).
5. Access to lockers and/or storage areas.
6. Access to tool room.
7. Access to controls for machinery and equipment (hand and foot controls may be necessary).
8. Nonskid floor surfaces.
9. Special guardplates for equipment, machinery and power tools.
10. Specially adapted tools for specific handicaps.

11. Sinks, faucets, outlets and emergency power switches should all be accessible.

## Working with Physically Handicapped Learners in Trade and Industrial Programs

Some general suggestions for T & I teachers who work with physically handicapped learners follow:

1. Seat students where they will be most comfortable and have the greatest access to materials, equipment, lavatory facilities and emergency exits.
2. Contact the special education teacher and/or the district nurse to learn about any medical considerations concerning these students. This would include such information as prescribed medication, possible side effects of medication, stamina limitations, physical limitations and possible emergency procedures.
3. Some students may have to be released from class periodically to use lavatory facilities, administer insulin injections, take medication, or go to the clinic for a short rest.
4. It is helpful to release students who have wheelchairs, crutches, canes or braces from class several minutes before the class ends so that they may get to their next class on time. A peer volunteer can be beneficial in assisting them to travel from one class to another. This would also foster positive interpersonal relationships.
5. Peer volunteers can be selected to use carbon paper to take duplicate notes during class lectures or discussions.
6. If adaptations have to be made in classroom/shop facilities or with equipment and machinery, ask physically handicapped students who will be using them to help determine exactly what changes must be made. They can often suggest modifications that are inexpensive and easy to create.
7. Place materials and supplies to be used by these students on lower shelves in storage areas.

8. Use the demonstration technique whenever possible to provide concrete instructional examples.

9. Allow these students longer periods of time to complete tasks, if necessary.

10. Allow students to tape assignments and tests if they are unable to write.

11. Many physically handicapped students will have orthopedic appliances such as wheelchairs, canes, crutches and braces. These appliances should be taken into consideration when adapting the program and facilities and/or instruction.

12. Overhead projectors will produce a larger image than writing on a chalkboard.

13. Special materials such as large print books, oversize pencils, pencil grips, clipboards and easy to grasp tools with larger handles should be provided as necessary.

14. Adaptive aids such as lapboards for wheelchairs, wrist harnesses to hold pens and bookholders attached to wheelchairs will help these students adapt to the program.

## MULTI-HANDICAPPED LEARNERS

"Multi-handicapped" means concomitant impairments (such as mentally retarded–blind, mentally retarded–orthopedically impaired, etc.), the combination of which causes such severe educational problems that the individual cannot be accommodated in a special education program designed for only one of the impairments. The term does not include deaf-blind (individuals). (Public Law 94–142, 121 a. 5).

Individuals who are classified as multi-handicapped have two or more handicapping conditions. It is important that each of these conditions be taken into consideration when education programs are planned. A thorough assessment of medical, psychological and academic records must be made to establish realistic goals and identify appropriate support services.

Examples of learners with multiple handicaps include (a) mentally retarded–speech impaired students, (b) mentally retarded–deaf students, (c) mentally re-

MEET FRANCIS, A MULTI-HANDICAPPED LEARNER . . .

Francis is 25 years old and is enrolled in a carpentry program at the post-secondary level. Francis is partially sighted and is also deaf in one ear. He has suffered emotional problems because of his disabilities.

Some modifications have been made in program instruction by Mr. Sanders, the carpentry teacher. Francis has been fitted with special lenses on his glasses and sometimes uses magnifying devices when working on laboratory activities. Francis has also participated in communications classes offered at the county school for the deaf. He has developed an ability to lipread through these classes. Mr. Sanders makes sure that he uses appropriate teaching techniques and large-print materials to meet Francis's needs. Because of this, Francis is progressing very well in the program. His success has helped decrease the number of emotional problems that probably erupted as a result of earlier frustration and failure.

Francis works closely with his vocational rehabilitation counselor. He has been assured that the vocational rehabilitation office will provide any adaptive devices or resources that he needs to succeed in the carpentry program. In addition, he will be provided with job placement assistance after he completes the program.

tarded–physically disabled students, (d) physically disabled–behavior disordered students, (e) deaf students who have speech impairments, (f) visually handicapped students who have cerebral palsy, (g) learning disabled students who have speech impairments, and (h) emotionally disturbed–deaf students.

It is important for the T & I teacher and cooperative planning personnel to analyze each handicapping condition separately as well as in relationship to one another when making program decisions. For example, in the case of a physically handicapped student in a wheelchair who also has a visual handicap, it would not suffice to merely make the classroom and laboratory accessible for the wheelchair. Other adaptations and techniques would also have to provide for the visual handicap so that the learner can succeed in the T & I program.

# DISADVANTAGED LEARNERS

MEET DAWN, A DISADVANTAGED LEARNER . . .

Dawn is 17 years old and enrolled in a building maintenance program. She is the seventh child in a family of ten. Her family is receiving support through public assistance; neither of her parents is employed. Dawn's school records show a series of failing grades, reading and math levels three grades below her peers, and a serious absentee and tardiness problem. In addition, the health records show that she has a history of health problems assumed to be the result of poor dietary habits and insufficient nutrition.

Dawn became interested in the building maintenance area during a career exploration activity in her freshman year. Mrs. Shepard, the building maintenance teacher, has noted a marked improvement in Dawn's attendance and personal hygiene since she has been in the program. Dawn has showed much more motivation and initiative since Mrs. Shepard placed her in a job situation through the cooperative education program several periods a day. The guidance counselor has also made arrangements for Mr. O'Connor, the school social worker, to work with the family and act as a liaison between the school and the home.

"Disadvantaged" means persons (other than handicapped persons) who (a) have academic or economic disadvantages and (b) require special services, assistance, or programs to enable them to succeed in vocational education programs. (Public Law 94–482)

Illustration 2.9 provides an overview of general characteristics often associated with disadvantaged learners.

In order to be eligible to participate in special programs for the disadvantaged, an individual must have problems in one of the following areas due to an academic or economic disadvantage:

1. Lack the prerequisites for success in the vocational program upon entering the program.

2. Require support services or special program modifications to help them to meet the requirements established by the state or local educational agency for the program (Public Law 94–482).

Individuals in this category often have problems displaying appropriate attitudes for participation in vocational programs. The background of the student is usually the greatest contributor to the problem. Some students may display defiant behavior, rebel against authority and be unable to establish realistic goals for their educational programs. They do not exercise accepted social behaviors in school-related situations and are often disruptive.

Others in this group may exhibit passive attitudes. They show no interest in school assignments and are often called "underachievers." Their poor sense of self-esteem and lack of motivation make them prime candidates for dropping out of school.

## Academically Disadvantaged Learners

Academically disadvantaged means that an individual (a) lacks reading and writing skills, (b) lacks mathematical skills, or (c) performs below grade level (Public Law 94–482).

Individuals in this group have problems in their general academic achievement. They have low motivation to succeed in school. As a result, these learners frequently have low scores on achievement tests and poor attendance records. Many are potential dropouts.

Academically disadvantaged students may have poor backgrounds in mathematics. They have difficulty performing mathematical problems and cannot apply math concepts to problem-solving situations or task-related activities in vocational programs. They also may have difficulty reading and writing. A lack of vocabulary development prevents them

## Illustration 2.9

## OVERVIEW OF GENERAL CHARACTERISTICS
## OF DISADVANTAGED LEARNERS

Some of the general characteristics that disadvantaged learners *may* exhibit are shown in this illustration. Remember that not every disadvantaged learner will display all of these characteristics.

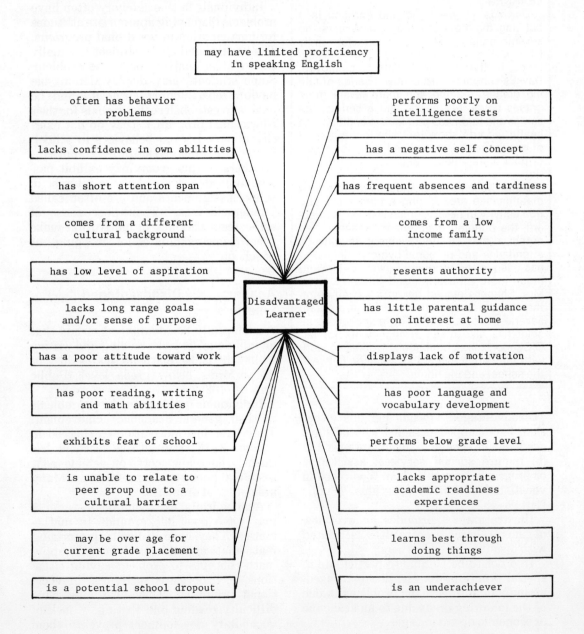

from reading or writing at the minimum level necessary for success in a vocational program. Often they read two or more years below grade level. They frequently have difficulty putting their thoughts into writing and also have problems following written directions to perform tasks.

This group of students often has language problems. Characteristics include poor speech patterns, limited use of English, trouble comprehending vocabulary and technical terms, difficulty in pronouncing words, problems constructing a proper sentence, and difficulty in carrying on a conversation with others. Because of the difficulty they have with verbal communication, they appear to have a limited ability to learn.

## Economically Disadvantaged Learners

Economically disadvantaged means that one or more of the following conditions exists:

1. The family income of the individual is at or below the national poverty level.

2. The individual or the parent/guardian is unemployed.

3. The individual or the parent is receiving public assistance funds.

4. The individual is institutionalized or under state guardianship (Public Law 94–482).

A lack of money is usually the primary cause of the problems of these individuals. The lack of financial support at home can affect nutrition, hygiene, and/or medical and dental care. They are frequently absent from school because they do not have enough money for clothes and transportation.

## Working with Disadvantaged Learners in Trade and Industrial Programs

Some general suggestions for T & I teachers who work with disadvantaged learners follow:

1. Use demonstration techniques whenever possible to present concrete examples.

2. Develop hands-on laboratory activities and experiments to reinforce lectures and demonstrations. These students learn best by doing.

3. Reinforce these students frequently. This will increase their motivation. Any feedback or praise that they receive will be helpful in encouraging them to continue or increase their performance level. It will also help to improve their self-concept.

4. Minimize the chance of failure as much as possible when developing activities and assignments. These learners suffer from low self-esteem and failure situations may cause them to stop trying.

5. Work with support staff to develop and implement appropriate behavior modification techniques for those students who display hostile or defiant behavior. Occupationally accepted behavior should always be stressed in working with them.

6. Whenever possible, encourage students to assume responsibility. These students generally learn to assume responsibility at an early age. Placing them in a position where they can demonstrate responsibility and leadership ability will allow them to actively participate in program activities rather than having to sit passively in the classroom and listen. Techniques that actively involve these learners are best suited to their needs.

7. Student-teacher contracts are an effective approach to allow students to proceed at their own pace while still assuming the responsibility for completing assignments within a specified time period.

8. Field trip and "shadowing" experiences are helpful in providing exposure to people who hold jobs associated with the program. Many of these students have no role model to follow in selecting or pursuing a career objective.

9. Present examples of successful workers from various cultural or minority groups to serve as examples and role models for these students.

10. Invite workers in the community

from various cultural or minority groups to come to the class and share their experiences with these students.

11. Assign these students to interview community leaders and workers from various cultural or minority groups.

12. Encourage students who are proficient in hands-on skills to become peer tutors for learners. This situation can serve as a motivating activity, as a way for disadvantaged students to increase their academic skills by reviewing related reading and math material, and as a reinforcer for positive peer relationships.

13. Identify the reading and math levels for these students. Use this information in selecting or developing instructional materials.

## SUMMARY

Special needs learners are those students identified as handicapped or disadvantaged who have difficulty succeeding in regular vocational programs without the aid of support services, instructional materials and techniques and/or supplementary aids and devices.

Handicapped students are classified into categories according to the nature and needs of their handicap. Recognized categories of handicapped learners include mentally handicapped, behavioral or emotionally handicapped, learning disabled, visually impaired, hearing impaired, speech impaired, physically handicapped and multi-handicapped.

Disadvantaged students are classified as having an academic or economic disadvantage that may interfere with their ability to learn and progress in a regular vocational program.

Trade and industrial teachers need to become familiar with the nature and needs of special needs learners if they are to lend their technical expertise toward preparing them for the world of work.

## REFERENCES

American Institute of Research. *Mainstreaming the handicapped in vocational education: Serving the communication impaired.* Palo Alto, California: Author, 1977.

American Institute for Research. *Mainstreaming the handicapped in vocational education: Serving the visually handicapped.* Palo Alto, California: Author, 1977.

Birch, Jack. *Hearing impaired children in the mainstream.* Reston, Virginia: The Council for Exceptional Children, 1975.

Brolin, Donn E. *Vocational preparation of retarded citizens.* Columbus, Ohio: Charles E. Merrill Publishing Co., 1976.

D'Alonzo, B., and Milter, S. A management model for learning disabled adolescents. *Teaching Exceptional Children,* 1977, *9* (3), 58–60.

Davis, Kay. *It's about time learning impairments came out in the open—Parts I, II, III.* Madison Wisconsin: University of Wisconsin–Madison, Wisconsin Vocational Studies Center, 1976–1977.

Grossman, H. J. *Manual on terminology and classification in mental retardation.* (Rev. ed.) American Association on Mental Deficiency. Baltimore, Maryland: Garamond/Pridemark Press, 1973.

Gugerty, John. *It's about time emotional disturbance came out in the open!* Madison, Wisconsin: University of Wisconsin–Madison, Wisconsin Vocational Studies Center, 1977.

Haring, M. (Ed.) *Behavior of exceptional children* (2nd ed.). Columbus, Ohio: Charles E. Merrill, 1978.

Kirk, Samuel. *Educating exceptional children.* Boston: Houghton Mifflin Company, 1972.

Sheppard, N., and Vaughn, D. *Guidelines for methods and techniques of teaching disadvantaged students.* Blacksburg, Virginia: Virginia Polytechnic Institute and State University, Division of Vocational and Technical Education, 1977.

The National Center for Research in Vocational Education. *Let's find the special people: Identifying and locating special needs learners.* Columbus, Ohio: The Ohio State University, 1979.

## SELF ASSESSMENT: WHO ARE SPECIAL NEEDS LEARNERS?

1. Describe the following populations:
   a. handicapped learners
   b. disadvantaged learners
   c. special needs learners.
2. Why is it important to keep individual differences in mind when working with special needs learners?
3. Who are mentally handicapped learners?
   a. What are some general characteristics usually associated with this group?
   b. Identify some techniques that you can use to help these learners succeed in your program.
4. Who are learners with emotional or behavior problems?
   a. What are some general characteristics usually associated with this group?
   b. Identify some techniques that you can use to help these learners succeed in your program.
   c. What would be the most effective way to handle an outburst by one of these students that is disrupting your class?
5. Who are visually handicapped learners?
   a. What are some general characteristics usually associated with this group?
   b. Identify some techniques that you can use to help these learners succeed in your program.

   c. What are some examples of special equipment, materials and/or aids which can help these learners to succeed in the program?
6. Who are hearing impaired individuals?
   a. What are some general characteristics usually associated with this group?
   b. Identify some techniques that you can use to help these learners succeed in your program.
   c. What are some examples of special equipment, materials and/or aids which can help these learners to succeed in the program?
7. Who are learning disabled students?
   a. What are some general characteristics usually associated with this group?
   b. Identify some techniques that you can use to help these learners succeed in your program.
8. Who are speech impaired learners?
   a. What are some general characteristics usually associated with this group?
   b. Identify some techniques that you can use to help these learners succeed in your program.
9. Who are health impaired learners?
   a. What are some general characteristics usually associated with this group?
   b. Identify some techniques that you can use to help these learners succeed in your program.
10. Who are physically handicapped learners?

a. What are some general characteristics usually associated with this group?

b. Identify some techniques that you can use to help these learners succeed in your program.

c. What are some examples of special equipment, materials and/or aids which can help these learners to succeed in the program?

11. Who are multi-handicapped learners?

a. What is the most important consideration to keep in mind in modifying programs for these individuals?

12. Who are disadvantaged learners?

a. What are some general characteristics usually associated with this group?

b. Identify some techniques that you can use to help these learners succeed in your program.

## ASSOCIATED ACTIVITIES

1. Contact the special education personnel in your school to discuss the possibility of developing an in-service presentation for the other T & I teachers. The topic would be "Who Are Special Needs Learners?" There are many simulation activities, guest speakers and films that could be used for this purpose.

2. Contact a special education teacher who works with high school mentally retarded students. Discuss the general characteristics of these students as well as appropriate techniques that can be used to meet their needs. Explain the nature of your program and discuss ways in which realistic vocational training opportunities can be developed for these students.

3. Contact a special education teacher who works with high school students who have an emotional or behavioral handicap. You may find this teacher in a resource room rather than a self-contained classroom. Discuss the general characteristics of these students as well as appropriate techniques that can be used to meet their needs. Explain the nature of your program and discuss ways in which realistic vocational training opportunities can be developed for these students.

4. Contact a special education teacher who works with high school students who are visually impaired. You may find that one teacher travels from school to school within the district to serve all these students. Discuss the general characteristics of these students as well as appropriate techniques that can be used to meet their needs. Explain the nature of your program and discuss ways in which realistic vocational training opportunities can be developed for these students.

5. Contact a special education teacher who works with high school students who are hearing impaired. You may find that one teacher travels from school to school within the district to serve all these students. Discuss the general characteristics of these students as well as appropriate techniques that can be used to meet their needs. Explain the nature of your program and discuss ways in which realistic vocational training opportunities can be developed for these students.

6. Contact the speech therapist who works with high school students who are speech impaired. Discuss the general characteristics of these students as well as appropriate techniques that can be used to meet their needs. Explain the nature of your program and discuss ways in which realistic vocational training opportunities can be developed for these students.

7. Contact a special education teacher who works with high school students who have a learning disability. You may find this teacher in a resource room rather than a self-contained

classroom. Discuss the general characteristics of these students as well as appropriate techniques that can be used to meet their needs. Explain the nature of your program and discuss ways in which realistic vocational training opportunities can be developed for these students.

8. Contact a special education teacher or rehabilitation counselor who works with physically handicapped high school students. Discuss the general characteristics of these students as well as appropriate techniques that can be used to meet their needs. Explain the nature of your program and discuss ways in which realistic vocational training opportunities can be developed for these students.

9. Contact a counselor or social worker who works with high school students who are health impaired. Discuss the general characteristics of these students as well as appropriate techniques that can be used to meet their needs. Explain the nature of your program and discuss ways in which realistic vocational training opportunities can be developed for these students.

10. Contact a teacher or counselor who works with high school disadvantaged students. Discuss the general characteristics of these students as well as appropriate techniques that can be used to meet their needs. Explain the nature of your program and discuss ways in which realistic vocational training opportunities can be developed for these students.

## CASE HISTORY: ANDY'S STORY

Andy is a moderately handicapped learner enrolled in a food service program. He enrolled in a special education program for trainable mentally retarded students. Until last year the class for trainable students was housed in a separate building. This year the class was moved to the high school to make the learning environment "least restrictive" for these students.

A modified curriculum has been developed cooperatively by the food service instructor and the special education teacher. They have already agreed that extended time will be necessary for Andy to successfully complete the goals and objectives that were developed in his IEP. The career goal that has been identified by Andy, his parents, the special education teacher and the food service instructor is that of a dishwasher operator.

Andy does not attend classes in the food service program on a full-time basis. The special education teacher and the food service instructor have developed a schedule for Andy to attend laboratory sessions during certain segments of the program. In addition, plans have been made to place Andy in an in-school work study program in the high school cafeteria operating the dishwashing machine during the lunch hours. As he demonstrates success in the vocational program and in the cafeteria, Andy will participate in the special education cooperative work study program. He will be placed in a hospital, restaurant, school or nursing home as a dishwasher operator.

The special education teacher is working with Andy to improve his self-help skills and prevocational skills. They are currently working on a unit on community transportation so that Andy will be able to get to and from work independently.

## CASE HISTORY ACTIVITY

Joyce has just enrolled in your program. She is in a special education program for trainable mentally retarded students in your school. You have had an opportunity to meet the special education teacher and do some cooperative planning. Joyce has developed appropriate self-help skills for enrollment in a regular vocational program, although it may not be on a full-time basis.

Based on this information, complete the case history profile worksheet for Joyce's participation in your program.

## CASE HISTORY PROFILE WORKSHEET

Student: _____ Page: _____

Handicapping Condition(s): _____

T & I Program: _____ Academic Levels: _____

Career Goal/Occupational Interest: _____

Considerations (e.g., medication, behavior): _____

_____

| Adaptation | Specific Services Needed | Where to Obtain Service |
|---|---|---|
| Cooperative Planning (School Personnel) | | |
| Support Services | | |
| Architectural Changes | | |
| Adaptive Equipment | | |
| Curriculum Modification | | |
| Instructional Materials/ Supplies | | |
| Teaching Techniques | | |
| Agency Involvement | | |
| Possible Job Placement | | |

# MODULE 3

## Referral, Assessment and Placement of Handicapped Students

One of the most important provisions of the Education for All Handicapped Children Act of 1975 (Public Law 94–142) is the requirement of due process rights for handicapped individuals. These rights are granted to guarantee that appropriate testing and placement procedures occur before an individual is labeled as handicapped. Specific procedures for the referral and assessment of handicapped students must be completed before the students can be placed in a special education program.

When a student has been identified as handicapped and placed in a special education class, an appropriate educational plan must be developed. The student must be placed in regular classes with nonhandicapped peers as often as possible. This is referred to as placing the student in the "least restrictive alternative." Support services and aids necessary to help the student achieve success in the regular program must be supplied by the school district. Trade and industrial programs represent one area where handicapped students can be educated in the least restrictive alternative. A variety of placement options should be available to allow these students to participate in T & I programs.

Specific sections of this module include: (a) The Effects of Labeling, (b) The Right of Due Process, (c) Vocational Education Delivery Options, (d) Placing Handicapped Learners in Trade and Industrial Programs, and (e) Delivery Options for Trade and Industrial Programs.

## MODULE OBJECTIVES

After you have finished reading and reviewing this module, studying the case history, completing the self-assessment questions and relating to the associated activities, you should develop the ability to:

1. Describe the importance of due process.
2. Describe the referral and assessment procedures for handicapped students.
3. Describe the role and responsibilities of T & I teachers in the identification and assessment procedure for handicapped students.
4. Explain the meaning of *least restrictive alternative*.
5. Identify the delivery options available to enroll handicapped students in vocational programs.
6. Identify several delivery options that can meet the needs of handicapped individuals who wish to participate in T & I programs.

## THE EFFECTS OF LABELING

Precise referral and assessment procedures must be established and followed carefully if students with special needs are to be provided with appropriate assistance and support services. Appropriate identification and assessment procedures can be used to avoid hasty, false labeling of students.

For example, in the past many students from minority and low income families were labeled as mentally handicapped or behavior disordered because they did not do well on standardized I.Q. tests. The effect of the home environment in these cases was not taken into consideration before a label was assigned. The educational needs of these learners were not correctly identified.

The due process requirements established by law for handicapped learners mandate that specific referral, assessment and review procedures must be followed before a student can be assigned to a special education program. These regulations guarantee that the specific needs of the individual will be met through appropriate special education services.

Labeling is a practice that has often been observed to result in negative effects for both students and teachers. By emphasizing the differences between special needs learners and other learners, labels tend to obscure the fact that these individuals are more like their peers than they are unlike them. They have strengths and weaknesses, likes and dislikes, desires and fears just as all of us do. The majority of this population lacks career education, prevocational education and vocational background exposure because they have not been provided with appropriate opportunities.

## THE RIGHT OF DUE PROCESS

The Education for All Handicapped Children of 1975 (Public Law 94-142) assures that every handicapped student will be provided with a free, appropriate public education. To accomplish this objective we must make sure that students are properly placed in special education programs. No longer can a single test be used to label an individual as handicapped. No longer can culturally biased tests be used to label minority students as low functioning. No longer can students be tested, evaluated and placed in special education programs without the involvement or consent of parents or guardians. Due process proceedings are now a right of individuals before labeling and placement in a special education environment can take place.

### Requirements of the Due Process Procedure

There has been extensive criticism over the effects of labeling individuals. Yet proper classification of handicapped students can be helpful in developing appropriate educational plans and providing

necessary support services for this population. Therefore, specific procedures for referring, evaluating, assessing and placing students in special education programs must be carefully followed. When assessment and classification procedures are monitored correctly through due process procedures, individuals will receive the specialized services needed to help them overcome their learning problems. Parents and guardians will also be given an opportunity to communicate with school officials and to contribute to the placement decision.

Each state Board of Education has developed specific policies and procedures for referring, screening, assessing and placing handicapped individuals according to the mandates of Public Law 94-142. Similarly, each local district must follow a specific identification process mandated by the state to evaluate and place handicapped individuals. Most states follow the general steps described in the following material. Students who are referred for evaluation will remain in the program or class where they are first identified until these steps have been completed and a final decision is made.

1. Initial Referral—A referral should be made to identify a student in a regular education program thought to have a learning problem resulting from a physical, mental or emotional handicap. The objective of this initial referral is to diagnose and evaluate the needs of the student so that an appropriate educational program can be developed along with the necessary support services needed for the student to succeed in school.

The referral can be made from a number of sources, including: teachers, guidance counselors, administrators, judicial officers, social workers, parents/guardians, and physicians. The referring party should provide a written assessment of the individual's strengths and weaknesses. Specific observations made while the learner is involved in classroom or laboratory activities should be documented in writing for future reference.

2. Parent/Guardian Notification—Parents or guardians must be notified of the referral. The notification must be made in writing in the primary language spoken in the home. The notification includes:

    a. The reason for the referral.

    b. An explanation of the evaluation process.

    c. A statement of parent/guardian right of access to all school records concerning the child.

The letter encourages the parent/guardian to contact the school if there are any questions about the contents of the letter. Written permission is requested in the letter to allow the school to evaluate the student to determine his/her unique needs. The parent/guardian has the right to attend the evaluation session. The letter also promises to inform the parent/guardian of the results of the evaluation process within a specific amount of time. All signed parent/guardian permission forms must be kept on file.

3. Student Evaluation Process—A comprehensive diagnostic evaluation is completed by a team of specialists. The general assessment areas for the student evaluation include:

    a. Educational information: initial referral forms, observation reports, intelligence tests, review of school records, aptitude scores, teacher reports, review of speech, language, and motor development.

    b. Social history: information about the family background of the student as well as the current home environment. This information is usually provided by the school social worker or a social agency.

    c. Medical information: a comprehensive physical examination, vision test, hearing test, review of past medical records, review of effects of any prescribed medication.

A decision about placing an individual in a special education program must be based on the results of several tests rather than on a single test. In this way a thorough assessment is assured rather than a quick decision based on a single test. When assessment procedures and specific instruments are selected, necessary adjustments must be made for students who have different cultural or linguistic backgrounds. Testing situations, by law, cannot discriminate against such students because of their differences. For example, a psychological examination must be administered in the language spoken by individuals if they are not proficient in English.

Test and evaluation results must be current. Even after learners are placed in special education programs, they must be reevaluated periodically to assure that the placement is meeting their needs.

4. Committee Review Evaluation Results—A committee composed of professional personnel reviews the results of the student evaluation process. This team may include, among others: (a) administrator, (b) guidance counselor, (c) special education teacher, (d) social worker, (e) psychologist, (f) psychiatrist, (g) vocational evaluator, (h) nurse, (i) speech therapist, (j) audiologist, (k) person making the referral, (l) parent/guardian and (m) any other personnel who can contribute to the committee review and placement recommendation.

It is the responsibility of this committee to carefully review the results of all tests, reports, school records, medical history, social background and referral information.

5. Committee Placement Recommendation—Once the committee has reviewed the information from the comprehensive evaluation, a placement recommendation is made. The parent/guardian has the right to attend and participate in the committee meeting. The parent/guardian must be notified of the placement recommendation made by the committee. This must be done in writing and must describe the program or service that is being recommended. They must be informed of their right to review all records concerning their son/daughter. They can also challenge any of this information.

The parent/guardian must also be given an opportunity to present additional information that could affect a placement decision. Agencies in the community can often provide an independent evaluation for review by the committee.

Finally, the parent/guardian must be informed of appeal procedures to which they can refer if they are dissatisfied with the committee recommendation.

6. Parent/Guardian Options—The parent/guardian may agree to the placement recommendation made by the committee. Once written permission is obtained, the student is placed in the special education program that was recommended.

The parent/guardian may wish to have an independent evaluation conducted. In this case, the committee will meet again to review the results and discuss the placement recommendation once again. At this time, the parent/guardian may either accept or refuse the recommendation.

The parent/guardian may refuse to accept the placement recommendation, with or without an independent evaluation. An appeal must be made.

7. Appeal Process—If the parent/guardian appeals the placement recommendation, another review is made by a different committee or ultimately by a court. The placement decision arrived through the appeal process is binding.

A student placed in a special education program as a result of the process outlined above must be evaluated periodically to determine whether the current placement is meeting his/her needs. Illustration 3.1 shows the general process for referring, assessing, and placing students in a special education program.

## Role of Trade and Industrial Teachers in Referral and Placement Process

If the T & I teacher notices that a student enrolled in a program seems to be having difficulty, the student should be carefully observed. The teacher should note the specific behaviors that the student demonstrates. The general characteristics found in Module Two (Identifying Special Needs Learners and Helping Them Succeed in Your Program) may help the teacher identify a student in need of referral and evaluation. Details of the student's behavior should be documented in writing to provide important information during the evaluation process.

The first step in the identification and placement process is an initial referral. The T & I teacher who feels that a student is in need of evaluation should contact the person in the school who handles the initial referral forms. This could be an administrator, a guidance counselor, a special education teacher or another professional in charge of this step in the identification and placement process.

The T & I teacher will complete the initial referral form, providing specific details about the behavior of the student. Once this referral has been made, the parent/guardian is notified in writing of the referral. The letter asks the parent/guardian for permission to evaluate the student.

When permission to evaluate the student has been obtained, the review committee collects relevant information, test data and records that will be used to determine the placement recommendation. After the comprehensive evaluation process is completed, the committee reviews all the information relative to the student. The T & I teacher, as the person who submits the initial referral, usually contributes to the review committee by discussing the reason for the referral as well as the specific learning problems and behavioral characteristics that the student has displayed in class.

When a final placement decision has been agreed upon by all parties, the T & I teacher may still work with the student in the T & I program if it is determined that he/she can succeed with the aid of support help. Placement in a special education program means that support services are made available to students enrolled in regular educational programs.

## Illustration 3.1

## REFERRAL AND PLACEMENT PROCESS:
## GENERAL PROCEDURE

*Objective:* To (a) identify students who have learning problems, (b) diagnose and evaluate their special needs and (c) develop an appropriate special education program for them.

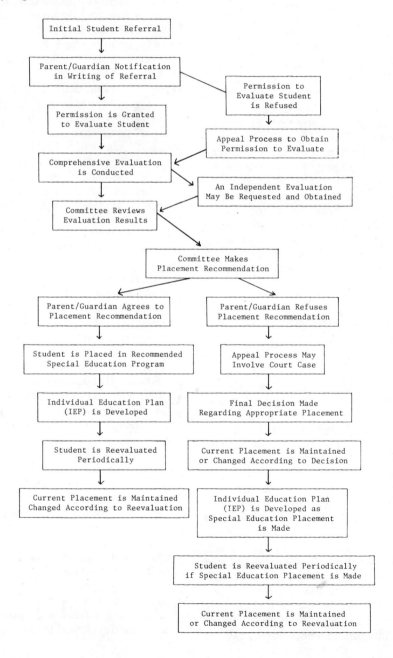

## Comprehensive Policy Statement

The Commission of Education issued a position statement regarding comprehensive vocational education for handicapped persons in September, 1978. This statement assures that "an appropriate comprehensive vocational education will be available and accessible to every handicapped person" (*Federal Register*, 1978).

The position statement was developed cooperatively between the Bureau of Occupational and Adult Education and the Bureau of Education for the Handicapped. It assumes that providing this "appropriate comprehensive vocational education" will depend on personnel in all educational areas. The role of vocational education in the comprehensive delivery of services, for example, is to "provide the education and training to develop occupational competencies" (*Federal Register*, 1978). Other disciplines, such as special education, should also assume a role in this process so that occupational readiness is reached before a student is placed in a vocational program.

## VOCATIONAL EDUCATION DELIVERY OPTIONS

A variety of delivery options should be available for handicapped individuals. Vocational education should not be expected to assume the total responsibility for providing occupational preparation skills for the handicapped population. Not all handicapped individuals can benefit fully from being enrolled in regular vocational programs.

The nature and severity of the person's handicapping condition(s) will greatly influence the extent to which vocational education will be able to provide appropriate opportunities. Many of these individuals will undoubtedly be able to succeed in regular vocational programs. In this case, vocational teachers would have the primary responsibility for providing services. Individuals with more severe handicapping conditions may be more successful in a more sheltered environment. In this case, vocational teachers may assume a secondary role in providing services as resource personnel and/or consultants.

The National Association of State Boards of Education (1979) released a state of the art report that mentioned a series of five vocational education delivery options for handicapped individuals. This variety should allow individual learners to successfully develop their vocational potential to the maximum. The five vocational education delivery options included:

1. *Regular vocational education programs* allow learners to participate in regular programs on a full-time basis, including classroom and laboratory activities. Slight modifications and/or resources may be necessary to ensure successful experiences. These might include speech therapy, social worker consultation, vocational counseling, adaptive devices and minor architectural changes. Vocational personnel should assume the primary responsibility for vocational instruction in this delivery option. Special education and other personnel should function in a support role to provide supplementary or remedial services. A positive, cooperative working relationship among professionals is important.

2. *Adapted vocational education programs* usually require specific adaptations in the program curriculum, teaching techniques and/or instructional materials for learners to experience success. Vocational personnel should assume the primary responsibility for vocational instruction in this delivery option also. However, support help and remedial assistance from special education is often necessary. Essential modifications might include remedial academic assistance from resource room teachers, specific curriculum modifications and/or materials written on a lower reading level. Again, a positive cooperative working relationship among professionals is important.

3. *Special vocational education programs* are developed for learners who are

unable to succeed in a regular vocational education program on a full-time basis because of the severity of their disability. Instruction is usually provided in a self-contained special education classroom. Special education personnel normally assume the primary responsibility for vocational instruction in this delivery option. Vocational education personnel should assume a secondary role and function in a support or resource capacity to ensure successful experiences. For example, vocational teachers can act as consultants to special education teachers by identifying appropriate prerequisite entry-level skills necessary for entry into the labor market.

4. *Individual vocational training programs* are individually prescribed to meet the specific needs of learners who cannot succeed in regular vocational education programs. The primary responsibility for vocational training in this delivery option should be assumed by special education personnel, vocational rehabilitation personnel, or a combination of both. Programs are developed to provide learners with appropriate prerequisite skills for specific jobs. Work-study programs and on-the-job training situations are examples of avenues to implement this option. Vocational teachers can be supportive by acting as resources or consultants.

5. *Prevocational evaluation programs* are developed for learners whose disabilities are so severe that they are unable to participate in activities found in the regular education environment. The primary objective of this delivery option is to complete a comprehensive prevocational skills assessment and subsequently provide placement in appropriate employment or training situations. Examples of avenues to implement this option include rehabilitation-sponsored facilities, work activity centers and sheltered workshops. Vocational rehabilitation personnel should assume the primary responsibility for vocational training in this delivery option. Special education and vocational education personnel both should assume a sec-

ondary role as consultants.

Illustration 3.2 provides an overview of the comprehensive system of vocational education delivery options.

## PLACING HANDICAPPED LEARNERS IN TRADE AND INDUSTRIAL PROGRAMS

According to the Education for All Handicapped Children Act of 1975 (Public Law 94–142), handicapped students must be placed in the "least restrictive alternative." This regulation requires that handicapped students be placed in regular education programs whenever possible. Handicapped students must be provided with equal opportunities to succeed in the same programs as nonhandicapped students. Their abilities cannot be restricted by placing them in separate classes or programs away from their peers. Support services and aids necessary to help the handicapped student succeed in the regular program must be provided.

After the identification, assessment and special education placement process has occurred, an appropriate education plan is developed for the handicapped student. At this point a decision is made concerning the ability of the student to benefit from participation in regular education programs. This includes enrollment in T & I programs.

## DELIVERY OPTIONS FOR TRADE AND INDUSTRIAL PROGRAMS

As illustrated in the previous section describing the comprehensive system of vocational education delivery options, a variety of placement options should also be developed for handicapped individuals who wish to participate in T & I programs. Suggested delivery options follow:

1. *Full-time participation in regular T & I programs* would be appropriate for

**Illustration 3.2**

## COMPREHENSIVE SYSTEM OF VOCATIONAL EDUCATION DELIVERY OPTIONS

*Handicapped Learners:* According to the nature and severity of their handicapping conditions and their specific abilities and needs can be placed in one of the following delivery options. Changes in program placement can be made as learner is continuously assessed.

| Regular Vocational Education Program – | Adapted Vocational Education Program – | Special Vocational Education Program – | Individual Vocational Training Program – | Prevocational Evaluation Program – |
|---|---|---|---|---|
| Full-time participation in regular vocational education program with slight modifications and/or resources. | Participation in regular vocational education program with specific adaptations in the program curriculum, teaching techniques and/or instructional materials. | Participation in a self-contained special classroom vocational program. | Participation in programs which are individually prescribed to meet the specific training needs of each learner in an attempt to develop appropriate prerequisite skills for a specific job. | Participation in activities which result in a comprehensive prevocational assessment and subsequent placement in appropriate employment or training situations. |
| Examples: | Examples: | Example: | Examples: | Examples: |
| Social Worker | Resource Room Assistance | Development of appropriate prerequisite entry-level skills necessary for entry into the labor market | Work-study programs | Rehabilitation sponsored facilities |
| Vocational Counseling | Specific Curriculum Modifications | | On-the-job training situations | Work activity centers |
| Speech Therapy | Materials written on lower reading level | | | Sheltered workshops |
| Minor Architectural changes | | | | |

(Adapted from *Vocational education of handicapped youth: State of the art*, Washington, D. C.: National Association of State Boards of Education, 1979.)

handicapped learners who may require only slight modifications and/or support services such as minor architectural changes, vocational counseling, speech therapy, special seating arrangements and early dismissal. Special education personnel should assume a support role to provide services necessary for these learners to succeed.

2. *Adapted T & I programs* would be appropriate for handicapped learners who cannot succeed in regular programs without specific adaptations made to the curriculum, teaching techniques, and/or instructional materials. Special education personnel can be an invaluable resource to both the student and the T & I teacher in the form of remedial instruction, extended time to complete program requirements, curriculum modification, material adaptation (e.g., lower reading level, large print, braille, taped instruction, programmed instruction), identification and implementation of appropriate teaching techniques, flexible scheduling, and in-class assistance (e.g., teacher aide, tutor, reader, interpreter).

3. *Individualized T & I programs* would be appropriate for handicapped learners whose disabilities are serious enough to prevent them from completing the entire program. In this case, the program would have to be modified and individually prescribed to meet the specific abilities and needs of each individual. In this manner, the appropriate prerequisite skills could be developed for a specific job in the T & I area. An individualized approach to vocational instruction and/or time limitations for completion of tasks may have to be altered. Extensive modifications of the classroom environment, furniture, tools and equipment may have to be considered. An open-entry/open-exit situation is often the best way of implementing this option. Special education personnel should be directly involved in cooperative planning efforts to ensure success.

4. *Participation in select laboratory activities* can be an option offered to handicapped individuals. By taking advantage of this delivery option, these learners can develop specific hands-on skills for vocational or avocational purposes. An example might be a specific student who may attend laboratory/shop sessions in a transportation program during the time the instructor is teaching engine tune-up. They could benefit from the laboratory activities without having to attend classroom lectures or read a textbook that may be too difficult for them. Cooperative planning between special education and vocational education personnel is very important.

5. *Informal vocational evaluation activities* can be established in regular T & I programs to assess the abilities of handicapped individuals wishing to participate in a specific program. Special education and vocational education personnel should function as a team to observe and analyze learner performance on tasks relating to successful performance in the T & I program. This team can then cooperatively select the best delivery option for the individual as well as plan appropriate program modifications.

6. *Career exploration activities* can be established in regular T & I programs to provide handicapped individuals with an opportunity to explore the "world of trade and industrial education." These activities will be helpful in identifying the specific program that is best suited to the interests and abilities of the specific learner.

Illustration 3.3 provides some suggested delivery options that could be offered to handicapped learners who want to participate in T & I programs.

## SUMMARY

Public Law 94–142 (The Education for All Handicapped Children Act of 1975) assures that every handicapped individual aged 3 to 21 will be provided with an appropriate education. It is essential that these students be evaluated correctly before they are placed in special education classes.

## Illustration 3.3

### SUGGESTED DELIVERY OPTIONS FOR PLACING HANDICAPPED STUDENTS IN TRADE AND INDUSTRIAL PROGRAMS

*Handicapped Learners* wishing to participate in trade and industrial programs may be provided with a series of delivery options according to the nature and severity of their handicapping conditions and their specific abilities and needs.

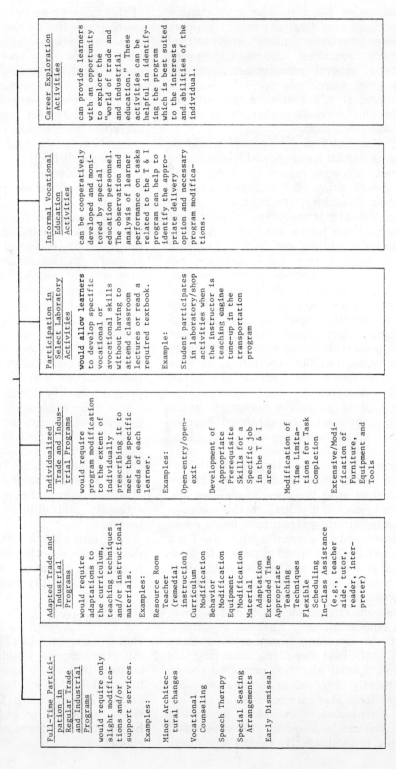

**Full-Time Participation in Regular Trade and Industrial Programs**

would require only slight modifications and/or support services.

Examples:

Minor Architectural changes

Vocational Counseling

Speech Therapy

Special Seating Arrangements

Early Dismissal

**Adapted Trade and Industrial Programs**

would require adaptations to the curriculum, teaching techniques and/or instructional materials.

Examples:

Resource Room Teacher (remedial instruction)

Curriculum Modification

Behavior Modification

Equipment Modification

Material Adaptation

Extended Time

Appropriate Teaching Techniques

Flexible Scheduling

In-Class Assistance (e.g., teacher aide, tutor, reader, interpreter)

**Individualized Trade and Industrial Programs**

would require program modification to the extent of individually prescribing it to meet the specific needs of each learner.

Examples:

Open-entry/open-exit

Development of Appropriate Prerequisite Skills for a Specific Job in the T & I area

Modification of Time Limitations for Task Completion

Extensive/Modification of Furniture, Equipment and Tools

**Participation in Select Laboratory Activities**

would allow learners to develop specific vocational or avocational skills without having to attend classroom lectures or read a required textbook.

Example:

Student participates in laboratory/shop activities when the instructor is teaching engine tune-up in the transportation program

**Informal Vocational Education Activities**

can be cooperatively developed and monitored by special education personnel. The observation and analysis of learner performance on tasks related to the T & I program can help to identify the appropriate delivery option and necessary program modifications.

**Career Exploration Activities**

can provide learners with an opportunity to explore the "world of trade and and industrial education." These activities can be helpful in identifying the program which is best suited to the interests and abilities of the individual.

Due process proceedings guarantee appropriate procedures for referring, assessing, evaluating and placing individuals in special education programs. Certain basic steps in the identification and placement process for the handicapped are: (a) initial referral, (b) parent/guardian notification, (c) student evaluation process, (d) committee review of evaluation results, (e) committee placement recommendation, (f) parent/guardian options, including an acceptance of the recommendation, a request for an independent evaluation or referral to accept the recommendation, and (g) appeal process.

The T & I teacher who identifies a student suspected of having a learning problem will have an important role in this process. An initial referral form must be filled out indicating the reason for the referral. The teacher may also be asked to attend the committee meeting and review the student's record of achievement and behavior pattern.

Once the referral, assessment and placement procedures have been completed, an appropriate educational plan is developed for the student. At this time, it is decided whether the student, with necessary support services and aids, can benefit from participation in a vocational education program. Enrollment in a T & I program would be one possible choice. A series of delivery options should be developed to meet the needs of handicapped individuals.

## REFERENCES

Davis, S. and Ward, M. *Vocational education of handicapped students: A guide for policy development.* Reston, Virginia: The Council for Exceptional Children, 1978.

Evans, R., Albright, L. and Fabac, J. *Introduction to the identification and assessment system.* Champaign, Illinois: University of Illinois at Urbana-Champaign, Bureau of Educational Research.

*Federal Register.* Vocational education of handicapped persons: Position statement. 43, 186, September 25, 1978.

Hewett, F. and Forness, S. *Education of exceptional learners.* Boston: Allyn and Bacon, Inc., 1977.

Klein, N. Least restrictive alternative: An educational analysis. *Education and training of the mentally retarded,* (131), 1978, pp. 102–114.

Moore, J. and Engleman, V. (Ed.). *Administrators manual programming for handicapped students at the secondary level: Responding to public laws.* Salt Lake City, Utah: The Southwest Regional Resource Center, 1977.

National Association of State Boards of Education. *Vocational education of handicapped youth: State of the art.* Washington, D.C.: Author, 1979.

Phelps, L.A. A proposed system for the identification, assessment and evaluation of special needs learners. *Journal of Industrial Teacher Education,* 1977, *14* (3), 19–35.

Tindall, L. and Gugerty, J. *Least restrictive alternative for handicapped students.* Columbus, Ohio: The Ohio State University, National Center for Research in Vocational Education, 1979.

Weintraub, Ballard and LaVor (Eds.). *Public policy and the education of exceptional children.* Reston, Virginia: The Council for Exceptional Children, 1976.

## SELF ASSESSMENT: IDENTIFICATION, ASSESSMENT AND PLACEMENT OF HANDICAPPED STUDENTS

1. What effect has labeling had on the placement of students in special education programs in the past?
2. What law guarantees due process rights to handicapped individuals?
3. What are the due process procedures?
4. Why is the due process procedure guaranteed to handicapped individuals?
5. Identify the steps in the identification and assessment procedures for handicapped students.
6. Describe the referral process. What must be done?
7. Describe the evaluation process. What information is collected?
8. What is the role of the T & I teacher in the referral and assessment procedure for handicapped students?
9. What is the role of the parent/guardian in the identification and assessment procedure for handicapped students?
10. What is the role of the school in the identification and assessment procedure for handicapped students?
11. What is the "least restrictive alternative" for handicapped students?
12. If the student is placed in a special education program, what must be provided for him/her?
13. If a student is placed in a special education program, does this mean that he/she will no longer participate in the T & I program?
14. What guarantee does the comprehensive policy statement give? What is the responsibility of vocational education in this position statement?
15. Describe several vocational delivery options that should be made available to handicapped students.
16. Describe several delivery options that could be made available to handicapped individuals who want to participate in T & I programs.

## ASSOCIATED ACTIVITIES

1. Locate the person in your school who is responsible for the initial referral forms for the identification and assessment procedure. Obtain a copy of the referral form and review it. Keep it in your desk in case you identify a student in your program whom you feel should be referred for evaluation.
2. Talk to the special education personnel in your school about the referral and assessment procedure for handicapped students. Become familiar with the specific process in your state so that you will be prepared to participate if a student in your program is referred.
3. Talk to the special education personnel in your school about your role in the referral and assessment procedures for handicapped students. Become familiar with the role that you would take in this process as a referring teacher.
4. Identify support personnel available to work with handicapped students in your school and/or district. Talk to these people to find out exactly how they assist handicapped students to succeed in the least restrictive alternative.
5. Consult with the special education personnel in your building/district to discuss the delivery options that could be offered to allow handicapped learners to participate in your program.

## CASE HISTORY: BRIDGET'S STORY

Bridget is a student who is in a special education program for students with emotional and behavior problems. She has normal intelligence, although her grades in other classes are mostly Cs or below. She can read and compute math problems on the same level as her peers when she puts forth the effort.

Bridget has enrolled in the appliance servicing program. After completing a period of time in the vocational assessment laboratory at the area vocational technical school, she was found to have above average mechanical aptitude. Her coordination and dexterity skills are very good. She has also had experiences in industrial arts and in the mechanical drawing program during her freshman year. Both instructors indicated that Bridget performed well in laboratory activities and during demonstrations but had problems paying attention during class discussions and lectures.

The instructor in the appliance servicing program has been working closely with the special education teacher. Several times during the past month Bridget has displayed outbursts of temper in class. This inappropriate behavior makes it difficult for the instructor to maintain control of the rest of the class. A conference was recently held between Bridget, the T & I instructor and the special education teacher. The class rules and regulations were firmly emphasized and the consequences were also discussed. Later the special education teacher worked cooperatively with the T & I instructor to establish a system of simple behavior modification techniques that could be reinforced in both class environments.

A student-teacher contract system was developed for Bridget's program of study in appliance servicing. She had no problems succeeding in the blueprint reading, sketching, and basic electricity units. However, she became frustrated while working on the pipefitting and refrigeration units. This seemed to provoke her emotional outbursts.

The contracts have been set up so that the work is self-paced. Since Bridget contributed to the planning of the contract, she feels more confident of succeeding. The contract system has proven to be an effective motivating technique. Her behavior has been steadily improving. Her test grades have all been good since the special education teacher has been reviewing the material from the T & I program.

## CASE HISTORY ACTIVITY

Frank has just enrolled in your program. He is an emotionally disturbed learner and attends special education classes. Frank is very hyperactive and finds it difficult to concentrate on tasks or to remain in his seat for long periods of time. He often wanders around the room during laboratory activities.

Frank has average intelligence but his grades in school have always been below average. Because of this his self-concept is poor. He has also been having problems developing friendships with his peers in the class.

Based on this information, complete the case history profile worksheet for Frank's participation in your program.

# CASE HISTORY PROFILE WORKSHEET

Student: _____ Page: _____

Handicapping Condition(s): _____

T & I Program: _____ Academic Levels: _____

Career Goal/Occupational Interest: _____

Considerations (e.g., medication, behavior): _____
_____

| Adaptation | Specific Services Needed | Where to Obtain Service |
|---|---|---|
| Cooperative Planning (School Personnel) | | |
| Support Services | | |
| Architectural Changes | | |
| Adaptive Equipment | | |
| Curriculum Modification | | |
| Instructional Materials/ Supplies | | |
| Teaching Techniques | | |
| Agency Involvement | | |
| Possible Job Placement | | |

# MODULE 4

## The Individualized Education Program

The Education for All Handicapped Children Act of 1975 (Public Law 94–142) mandates an individualized education program (IEP) be established for each handicapped student age 3 to 21, to assure that these individuals receive an education that meets their specific needs. The 1976 Amendments to the Vocational Education Act (Public Law 94–482) parallel this mandate by assuring that handicapped students will be placed in vocational education programs according to the goals and objectives developed in the IEP.

It is important for T & I personnel to be involved in the IEP process when handicapped students are enrolled in existing programs. Trade and industrial personnel alone have the expertise and background to develop realistic and appropriate goals and objectives for their programs. Therefore, they should be instrumental in developing the vocational education component of the IEP as well as in evaluating the extent to which the student has met them.

This module presents information about the IEP process, the necessary components of the IEP, the role and responsibilities of T & I personnel in the IEP process, and the benefits that T & I personnel can gain from participating in the planning, implementation and review phases of the IEP.

Specific sections in this module include (a) an introduction to the Individualized Education Program, (b) purposes of the IEP, (c) the IEP team, (d) role and responsibilities of Trade and Industrial personnel, (e) components of the IEP, and (f) benefits for Trade and Industrial personnel participating in the IEP process.

## MODULE OBJECTIVES

After you have read and reviewed this module, studied the case history, reviewed the self-assessment questions and completed the associated activities, you should be able to:

1. Discuss the importance of the IEP as a management tool in providing appropriate educational experiences for handicapped individuals.

2. Describe the IEP team meeting, the purpose for this meeting, the required participants and the role of the T & I personnel at this planning session.

3. List the required components of the IEP and describe the function of each component.

4. Describe the benefits for T & I personnel participating in the IEP process.

## INTRODUCTION TO THE INDIVIDUALIZED EDUCATION PROGRAM

The Education for All Handicapped Children Act of 1975 (Public Law 94–142) guarantees certain rights for handicapped individuals. One of these guarantees is the requirement that handicapped learners be provided with a free, appropriate education in an environment that is "least restrictive" to their abilities. In order to assure that the educational program for each of these learners is individually prescribed, carefully planned and frequently monitored, this Act requires that a written individualized education program (IEP) be developed and reviewed at least annually for each handicapped individual age 3 to 21. The mandate assures that this population will be provided with appropriate special education and related services necessary for them to succeed in the specific educational program designed to meet their needs.

The 1976 Amendments to the Vocational Education Act (Public Law 94–482) provide that handicapped learners be given an opportunity to participate in existing vocational education programs whenever possible. These learners will be placed in vocational education programs according to the goals and objectives set forth in the IEP.

## PURPOSES OF THE IEP

The basic philosophy behind the IEP is the apparent need to develop a comprehensive plan to guarantee special education programming to all handicapped youth who require these services and to ensure that appropriate and realistic decisions are made regarding educational opportunities that are provided for them. The IEP acts as a management tool to assist educators in scheduling, implementing and evaluating essential services and activities to meet the needs of these learners.

One important purpose of the IEP is to plan an educational program that is individually prescribed to meet the assessed needs of each handicapped individual. The IEP is a general guide by which personnel can determine the most realistic direction to take in providing an appropriate education for the learner. Goals and objectives help to determine instructional activities that can facilitate student progress.

Another important purpose of the IEP is to provide a system of accountability for providing educational services to handicapped individuals. This accountability can be assured for a number of reasons. First, the IEP identifies specific personnel who will have the responsibility for implementing the contents of individualized programs. Second, a system for continuously monitoring student progress is provided through the short-term instructional objectives and the criterion levels identified for each one.

A third important purpose of the IEP is to provide for an open channel of communication among all personnel working with the individual. In this manner, a comprehensive, coordinated and orga-

nized plan of action can be developed to meet the needs of the learner. The degree to which this coordinated effort is planned, implemented and monitored will greatly affect the level of success that the student will experience in achieving the annual goals and short term objectives developed in the IEP.

## IEP TEAM

A team of individuals is responsible for developing the IEP. This team must include the following members:

1. An administrator or representative of the local education agency.
2. The student's parents/guardians.
3. The teachers (special and classroom) who will be responsible for working with the student.
4. The student, if appropriate.

Each of these participants provides a unique element to the development of the IEP. The administrator determines what support services and resources are available in the school or district as well as the local community and can help to ensure that appropriate support services are provided to meet the needs of the student. The administrator will also be instrumental in scheduling these services or obtaining sufficient funds to purchase necessary resources.

The parent or guardian can provide essential background information about the needs of the student. Federal law now recognizes the rights of these parents to be active participants in the educational planning of their handicapped children. Therefore, they must be given an opportunity to be involved in the decision-making and planning process that occurs during the IEP meeting.

The teacher(s) involved in the development of the IEP will be responsible for implementing and monitoring the contents of the individual program. Representatives can include special education teachers as well as regular classroom teachers who will have the handicapped student in their class or program. These team members can help to interpret diagnostic information, identify the specific educational needs of the learner, develop appropriate goals and objectives to meet these needs, and identify the support services and resources that will be required.

Last, but certainly not least, the student can be involved as a contributing member of the team to develop the IEP. Frequently, students have been eliminated from planning sessions that determine the direction of their educational program. Federal law now guarantees that handicapped students be given an opportunity, when appropriate, to participate in developing their educational program. (Illustration 4.1 describes the IEP process for handicapped students.)

## ROLE AND RESPONSIBILITIES OF TRADE AND INDUSTRIAL PERSONNEL

Trade and industrial personnel should be instrumental in developing the vocational education component of the IEP and in evaluating the extent to which the student has succeeded in accomplishing the goals stated in the IEP.

When handicapped students are mainstreamed in vocational education programs it is important that vocational education personnel be represented on the IEP team. Vocational education representatives can include the vocational administrator and/or vocational supervisor, a vocational counselor, and vocational education teachers who will be responsible for instructing the student. (see Illustration 4.2).

Special education personnel often do not have an understanding of trade and industrial education and thus cannot develop realistic goals for the student who is to be placed in a specific program. Therefore, it is essential that T & I personnel be involved in the IEP process when handicapped students are enrolled

in existing programs.

Illustration 4.3 is an example of a case study report of an IEP meeting, and illustration 4.4 shows the various responsibilities of team members.

## COMPONENTS OF THE IEP

The format of the IEP varies among school systems; however, each form includes the same basic parts. The essential components of the IEP include (a) a statement of the present level of educational performance, (b) annual goals and short-term instructional objectives, (c) specific educational services to be provided, including the anticipated date they will begin and how long they will be needed, (d) the extent to which the student will participate in regular educational programs/activities, and (e) appropriate objective criteria and evaluation at least once a year to determine whether instructional objectives are being achieved.

Each of these essential components will be discussed in this section. Examples will be provided to illustrate information available in an IEP. In addition, the role of the T & I teacher will be reviewed as it relates to each of the necessary elements of the IEP. Illustration 4.5 illustrates the mandated components of the IEP.

### Present Level of Educational Performance

A statement of the student's present level of educational performance is the first component that should be present in each IEP. This statement includes performance levels in a variety of educational content areas, including academic achievement, personal-social skills, psychomotor skills, self-help skills, and prevocational and vocational skills.

The information necessary to determine the present level of performance for a particular student is gathered from a variety of sources. These sources include (a) consultations with school personnel, parents and/or community agencies, (b)

**Illustration 4.1**

## IEP PROCESS FOR HANDICAPPED STUDENTS

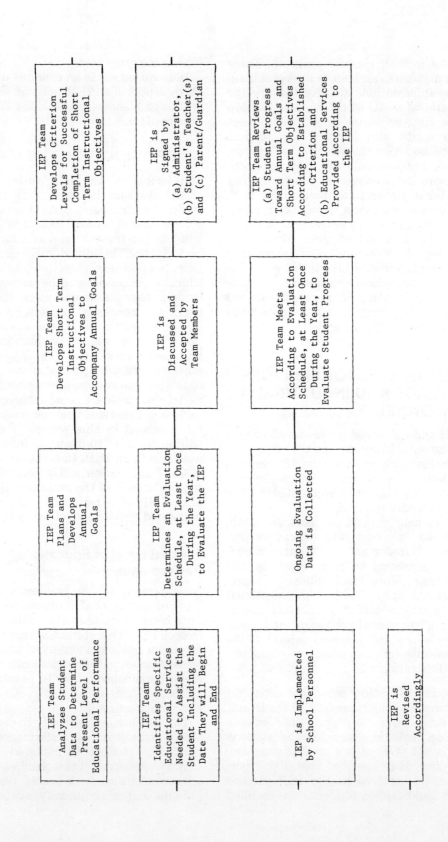

## Illustration 4.2

## SUGGEST IEP TEAM MEMBERSHIP FOR HANDICAPPED STUDENTS ENROLLED IN A TRADE AND INDUSTRIAL PROGRAM

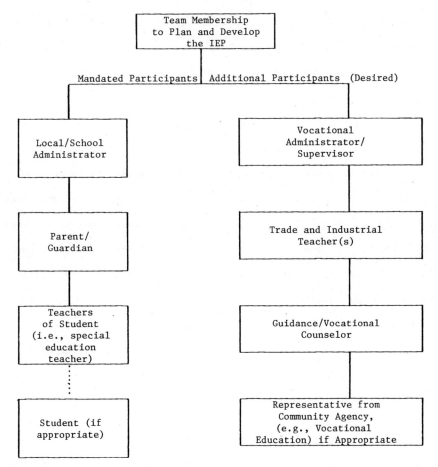

## Illustration 4.3

## CASE STUDY: IEP TEAM MEETING

Mr. Anderson is the construction teacher at Dunkirk High School. In early September he was contacted by Mrs. Proper, the special education teacher, to discuss the possibility of enrolling a student with behavior problems in the construction program during the coming year. They arranged to meet during their lunch hour the following week to discuss the student.

Illustration 4.3 (continued)

Mr. Anderson learned that the student, Jeremy Bartlett, had participated in a series of career exploration activities the previous year,
including a variety of hands-on experiences in the areas of masonry,
carpentry and plumbing in the construction program.  He remembered that
Jeremy had performed very well despite several instances of inappropriate behavior.  After completing the career exploration activities
Jeremy expressed a desire to be enrolled in the construction program.

Mrs. Proper then asked Mr. Anderson to attend the IEP team meeting
to be held at the end of the week.  Mr. Anderson noted that he was free
during the period when the team meeting was to be held and agreed to
attend.  He and Mrs. Proper then discussed his role and responsibilities
for this planning session.  Mrs. Proper told him that his expertise
was needed to help plan realistic goals and objectives for Jeremy in
relationship to the construction program.  She also emphasized that she
was very eager to plan cooperatively in order to provide both Mr. Anderson
and Jeremy with appropriate support help.

When Mr. Anderson arrived at the conference room for the IEP team
meeting he found several other participants there.  Attending the planning
session were:  (a) special education supervisor, (b) vocational supervisor, (c) Mrs. Proper, (d) Jeremy's parents and (e) Jeremy.

Once the initial introductions had been made the special education
supervisor, as a representative of the local school district, brought the
meeting to order and explained the tasks that were before them.  These
tasks included reviewing information about Jeremy and developing an
appropriate IEP for the coming year.

The team first examined school records, test data, attendance records,
and vocational assessment reports to determine Jeremy's present level of

educational performance. Jeremy has been in a special education program for students with behavior problems for the past three years. During this time he has received assistance from Mrs. Proper; she feels that he has made great strides. The team discussed the efforts that had been made during the previous year, especially the progress that Jeremy made in the two regular classes (programs) that he attended.

The next step was to determine the general scope of Jeremy's educational program for the year and to develop appropriate annual goals to give direction to his program. Jeremy and his parents actively participated in this discussion by providing information about his interests and personal goals. One important point of discussion was his desire to participate in the construction program. The vocational assessment information was reviewed along with Mr. Anderson's observations made during the exploration activities. Both sources indicated that he possessed general work habits and attitudes, vocational aptitude and personal interest that would benefit him. It was decided that Jeremy would be enrolled in the construction program, beginning in the carpentry area.

Mr. Anderson then had an opportunity to tell the other team members about the goals and objectives of his program. He was instrumental in developing the annual goals and short term instructional objectives that were appropriate for Jeremy. Criterion levels for successful mastery of goals and objectives were also discussed. Finally, Mr. Anderson had an opportunity to identify the support services and instructional materials that he would need to help Jeremy succeed. Mrs. Proper assured him that cooperative planning would follow throughout the year. They agreed to establish and maintain an open system of communication and sharing as well as a process of periodic evaluation to determine whether the IEP was meeting Jeremy's needs.

Illustration 4.3 (continued)

After the IEP had been developed and discussed, a date was scheduled at the end of the year for the IEP team to meet and review the IEP.

Mr. Anderson felt more confident about his ability to work with Jeremy in the construction program after the IEP team meeting for the following reasons:

1.    he felt that he better understands the problems that Jeremy has relating to his emotional handicap and can deal with situations that might occur in the construction class/laboratory;

2.    he felt reassured to know that there will be support help available for Jeremy in the form of special education personnel—cooperative planning will definitely make his job easier;

3.    he felt more like a contributing member of the IEP because he had an opportunity to establish realistic annual goals and accompanying objectives for Jeremy to attain in the construction program as opposed to having these goals and objectives developed by individuals who had no knowledge of the T & I area.

interviews with the student, (c) rating scales, checklists and inventories, (d) standardized tests, (e) criterion referenced tests, (f) evaluation results available from student records, and (g) evaluations by teachers, counselors, psychologists, and a psychometrist.

Certain criteria should be met in gathering assessment information. The information used should come from a variety of tests and batteries. Examples include standardized tests to determine I.Q., vision and hearing tests, performance tests to determine reading and math achievement levels, work sample batteries, aptitude tests, and interest batteries.

Tests should also be nondiscriminatory. For instance, students who speak limited English should be tested in the language spoken in the home so that the results will be a better predictor of the student's abilities and interests. Modifications may have to be made in the testing procedure for a specific handicapped individual. Deaf individuals may need an interpreter to aid them in understanding test items. Visually impaired individuals may need extended time when taking tests.

Finally, information obtained from tests should be recent in order to be helpful in assessing the present level of performance. Therefore, students must be

## Illustration 4.4

## RESPONSIBILITIES OF IEP COMMITTEE MEMBERS

| Responsibility | T & I Teacher | Special Education Teacher(s) | Guidance/Vocational Counselor | Administrator (Vocational Supervisor, Special Education, Local/School Administrator) | Representative from Community Agency | Parent/Guardian | Student |
|---|---|---|---|---|---|---|---|
| Gather background information concerning a particular student | X | X | X | X | X | X | X |
| Develop appropriate annual goals for participation in the T & I program | X | X |  | X | X | X | X |
| Develop realistic short term instructional objectives to accompany IEP | X | X |  |  |  | X |  |
| Develop specific criterion levels for successful achievements of short term objectives | X | X |  |  |  |  |  |
| Identify support services that will be necessary to aid the student | X | X |  | X | X | X |  |
| Provide necessary support services | X | X |  | X | X |  |  |
| Develop appropriate lesson plans that will implement the content of the IEP | X | X |  |  |  |  |  |
| Utilize appropriate teaching techniques | X | X |  |  |  |  |  |
| Supply remedial assistance |  | X |  |  | X | X |  |
| Periodically assess student progress in achieving the goals and objectives | X | X |  |  |  |  |  |
| Document student progress for use in evaluating the IEP | X | X |  |  |  |  |  |
| Participate in the annual review of the IEP | X | X |  | X | X | X | X |

## Illustration 4.5

## MANDATED COMPONENTS OF THE IEP

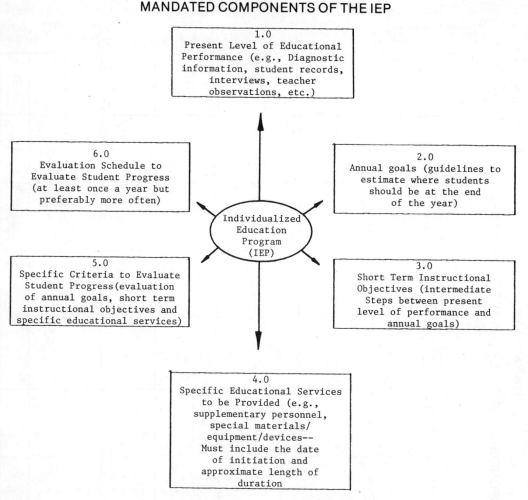

1.0
Present Level of Educational
Performance (e.g., Diagnostic
information, student records,
interviews, teacher
observations, etc.)

6.0
Evaluation Schedule to
Evaluate Student Progress
(at least once a year but
preferably more often)

2.0
Annual goals (guidelines to
estimate where students
should be at the end
of the year)

Individualized
Education
Program
(IEP)

5.0
Specific Criteria to Evaluate
Student Progress (evaluation
of annual goals, short term
instructional objectives and
specific educational services)

3.0
Short Term Instructional
Objectives (intermediate
Steps between present
level of performance and
annual goals)

4.0
Specific Educational Services
to be Provided (e.g.,
supplementary personnel,
special materials/
equipment/devices--
Must include the date
of initiation and
approximate length of
duration

periodically reevaluated so that current performance levels are known to personnel developing the IEP. Currently, reevaluations are required every three years.

*Role of Trade and Industrial Personnel.* The T & I teacher should identify information about the student that would be helpful in developing realistic goals, objectives, and necessary services to help the student succeed in the program. Examples of pertinent information relating to the student's present level of educational performance are:

1. Reading level.
2. Math level.
3. Results of vocational interest and/or aptitude results.
4. Results of work sample batteries.
5. Previous vocational/T & I courses taken.
6. Communication skills.
7. Gross motor skills.
8. Fine motor skills.
9. Interpersonal relationship skills.
10. Medication that may affect physical and/or behavioral performance.
11. Overt behavior problems.

12. Strong learning style (i.e., visual, auditory).
13. Ability to work in groups.
14. Work experience.
15. Prevocational background.
16. Ability to follow safety rules.

Special education can help to provide this information or arrange for appropriate testing that will provide the information. This will assist the T & I teacher in planning an appropriate program for the student.

Trade and industrial personnel who will be working with handicapped learners can positively contribute to developing a pupil profile through the identification and establishment of the present level of educational performance. Some examples of responsibilities that can be assumed by T & I personnel to foster a positive cooperative working relationship with special education personnel and to ensure that this portion of the IEP is realistic are as follows:

1. Analyze the prevocational and/or vocational education background of the student to determine the most appropriate program goals for the student.

2. Ascertain the physical accessibility of the T & I classroom and laboratory to determine any necessary architectural and/or equipment modifications.

3. Identify academic, prevocational and/or skill prerequisites that will help to determine whether the student is prepared to enroll in the T & I program and/or identify necessary services to assist the student in succeeding (i.e., ability to read a ruler, ability to follow safety rules, ability to recognize specific vocational vocabulary terms essential to the T & I program).

4. Identify important T & I program information that will help to determine appropriate goals and objectives relating to the abilities of the student (e.g., proficiency skills necessary for entry level employment, appropriate instructional areas/units in the T & I program, specific safety standards that must be observed).

5. Assist in providing vocational education exploration activities for handicapped students to assist them in identifying their interests (e.g., informal "hands-on" activities, information about jobs that can be obtained after completion of program/course requirements).

## Examples of Present Level of Educational Performance

Following is an example of information describing the present level of educational performance for a student who plans to enroll in a T & I program.

## Annual Goals and Short-Term Instructional Objectives

The second component present in each IEP includes statements of annual goals and specific short-term instructional objectives. These goals and objectives should be based on the student's present level of educational performance.

The annual goals indicate the general direction the student will follow during the year and describe the performance to be demonstrated by the student at the end of the year. These goals should be realistic and reasonable in relation to the abilities, performance, and interests of the student. The goals are generally developed in the performance areas addressed in the present level statements (i.e., academic skills, personal-social skills, psychomotor skills, self-help skills, and prevocational and vocational skills). The performance areas and annual goals to be included in the IEP depend on the specific needs of the individual student. The number of goals developed for a specific student depends on the nature and/or severity of the handicapping condition(s).

Once the destination for a student's educational program has been described in the annual goal statements, short-term instructional objectives are developed. These objectives represent intermediate

INDIVIDUALIZED EDUCATION PROGRAM

Student's Name: _Michael Moore_

Birthdate: _December 8, 1964_     Age: _16_

Grade: _10_     Dominant Language Spoken in Home: _English_

Health Conditions (Including Prescribed Medication): _diabetic (home insulin injections)_

Placement: _Learning Disabilities Program_

Strong Learning Mode: _Visual_

Date of IEP Planning: _September 18, 1980_

Date of Annual Review: _May 30, 1981_

PRESENT LEVEL OF EDUCATIONAL PERFORMANCE:

Academic Skills: _Michael performed at the following levels on recent achievement tests: Reading 3.5 (greatest difficulty in word attack skills) Math 4.0 (deficiency in the areas of measurement and long division) Michael's performance in his regular academic classes has resulted in "C" grades during the past year. He has received related academic assistance in a resource room during one period each day._

Psychomotor Skills: _Michael was observed carefully during exploratory activities and was given a series of exercises to determine gross and fine motor skills. As a result, he exhibited a slight weakness in fine finger dexterity._

Personal-Social Skills: _Michael is shy and withdrawn. His regular classroom teachers have noted that he has difficulty in communicating with his peers when placed in a group activity situation. He has stated a preference of working by himself on several occasions rather than be put into a situation where he would have to react with others in the class._

Self-help Skills: *Michael has no significant problems in the area of self-help skills that differ from his peer groups. Michael is able to administer the insulin injection at home daily to meet the needs of his diabetic condition.*

Prevocational/Vocational Skills: *Michael had an opportunity to participate in a series of career exploration activities during the past year to help him determine which vocational program met his abilities and interests. After experiencing exploratory activities in several areas, Michael indicated that he preferred the auto body repair program. He also has had career education classes provided by his special education teachers at the junior high school level.*

1.  Trade and Industrial Program:  Construction (Masonry)

    Annual Goal(s):  By the end of the year the student will be able to demonstrate competence in fundamental trowel handling, tool manipulation, laying brick to a line, and the use of brick spacing rules.

| Short Term Instructional Objectives | Specific Criteria for Successful Completion |
|---|---|
| 1.1  The student will display the proper use of a trowel in spreading mortar. | 1.1  Performance check to the satisfaction of the instructor. |
| 1.2  The student will display the proper use of a trowel, jack lines and deadman to lay brick to the line on prebuilt wooden or metal leads. | 1.2  Performance checklist by the instructor according to standardized masonry evaluation. |
| 1.3  The student will display the proper use of a spacing rule to determine layout height for standard brick size. | 1.3  Performance check to the satisfaction of the instructor. |
| 1.4  The student will display the proper use of a brick hammer, brick set and brick saw to cut bricks and blocks. | 1.4  Measurement of cuts by the instructor. |

2. Trade and Industrial Program: Metal Fabrication (Machine Shop)

Annual Goals: By the end of the year the student will be able to identify and operate the parts of the lathe with accuracy.

| Short Term Instructional Objectives | Specific Criteria for Successful Completion |
|---|---|
| 2.1 The student will display the appropriate method of manipulating the lathe by identifying the major parts, demonstrating lathe safety techniques and operating lathe controls. | 2.1 Written test at the end of the unit in coordination with instructor observation (minimum 85% score). |
| 2.2 The student will display the appropriate procedure for grinding tool bits after selecting the correct lathe tool bits. | 2.2 Instructor checklist of process and procedures according to appearance and accuracy. |
| 2.3 The student will demonstrate appropriate procedures for the following lathe operations:<br><br>a. rough turning<br>b. finish turning<br>c. threading<br>d. cutting and grooving with parting tool<br>e. turning between centers<br>f. drilling<br>g. boring<br>h. reaming<br>i. cutting threads with tap and die. | 2.3 Instructor checklist on process and product according to set-up, appearance and accuracy on a project or task. |

3. Trade and Industrial Program: Cosmetology

Annual Goals: By the end of the year the student will be able to a) develop a basic understanding of specific vocabulary related to cosmetology, b) develop a basic understanding of the structure and function of the hair, c) display a knowledge of the theory of shampoos, d) demonstrate competence in basic pin curls.

| Short Term Instructional Objectives | Specific Criteria for Successful Completion |
|---|---|
| 3.1 The student will demonstrate a basic knowledge of hair and | 3.1 Objective written test on hair (85% accuracy). |

| | |
|---|---|
| its related functions, including hair structure and chemistry. | |
| 3.2 The student will show a basic knowledge of various common shampoos and rinses. | 3.2 Written test (90% accuracy). |
| 3.3 The student will display competence in recognizing abnormal hair/scalp conditions and select shampoos accordingly. | 3.3 Instructor's satisfaction on practical test in addition to a one-to-one review discussion between instructor and student. |
| 3.4 The student will identify the parts of pin curls and demonstrate the proper rolling procedure of basic pin curls. | 3.4 Objective written test on pin curls (85% accuracy) and instructor satisfaction in observation practical demonstration on a manikin. |

steps between the student's present level of educational performance and the annual goals.

These objectives, written in behavioral terms, will act as specific guidelines for accomplishing the annual goals. They specify for the student what will be required for successful completion of the goal. Thus, the student can follow a sequential pattern leading to satisfactory completion of established goals.

*Role of Trade and Industrial Personnel.* Annual goals developed for the student enrolled in a T & I program should be general and comprehensive, should take into consideration the student's present level of educational performance, and should be a realistic estimate of what he/she can accomplish in the specific program during the year.

Short-term instructional objectives should be sequential steps that will help the student to progress from the present level of educational performance to the desired achievements stated in the annual goals for the T & I program.

Sources that can help T & I personnel in developing annual goals and accompanying objectives include curriculum guides, job related employability skills listed, current employment prerequisite information obtained from industry, V-TECS catalogs, and competency-based checklists.

Some examples of responsibilities that can be assumed by T & I personnel to foster a positive cooperative working relationship with special education personnel and to ensure that this portion of the IEP is realistic are as follows:

1. Help to identify an appropriate occupational goal based on the abilities, performance, and interests of the student.

2. Develop appropriate annual goal statement(s) for the T & I program based on the student's abilities, interests, and occupational goal.

3. Develop a sequence of short-term instructional objectives for each annual goal.

4. Identify appropriate criterion levels to determine whether each short-term objective has been met.

5. Revise annual goals and short-term objectives as necessary during the year as a result of observing and evaluating pupil progress.

6. Revise occupational goals, if necessary, as a result of observing and evaluating pupil progress during the year.

*Examples of Annual Goals and Short-Term Instructional Objectives.* Examples of annual goal statements developed for a student being enrolled in a T & I program follow. In accordance with the mandates of the law regarding IEP development, each annual goal statement is accompanied by short-term instructional objectives and associated criterion levels of expected performance.

## Specific Educational Services to be Provided

Another component in each IEP is the identification of specific educational services that should be provided to assist the student in attaining the annual goals. These services may include such related services as supplementary personnel, special equipment/devices/materials, and services from outside agencies. The following are examples of educational services that may be requested on the IEP:

a. *Supplementary Personnel*
   1. Psychologist or psychometrist (to administer psychological tests, interpret results and/or provide counseling)
   2. Audiologist (to administer and interpret hearing tests and/or provide auditory training)
   3. Social worker
   4. Itinerant teacher (to travel to various schools to assist teachers who have handicapped students in their classes)
   5. Resource room teacher
   6. Speech therapist
   7. Occupational therapist
   8. Physical therapist
   9. Interpreter
   10. Vocational/career counselor
   11. Work-study program/coordinator
   12. Teacher aide
   13. Remedial math teacher
       Remedial reading teacher
   14. Curriculum specialist
   15. Medical consultant (e.g., neurologist, orthopedist, psychiatrist)

b. *Special Equipment/Devices/Materials*
   1. Prosthetic devices
   2. Equipment modification
   3. Curriculum modifications
   4. Special curriculum guides
   5. Special instructional materials for instruction (e.g., captioned films, large print books, recordings of books)
   6. Transportation services (e.g., revised time schedules, attendants for physically handicapped, assistance for blind students)
   7. Classroom/laboratory modification to assure accessibility
   8. Special equipment (e.g., hardware such as machinery or furniture, braille typewriter, stylus for writing braille)

c. *Services from Outside Agencies*
   1. Vocational Rehabilitation
   2. Comprehensive Employment and Training Act (CETA) programs
   3. Community services (e.g., mental health services, special clinics)
   4. Employment service
   5. Family and Child Services
   6. Department of Human Resources
   7. Advocacy organizations

Once the specific educational services have been determined, the team developing the IEP projects when each service will be required. These dates are not binding but merely help the team to plan for the services that a particular student will require. The IEP can be modified whenever the committee deems necessary.

*Role of Trade and Industrial Personnel.* Trade and industrial personnel working with handicapped students should assume the same responsibilities that are associated with other students enrolled in T & I programs. Specifically, T & I teachers should (a) assume responsibility for specific instruction in the T & I program, (b) provide relevant hands-on laboratory experiences, and (c) encourage and assist students to become actively involved in youth group activities.

Some examples of responsibilities that can be assumed by T & I personnel to foster a positive cooperative working relationship with special education personnel

| Annual Goals | Objectives | Criteria for Mastery | Evaluation | Date of Evaluation | MASTERY | |
|---|---|---|---|---|---|---|
| | | | | | Complete | Incomplete |
| 1. Identify the key points of each graphic arts lab area as well as the function of each piece of equipment | a. Student will identify and describe shop organization procedures relating to shop safety regulations and lab clean-up procedures | Satisfactory completion on shop organization checklist (teacher developed) | | | | |
| | b. Student will describe the proper procedure for daily and long range equipment maintenance | Written quiz on written handouts on equipment maintenance (85% accuracy) and laboratory demonstrations by instructor | | | | |
| | c. Student will identify and describe the function of the equipment used in the graphic arts industry: | One-to-one review discussion with instructor. Evaluation based on laboratory activities, written handouts and class lectures. | | | | |
| | 1. Layout tables | | | | | |
| | 2. Typesetters | | | | | |
| | 3. Printing presses | | | | | |
| | 4. Cameras | | | | | |
| | 5. Contact frames | | | | | |
| | 6. Enlargers | | | | | |
| | 7. Sinks | | | | | |
| | 8. Safelights | | | | | |
| | 9. Paper cutters | | | | | |
| | 10. Joggers | | | | | |
| | 11. Folders | | | | | |
| 2. Perform all the basic tasks necessary for design, layout and completion of paste-up art to make camera ready art | a. Student will make a thumbnail sketch | Approval of instructor | | | | |
| | b. Student will construct a rough design for a layout | Approval of instructor | | | | |
| | c. Student will complete a sample layout design for an advertising brochure | Approval of instructor | | | | |
| | d. Student will identify by the correct name and function the following: | Instructor checklist to accompany small group discussion and written quiz (85% accuracy) | | | | |
| | 1. supplies, tools and material used in layout work; | | | | | |
| | 2. most frequently used styles and sizes of type; | | | | | |
| | 3. most frequently used proof reader marks. | | | | | |
| | e. Student will properly set type with typewriter, photo-compositor and/or instant pre-prepared art and lettering | Satisfaction of instructor | | | | |
| | f. Student will develop a rough design layout of a job | Satisfaction of instructor | | | | |

87

and to ensure that this position of the IEP is realistic are as follows:

1. Identify and secure appropriate instructional materials for use in the T & I program in cooperation with special education personnel.

2. Develop and/or modify instructional materials for use in the T & I program in cooperation with special education personnel.

3. Identify and utilize appropriate instructional techniques in cooperation with special education personnel in order to meet the learning needs of the student (e.g., develop task analyses of instructional activities).

4. Arrange for extended time arrangements when necessary.

5. Identify remedial assistance necessary for the student to succeed in the program.

6. Identify specific equipment or devices necessary for the student to succeed in the program.

7. Identify specific services necessary for the student to succeed in the program.

*Examples of Specific Educational Services.* Several examples of specific educational services to be provided for handicapped students, as documented in the IEP, are shown in Illustration 4.6. In addition to identifying the specific services that will be necessary to assist the student in meeting the annual goals and short-term instructional objectives, the person/agency responsible for providing the service is named, as well as the frequency of time needed and the approximate beginning and ending dates of the service.

## Extent of Participation in Regular Educational Programs/Activities

The IEP, in meeting the requirements of this component, must include information regarding the type of regular education program or activity, justification for this type of placement and the amount of time the student can be expected to participate. As the IEP progress of the student is reviewed periodically throughout the year, the extent of participation can be increased or decreased as necessary.

*Role of Trade and Industrial Personnel.* Handicapped students have the right to participate in T & I programs and activities to the maximum extent possible. This does not mean that all handicapped students will automatically be enrolled full-time in T & I programs. A range of options is available in placing these learners in existing programs. Trade and industrial personnel should work cooperatively with special education personnel to plan the extent to which the student will participate in the program. These options are discussed in more detail in Module 3.

This range of placement options is in response to the "least restrictive environment" requirement of Public Law 94–142. The placement option selected should depend on the abilities and interests of the student as well as the nature and severity of the handicap. Further information on placement options can be found in Module 3.

Some examples of responsibilities that can be assumed by T & I personnel to foster a positive cooperative working relationship with special education personnel to ensure that this portion of the IEP is realistic are as follows:

1. Work with special education personnel to match the abilities and interests of the student with an appropriate placement option.

2. Review pupil progress periodically to determine whether the placement is still appropriate.

3. Revise the placement option as necessary based on pupil progress.

*Examples of Extent of Participation in Regular Educational Programs/Activities.* Several examples of statements describing the extent to which a handicapped student is to participate in a T & I program are as follows:

1. The student will participate in the cosmetology program for a three-hour period of classroom instruction and a one-

**Illustration 4.6**

**EXAMPLES OF SPECIFIC EDUCATIONAL SERVICES**

| SPECIFIC EDUCATIONAL SERVICES | FREQUENCY | PERSON/AGENCY RESPONSIBLE | BEGINNING DATE | ENDING DATE |
|---|---|---|---|---|
| Speech Therapy | Twice a week, one hour per session | District Speech Therapist | October 1 | May 15 |
| Resource Room | One period per day | School Resource Room Teacher | September 30 | June 1 |
| Social Worker | As needed, preferably one home visit per month | District Social Worker | November 1 | March 30 |
| Vocational Counseling | As needed | Guidance Counselor | September 15 | January 30 |
| Curriculum Modification (related materials written on an appropriate reading level) | Materials appropriate for units of instruction | Local School | ----------- | ----------- |

hour period of related laboratory instruction three times a week for the first semester of this academic year.

2. The student will participate in the graphic arts program for a period of one hour a day, five days a week, during this academic year.

3. The student will be enrolled in the welding program for a period of two hours a day during the first quarter of this academic year.

4. The student will participate in the carpentry program and related laboratory sessions for a period of one hour, three times a week, during this academic year.

## Criteria for Evaluating Objectives and Schedule for Review

The last component that must be present in each IEP includes appropriate objective criteria to be used at least once a year to evaluate the extent to which the annual goals and short-term instructional objectives have been met. This evaluation should be considered as an opportunity to determine to what extent the IEP is meeting the specific needs of the student. It should provide information to assist in improving this important management tool in order that realistic objectives and appropriate resources are provided.

One method of effectively evaluating student progress during the year is to establish behavioral statements for each short-term instructional objective. These statements describe criterion levels or specific conditions necessary for mastering that objective. A system of record-keeping and a schedule for evaluation should be developed by all personnel working with handicapped students so that progress can be monitored. The criterion levels established for each objective will help to determine the method of recording and evaluating student progress. Some examples include recording specific behaviors during observation and teacher-prepared skill checklists.

Specific educational services provided in the IEP must also be evaluated. Each service should be addressed periodically during the year to determine whether the service is assisting the student to achieve success and whether the service is still necessary. Again, evaluation of educational services should be documented in written form so that progress can be discussed and the IEP can be revised as needed. In cases where necessary services were not provided, justification has to be documented.

*Role of Trade and Industrial Personnel.* In order to positively contribute to the annual IEP review procedure, the T & I teacher should develop a system to evaluate and record student progress during the year. This can be accomplished by monitoring the specific criteria developed for the short-term objectives. Some form of written data should be maintained.

If short-term objectives have not been met, the reason(s) for the failure should be discussed by all the participants at the IEP review meeting. Along with this, the specific services provided for the student should be reviewed to determine whether they were adequate. This annual review process will assist the IEP team in planning future goals and objectives that are realistic.

Some examples of responsibilities that can be assumed by T & I personnel to foster a positive working relationship with special education personnel to ensure that this portion of the IEP is realistic are as follows:

1. Analyze and record student performance relating to short-term objectives according to specific criteria established.

2. Establish continuous evaluation procedures to provide feedback relative to student progress (e.g., proficiency profiles, activity checklists).

3. Actively participate in and contribute to review conferences.

4. Utilize evaluation feedback as a management tool to revise goals, objectives and services to meet the needs of the student.

*Examples of Criteria for Evaluating Objectives.* Several examples of statements describing criteria specifications that can be used by T & I teachers to evaluate student progress in meeting the short-term instructional objectives and, ultimately, the annual goals are as follows:

1. The student will score a minimum of 85 percent correct answers on a written review test.

2. The student will score a minimum of 90 percent correct answers on an oral review test.

3. The student will remain on tasks for a minimum of 90 percent of the time spent in the T & I classroom/laboratory.

4. The student will demonstrate proficiency on the stated task according to the criterion specifications established by the manufacturer.

5. The student will perform the assigned laboratory task with a minimum accuracy level of 95 percent as evaluated by the daily observation of the T & I teacher.

6. The student will meet the specific criterion on a teacher-developed checklist with at least the minimum level of accuracy (e.g., 85 percent accuracy, 90 percent accuracy).

Illustration 4.7 provides a sample of the vocational component of an IEP developed for a hearing impaired student enrolled in a graphic arts program at the secondary school level.

# BENEFITS FOR TRADE AND INDUSTRIAL PERSONNEL PARTICIPATING IN THE IEP PROCESS

Participating in the IEP process can be beneficial to T & I teachers who work with handicapped students in a variety of ways. Some suggestions follow for ways in which the IEP process can aid T & I teachers to organize, teach, monitor and evaluate ongoing program content and activities as well as assume the responsibility for developing the vocational education component.

1. Assist the teacher in understanding the strengths, abilities, interests and needs of the handicapped student to be enrolled in the T & I program.

2. Encourages the teacher to analyze specific program content in relation to the strengths, abilities, interests and needs of the student.

3. Helps the teacher organize the curriculum for the program.

4. Assists the teacher to work as a team member with special education personnel to analyze the student's present level of educational performance, abilities and interests in order to identify a realistic occupational goal.

5. Assists the teacher in identifying appropriate and realistic annual goals that can be achieved by the student during the year.

6. Aids the teacher in developing short-term instructional objectives that will lead to successful completion of the annual goals established for the student.

7. Helps the teacher identify specific criterion levels that must be demonstrated before success is met regarding short-term instructional objectives.

8. Enables the teacher to use specific criterion levels and short-term instructional objectives in making continuous revisions and improvements in the program.

9. Enables the teacher to develop appropriate lesson plans for use with the student.

10. Assists the teacher in selecting appropriate teaching procedures and materials to meet the needs of the student.

11. Provides the teacher with an opportunity to communicate the T & I program goals and objectives to administrators, parents and special education personnel during the IEP team process.

12. Enables the teacher to work cooperatively with other school personnel to meet the needs of the student.

## Illustration 4.7

## SAMPLE INDIVIDUALIZED EDUCATION PROGRAM
### (Vocational Component)

The following is an illustration of an IEP developed for a 17 year old hearing impaired student who will be attending regular classes and also be enrolled in the graphic arts program. She will be provided assistance by an itinerant teacher for the hearing impaired, a speech therapist, a resource room teacher and an interpreter, if necessary.

STUDENT INFORMATION

Name: _Patricia Berry_                                    Age: _16_

Address: _8 Tradewinds, Apartment A_          Grade: _10_

_Littletown, New York_                                   Birthdate: _6/30/63_

School: _Grover Cleveland High School District - Erie County_

Special Education Program: _Itinerant Program for Hearing Impaired_

Parent/Guardian: _Mr. & Mrs. Thomas Berry_          Phone: _689-6576_

Primary Language of: Home _English_     Student _English_

Learning Style: _Visual_          Teacher: _Mrs. Marshall*_

Vocational Program: _Graphic Arts_          _Mr. Townsend**_

Date of IEP meeting : _September 29, 1981_

Date of annual review: _June 15, 1982_

*_(special education itinerant teacher for hearing impaired)_
**_(vocational education)_

Statement of Integration in Regular Class: _Patricia will be enrolled in regular academic classes in the 10th grade curriculum this year. In addition, Patricia will be enrolled in the graphic arts program during the 1981-82 academic year for a two-hour time block 5 days a week. She will receive related remedial reading and math instruction which will be provided in a resource room one hour each day. Participation in these programs will begin in October 1981 and is expected to continue throughout the year._

PRESENT LEVEL(S) OF EDUCATIONAL PERFORMANCE

Academic: _Patricia is currently reading at a 4.5 grade level. She is able to read independently at the 4.0 - 5.0 grade level and, given more assistance, can also function at the 5.0 grade level. However, material written above the 5.5 grade level is too difficult and results in frustration._

The results of the Peabody Individual Achievement Test (PIAT) showed that Patricia has difficulty with word attack and comprehension skills.

Patricia is currently working at the 8th grade level in mathematics according to the Peabody Individual Achievement Test (PIAT). Although she requires help in reading some word problems, she has good reasoning processes and can solve problems independently. Her logical thinking abilities are also very good.

Patricia spent the first 8 years of school in the Erie County School for the Deaf. While there she learned appropriate communication techniques, including lipreading and sign language. She is therefore able to participate in regular class activities and can generally understand the teacher.

Personal-Social: Patricia is shy and withdrawn when first introduced to new people. This behavior originates from her feelings of inadequacy in understanding others and communicating with them. Once people realize that she is hearing impaired and make certain accommodations in communicating with her (e.g., facing her when talking to her so that she can lipread) she is much more comfortable.

Her level of self-confidence makes her feel more comfortable in small groups. She communicates most effectively in small groups or one-to-one situations.

She has adapted well to her regular classes during the past year with the assistance of the itinerant teacher and the speech therapist. Her withdrawn behavior has decreased as a result of the success she has been experiencing in school.

Psychomotor: Patricia has average gross motor skills. Her fine motor control is well developed and requires no special remediation. Her psychomotor skills were observed during the previous year when she was involved in a series of informal hands-on activities in several vocational programs offered in the school. These activities were developed cooperatively between the itinerant teacher and the vocational education teachers.

Self Help: Patricia's self-help skills are comparable to her peer group.

There is no need to provide her with any assistance in this area.

**Prevocational/Vocational:** *During the past year, Patricia was involved in a number of hands-on exploratory activities in order to determine her abilities and interests. Graphic arts was one of the programs that she sampled. After completing a variety of hands-on activities and participating in a counseling session with the itinerant teacher, special education resource room teacher and her parents. Patricia expressed an interest in the graphic arts program.*

*The itinerant teacher then contacted the graphic arts teacher to discuss whether this would be a realistic placement. He agreed to work with Patricia in the program and commented that she had performed very well on the exploratory tasks.*

*Patricia has had no other vocational education experiences. She did have a class in prevocational education and another in career awareness while enrolled at the Erie County School for the Deaf.*

SPECIAL EDUCATIONAL SERVICES TO BE PROVIDED

| Service | Date Services Begin | Date Services End |
|---|---|---|
| Speech Therapy | October 1980 | June 1980 |
| Resource Room (remedial reading, coordinated with itinerant teacher) | October 1980 | June 1980 |
| Itinerant teacher for the hearing impaired | October 1980 | June 1980 |
| Teacher aide | October 1980 | June 1980 |

ANNUAL GOALS

At the end of the year, Patricia will be able to:

1. Identify the key points of each graphic arts lab area as well as the function of each piece of equipment;

2. Perform all the basic tasks necessary for design layout and completion of paste-up art to make camera ready copy.

13. Provides the teacher with useful information regarding support services and remedial assistance available in the school/district to help the student succeed in the program.

14. Provides the teacher with useful information regarding community agencies, organizations and advocacy groups that are available to help the student succeed in the program.

15. Assists the teacher to utilize the IEP as an evaluation tool to assess student progress in the program.

## SUMMARY

One of the most important guarantees of the Education for All Handicapped Children Act of 1975 (Public Law 94-142) is the requirement that every handicapped individual age 3 to 21 be provided with a written individualized education program (IEP). This program describes the specific educational opportunities that the local school district will provide for the student. It must be developed and reviewed at least once annually.

The 1976 Amendments to the Vocational Education Act (Public Law 94-482) states that the goals and objectives developed in the IEP will be used to place students in vocational education programs.

The three basic purposes of the IEP are (a) to provide an individually prescribed educational program to meet the needs of each handicapped individual, (b) to provide a system of accountability for providing educational services to handicapped individuals and (c) to provide for an open channel of communication among all personnel working with the individual.

The IEP team that meets to develop this program must include: (a) an administrator or representative of the local education agency, (b) the student's parent/guardian, (c) the teacher(s) who will be responsible for working with the student and (d) the student, if appropriate.

When handicapped students are mainstreamed into T & I programs, it is important that the teacher be a member of the IEP team and actively participate in the IEP process to assure that the goals, objectives and educational services are appropriate.

The necessary components of the IEP include: (a) present level of educational performance of the student, (b) annual goals and short-term instructional objectives, (c) specific educational services to be provided, (d) extent to which the student will participate in regular educational programs/activities and (e) specific criteria for evaluating objectives and schedule for review.

Participating in the IEP process can be beneficial to T & I personnel in a variety of ways. It can: (a) assist them in better understanding the needs of the handicapped individual, (b) help them to organize, present and evaluate the curriculum, (c) aid them in developing realistic, appropriate goals and objectives to meet the specific needs of the learner, (d) assist them in evaluating student progress in the program and (e) provide them with an opportunity to work cooperatively with other personnel.

### References

Cegelka, P., and Phillips, M. Individualized education programming at the secondary level. *Teaching Exceptional Children*, 1978, *10* (3), 84-87.

Dahl, P., Appleby, J. and Lipe, D. *Mainstreaming guidebook for vocational educators*. Salt Lake City, Utah: Olympus Publishing Company, 1978.

Godia, L. Program changes to accommodate handicapped students. *American Vocational Journal*, 1978, *53* (3), 29.

Hayes, R. The what, who, how, etc., of the IEP. *School Shop*, April 1978, *37* (8), 57-60.

Kalfas, R. and Batsche, C. *The role of the vocational educator in the IEP.* From Proceedings of the Conference on Mainstreaming Handicapped Students in Vocational Education Programs. Blacksburg, Virginia: Virginia Polytechnic Institute and State University, The Division of Vocational and Technical Education, February 1978, 77–92.

Larsen, S. and Poplin, M. *Methods for educating the handicapped: An individualized education program approach.* Boston, Massachusetts: Allyn and Bacon, 1980.

McKinney, L. and Seay, D. *Development of individualized education programs (IEPs) for the handicapped in vocational education.* Columbus, Ohio: The Ohio State University, National Center for Research in Vocational Education, 1979.

Parrish, L. *Instructional planning for the handicapped: Developing individual education programs.* College Station, Texas: Texas A & M University, Center for Career Development and Occupational Preparation, 1978.

Torres, S. (Ed.). *A primer on individualized education programs for handicapped children.* Reston, Virginia: The Foundation for Exceptional Children, 1977.

Weintraub, F., Baeson, A., Ballard, J. and LaVore, M. (Eds.). *Public policy and the education of exceptional children.* Reston, Virginia: The Council for Exceptional Children, 1976.

## SELF ASSESSMENT: INDIVIDUALIZED EDUCATION PROGRAM

1. Describe the relationship between the IEP and recent federal legislation.
2. Describe the three general purposes of the IEP.
3. For whom is the IEP developed?
4. List the individuals who must be involved in developing the IEP.
5. Describe the role and responsibilities of each member of the IEP team.
6. What is the role and responsibilities of the T & I personnel participating in the IEP team meeting?
7. Describe what happens during an IEP team meeting.
8. Identify the required components of the IEP.
9. Discuss the importance of identifying the student's present level of educational performance for use in the IEP.
10. Discuss the importance of developing annual goals and accompanying short-term instructional objectives for the IEP.
11. Discuss the importance of identifying specific educational services to be provided for the student.
12. Discuss the importance of describing the extent to which the student will participate in regular classroom/program activities.
13. Discuss the importance of establishing specific criteria for use in evaluating annual goals and short-term instructional objectives.
14. Discuss the importance of scheduling a date for reviewing the IEP.
15. How often must the IEP be reviewed?
16. List the benefits for T & I personnel participating in the IEP process.

## ASSOCIATED ACTIVITIES

1. Work cooperatively with special education personnel to establish some informal hands-on assessment activities for use in determining the student's present level of educational performance in psychomotor skills and/or vocational skills.

2. Prepare a list of prerequisite skills and/or knowledge that would be useful for a handicapped individual to have prior to enrolling in your program. Use this list as a basis for discussion and decision-making during the initial IEP team meeting.

3. Identify, in cooperation with special education personnel, the support services and supplementary aids that are available in your school/district to meet the identified needs of handicapped students. You can then use this information to determine the specific educational services that a handicapped student will need when he/she is enrolled in your program. This should be documented in the IEP.

4. If you are currently working with handicapped students in your program, contact the special education teacher and request to see a copy of the IEP developed for each student. If you were not included in the initial development phase, check the goals, objectives and services as they relate to student participation in the T & I program. Cooperatively plan any necessary modifications or revisions with the special education teacher. Request that you be included in future IEP team meetings to assure that the vocational education component of the IEP will be realistic and relevant.

5. Establish a file to keep a copy of current IEPs (or, at a minimum, the vocational education component) so that you can refer to them for assistance in organizing the curriculum, developing instruction and monitoring student progress.

6. Develop specific criteria for mastering tasks in your program. These criteria can be in the form of activity checklists, proficiency profiles, written tests/quizzes and criterion reference performance tests. These criteria can be used in developing the IEP and in evaluating student performance.

7. Develop an efficient record-keeping system to periodically evaluate student progress in the T & I program relative to the objectives established in the IEP.

8. Contact other vocational education teachers in your school or district who have worked with a particular handicapped student. Discuss the direction they took in the IEP process for this student.

## CASE HISTORY: DALE'S STORY

Dale is a blind student enrolled in a program to train medical secretaries. He has had mobility training at the state school for the blind and uses a cane to help him get around. An itinerant teacher for the visually handicapped has been provided by the district to assist Dale. This support teacher works cooperatively with the program instructor in addition to working with Dale.

Dale can read braille. He utilizes a cassette recorder during classroom lectures, demonstrations and discussions. The area Talking Books association has been very helpful by providing taped versions of textbook material used in the medical secretary program.

The program is comprised of components designed to develop necessary skills in typing, dictation, transcription, operation of office machines and medical secretarial procedures. The phase of the secretarial program that most interests Dale is the one that deals with medical terminology and medical transcription skills.

The itinerant teacher, the program instructor, Dale's parents and Dale have had several conferences to identify a realistic career goal. Based on Dale's interests and performance in the program, a career goal of medical library clerk has been identified. Dale hopes to complete the requirements for certification by the American Medical Records Association before exiting the program. This goal has been put into Dale's IEP and appropriate objectives have been developed.

The itinerant teacher will continue to work with the program instructor and with Dale to help him meet his goal. In addition, a Vocational Rehabilitation counselor has been assigned to assist Dale. Vocational Rehabilitation has agreed to provide him with any adaptive devices he may require in the program or on the job. Job placement assistance will also be provided when Dale is ready to exit from the program.

## CASE HISTORY ACTIVITY

Eileen is a partially sighted student who has just enrolled in your program. Eileen's reading and math levels are at the sixth grade level. It is helpful for her to have written materials prepared in large print.

Eileen is currently working closely with an itinerant teacher for the visually handicapped, a resource room teacher and a vocational rehabilitation counselor.

Based on this information, complete the case history profile worksheet for Eileen's participation in your program.

## CASE HISTORY PROFILE WORKSHEET

Student: _____  Page: _____

Handicapping Condition(s): _____

T & I Program: _____  Academic Levels: _____

Career Goal/Occupational Interest: _____

Considerations (e.g., medication, behavior): _____

_____

| Adaptation | Specific Services Needed | Where to Obtain Service |
|---|---|---|
| Cooperative Planning (School Personnel) | | |
| Support Services | | |
| Architectural Changes | | |
| Adaptive Equipment | | |
| Curriculum Modification | | |
| Instructional Materials/ Supplies | | |
| Teaching Techniques | | |
| Agency Involvement | | |
| Possible Job Placement | | |

# MODULE 5

## Vocational Assessment and the Cooperative Planning Process

Vocational assessment is a process that provides information about an individual's vocational potential. The process of vocational assessment can occur before an individual is placed in a specific program and/or at the time the individual enters the program.

Results from the vocational assessment process include useful information concerning aptitudes, interests, work habits, socialization skills, work attitudes and work tolerance. The purpose of the assessment process is to develop a comprehensive profile of an individual's assets and limitations as they relate to vocational possibilities.

Vocational assessment requires cooperation from a variety of professionals if realistic vocational employment opportunities are to be identified for special needs populations. The cooperative planning process is a coordinated effort by various individuals and agencies to provide a realistic instructional plan for a specific learner. The cooperative planning process is necessary if the vocational potential of special needs learners is to be developed to the maximum.

This module will present information regarding the specific component of vocational assessment. Each component will be discussed and illustrated. Information will also be presented about the importance of the cooperative planning process and the important components of this process.

Sections in this module include: (a) compiling a learner profile, (b) commercial work samples, (c) informal work samples, (d) job analysis, (e) situational assessment, and (f) cooperative planning.

## MODULE OBJECTIVES

After you have read and reviewed this module, studied the case history, reviewed the self-assessment questions, and completed the associated activities, you should be able to:

1. Discuss the purpose of the vocational assessment process.
2. Explain the importance of the vocational assessment process.
3. List the major components of the vocational assessment process and briefly discuss the importance of each component.
4. Identify the specific information that can be provided by vocational assessment.
5. Explain why the cooperative planning process is important.
6. List the major components of the cooperative planning process and briefly discuss the importance of each component.

## VOCATIONAL ASSESSMENT OF SPECIAL NEEDS LEARNERS

### Purpose of Vocational Assessment

Vocational assessment, or vocational evaluation, is a process that provides information relating to an individual's vocational potential. This information should be obtained over a period of time through real-life work situations and/or simulated work activities. Vocational potential is measured in such areas as: (a) vocational aptitudes, (b) vocational interests, (c) work habits, (d) socialization skills, (e) personal adjustment skills, (f) work attitudes, and (g) work tolerance. The purpose of the vocational assessment process is to develop a comprehensive profile of the individual's assets and limitations as they relate to vocational possibilities.

Vocational assessment should not be a solitary activity. In order for the information collected from the process to be effected, it should be a continuous activity. The onset of vocational assessment usually occurs before a program placement decision is made for a specific learner and/or at the time the student enters the vocational program.

In the past, vocational evaluation results have often been used to screen individuals out of vocational education programs. Today, information gathered through vocational assessment is carefully analyzed and used to determine appropriate program placement and planning for special needs learners according to their abilities, interests, and needs.

If weaknesses are observed during the evaluation process, they can usually be strengthened through a combined effort by various disciplines. Therefore, the vocational assessment procedure can identify specific areas that can be accommodated and/or remediated to allow the individual to profit from participation in an appropriate vocational program.

A comprehensive vocational assessment process should: (a) assess the vocational potential of learners, (b) use evaluation information as a basis for vocational counseling, (c) place learners in appropriate vocational program or job training situations, (d) design and implement individualized vocational training programs, and (e) motivate special needs students who have consistently had failure experiences in school.

The vocational assessment process can be helpful in identifying realistic vocational placement options and developing appropriate program objectives for special needs learners. The evaluation process provides students with an opportunity to experience hands-on exploration activities that will help them to identify their interests.

Illustration 5.1 shows information that can be obtained through a comprehensive vocational assessment process.

## COMPILING A LEARNER PROFILE

An important component of the vocational assessment process is the collection of relevant background information. This information can be organized into a learner profile for use during the vocational assessment process. The profile should obtain information in the following areas: (a) educational/academic/psychological, (b) physical/medical, (c) social/interpersonal relations, and (d) prevocational/vocational.

There are a variety of sources that could be helpful in providing relevant background information for a specific learner. These sources include: (a) attendance records, (b) school/academic records, (c) psychological reports, (d) anecdotal reports, (e) teacher observations, (f) achievement profiles, (g) health/medical records, (h) personal interview with special needs learner and/or parent/guardian, and (i) reports from vocational/guidance counselor.

### Educational, Academic and Psychological Component

The educational, academic and psychological component of the learner profile should be compiled and used as a guide to the individual's achievement and potential in academic areas. Academic ability is certainly not the only consideration for vocational and employment placement. However, information compiled in this section of the learner profile can be beneficial in analyzing and applying the educational strengths and weaknesses of a specific individual as they relate to vocational development and eventual employment opportunities. This information should also be used in identifying necessary program modifications.

Illustration 5.2 suggests some basic background information that could be integrated into the educational, academic and psychological component of the learner profile.

### Physical and Medical Component

The physical and medical component of the learner profile should be compiled and used as a guide to the individual's general

## Illustration 5.1

## INFORMATION OBTAINED THROUGH
## VOCATIONAL ASSESSMENT

Information which can be obtained through a comprehensive, on-going vocational assessment process includes, but is not limited to, the following areas:

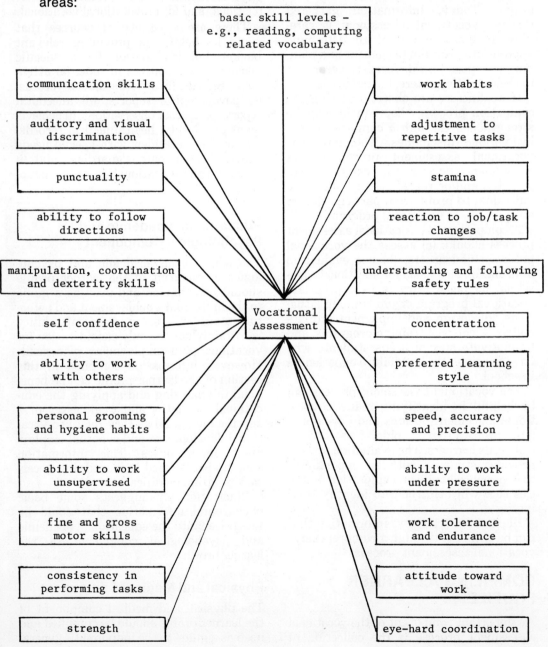

- basic skill levels – e.g., reading, computing related vocabulary
- communication skills
- auditory and visual discrimination
- punctuality
- ability to follow directions
- manipulation, coordination and dexterity skills
- self confidence
- ability to work with others
- personal grooming and hygiene habits
- ability to work unsupervised
- fine and gross motor skills
- consistency in performing tasks
- strength

Vocational Assessment

- work habits
- adjustment to repetitive tasks
- stamina
- reaction to job/task changes
- understanding and following safety rules
- concentration
- preferred learning style
- speed, accuracy and precision
- ability to work under pressure
- work tolerance and endurance
- attitude toward work
- eye-hard coordination

## Illustration 5.2

## SUGGESTED BACKGROUND INFORMATION FOR LEARNER PROFILE—
## EDUCATIONAL/ACADEMIC/PSYCHOLOGICAL COMPONENT

The following educational, academic and psychological information would be helpful in developing a pupil profile to contribute to the vocational assessment process:

1. Overall performance levels (i.e., standardized achievement results):

    a. Reading level _____

    b. Comprehension level _____

    c. Mathematics level _____

    d. Spelling _____

2. School Achievement Records (e.g., rate of learning = below average, average, above average): _____

3. Permanent Record/Transcripts (i.e., grades): _____

4. Language development (speech or comprehension difficulty): _____

    a. listening skills: _____

    b. relating messages/information: _____

5. Psychological assessment:   a. Test used _____

                                    b. Date _____

                                    c. Test results _____

6. Communication skills (e.g., conversation skills, writing skills):

_____

7. Attendance records (i.e., attendance history, reasons for excessive absences:

_____

8. Student's Strong Learning Style:

      Visual (i.e., reading, demonstration): _____

      Auditory (i.e., lecture, oral directions): _____

      Kinesthetic (i.e., motor or hands-on activities): _____

9. Appropriate instructional techniques: _____

10. Perceptual – motor skills development: _____

11. Specific problems the student is experiencing in academic areas:

_____

12. Student academic strengths: _____

13. Student academic weaknesses: _____

14. Results of vocational interest batteries: _____

15. Specific teacher observation reports: _____

health, disabilities, and physical capacities as they relate to vocational development and eventual employment opportunities. This information should also be used in identifying necessary program or job modifications.

Illustration 5.3 suggests some basic background information that could be integrated into the physical and medical component of the learner profile.

## Social and Interpersonal Relations Component

The social and interpersonal relations component of the learner profile should be compiled and used as a guide to the individual's social skills and ability to get along with others. Important information in this area includes observation and data relating to maturity, work attitudes and habits, personal hygiene, family background, and relationship to peers and authority figures.

Illustration 5.4 suggests some basic background information that could be integrated into the social and interpersonal relations component of the pupil profile.

## Prevocational and Vocational Component

The prevocational and vocational component of the learner profile should be compiled and used as a guide to the individual's background preparation in prevocational skills, experiences in vocational education, employment history, and expressed career goal.

Illustration 5.5 suggests some basic background information that could be integrated into the prevocational and vocational component of the pupil profile.

## COMMERCIAL WORK SAMPLES

Work samples simulate tasks that are closely associated with jobs in the labor market. The activities performed in work sample situations are as realistic as possible. They incorporate the tools and standards associated with the actual job. Work samples are a common component of the vocational assessment process because they emphasize performance skills rather than the verbal or written skills that are expected on most tests.

The special needs learner profits from work sample activities because they provide practical hands-on experiences. These experiences can assist learners in identifying their strengths and weaknesses and can also assist in determining a realistic career goal.

At the same time, work sample activities provide the evaluator with observation information concerning the work habits, manipulative skills, physical abilities, interpersonal skills and work capacity of the specific learner. This information is helpful in analyzing vocational potential, selecting appropriate training programs and identifying necessary program modifications. The results of work sample evaluation can be a useful tool in career counseling program development and job placement.

There are several advantages of using commercial work samples in the vocational assessment process. They tend to motivate students because the work samples are more like real job tasks than paper and pencil assignments. Although an individual's performance on work samples cannot guarantee success in actual job situations, it can provide the evaluator with important observation information that can help to predict functional ability, attitude, aptitude, tolerance and limitations. It also provides experiences for hands-on testing and following oral directions. Finally, work samples allow for experiences that will be helpful in program and career planning.

There are several disadvantages of using commercial work samples in the vocational assessment process. The systems are often expensive and time-consuming to administer. Some work samples that are supposed to represent various

## Illustration 5.3

## SUGGESTED BACKGROUND INFORMATION FOR LEARNER PROFILE— PHYSICAL/MEDICAL COMPONENT

The following physical and medical information would be helpful in developing a pupil profile to contribute to the vocational assessment process:

1. Condition of general health: _____

    a. Results of general medical examination: _____

    b. Date of general medical examination: _____

2. Physical capacities/limitations (i.e., strength, stamina, chronic illnesses, physical disabilities, etc.): _____

_____

3. Sensory Development: _____

4. Motor Development: _____

    a. Fine motor skills: _____

    b. Gross motor skills: _____

5. Vision Ability: _____

6. Hearing Ability: _____

7. Manual and finger dexterity: _____

8. Eye-hand coordination: _____

9. Ability to cope physically in classroom/laboratory/job situations:

_____

10. Modifications necessary in classroom/laboratory/job environment:

_____

11. Modifications necessary in equipment/machinery/tools: _____

_____

12. Is the student currently on medication?: _____

13. If yes, what is the medication used for?: _____

14. Possible side effects of the medication: _____

    a. Possible effect(s) of the medication on the social ability of the individual: _____

    b. Possible effect(s) of the medication on the emotional stability of the individual: _____

    c. Possible effect(s) of the medication on the academic ability of the individual: _____

    d. Possible effect(s) of the medication on the ability of the individual to perform/complete job assignments: _____

_____

## Illustration 5.4

## SUGGESTED BACKGROUND INFORMATION FOR LEARNER PROFILE—
## SOCIAL/INTERPERSONAL RELATIONS COMPONENT

The following social and interpersonal relations information would be helpful in developing a pupil profile to contribute to the vocational assessment process:

1. Ability to cope socially in classroom/laboratory/job situation:

   _____

2. Ability to cope emotionally in classroom/laboratory/job situation:

   _____

3. Ability to cope in group activities: _____

4. Attitude:

   _____ defiant/hostile

   _____ antisocial

   _____ passive

   _____ moody

   _____ aggressive

   _____ withdrawn

   _____ other (specify): _____

5. Motivation level: _____

6. Relationship with peers: _____

7. Relationship with teacher: _____

8. Personality Characteristics:

   General Attitude toward School: _____

   Accepts Authority: _____

   Cooperation with Adults: _____

   Cooperation with Peers: _____

   Appropriate conduct: _____

   Decision-making Skills: _____

   Assumes responsibility: _____

   Maturity: _____

   Self-control: _____

   Reaction to criticism: _____

   Other (specify): _____

9. Grooming/Personal hygiene habits: _____

10. General Family Situation: _____

   _____

## Illustration 5.5

### SUGGESTED BACKGROUND INFORMATION FOR LEARNER PROFILE—
### PREVOCATIONAL/VOCATIONAL COMPONENT

The following prevocational and vocational information would be helpful in developing a pupil profile to contribute to the vocational assessment process:

1.  Results of formal vocational assessment (standardized tests, formal work samles, formal activities): _____

    _____

2.  Results of aptitude tests: _____

3.  Results of informal vocational assessment activities (exploration activities, job tryouts, situational assessment): _____

    _____

4.  Results of interest surveys: _____

5.  Results of student interview:

    Student interest: _____

    Career goal: _____

6.  Prevocational background: _____

7.  Work study experience: _____

8.  Work history (including employer's comments): _____

9.  Vocational classes taken: _____

10. Student self assessment (e.g., analysis of abilities, limitations, projected lifestyle): _____

11. Knowledge of tool usage: _____

12. Are work habits consistent with employment demand: _____

    _____

13. Vocational strengths: _____

14. Vocational weaknesses: _____

occupational areas are too simple and do not present a realistic view of what the job is really like. The norms provided for work sample performance may not relate to the population being evaluated (e.g., work samples normed on the performance of nonhandicapped individuals will not be relevant or valid for handicapped individuals being evaluated). The following example illustrates how the work sample assessment procedure is used.

### Example of a Commercial Work Sample

Suzanne Cope has been referred by the special education teacher for vocational assessment to the vocational evaluation center at the area vocational-technical school. A number of commercial work sample batteries are used by the evaluator at this center. One system that is available is the Singer Graflex system. It is used because of the close relationship between the work samples and the available vocational training programs in the district.

Suzanne selects several work sample areas in which she has an interest, including carpentry, needle trades, and drafting. The evaluator starts her at the work station relating to carpentry. The work station is situated at a self-contained desk area with partitions on each side of the desk.

Suzanne sits at the work station and sees a variety of tools that are used in carpentry. She also finds an audiovisual Caramate projector with a remote control operating panel, a filmstrip, and a tape cartridge.

An audiovisual presentation shows Suzanne how to operate the machine and presents information about jobs that are associated with the carpentry area. Another filmstrip/cassette presentation orients her to the tools that are in front of her at the work station. When this phase has been completed the evaluator asks Suzanne if she is interested in any of the jobs she saw and heard about. Suzanne responds that she is interested in several.

The next phase takes Suzanne through a step-by-step simulation activity associated with carpentry using the tools and materials at the work station. In the carpentry work sample the task is to make a napkin holder out of dowels, a board and plywood. The task operations involve measuring, laying out, cutting, hammering, chiseling and drilling the pieces for fabrication. The slide/cassette presentation on the Caramate projector instructs and illustrates each step of the task. Suzanne watches the screen, listens and follows the directions given to her. She is allowed to stop the presentation if she is having trouble keeping up with the task.

While Suzanne is working on this task the evaluator is observing her performance. She will be rated on speed and quality of her work. Her scores can be compared to norm group scores to see how she performed as compared to others. At the end of the task, the evaluator also asks Suzanne to rate herself for speed and quality.

## Commercial Vocational Evaluation Systems and Component Work Samples

The following pages describe some common commercial vocational evaluation systems currently available for use. Each system consists of a variety of work samples that simulate tasks required in a specific vocational area and/or in business and industry.

Work samples to be used should be analyzed in terms of how the evaluation information relates to the skills necessary for successful participation in the T & I program. It is also important to check the target groups on which these batteries are normed. Some systems were developed especially for one or two areas of handicapping conditions (e.g., mentally retarded, physically handicapped). Others are more general and were developed for use with all special needs populations (handicapped and disadvantaged individuals).

Selection of appropriate commercial systems should also take into consideration the following factors:

1. Range of jobs available in the community and scope of jobs represented in the work sample;

2. Validity and reliability for the client population to be served;

3. Purpose of the evaluation—(a) occupational information through a hands-on experience, (b) assessment of present skills and aptitudes without relating information to career functions, and (c) a thorough evaluation of student aptitudes and work behaviors, (d) occupational information and dissemination, and (e) occupational exploration. (Revell, Kriloff and Sarkees, 1980, p. 80)

The commercial vocational evaluation systems that follow do not represent a total list of all the batteries that are available nor an endorsement for any single commercial system. They are presented as examples of systems that are on the market. (See pages 110-113.)

## INFORMAL WORK SAMPLES

Work sample activities can be developed by T & I personnel to evaluate the abilities of learners to perform specific work tasks. Informal work samples are generally not as expensive as commercial work sample systems. The tools, equipment and supplies used in the regular T & I activities are used in informal work sample experiences. These activities usually reflect proficiencies necessary for entry-level jobs associated with the program. These samples cannot always represent the total job but include tasks that are necessary to successful performance of the job.

Several steps should be considered. Trade and industrial teachers should follow a sequence of basic steps such as those suggested by Brolin (1976) when developing a work sample.

1. Survey the local community to determine jobs that will be available to students after they complete the program.

2. Based on the information collected during the community survey, decide what work samples are to be developed.

3. Analyze the job to be simulated in the work sample. It is very important that the skills required for the job are the same as those represented in the work sample. If the skills are not the same, the work sample will not be valid.

4. Design the work sample by developing activities that simulate the tasks expected for a specific job. Keep in mind (a) prerequisite skills that may be necessary, (b) tools, equipment and materials used on the job, (c) working conditions or work environment associated with the job, and (d) criteria for successfully completing the work sample.

5. Determine how the work sample will be explained and/or demonstrated to special needs learners. It is a good idea to have the sample reviewed by workers who actually do the job before using it as an assessment tool. Community employees and/or advisory committee members can be helpful in accomplishing this.

6. Establish scoring criteria. The T & I teacher should identify what will be expected of students who complete the work sample. Considerations in scoring may include: (a) desirable work habits, (b) quality of work produced, (c) quantity of work produced, and (d) time required to complete the work sample.

7. Pre-test the work sample with special needs learners before using it as an evaluation tool in your program. This procedure will help to identify any problems that might arise while you are administering the work sample.

Informal work samples can be used (a) to provide career exploration activities for special needs learners, (b) to assess the work habits, coordination, physical capacity, and social skills of special needs learners before they are enrolled in a specific program, (c) to assess the abilities and limitations of special needs learners after they have enrolled in a specific program, and (d) to evaluate the skills that special needs learners have developed in the T & I program before they exit the program and/or are placed in a job situation.

Some examples of informal teacher-made work samples follow:

### Sample A: Masonry Program

*Objective/Purpose of Work Sample:* To observe and evaluate the learner's ability to build a brick column (16'' X 20'').

*Skills Necessary to Accomplish Work Sample Objective:* Given the proper tools, equipment and supplies, the learner will demonstrate the following:

1. Ability to use proper measurement.
2. Ability to spread mortar.

# COMMERCIAL VOCATIONAL EVALUATION SYSTEMS

Comprehensive Occupational Assessment and
Training System (COATS) Vocational Education System

Address: PREP, Inc.
1575 Parkway Avenue
Trenton, N.J. 08628

This system consists of twenty work samples covering 63 occupations.

The work samples include:

1. drafting
2. clerical/office
3. metal construction
4. sales
5. wood construction
6. food preparation
7. medical services
8. travel services
9. barbering/cosmetology
10. small engine
11. police science
12. masonry
13. electrical
14. accounting and bookkeeping
15. agri-business
16. climate control
17. electronics
18. clothing and textiles
19. fire science
20. real estate

Hester Evaluation System

Address: Hester Evaluation System
120 South Ashland Boulevard
Chicago, Illinois

This system consists of a series of separate tests which measure 28 independent ability factors. These tests include:

1. arm-hand steadiness
2. two-arm coordination
3. manual dexterity
4. finger dexterity
5. wrist-finger speed
6. two-hand coordination
7. machine feeding
8. hand/tool dexterity
9. perceptual accuracy
10. multi-limb coordination
11. perceptual speed
12. oral directions
13. aiming
14. visual-motor reversal
15. fine psychomotor coordination
16. decision speed
17. lifting ability
18. hand strength
19. reaction time
20. response orientation

21. abstract reasoning

22. language and numerical reasoning

23. reading grade level

24. mathematics grade level

Jewish Employment and Vocational Service (JEVS)
Vocational Evaluation System

Address: Vocational Research Institute, Incorporated
Jewish Employment and Vocational Service
1624 Locust Street
Philadelphia, Pennsylvania 19103

This system consists of 28 work samples organized into 10 worker trait groups including:

1. handling

2. sorting, inspecting, measuring and related work

3. tending

4. manipulating

5. routine checking and recording

6. classifying, filing and related work

7. inspecting and stock checking

8. craftsmanship and related work

9. costuming, tailoring and dressmaking

10. drafting and related work

Micro TOWER Group Vocational Evaluation System

Address: ICD Rehabilitation and Research Center
340 East 24th Street
New York, New York 10010

This system consists of 13 work samples arranged in five aptitude areas including:

Motor Skills

1. electronic connector assembly

2. bottle capping and packing

3. lamp assembly

Spatial

4. blueprint reading

5. graphics illustration

Clerical Perception

6. mail sorting

7. filing

8. zip coding

9. record checking

Verbal Skills

10. message taking

11. want ads comprehension

Numerical Skills

12. payroll computation

13. making change

Singer Graflex Vocational Evaluation System

Address:  Singer Education Division
          Education Systems
          3750 Monroe Avenue
          Rochester, New York  14603

This system consists of 20 independent work samples including:

1.  sample making
2.  bench assembly
3.  drafting
4.  electrical wiring
5.  plumbing and pipefitting
6.  carpentry
7.  refrigeration, heating and air conditioning
8.  soldering and welding
9.  office and sales clerk
10. needle trades
11. masonry
12. sheet metal
13. cooking and baking
14. engine service
15. medical service
16. cosmetology
17. data calculation and recording
18. soil testing
19. photo lab technician
20. production machine operator

Systematic Approach to Vocational Education (SAVE)

Address:  S.A.V.E. Enterprises
          P.O. Box 5871
          Rome, Georgia  30161

This system consists of work samples in 16 worker trait groups

including:

1.  sorting, inspecting, measuring and related work
2.  precision working
3.  manipulating
4.  signaling and related work
5.  feeding-offbearing
6.  handling
7.  modeling and related work
8.  set-up and adjustment
9.  driving/operating
10. tending
11. child and adult care
12. miscellaneous personal service work
13. accommodating work
14. miscellaneous customer service work
15. ushering, messenger service and related work
16. animal care

Testing, Orientation and Work Evaluation
in Rehabilitation (TOWER)

Address:  ICD Rehabilitation and Research Center
          340 East 24th Street
          New York, New York 10010

This system categorizes 93 work samples into 14 training areas

including:

1.  clerical
2.  drafting
3.  drawing
4.  electronics assembly
5.  jewelry manufacturing
6.  leathergoods
7.  machine shop
8.  lettering
9.  mail clerk
10. optical mechanics
11. pantograph engraving
12. sewing machine operating
13. welding
14. workshop assembly

VALPAR Vocational Evaluation System

Address:  VALPAR Corporation
          3801 34th Street, Suite 105
          Tucson, Arizona  85713

This system is composed of 18 work samples including:

1.  small tools mechanical
2.  size discrimination
3.  numerical sorting
4.  upper extremity range of motion
5.  clerical comprehension and aptitude
6.  independent problem solving
7.  multi-level sorting
8.  simulated assembly
9.  whole body range of motion
10. tri-level measurement
11. eye-hand-foot coordination
12. soldering and inspection
13. money handling
14. integrated peer performance
15. electrical circuitry and print reading
16. drafting
17. pre-vocational readiness battery
18. conceptual understanding through blind evaluation (C.U.B.E.)
    (videotaped instruction for hearing impaired individuals is
    also available).

3. Ability to determine appropriate spacing.
4. Ability to space bricks.
5. Ability to course bricks.
6. Ability to level brick courses.
7. Ability to build brick corners.
8. Ability to plumb brick corners.
9. Ability to strike joints.

*Socring Criteria:* The skills demonstrated by the learner will be evaluated according to the following code:
1. Learner can perform the skill independently and consistently.
2. Learner can perform the skill with supervision and/or assistance.
3. Learner displays proficiency below the acceptable performance level and will require further instruction.

## Sample B: Residential Wiring Program

*Objective/Purpose of Work Sample:* To observe and evaluate the learner's ability to successfully complete an electrical wiring activity.

*Skills Necessary to Accomplish Work Sample Objective:* Step-by-step instructions for this activity will be given by audiovisual equipment. Given an activity board, 36 inches of #14 gauge electrical wire, 6 electrical terminals, a screw driver, a 12-inch ruler, and wire cutting and crimping pliers, the learner will display the ability to:
1. Follow verbal directions.
2. Follow visual instructions.
3. Read a 12-inch ruler.
4. Operate appropriate hand tools.

*Tasks Included in the Work Sample:*
1. Measure the #14 gauge electrical wire to prescribed lengths using a 12-inch ruler.
2. Cut the electrical wire using the appropriate tool.
3. Attach the electrical terminals to the wire ends as directed.
4. Install the different length electrical

wires properly on activity boards containing 12 volt batteries, 12 volt electrical motors and electrical switches.

*Scoring Criteria:* The skills demonstrated by the learner will be evaluated according to the standards set by the instructor and will be judged after careful observation of task performance and examination of the final product.

## Sample C: Cosmetology Program

*Objective/Purpose of Work Sample:* To observe and evaluate the learner's ability to condition damaged hair.

*Skills Necessary to Accomplish Work Sample Objective:* Given a shampoo cape, hair brush, towels, shampoo, corrective treatment and written directions for treatment, the learner will display the ability to:
1. Identify damage to the hair.
2. Drape the patron to protect the clothing.
3. Sanitize hands and equipment.
4. Determine the extent of damage to the hair.
5. Read and follow the manufacturer's directions for treatment.
6. Brush hair for several minutes.
7. Give patron a mild shampoo.
8. Apply conditioning treatment to hair according to the written directions.

*Scoring Criteria:* The skills demonstrated by the learner will be evaluated according to the standards and specifications established by the state license examination in cosmetology.

## JOB ANALYSIS

Analyzing a job is another aspect of the vocational assessment process. This procedure provides information concerning what a worker does, how the job is done, and why it is necessary. When conducting a job analysis, T & I personnel should identify necessary performance requirements for the job. Performance requirements may include (a) the primary tasks involved in completing the job, (b) goods/services produced by the worker, (c) job knowledge necessary for the job, (d) requirements and physical worker traits necessary for the job, (e) specific responsibilities to be assumed by the worker, (f) equipment, machinery tools, materials and work aids used on the job, (g) working conditions, and (h) performance standards associated with the job.

Information obtained by a job analysis can be used to develop job samples or work samples for use in assessing vocational potential. The same machinery, equipment, tools, materials and aids used on the job should be incorporated in the work samples whenever possible. The tasks involved in the work sample as well as the performance standards should be the same as those expected on the job. It is very important that the tasks and performance standards used in the sample or work sample be valid so that a realistic and appropriate assessment of a learner's strengths and weaknesses can be made.

Illustration 5.6 shows an example of an information sheet that could be used to organize job analysis data.

A variety of sources can be used to collect job analysis information. Three of the most widely used sources are the *Dictionary of Occupational Titles,* the *Occupational Outlook Handbook,* and a community manpower survey. A description of each of these sources follows:

## Dictionary of Occupational Titles (DOT)

The *Dictionary of Occupational Titles* (DOT) is an inventory of occupations within our economy prepared by the United States Department of Labor. This resource provides information about the physical demands, working conditions, and aptitudes required for a specific job as well as identifying its relationship to people, data, and things. The information

is collected through observation of workers and job sites by occupational analysts.

The DOT consists of several volumes of current information about occupations. These volumes are revised periodically. It can be useful in describing the proficiencies and skills required for each job, as well as the relationship between one job and another.

Volume I of the DOT contains definitions of over 35,000 job titles that are arranged alphabetically by title. Each definition contains information about what is done on the job, how the job is done, and why it is done. Specific worker functions and requirements are also included in the definition statement. These definitions should provide the reader with an occupational picture of each job, including the industry/industries in which the job is located, and alternate job titles.

Volume II introduces the classification system used in the DOT. This system combines both an Occupational Group Arrangement Code number and a Worker Trait Arrangement number. Each job in the DOT is identified by a six-digit code number. The first three digits (Occupational Group Arrangement) represent the field of work associated with the job, including the specific occupational category, division, and group. The broad occupational categories are as follows:

0–1 Professional, technical, and managerial occupations
2 Clerical and sales occupations
3 Service
4 Farming, fishery, forestry, and related occupations
5 Processing occupations
6 Machine trade occupations
7 Bench work occupations
8 Structural work occupations
9 Miscellaneous occupations

The last three digits of the code number (Worker Trait Arrangement) indicate the relationship of the job to data, people, and things, in that order. The lower the number, the higher is the relationship. This information can be helpful in analyz-

**Illustration 5.6**

## JOB ANALYSIS INFORMATION SHEET

JOB ANALYSIS INFORMATION SHEET

1.  Job Title: _____

2.  D.O.T. Code Number: _____

3.  Occupational Cluster: _____

4.  Job Description:

5.  Tasks to be Performed:

| Task/Competency | Performance Standard Required |
|---|---|
|  |  |

Comments:

6.  Job Knowledge Necessary:

7.  Physical Requirements:

8.  Worker Traits:

9.  Specific Responsibilities to be Assumed by the Worker:

10.  Equipment, Machinery, Tools, Materials and Aids Used on the Job:

11.  Working Conditions/Work Environment:

12.  Goods/Services Produced by the Job:

13.  Additional Information:

ing the qualifications of the job in order to match a learner's abilities and interests to a realistic career objective.

The DOT, therefore, can be a useful tool in the job analysis process as well as a valuable source of information in developing appropriate work samples for use in the vocational assessment process. An example of a job title listed in the DOT follows.

*Example of a Job Title Listed in the DOT:* 620.281–026 BRAKE REPAIRER (auto ser.) brake mechanic; brake-repair mechanic; brakeshoe repairer. Repairs and overhauls brake systems in automobiles, buses, trucks,and other automotive vehicles: Pushes handle of hydraulic jack or pushes hoist control to raise vehicle axle. Removes wheels, using wrenches, wheel puller, and sledge hammer. Replaces defective brakeshoe units or attaches new linings to brakeshoes. Measures brakedrum to determine amount of wear, using feeler gauge. Inserts vacuum gauge into powerbrake cylinder, starts engine, and reads gauge to detect brake-line leaks. Repairs or replaces leaky brake cylinders. Repairs and replaces defective air compressor in airbrake systems. Replaces wheel on axle and adjusts drumshoe clearance, using wrench. Fills master brake cylinder with brake fluid, pumps brake pedal or uses pressure tank and opens valves on hydraulic brake system to bleed air from brake lines. Closes valves and refills master brake cylinder. May be designed according to speciality as BRAKE REPAIRER, AIR (auto. ser.); BRAKE REPAIRER, HYDRAULIC (auto. ser.); BRAKE REPAIRER, BUS (auto. ser.). (U.S. Department of Labor, *Dictionary of Occupational Titles–Fourth Edition,* 1977, p. 537)

## Occupational Outlook Handbook

The *Occupational Outlook Handbook* is a publication of the United States Department of Labor. This resource provides information concerning more than 850 occupations in a variety of major industries. The industries are grouped according to major divisions in our economy. These divisions include agriculture, mining, and petroleum; construction; manufacturing; transportation, communications and public utilities; wholesale and retail trade; finance, insurance, and real estate services; and government.

The Bureau of Labor Statistics works with the Department of Labor to continuously gather data about occupations and employment trends. This resource describes job opportunities in sales work, professional occupations, craft and service areas, clerical work, managerial and labor positions, and farm occupations.

Every two years a new edition is published with the most current employment data available. Specific information provided for each major job includes:

1. What the job is like—
   a. Major duties of workers in the occupation.
   b. Nature of the work.
2. Places of employment—
   a. Number of workers in the occupation.
   b. Whether the job is concentrated in a particular industry.
   c. Whether the job is concentrated in a specific geographic area.
3. Personal qualifications for the job—
   a. Social skills.
   b. Motivation.
   c. Likes and dislikes.
   d. Decision-making abilities.
   e. Supervision skills.
4. Training qualifications for the job—
   a. Coordination skills.
   b. Manipulation skills.
   c. Dexterity skills.
5. Educational qualifications for the job—
   a. College education.
   b. Post-secondary vocational-technical program.
   c. Private vocational education programs.
   d. Home-study courses.
   e. Government training programs.

f. Training in the armed forces.

g. On-the-job training experiences.

h. Secondary vocational education programs.

i. High school diploma.

j. Licensing.

6. Working conditions—
   a. Environment.
   b. Hazards.
   c. Physical demands.
   d. Type of work, including shift and overtime work.

7. Earnings—
   a. Wage or salary range.
   b. Fringe benefits.
   c. Which jobs pay the most.
   d. Salaries in different geographic locations.

8. Opportunities for advancement.

9. Sources of additional information—
   a. Libraries.
   b. Guidance personnel.
   c. Business and industrial firms.
   d. Public employment service.
   e. Private employment agencies.
   f. Trade unions.
   g. Professional organizations.
   h. Businessmen's associations.

(Department of Labor Statistics)

## Community Manpower Survey

A survey of manpower needs in the community can be helpful in collecting job analysis information. The survey of local industries can provide information relating to the types and numbers of available jobs, specific skills required for each job, and working conditions.

There are a variety of methods that can be used to collect community manpower information, including personal interviews, sending survey forms by mail, and collecting information by telephone conversations. The survey method selected should take into consideration the size of the community, the number of firms and industries available, and the amount of time to be spent on the survey. The local business and industrial firms to be included in the survey can be obtained from such sources as the Chamber of Commerce, the telephone directory, and community retail merchant groups.

Illustration 5.7 provides an example of information that might be useful to include in a community manpower survey. The survey form, however, should be developed to include information that will meet the specific needs of the community, the T & I program, and the learners to be served.

## SITUATIONAL ASSESSMENT

One of the most widely used vocational evaluation approaches is situational assessment. This assessment technique uses observation skills to record vocational behaviors and work habits which learners exhibit while performing specific work tasks. The work tasks can occur in a simulated environment or in an actual job situation. Learners are observed and evaluated while working in a group setting rather than on an individual basis. In this manner, the evaluator can observe hands-on skills as well as important interpersonal skills and social behaviors. Rating scales and behavior checklists are normally used during situational assessment activities to record work performance.

Brolin (1976) presents several advantages of the situational assessment approach in the vocational assessment process. This technique has several advantages:

1. It simulates a real work situation.

2. It allows the evaluator to observe social and interpersonal relationship behaviors as well as important hands-on skills necessary for the job.

3. It is less time-consuming than formal or informal work samples.

4. It is not expensive to develop activities for this approach.

5. It gives the individuals to be evaluated a chance to adjust to the activity in a more natural work environment than a regular testing situation.

**Illustration 5.7**

## COMMUNITY MANPOWER SURVEY GUIDELINES

1.  Source of data information:

    a.  Name of firm: _____

    b.  Address: _____

    _____

    c.  Phone Number: ( ) _____

    d.  Employer(s) providing information (include name and official
        title): _____

    _____

2.  Overview of employer and business (including number of full-time
    and part-time employees hired each year): _____

    _____

3.  Types and numbers of jobs relating to the T & I program which
    are available:

    | Job Title | Number of Available Openings |
    | --- | --- |
    |  |  |

4.  Job description information:

    | Job Title | Job Description |
    | --- | --- |
    |  |  |

5.  Specific skills required for each job:

    | Job Title | Specific Skills Required |
    | --- | --- |
    |  |  |

119

6. List of job tasks frequency of task performance and performance level(s) required:

| Job Title | Job Tasks | Frequency of Performance | Performance Level(s) Required |
|-----------|-----------|--------------------------|------------------------------|
|           |           |                          |                              |
|           |           |                          |                              |
|           |           |                          |                              |

7. Working conditions and environment:

| Job Title | Working Conditions/Environment |
|-----------|--------------------------------|
|           |                                |
|           |                                |
|           |                                |

8. Does your company receive assistance through federal contracts?

_____ Yes          _____ No

9. If yes, do you have an affirmative action program for the handicapped in compliance with Sections 503 and 504 of the Rehabilitation Act of 1973?

_____ Yes          _____ No

6. It provides an opportunity for several professionals to observe and interpret behavior in a cooperative planning process. These personnel can include teachers, vocational evaluators, and supervisors.

The following description provides an example of how a T & I teacher can work cooperatively with other school personnel to develop a situational assessment activity designed to evaluate the work potential of special needs learners enrolled in the program.

Mr. Garland, the T & I teacher, decided to develop a series of activities that could be used to help him evaluate the abilities and work habits of the special needs learners enrolled in his program. He had several planning sessions with the special education teacher and the coordinator for disadvantaged students. During these sessions it was decided that they would all participate in observing the special needs learners perform the work tasks involved in the situational assessment activities. A situational assessment checklist was also developed to record their observations.

The activities developed by Mr. Garland are composed of work tasks that have to be performed on the job. The tools, equipment, and materials used on the job are included in these tasks. Observations made during these activities will be used as a tool to discover how many basic skills the special needs learners possess.

Mr. Garland divides the class into small groups. Each group has an opportunity to participate in the situational assessment activities. At the beginning of each activity Mr. Garland introduces the tools, equipment, and materials to be used for the work tasks. He then explains the procedure for completing the work task.

While the groups perform the operations involved, Mr. Garland, the special education teacher, and the coordinator for disadvantaged students observe the performance of the special needs learners. They record their observations on the situational assessment checklist developed for this purpose. After the activity has been completed the cooperative team will discuss their observations and use the results to make realistic plans for these learners in the T & I program.

## A Cooperative Approach to Vocational Assessment

In the past, vocational evaluation has been conducted mainly by psychologists, evaluators, and rehabilitation personnel. The purpose in many cases was to analyze individual abilities so that specific training programs could then be considered or rejected. This philosophy often limited the appropriate use of evaluation results. Isolated results were used only to determine the work ability of the individual in regard to the vocational development opportunities that could be provided. The current practice (of using the vocational assessment process as a method of identifying program modifications to meet the specific abilities and needs of handicapped and disadvantaged learners) has increased the need of cooperation from experts in many disciplines. Cooperation among professionals is critical if the evaluation process is to lead to realistic and appropriate vocational and employment opportunities for special needs populations.

Illustration 5.8 provides an example of a checklist that could be used to record and evaluate an individual's performance during a situational assessment activity.

Observation information gathered from situational assessment activities can be used to develop appropriate vocational education goals and objectives for special needs learners. This technique can help to identify the specific hands-on skills that the individual can or cannot perform as well as indicating the work habits and social skills that need improvement.

Vocational assessment should be a cooperative process involving a variety of professionals and specialists who offer a continuum of services. Personnel who can provide relevant information and expertise for this process include (a) special education administrator/supervisor, (b) vocational education administrator/supervisor, (c) school/district administrator, (d) vocational evaluator, (e) vocational teacher, (f) vocational/guidance counselor, (g) speech clinician, (h) hearing clinician, (i) psychologist, (j) parent/guardian, (k) physical therapist, (l) occupational therapist, (m) special education personnel, (n) vocational rehabilitation personnel, (o) medical personnel, (p) prevocational/career education instructors, (q) social worker, and (r) special needs learner.

The number of personnel involved in the cooperative vocational assessment process and the extent of their involvement will depend on a number of factors, including the amount of time alloted for assessment, the availability of these professionals, and the nature or amount of relevant information requested for the evaluation.

Illustration 5.9 presents an overview of personnel who could be helpful in providing information or assistance in the vocational assessment process.

Illustration 5.10 is an example of a vocational assessment checklist.

## COOPERATIVE PLANNING

Cooperative planning is a coordinated effort by various individuals and agencies to provide a comprehensive and realistic instructional plan for a specific learner.

**Illustration 5.8**

## SITUATIONAL ASSESSMENT CHECKLIST

Student: _____

Date: _____

Observer(s): _____

_____

_____

Job Task: _____

| Observation | Rating | | |
|---|---|---|---|
| | Excellent | Satisfactory | Needs Improvement |
| 1. Work habits | | | |
| 2. Punctuality | | | |
| 3. Manipulation, coordination, dexterity | | | |
| 4. Personal grooming/hygiene | | | |
| 5. Ability to work unsupervised | | | |
| 6. Ability to work under pressure | | | |
| 7. Eye-hand coordination | | | |
| 8. Speed, accuracy and precision | | | |
| 9. Strength | | | |
| 10. Consistency in performing task(s) | | | |
| 11. Work tolerance/endurance | | | |
| 12. Understanding and following safety rules | | | |
| 13. Fine motor skills | | | |
| 14. Gross motor skills | | | |
| 15. Ability to work with others | | | |
| 16. Concentration | | | |
| 17. Reaction to job/task changes | | | |
| 18. Adjustment to repetitive tasks | | | |
| 19. Ability to follow directions | | | |
| 20. Quantity of work performance | | | |
| 21. Quality of work performance | | | |
| 22. Work attitude | | | |
| 23. Initiative | | | |

| Observation | Rating | | |
|---|---|---|---|
| | Excellent | Satisfactory | Needs Improvement |
| 24. Motivation | | | |
| 25. Accepts constructive criticism | | | |
| 26. Accepts constructive authority | | | |
| 27. Concentration | | | |
| 28. Communication skills (speech) | | | |
| 29. Completes assigned tasks | | | |
| 30. Follows directions | | | |
| 31. Remembers verbal directions | | | |
| 32. Assumes responsibility | | | |
| 33. Attention span | | | |
| 34. Care of equipment and materials | | | |
| 35. Frustration tolerance | | | |
| 36. Perseverance | | | |
| 37. Thoroughness | | | |

Comments:

Recommendations:

A team approach is used to accomplish this objective. The team members include professionals in the school, representatives of agencies and organizations, advisory committees, employers, administrators, and parents/guardians.

Several considerations must be addressed before the cooperative planning process can succeed. The individuals represented on the cooperative planning team must have a positive attitude toward special needs learners and a commitment to assist these learners in regular vocational programs. Appropriate placement options must also be available if realistic cooperative plans developed for the learner will depend on such variables as the flexibility of the learner's schedule and the availability of necessary support services. Cooperative planning is necessary if the vocational potential of special needs learners is to be developed to the maximum.

Illustration 5.11 shows the important components of the cooperative planning process. Each of these components will be discussed briefly.

## State and Local Cooperative Interagency Agreements

Many states have developed a cooperative interagency agreement that describes the role and responsibilities of vocational education, special education, and vocational rehabilitation in order to maximize the services provided for handicapped individuals. These agreements have been developed as a result of the current national drive to expand and improve the service delivery systems used to provide this population with appropriate vocational education opportunities. Interagency agreements are also important to prevent

## Illustration 5.9

### PERSONNEL WHO MAY BE INVOLVED IN THE COOPERATIVE VOCATIONAL ASSESSMENT PROCESS

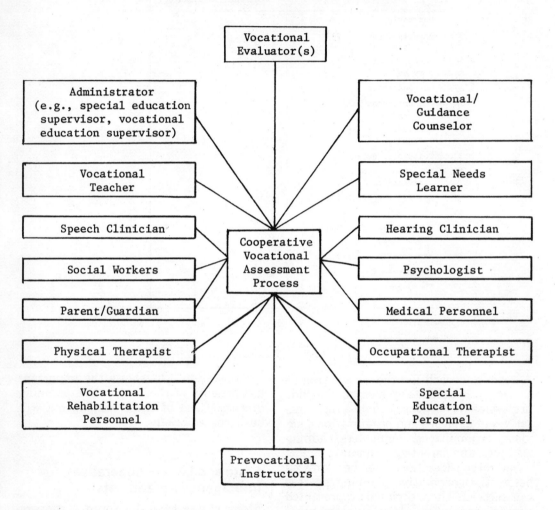

the duplication of services by two or more agencies.

The commitment on the part of vocational education, special education, and vocational rehabilitation is partially to assure that the rights of handicapped individuals to receive appropriate services are provided as mandated in the Education of All Handicapped Children Act of 1975 (Public Law 94–142), the Vocational Educational Amendments of 1976 (Public Law 94–482), and Section 504 of the Rehabilitation Act of 1973 (Public Law 93–112). For a review of these Acts refer to Module 1.

The cooperative agreement is a commitment by the agencies involved to work together toward providing comprehensive vocational education opportunities for handicapped individuals. The agreement usually covers cooperative services in the general areas of identification, evaluation, and vocational training.

An example of a state cooperative inter-

**Illustration 5.10**

# VOCATIONAL ASSESSMENT CHECKLIST

Student: _____

Date of Referral: _____

Individual(s) Involved in Assessment Process: _____

_____

_____

Directions:   Complete the information for the following components of
the vocational assessment process:

1.   Referral information (e.g., who made initial referral, eligibility
for vocational evaluation):

2.   Biographical information (e.g., student record information,
academic information, social/family information, vocational/
prevocational information, medical information):

3.   Student orientation to vocational assessment process (e.g., orientation process, who explained the process, student reaction to
orientation, possible problems):

4.   Psychometric testing results (e.g., name, date and results of
aptitude tests, dexterity tests, dexterity tests, interest
inventories):

5.   Work sample results (e.g., description, date and results of
student participation in commercial and/or information work
sample activities):

6.   Observation information (e.g., social/interpersonal relation
skills, work habits, work tolerance):

7.   Student interview (e.g., results of one-to-one conference with
student after completion of vocational assessment components):

8.   Situational Assessment information (e.g., student performance
on job related tasks in a vocational program and/or performance
on the job):

9.   Follow-up Information:

10.   Recommendations:

Illustration 5.11

## IMPORTANT COMPONENTS OF THE COOPERATIVE
## PLANNING PROCESS

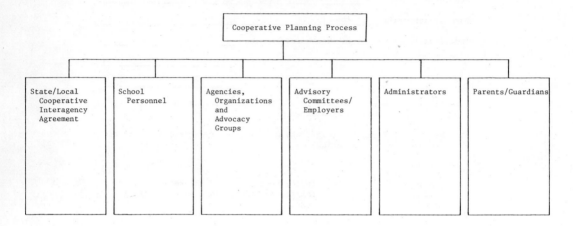

agency agreement might include the following provisions:

1. Vocational Education shall accept the responsibility for:
   a. Providing occupational preparation training to those handicapped individuals referred by Special Education and/or Vocational Rehabilitation.
   b. Complying with the requirements set forth in the state plan regarding handicapped individuals.
   c. Referring identified handicapped individuals for services from Vocational Rehabilitation when appropriate.
   d. Participating in the development of the Individualized Education Plan (IEP) for handicapped individuals enrolled in vocational education programs.
   e. Participating in the development of the Individualized Written Rehabilitation Program (IWRP) for handicapped individuals enrolled in vocational education programs.
   f. Participating in cooperative inservice and staff development

training activities with staff from Special Education and Vocational Rehabilitation.

2. Special Education shall accept the responsibility for:
   a. Providing technical assistance to local education agencies to insure that handicapped students are provided with appropriate personal-social and prevocational skills before being referred to Vocational Education.
   b. Placement of specific handicapped students in Vocational Education programs based on their IEPs.
   c. Involving Vocational Education and Vocational Rehabilitation in the development of the IEPs.
   d. Providing local education agencies with information concerning the services available from Vocational Rehabilitation and the requirements for client eligibility.

3. Vocational Rehabilitation shall accept the responsibility for:
   a. Accepting for screening referred handicapped students, age 16 or older, from Vocational Education and/or Special Education to deter-

mine their eligibility for services.

b. Identifying, evaluating, and providing rehabilitation services to eligible handicapped individuals.

c. Developing an IWRP for eligible students in cooperation with appropriate Vocational Education and/or Special Education staff.

d. Providing vocational rehabilitation services and benefits as specified in federal and state regulations and the state plan.

(Example taken from the State of Georgia Cooperative Interagency Agreement, 1979).

Local education agencies have the option of developing cooperative interagency agreements that reflect the guidelines established in the state cooperative interagency agreement. This provides an opportunity for local vocational education, special education, and vocational rehabilitation staff to jointly determine how services will be delivered, issues of local concern, and responsibilities of each discipline area.

Trade and industrial personnel working with special needs learners should check with the State Department of Education and local administrators to determine whether state or local cooperative interagency agreements have been developed. These agreements would provide information concerning specific roles and responsibilities of the disciplines involved in providing services to this population.

## Cooperative Planning with School Personnel

Vocational education personnel cannot be expected to accept the full responsibility of planning, implementing, and evaluating appropriate vocational training programs for special needs learners. Cooperative planning is essential if necessary services are to be provided. Whether or not these individuals succeed in vocational programs depends to a great degree on the cooperative relationships established among school personnel.

A team approach is usually the best method to ensure that handicapped and disadvantaged learners are provided with appropriate evaluation acitivities, guidance and counseling services, supplemental services, instructional materials, occupational competencies, and job placement opportunities. A list follows of school personnel who can be helpful in the cooperative planning process. Each of these individuals can lend a specific type of expertise to the cooperative planning team. These personnel include:

1. Psychologist.
2. Social worker.
3. Resource room teacher.
4. Itinerant teacher.
5. Speech therapist/communication specialist.
6. Work-study coordinator.
7. Prevocational coordinator.
8. Special education teacher.
9. Other vocational personnel.
10. Guidance counselor/vocational counselor.
11. Nurse/medical personnel.
12. Remedial math teacher.
13. Remedial reading teacher.
14. Remedial communications skills teacher.
15. Curriculum coordinator.
16. Bilingual teacher.
17. Teacher's aide.
18. Interpreter.
19. Media specialist.
20. Artist/illustrator.
21. Regular classroom teachers.
22. Hearing clinician.
23. Occupational therapist.
24. Physical therapist.
25. Peers in the classroom.
26. Tutors.
27. Handicapped/disadvantaged student.

## Cooperative Planning with Agencies and Organizations

Community agencies organizations and advocacy groups can often offer services and assistance that are not readily available in the school system. Cooperation with these groups should be developed to the maximum extent possible and existing services should be utilized to provide appropriate vocational programs and support services for special needs learners.

Vocational education programs should make initial contacts with outside agencies and community services, especially when they can effectively supplement vocational activities. In many cases, vocational education personnel do not possess the expertise and skills necessary to deliver services that are available from these outside sources.

One of the most important agencies that can provide services for handicapped individuals is Vocational Rehabilitation. Vocational rehabilitation services are frequently used to provide a coordinated approach to serving handicapped learners with vocational training and placement opportunities. Criteria for eligibility of services include (a) a physical or mental disability that represents or contributes to an employment handicap and (b) a reasonable expectation that services provided by vocational rehabilitation will benefit the individual to become employable.

Specific services that may be provided for eligible handicapped individuals include:

1. Vocational assessment and evaluation services.
2. Vocational adjustment services.
3. Vocational guidance and counseling services.
4. Physical restoration services.
5. Books, materials, and tools necessary for a specific training program.
6. Transportation services.
7. Interpreter services for the deaf.
8. Services for the blind, including reader services, orientation, and mobility training.
9. Technological aids and devices necessary for participation in a training program and/or employment situation.
10. Medical examinations and services.
11. Psychological examinations and services.
12. Job placement services.
13. Post-employment services necessary to help handicapped individuals keep their job.
14. Occupational licenses, equipment, tools, and supplies necessary for success on the job.
15. Referral to other appropriate agencies for services not available through vocational rehabilitation.

A list of other agencies, organizations and community groups that can be useful in providing services for special needs learners can be found in Appendix A.

## Cooperative Planning with Advisory Committees and Employers

Local advisory committees are groups of individuals from the community that advise vocational educators about planning, implementing, and maintaining programs. Under the provision of the Vocational Education Amendments of 1976, each local education agency must establish a vocational education advisory committee in order to receive funds.

Membership for vocational education advisory committees should be selected from a variety of community sources, although the major portion of the committee should be composed of representatives from the business and industrial sector. Other sources include (a) Chamber of Commerce, (b) Labor Department, (c) labor unions, (d) state and community agencies, (e) employers of program completers, (f) prospective employers, (g) local government, (h) clergy, (i) local media (radio and television), (j) local newspaper, (k) local management, (l) parents, and (m) handicapped and disadvantaged individuals/advocates.

The primary function of a vocational education advisory committee is to assist in planning a sound training program that will meet the needs of the students enrolled as well as the manpower needs of the community.

Cooperative planning with vocational education advisory committees can assist vocational personnel in providing appropriate opportunities for special needs learners. Specific services that can be provided by this valuable resource include:

1. Assistance in planning programs that would be appropriate and realistic for special needs learners.

2. Advice concerning appropriate program objectives, curriculum content, and occupational competencies to be included in programs.

3. Identification of community resources that may be useful in assisting special needs learners to succeed in programs.

4. Assessing the educational and manpower needs of the community (possibly through a needs survey).

5. Identification of entry-level job proficiencies.

6. Establishing and promoting positive community public relationships.

7. Advice concerning equipment, laboratory, and facilities modifications for special needs learners.

8. Assistance in locating potential on-the-job training sites for special needs learners who require further reinforcement during or after completion of a specific program.

9. Assistance in identifying job placement situations for special needs learners.

## Cooperative Planning with Administrators

The role of the administrator in planning, implementing, and evaluating vocational education programs to meet the needs of handicapped and disadvantaged learners is very important to the effectiveness of cooperative planning arrangements. Involvement of administrators in the formulation of cooperative agreements is equally important. Polities used to determine how programs will be coordinated and monitored to include special needs learners are usually formulated by administrators at the state and local level.

Administrators involved in planning, implementing, and evaluating vocational service options for these students will depend on the organization and structure at the local level. These administrators may include (a) director/supervisor of vocational education, (b) director/supervisor of special education, and/or (c) special needs coordinator. These individuals may be given full-time or part-time responsibility for special needs program management alone or in cooperation with others.

Administration support in the cooperative planning process can result in provision of the following services:

1. Appropriate service delivery options.

2. Support services necessary to aid special needs learners.

3. Flexible scheduling opportunities such as extended time, and open entry/open exit.

4. In-service/staff development activities to develop cooperative relationships between special education and vocational education personnel.

5. Funds to purchase appropriate instructional materials.

6. Modification of machinery and equipment.

7. Modification of classroom/laboratory facilities (accessibility).

## Cooperative Planning with Parents/Guardians

Parents/guardians are a very important component of the cooperative planning process. They probably know the student better than any professional in the school system. They have an enormous influence on the growth and development of the student. They have valid questions and concerns that should be addressed when planning an instructional program for the special needs individual. Some of the questions that they may raise during the cooperative planning process include:

1. Does the T & I program meet the needs of the student?

2. Is the T & I program the best available placement for the student? Have all realistic options been discussed? Has the student been provided with appropriate

career exploration activities and/or career counseling?

3. Will necessary support services be provided to help the student succeed in the program? Will the student be able to keep up with others in the program? Will extended time in the program be allowed if necessary?

4. Will the student be accepted by peers in the program?

5. Will the T & I teacher be understanding of the needs of the student? Will the teacher discriminate against the student because he/she has special needs?

6. Will there be a job for the student once he/she has successfully completed the program? Will the student have the necessary entry-level proficiencies upon completion of the program?

For many years schools assumed the responsibility of testing, placing, instructing and evaluating all students. There is now a strong emphasis on the role of parents/guardians in the educational planning process. An example of this is seen in the Education for All Handicapped Children Act (Public Law 94–142), which mandates that parents be included in the planning of the individualized education program (IEP) developed for each handicapped learner. Parents of handicapped learners are now entitled, by law, to share in the educational planning, confidential treatment of records, and involvement in advisory committee meetings. Parents have now been asked to take their rightful place in working with school personnel and outside agencies to provide the best possible educational opportunities for their sons and daughters.

When parents understand what is happening in school, they are much more willing to provide support help in meeting cooperative objectives. Parents have a right to know about the T & I program that their son/daughter is to be enrolled in. They need to be informed of pertinent information regarding program objectives, specific skills to be taught, entry-level job opportunities. Parents are usually very concerned that their children be placed in a program that will help them gain the skills they need to lead a productive and useful life.

There are many advantages to involving parents/guardians in the cooperative planning process. They can lend encouragement and reinforcement at home that will help to motivate the student. They can apply behavior modification techniques, assist the student in related instruction, lead and participate in career guidance discussions and report to school personnel any problems that arise at home relating to participation in the T & I program.

## SUMMARY

The vocational assessment process can provide valuable information about an individual's vocational potential. Specific information that can be provided as a result of this process includes vocational aptitudes, vocational interests, work habits, socialization skills, personal adjustment skills, work attitudes and work tolerance. This information can be obtained over a period of time through real life and/or simulated work situations.

The specific components of the vocational assessment process include collecting background information and compiling a pupil profile, the use of commercial work sample batteries, the use of informal work samples, job analysis, and situational assessment. Vocational assessment should be a cooperative endeavor involving a number of school and community based personnel.

The process of cooperative planning for special needs learners should be a coordinated effort by various individuals and agencies. It is essential that a team approach to planning be used in order to provide a comprehensive and realistic instructional plan for each learner.

The important components of the cooperative planning process include state and local cooperative interagency agreements; school personnel; agencies, organizations, and advocacy groups; advisory committees and employers; administrators; and parents/guardians.

# REFERENCES

Brolin, D. *Vocational preparation for retarded citizens.* Columbus, Ohio: Charles E. Merrill Publishing Company, 1976.

Dunn, D. *Situational assessment: models for the future.* Menomonie, Wisconsin: University of Wisconsin-Stout, Research and Training Center, 1973.

Pruitt, W. *Vocational (work) evaluation.* Menomonie, Wisconsin: Walt Pruitt Associates, 1977.

Revell, W., Kriloff, L. and Sarkees, M. Vocational evaluation. In P. Wehman and P. McLaughlin, *Vocational curriculum for developmentally disabled persons.* Baltimore, Maryland: University Park Press, 1980.

Sarkees, M. An overview of selected evaluation systems for use in assessing the vocational potential of handicapped individuals. *Diagnostique,* 1979, *4* (1), 42–51.

Shea, D. Diagnostic and assessment procedures for identifying individual characteristics and problems. In J. Wall (Ed.), *Vocational education for special groups.* Washington, D.C.: American Vocational Education Association, 1976.

Sitlington, P. The assessment process as a component of career education. In G. Clark and W. White, *Career education for the handicapped: current perspectives for teachers.* Boothwyn, Pennsylvania: Educational Resources Center, 1980.

## SELF ASSESSMENT: VOCATIONAL ASSESSMENT AND THE COOPERATIVE PLANNING PROCESS

1. What is the purpose of vocational assessment?
2. Why is the vocational assessment process important?
3. List some specific information that can be provided as a result of the vocational assessment process.
4. What is the purpose of collecting background information for a specific special needs learner?
5. What information is usually documented on a learner profile? Why is this information important to the vocational assessment process?
6. What are the advantages and disadvantages of using commercial work samples with special needs learners?
7. What factors should be taken into consideration when using commercial work samples results to place special needs learners in T & I programs?
8. Discuss the steps involved in developing an informal work sample.
9. What specific information can be obtained through job analysis that can be used in the vocational assessment process?
10. What information can be provided by the *Dictionary of Occupational Titles* (DOT)? How can this information be helpful in the vocational assessment process?
11. What information can be provided by the *Occupational Outlook Handbook*? How can this information be helpful in the vocational assessment process?
12. How can a community manpower survey be useful in providing job analysis information? What specific information can it provide? How can this information be used in the vocational assessment process?
13. What are the advantages and disadvantages of the situational assessment approach to vocational assessment?

14. Why should vocational assessment be a cooperative endeavor?
15. Name personnel who may be involved in the cooperative vocational assessment process.
16. Describe the importance of the cooperative planning process.
17. Name some personnel who should be included in the cooperative planning process.
18. What information is usually included in a state or local cooperative interagency agreement?
19. What contributions can school personnel make to the cooperative planning process?
20. What contributions can agencies, organizations and advocacy groups make to the cooperative planning process?
21. What contributions can advisory committees and employers make to the cooperative planning process?
22. What contributions can administrators make to the cooperative planning process?
23. What contributions can parents/guardians make to the cooperative planning process?

## ASSOCIATED ACTIVITIES

1. Contact personnel in your school or district who are in charge of vocational assessment for handicapped and disadvantaged individuals. These contacts may include special education personnel, guidance counselors, special education staff and vocational rehabilitation counselors. Discuss the initial referral process. Also ask to see a learner profile form. If none is used, suggest that a form be cooperatively developed for use in the future.
2. Check with vocational evaluation personnel to determine what commercial work sample batteries are used with special needs learners. Are these samples relevant to your program? Have these work samples been normed on the population(s) with which they will be used?
3. Work cooperatively with other staff members to develop informal work samples that can be used with special needs learners enrolled in your program. What specific information will you be looking for? How will this information help you to better plan for these learners in your program?
4. Develop a job analysis information sheet that can be used to collect important information for use in your program.
5. Locate or purchase a copy of the *Dictionary of Occupational Titles* and the *Occupational Outlook Handbook* for future reference.
6. Develop a community manpower survey that can be used to collect useful information for your program.
7. Develop a situational assessment checklist to use in observing special needs learners participating in work tasks. This checklist should involve other personnel who may also be observing these students.
8. Check to see whether your state and/or local district has developed a cooperative interagency agreement. What are the responsibilities of vocational education, special education, and vocational rehabilitation according to this agreement?

## CASE HISTORY: CHRISTINA'S STORY

Christina is a deaf student enrolled in an industrial and residential wiring program. Christina has been deaf since she was five years old. She spent the next ten years attending the area school for the deaf. During that time she received training in lipreading, oral speaking, and signing.

Since she has returned to the public schools Christina has been working with a speech therapist, an itinerant teacher for the hearing impaired, an interpreter, and a vocational rehabilitation counselor. These resource personnel have also been working cooperatively with regular class instructors who are working with her in their programs.

Christina became interested in the industrial and residential wiring program as a result of the vocational evaluation she participated in last year at the rehabilitation center.

The program instructor is pleased with Christina's performance in class. He feels comfortable working with her because of the support help they are receiving from the resource personnel. The speech therapist is helping Christina with her speech problem. The itinerant teacher visits the classroom each week to work with Christina and the instructor.

Christina has demonstrated proficiency in the areas of blueprint reading, residential wiring, romex wiring, and the proper use of necessary tools. However, she is experiencing some difficulty learning the codes and ordinances that are necessary for successful completion of the program. In this case, an interpreter was provided to help Christina with this unit. The vocational rehabilitation counselor has offered to provide any necessary services in the form of adaptive aids and job placement assistance.

## CASE HISTORY ACTIVITY

Daniel is a hard-of-hearing student who has recently enrolled in your program. He has a slight speech defect as a result of his hearing loss. He is very self-conscious about his handicap. Therefore, he is reluctant to participate in group activities or class discussions. He is very good at mathematical problems but has a lower reading level than his peers. Daniel has problems reading the textbook and the handouts used in the program.

Based on this information, complete the case history profile worksheet for Daniel's participation in your program.

# CASE HISTORY PROFILE WORKSHEET

Student: _____ Page: _____

Handicapping Condition(s): _____

T & I Program: _____ Academic Levels: _____

Career Goal/Occupational Interest: _____

Considerations (e.g., medication, behavior): _____

_____

| Adaptation | Specific Services Needed | Where to Obtain Service |
|---|---|---|
| Cooperative Planning (School Personnel) | | |
| Support Services | | |
| Architectural Changes | | |
| Adaptive Equipment | | |
| Curriculum Modification | | |
| Instructional Materials/ Supplies | | |
| Teaching Techniques | | |
| Agency Involvement | | |
| Possible Job Placement | | |

# MODULE 6

## Teacher Concerns and Abilities of Trade and Industrial Teachers in Working with Special Needs Students

Trade and industrial teachers often express a number of concerns about working with special needs learners. The primary concern, however, is a feeling of inadequacy. These teachers feel that they lack the specialized training that is essential to help special needs students develop the personal-social qualities, knowledge, and skills required to be employable.

Other specific teacher concerns include (a) providing a safe environment, (b) motivating special needs learners, (c) developing peer relationships, (d) maintaining program standards, (e) selecting and/or developing appropriate instructional materials, (f) controlling student behavior, (g) facilitating classroom or laboratory accessibility, (h) modifying equipment for the handicapped, and (i) evaluating student achievement.

Many of these concerns expressed by T & I teachers are grounded in misinformation and often take the shape of myths that lead to the development and maintenance of stereotyped thinking and negative attitudes. Before special needs learners can be successfully integrated into existing trade and industrial programs, these myths held by teachers must be dissolved and replaced with factual information. Teachers must develop positive, open-minded attitudes toward helping special needs students to develop the personal-social qualities, knowledge, and skills required to become a successful worker.

Module 6 presents an overview of the nature of trade and industrial education, including the types of instructional programs available to meet the needs of a variety of students who choose to enroll in these programs. The module also addresses concerns expressed by T & I teachers asked to work with special needs students and includes factual information about these concerns to help destroy stereotypes, dissolve myths, and replace negative attitudes with positive ones. The personal-social qualities and competencies of T & I teachers that are beneficial in working with special needs students are also discussed. The module is organized into four sections: (1) the nature of trade and industrial programs, (2) types of instructional programs within trade and industrial education, (3) concerns of trade and industrial teachers in working with special needs learners, and (4) personal-social qualities and specific competencies needed by trade and industrial teachers.

## MODULE OBJECTIVES

After you have read and reviewed this module, studied the case history, reviewed the self-assessment questions, and completed some of the associated activities, you should be able to:

1. Describe the nature of trade and industrial programs.

2. Identify and describe the types of instructional programs within trade and industrial education.

3. List the major concerns of T & I teachers about working with special needs students and briefly explain how each concern can be reduced or eliminated.

4. Identify and describe personal-social qualities that are beneficial in T & I teachers who work with special needs learners.

5. Identify and describe specific competencies that are beneficial in T & I teachers who work with special needs students.

## NATURE OF TRADE AND INDUSTRIAL PROGRAMS

Worker performance differs for people employed in trade, industrial, and technical occupations. In educational practice, the terms *trade* and *industrial* are often combined to form the *trade and industrial* education program, with technical education being a different type of program.

The following definitions from the American Vocational Association's publication, *Vocational-Technical Terminology* (1971), should help clarify some relevant terms.

### Trade and Industrial Education

Trade and industrial education, sometimes referred to as vocational industrial education, is a broad, vocationally oriented instructional area that includes training in a variety of occupations. It is offered at the secondary, post-secondary, and adult level in public education institutions as well as in business, industry, and private educational settings. The broad purpose of trade and industrial education programs is to prepare people with the basic manipulative skills, technical knowledge, and related occupational information necessary for initial employment, retraining, or advancement in trade and industrial occupations.

As identified in the Vocational Amendments of 1963 and continuing in the Amendments of 1976, the individuals eligible for training include (a) full-time students in secondary and post-secondary institutions, (b) employed persons who need training or retraining to maintain or advance their positions, and (c) students who are disadvantaged and handicapped.

### Technical Education

Technical education is a vocationally oriented instructional area. It is a generic term that encompasses various levels and types of technicians. This area of education is devoted to education and training that is generally of a higher level than the craftsman or trade level, but not professional in nature. Technical education programs are primarily offered at the post-secondary and adult levels in educational institutions. They are available in public, private, and industrial training settings. Technical education programs emphasize the development of a solid background of science and mathematics and the application of technology to a particular field or job.

The nature of technical education in terms of field-oriented and job-oriented technicians is addressed in the U.S. Office of Education Publication, *Criteria for Technical Education—A Suggested Guide* (1968). Field-oriented technicians are usually interested in a broad technical area. They combine a minimum of manipulative skills with a maximum of mathematical and scientific principles. Examples of field-oriented technicians include chemical, forestry, and mechanical design technicians.

Job-oriented technicians, on the other hand, have a narrow field of interest. They possess varying degrees of manipulative skills. Their related knowledge of mathematics and science depends on the specific area of technology. These individuals are normally charged with a specific area of responsibility in a field or occupation. Examples of job-oriented technicians include dental hygienists, dental laboratory technicians, electronics technicians, and hospital equipment technicians.

Technical education, as a specific level of education, depends upon other instructional areas for the prerequisites needed by individuals who plan to prepare for jobs as technicians. Due to this dependence upon support areas, there is a great deal of misconception about technical education. One way to differentiate among the occupational levels is to identify the varying levels of manipulative skills, mathematics, and scientific knowledge required. As one moves from laborer to technician, the amount of manipulative skills required decreases, while the knowledge of mathematics and scientific principles needed increases sharply.

# TYPES OF INSTRUCTIONAL PROGRAMS WITHIN TRADE AND INDUSTRIAL EDUCATION

## Day Trade Classes

Trade and industrial educators have developed different types of classes or instructional programs to meet the needs of a variety of persons. One type of instructional program is commonly called *day trade classes*. These classes are designed to serve full-time students at the secondary or post-secondary level. At the secondary level these classes are provided in traditional or "comprehensive" high schools, in special-purpose vocational or technical high schools, and in area vocational high schools. In the case of area vocational high schools, students typically attend the area school part of the day and their regular high school for the remainder of the day. Secondary day trade students typically spend from one to four hours per day in vocational classes.

At the post-secondary level, day trade classes are conducted in (a) post-secondary area vocational-technical schools, (b) junior or community colleges, (c) public or private trade schools, (d) technical institutes, and (e) four-year institutions of higher education. Post-secondary day trade students typically spend six hours per day in training. However, the time varies considerably depending upon the type of institution and its occupational objectives.

## Cooperative Education Programs

A second type of trade and industrial class is a cooperative education program in which students spend a part of the day in school and the remainder of the day in an employment situation. Cooperative programs are known by different titles in various states; the two most common types are Diversified Occupations (DO) and Industrial Cooperative Training (ICT) programs.

In secondary trade and industrial cooperative education programs, the student attends a number of regular classes and at least one related instruction class each day. The teacher-coordinator provides students with general occupational information as well as information relating to specific occupations. Individualized instructional materials are used to deliver this instruction. The student spends the remaining part of the school day in a trade or industrial occupation under the supervision of a training supervisor. The on-the-job part of a student's instructional program is not left to chance. It is carefully planned with input from the employer, the instructor, the student, and the parents. A cooperative trade and industrial education program is not merely a work experience program but rather a vocational education program that emphasizes educational preparation for employment.

## Apprenticeships

A third type of instructional program prepares apprentices. The content of these classes is jointly planned by the apprenticeship committee and the school. These classes may be conducted during the regular school day, at night or on Saturdays. The bulk of the content for apprenticeship classes is comprised of classroom-type work, even though it is often educationally desirable to provide some training in skills, particularly where these skills may be learned more efficiently in school.

## Part-Time Classes

A fourth type of instructional program is commonly known as part-time or adult education classes. In part-time classes instruction may be provided in any trade and industrial occupation for purposes of upgrading present job competencies or learning new ones. Instruction may vary from a few hours to several years. Content may include classroom instruction, skill training in a shop or laboratory setting, or a combination of both. Part-time classes are usually offered at night when facilities are more readily available. Instructors may be regular school staff or part-time instructional staff employed from trade or industry.

## CONCERNS OF TRADE AND INDUSTRIAL TEACHERS IN WORKING WITH SPECIAL NEEDS LEARNERS

Trade and industrial teachers should accept the reality of mainstreaming and should modify their teaching techniques, tools, materials, and classroom and laboratory facilities to accommodate special needs learners. Thus they should be willing to enter into cooperative planning and working relationships with special education personnel and other appropriate professionals who have expertise in working with handicapped and disadvantaged students.

Trade and industrial teachers should adopt the philosophy of individual differences. They should realize that, without lowering program standards, they can provide the instruction and support services that will allow special needs students to develop occupational skills. In some cases special needs students may require more time to develop occupational skills than their fellow classmates, but the important point is that they can develop entry-level skills and they can succeed in employment situations.

Competencies necessary for T & I instructors who work with special needs students do not differ significantly from those needed to work with all students. This is because special needs learners are more like other learners than they are unlike them.

The qualities of patience, consistency, and perseverance are beneficial in promoting success for special needs students in trade and industrial programs. State and local staff development activities and in-service training programs, both voluntary and mandatory, help T & I instructors develop specific competencies in working more effectively with special needs learners, developing appropriate teaching techniques, and using available support services. These competencies and qualities coupled with those expected of any teacher should result in an instructional program in which all students can succeed in reaching their educational and training goals.

The major concerns generally expressed by T & I teachers about working with special needs learners usually arise from a lack of understanding of their own abilities and a feeling of inadequate preparation. Several of these concerns are discussed in this section of the module.

### Providing a Safe Environment

Basic principles of accident prevention are essential to the operation of any trade and industrial program. Special needs students can be taught the proper use of machinery, equipment, and tools as effectively as their peers can be taught. It is natural to assume that every T & I teacher is concerned with the general safety environment and welfare of all the students enrolled in the program. It is also understandable that because of the lack of preparatory training and exposure to handicapped and disadvantaged students, these teachers are apprehensive about safety and liability considerations.

Special needs learners should receive the same safety instruction and reinforcement that is provided for all students. Each student must develop the ability to recognize potential safety hazards and develop safety procedures that will reduce or eliminate potentially dangerous situations. Students need to develop a positive attitude toward safety and develop safety habits that are essential for maintenance of an accident-free environment.

Generally, the same safety precautions and techniques required for other students can be successfully taught to special needs students. It is true that specific modifications will have to be made for some of these learners. For example, additional time for learning may be required before the student can demonstrate a specific safety technique. These changes necessary for teaching appropriate safety procedures to special needs learners should be made according to the individual needs of each student.

There is no evidence to indicate that special needs learners are a greater safety risk than other learners. As an example, employer surveys indicate that handicapped workers have safety records that are as good as, if not better than, those of nonhandicapped workers.

The primary causes of accidents in a laboratory setting result from lack of understanding of safety rules, confusion, and inattentiveness on the part of students. These circumstances can occur with any student if proper precautions are not taken before independent work is allowed in the lab area.

A good procedure to follow with all students enrolled in a trade and industrial program is to develop and implement a comprehensive safety training orientation program. This program should include general information on safety rules and practices, protective equipment, proper use of tools and equipment, and proper operation of machinery in the laboratory setting. As each student demonstrates appropriate safety habits when using equipment and machinery, a safety profile can be developed. Using this method, T & I teachers can be certain that students are able to operate machinery and equipment safely before they are allowed to work independently in the laboratory.

Support staff such as special education personnel and resource room teachers can help special needs students in safety orientation instruction. The rules that are covered in the trade and industrial program can be reinforced and reviewed during the time the students are with the support personnel. This reinforcement can be considered to be remedial academics. Cooperative planning between T & I teachers and support staff will help these learners to successfully demonstrate appropriate safety habits.

*Developing a Student Safety Profile.* The Student Safety Profile is an organized method of documenting student progress in the safety orientation to an instructional program. Illustration 6.1, designed for a machine shop program, summarizes the components of a comprehensive safety orientation program. Modification of the sample form will be necessary for other instructional programs, particularly in the area of tools and equipment.

The form is arranged by specific objectives of the orientation program and provides a method of documenting when a student has accomplished each of these objectives. In addition, specific behaviors that are involved in accomplishing each major objective are listed and space is provided for documenting the completion of each.

Another approach to assure a safe working environment in the laboratory is to develop a brief safety checklist. An instructor can check the crucial areas of safety performance as the student demonstrates appropriate safety techniques. Several examples of safety checklists that could be modified to meet the needs of a trade and industrial laboratory situation are provided in Illustrations 6.2 and 6.3.

Safety checklists can be used in addition to the general laboratory safety demonstration profile or as a separate method of evaluating the ability of the student to work safely in the laboratory.

*Safety Considerations for Special Needs Students.* To insure a safe and accessible environment for special needs students, specific modifications will have to be

## Illustration 6.1

## SAFETY DEMONSTRATION PROFILE

General Laboratory

Student: <u>Timothy Reuel</u>                                         Date: <u>9/2/80</u>

Trade and Industrial Program: <u>Machine Shop</u>

Instructor: <u>Robert Hogan</u>

Date of Entry: <u>9/2/80</u>

Date of Safety Orientation: <u>9/4/80</u>

Date Student Completes Specific Objectives of Safety Orientation: _____

---

| Specific Objectives: | Date Accomplished |
|---|---|
| Develops an awareness of hazard and becomes more safety conscious | _____ |
| Develops a serious attitude toward safety | _____ |
| Prepares for safety before entering work area | _____ |
| Prepares for safety at work stations | _____ |
| Understands color coding | _____ |
| Practices safety procedures | _____ |
| Prepares for safety on leaving shop | _____ |

| Develops an awareness of hazards and becomes more safety conscious (successfully respons to the following:) | Competence Demonstrated (Date) |
|---|---|
| 1. Why provide safety for yourself and others? | _____ |
| 2. How does shop safety produce project and fun? | _____ |
| 3. What laws and agencies regulate shop safety? | _____ |
| 4. What are the causes of shop accidents? | _____ |

Develops a serious attitude toward safety

| | |
|---|---|
| 1. Gives serious thought to work safety | _____ |
| 2. Remains alert in the shop area | _____ |

3. Works carefully       _____

4. Remains calm and hold temper     _____

5. Focuses attention on what is being done   _____

6. Assumes responsibility for own safety and safety of others

Prepares for safety before entering shop

1. What are the characteristics of a training program?

    a. Determines what tools, machines, and materials are required   _____

    b. Determines what hazards are involved   _____

    c. Determines what skills are needed   _____

Competence
Demonstrated (Date)

2. What clothing and safety equipment to wear?

    a. Recognizes types of clothing suitable for shop area   _____

    b. Recognizes types of foot and leg covering   _____

    c. Recognizes types of head covering   _____

    d. Recognizes types of eye and face protection   _____

    e. Recognizes types of hearing protection   _____

    f. Recognizes types of hand and arm protection   _____

    g. Recognizes types of lung and breathing protection   _____

Prepares for safety on entering the shop

1. What safety provision to locate?

    a. Locates exits   _____

    b. Locates emergency fire equipment   _____

    c. Locates emergency aids   _____

    d. Locates main power disconnect areas   _____

    e. Locates safety zones and lanes

2.   What potential hazards to keep in mind?

    a.   Identifies flammable materials      _____

    b.   Identifies mobile equipment      _____

    c.   Identifies activities of others      _____

Competence
Demonstrated (Date)

Prepares for safety at work station

1.   Obtaining tools and materials

    a.   Remembers where tool was obtained    _____

    b.   Follows established procedures for
       obtaining tools    _____

    c.   Checks condition of tool upon
       receipt    _____

    d.   Uses care in handling tools    _____

2.   What safety precautions to observe?

    a.   Checks for the condition of floor
       openings and storage areas    _____

    b.   Checks for proper lighting    _____

    c.   Checks for proper ventilation    _____

    d.   Checks for caution areas and
       protective signs    _____

    e.   Checks for guard rails    _____

3.   What power is available?

    a.   Uses electric power safely    _____

    b.   Uses air power safely    _____

    c.   Uses hydraulic power safety    _____

4.   What solvents and chemicals are present?

    a.   Checks the parts cleaning area    _____

    b.   Check the dispensing containers    _____

Practicing shop safety skills

1. Recognizes how to prevent bodily injuries

    a. Understands how to prevent slipping or falling     _____

    b. Understands how to avoid injuries from lifting     _____

    c. Understands how to avoid crushing injuries     _____

    d. Understands how to avoid hand and arm injuries     _____

2. Develops tool and machine safety skills

    a. Demonstrates hand tool safety skills     _____

    b. Demonstrates power tool safety skills on the following machines:

        (1) Milling machines     _____

        (2) Lathes     _____

        (3) Shapers     _____

        (4) Drill presses     _____

        (5) Power hacksaws     _____

        (6) Band saws     _____

        (7) Electrical discharge machines     _____

Understands color coding

1. Recognizes safety color codes for shop machines and equipment     _____

Prepares to leave the school shop

1. Stores tools, machines and materials

    a. Stores hand and portable power tools     _____

    b. Secures stationary power tools     _____

    c. Stores usable materials and supplies     _____

2.   Disposes of waste materials

    a.   Disposes of scrap metal, filings and chips  _____

    b.   Disposes of hot metal

    c.   Disposes of waste liquids

    d.   Disposes of sawdust and absorbent
       compounds  _____

3.   Cleans the workbench and floor  _____

4.   Stores safety equipment  _____

5.   Cleans hands and other parts of body  _____

6.   Performs final check of shop area  _____

and equipment. These modifications will have to be made according to the needs of each student. Illustration 6.4 is an example of a checklist appropriate for recording the modifications necessary for trade and industrial classroom and laboratory facilities (see Illustration 6.4). Further details about modifying equipment and facilities for handicapped students can be found in Module 7.

## Motivating Special Needs Learners

A key factor in student motivation is teacher attitude. Once special needs learners realize that a T & I teacher respects their abilities, respects them as individuals and is willing to make adjustments and modifications in the instructional program to allow for individual differences, insecurity and low motivation will often be replaced by a strong desire to succeed.

Many problems involving the motivation of special needs learners in regular programs result from their background of failure experiences in school. Their reluctance to put forth enthusiasm and effort often stems from failures experienced in the past. It is to be expected that students who have never had successful experiences in school will exhibit negative or apathetic attitudes toward new situations.

There are several techniques that are effective in motivating special needs learners. The first technique relates to the theory that a taste of success will generally ignite enthusiasm and motivation in a learner. The T & I teacher can promote student motivation by providing classroom activities and laboratory experiences that will lead to success for each student. This objective can often be accomplished through individualized instruction and cooperative working relationships with other professionals involved in planning the educational program of the special needs students.

A special needs learner often exhibits inappropriate behavior as a means of attracting attention. Since they generally have not been successful in gaining attention in a positive manner, they may assume that negative attention is better than no attention at all. The instructor can help to eliminate negative behaviors by making an effort to reinforce the positive efforts of the student. Positive reinforcement serves not only to prevent inappropriate behavior but also to motivate students to try harder.

Once the instructor identifies the strengths and weaknesses of the special needs learner and begins to incorporate this information into individualized planning, success will result. As an added

## Illustration 6.2

## SAFETY CHECKLIST

Student: _____

Instructor: _____

Program:  <u>Machine Shop</u>

Criterion:  <u>The student will demonstrate appropriate safety techniques
in each of the following areas with 100% accuracy prior to
working independently in the laboratory.</u>

| Safety Area | Date | Instructor Initials |
|-------------|------|---------------------|
| 1.  General Safety Rules | | |
| 2.  Hand Tools | | |
| 3.  Engine Lathe | | |
| 4.  Turret Lathe | | |
| 5.  Vertical Milling Machine | | |
| 6.  Horizontal Milling Machine | | |
| 7.  Drill Press | | |
| 8.  Radial Drill Press | | |
| 9.  Horizontal Band Saw | | |
| 10.  Vertical Band Saw | | |
| 11.  Pedistal Grinder | | |
| 12.  Surface Grinder | | |
| 13.  Jig Bone Machine | | |
| 14.  Meat Treating Equipment | | |
| 15.  Fire Extinguishers | | |
| 16.  Emergency Exit Charts | | |
| 17.  Emergency Exit Procedures | | |
| 18.  Emergency Electrical Circuit Breakers | | |

Comments:

_____
Instructor Signature

**Illustration 6.3**

## SAFETY CHECKLIST

Student: _____

Instructor: _____

Program:  Heating and Air Conditioning

| Safety Demonstration | Date | Evaluation |
|---|---|---|
| 1.  Safety Statement Signed/Filed | | |
| 2.  Fire Extinguisher | | |
| 3.  Building Emergency Exit Procedures/Routes | | |
| 4.  Electric Drills | | |
| 5.  Electric Grinder | | |
| 6.  Handling of Refrigerants | | |
| 7.  Prestolite Torch | | |
| 8.  Turbo Torch | | |
| 9.  Acetylene/Oxygen Torch | | |
| 10.  Electric Pipe Threader | | |
| 11.  Electrical Circuit Testing | | |
| 12.  Furnace Lighting Procedures | | |

Comments:

Instructor Evaluation Code:

| | |
|---|---|
| + | Student is able to perform all tasks of the operation of the tool/equipment. |
| ✓ | Student needs more help in appropriate safety techniques for the tool/equipment. He/she may require assistance from the instructor and/or a partner in completing laboratory activities. |
| - | Student will not be allowed use of tool/equipment until observed again to determine appropriate safety techniques. |

_____
Instructor Signature

## Illustration 6.4

### CHECKLIST: SAFETY CONSIDERATIONS FOR SPECIAL NEEDS STUDENTS

Architectural barriers removed                                    Yes      No

A.   Doorways and walkways accessible                          _____  _____

B.   Classroom facilities accessible                           _____  _____

C.   Work station areas accessible                             _____  _____

D.   Tool cabinets and tool boards accessible                  _____  _____

E.   Stock, materials and supplies accessible                  _____  _____

F.   Restroom facilities accessible                            _____  _____


Modifications of machinery/equipment

A.   Switches and/or controls on machinery and
       equipment accessible                                    _____  _____

B.   Work station tables at proper height                      _____  _____

C.   Labeling/directions done in large print,
       thermoform print and/or Braille                         _____  _____

D.   Appropriate jigs/fixtures available to
       meet student needs                                      _____  _____

E.   Additional guards on machines provided
       to meet student needs                                   _____  _____

bonus, the student's self-concept will be positively affected and enthusiasm, determination, and motivation will replace inappropriate behavior.

Performance contracts can also be a successful technique to motivate some students. An example is shown in Illustration 6:5. Support staff and parents both can contribute to planning contracts and reinforcing student efforts.

An agreement of tasks to be completed is the basis of a performance contract. These tasks should be clearly understood and listed so that the student and the teacher can keep track of student progress. As each task or assignment is satisfactorily completed, the instructor dates the performance contract. This serves as an updated progress report as well as an immediate reinforcement for the student.

Performance contracts include the student in the planning process and places the responsibility of completing program requirements on the student. The learning then becomes self-managed and individually paced.

## Developing Peer Relationships

Trade and industrial instructors can use a variety of techniques to promote peer acceptance of special needs students. For example, the instructor and/or special needs teacher might conduct an informal

# Illustration 6.5

## PERFORMANCE CONTRACT

Student: <u>Francis Joseph</u>      Date: _____

Program: <u>Residential Wiring</u>

Instructor: <u>Joe Smith</u>

Unit/Module: <u>Switching Circuits</u>

Approximate Time for Completion: <u>Six weeks</u>

| Task/Assignment | Date Completed |
|---|---|
| 1. Install 110V lamp controlled by a special switch. | |
| 2. Install 2-110V lights in parallel. | |
| 3. Install 110V lights and duplex receptacle in parallel with light controlled by special switch. | |
| 4. Install 1-110V light controlled by 2-3 way switches. | |
| 5. Install 1-110V light controlled by 2-3 way switches and 1-4 way switch. | |
| 6. Install 1-110V light controlled by two-three way and two-four way switches. | |
| 7. Install a circuit with 4 receptacles and 1 special switch so it controlls one receptacle while others remain hot. | |
| 8. Install a light dimming system. | |

Comments: (include pertinent comments and suggestions about handicap
from the student and support personnel.

Francis has limited use of his left arm. He cannot use this arm for any
tasks requiring strength and power. He has exceptional strength in his
right arm and can perform most tasks using it. Adaptations may be
required for tasks requiring two arms.

| | |
|---|---|
| _____ Date _____ | _____ Student Signature _____ |
| _____ Date _____ | _____ Instructor Signature _____ |

148

orientation session for the class before the student is enrolled. An orientation session should create a general awareness among students in the class of the nature and needs of a special needs student and encourage acceptance of the student.

Once a special needs student enters the class, there are several techniques that may be used to ensure a smooth transition. One technique is the *buddy system,* in which a special needs student is paired with one or more fellow classmates for support, aid or assistance. An advantage of the buddy system is that it promotes positive interpersonal relationships with classmates in addition to providing a source of remedial aid when necessary.

Another successful technique is *peer tutoring.* This involves selecting volunteers from the class who have abilities to work with a special needs learner on a one-to-one basis in a specific area of instruction. Peer tutoring is usually effective because student tutors are often enthusiastic and become very involved in the tutoring process. Peer tutoring can benefit the special needs students because they receive individualized assistance and experience the opportunity to socialize with their peers. Successful use of this technique allows the teacher to spend time supervising instruction of all students.

Grouping arrangements for activities, projects, and laboratory assignments should be flexible to provide special needs students with a variety of interpersonal experiences. Flexible groups provide special needs students with opportunities to interact with different people in various situations. They also learn to apply appropriate social skills and attitudes to training, social, and work-related situations.

## Maintaining Program Standards

Trade and industrial instructors are not expected to lower program standards to successfully integrate special needs students into their classes. If these students are to be employable upon completion of the program, certain proficiency and employability standards must be met. Rather than lowering program standards for these students, T & I teachers need to exercise flexibility in planning programs and in identifying employment options for this population.

Trade and industrial teachers should recognize the importance of an extended time approach when working with special needs learners. This approach would provide students with an opportunity to enter a program after prerequisite skills have been mastered, to develop entry-level skills in an individualized, self-paced environment, and to exit from the program when a realistic vocational goal has been met. There are multiple exit points that can be identified in each trade and industrial program that will enable the teacher to match the abilities and proficiencies of special needs students with realistic employment opportunities.

Flexible scheduling should be utilized so that students can be given extended time if necessary to successfully complete program requirements. It is more realistic to allow these learners a longer period of time to develop a salable skill than to withhold vocational opportunities because they cannot keep up with a predetermined pace.

Cooperative planning with support personnel can aid the special needs learner by providing remedial instruction relating to work introduced in the trade and industrial program. This is one way to identify the pace of learning for each student and to aid them in meeting the requirements for competitive employment.

## Selecting and/or Developing Appropriate Instructional Materials

Trade and industrial teachers, in cooperation with special education and support personnel, may need to modify existing instructional materials so that they can be used by special needs learners. The learning characteristics and ability levels of the students should be known so that instructional materials may be appropriately and effectively adapted or developed. The level of difficulty of the materials should be consistent with the current functioning level of the student. Often information about the student's functioning levels can be obtained from student files or from special education and support personnel.

There are several simple readability formulas available that can be used to test the reading level of an instructional material. Among these are the Fry method, the Smog method, and the Flesch method. These readability formulas can be found in Appendix B. They can be used quickly and effectively to determine the reading level of a specific material. A comparison should then be made with the current reading level of the student.

Personnel such as classroom paraprofessionals, special education teachers, and resource room staff can help with the task of modifying instructional materials. There are commercial materials that can be purchased for special needs students or used as models for developing materials that relate to their needs and interests. Special materials are also available in the form of film loops, recordings, slide presentations, and videotapes. These can be effectively used in coordination with classroom instruction.

A sample of companies and organizations that produce and distribute instructional materials appropriate for special needs are listed in Illustration 6.6. It should be noted that this is a partial list. Appropriate instructional materials may be available from local school or state department sources. It is suggested that T & I personnel who are interested in locating sources that may have instructional materials appropriate for a specific program area contact these sources to request a catalog of available materials.

When reviewing instructional materials to determine whether they are appropriate for a specific student and/or the trade and industrial program, some general guidelines should be used. Illustra-

tion 6.7 presents a list of suggestions that may be helpful in reviewing materials.

Some instructional materials may need further modification to meet the specific needs of the student and/or program. Illustration 6.8 offers guidelines to keep in mind when revising instructional materials.

Further information regarding curriculum modification and the development of teacher-made instructional materials can be found in Module 8.

## Controlling Student Behavior

Controlling student classroom behavior is a constant concern of all teachers. If inappropriate behavior is permitted in the classroom on a regular basis it can seriously affect the learning process. Trade and industrial teachers are particularly concerned about student behavior because of the potential danger that exists in classroom and laboratory situations. They often express concern that special needs students will exhibit inappropriate behavior that will be difficult to modify or control.

Teachers are most effective in maintaining a good learning environment when they use techniques that allow students to experience security and confidence. One method of achieving this is to identify realistic objectives for them. These learners may display disruptive and inappropriate behavior if they feel threatened by a new situation or by one they perceive as impossible to reach. Trade and industrial teachers should identify and sequence realistic objectives for special needs learners so that they can experience success on a regular basis. These successful experiences will help students develop a high degree of motivation and self-direction.

Incentives should be available to motivate all learners. A basic incentive that is successful with most learners is to identify and meet their needs within the framework of the instructional program. The specific needs of a handicapped or

## Illustration 6.6

## SOURCES OF INSTRUCTIONAL MATERIALS FOR USE
## WITH SPECIAL NEEDS LEARNERS

1.  Academic Therapy Publications
    P.O. Box 899
    1539 Fourth Street
    San Rafael, California  94901

2.  American Association for Vocational Instructional Materials
    Engineering Center
    University of Georgia
    Athens, Georgia  30602

3.  American Institutes for Research
    P.O. Box 1113
    1791 Arastradero Road
    Palo Alto, California  94302

4.  American Foundation for the Blind
    15 West 16th Street
    New York, New York  10011

5.  American Visuals Corporation
    New York, New York

6.  Board of Cooperative Educational Services of Nassau County
    Division of Occupational Education/Division of Special Education
    Westbury, New York

7.  Career Related Instructional Modules
    Capital Area Career Center
    611 Hagadorn Road
    Mason, Michigan

8.  CAP Materials
    Center for Studies in Vocational and Technical Education
    University of Wisconsin – Madison
    Madison, Wisconsin

9.  Clearing house on the Handicapped
    Office of Handicapped Individuals
    Department of HEW
    3380 Hubert F. Humphrey Building
    200 Independence Avenue, S.W.
    Washington, D. C. 20201

10. Educational Opportunities Division
    Division of Follett Publishing Company
    1010 West Washington Boulevard
    Chicago, Illinois  60607

11. Educational Resources Division
    Educational Design, Incorporated
    47 West 13 Street
    New York, New York  10011

12. Frank E. Richards Publishing Company, Incorporated
    324 First Street
    Liverpool, New York  13088

13. Instructional Materials Laboratory
    10 Industrial Education Building
    University of Missouri - Columbia
    Columbia, Missouri  65201

14. Instructional Materials Laboratory
    College of Education
    324 Fairchild Hall
    Illinois State University
    Normal, Illinois  61761

15. Instructional Materials
    Trade and Industrial Education
    P.O. Box 2847
    University of Alabama
    Tuscaloosa, Alabama  35401

16. Job Corps Occupational Training Guides
    Job Corps
    Development Division
    Manpower Administration
    U.S. Department of Labor
    1111 18th Street, N.W.
    Washington, D. C.  20210

17. Link Educational Laboratories
    Box 25
    Hope Hull, Alabama  36043

18. Materials Development Center
    Stout Vocational Rehabilitation Institute
    School of Education
    University of Wisconsin - Stout
    Menomonie, Wisconsin  54751

19. Mid-American Vocational Curriculum Consortium, Incorporated
    1515 West Sixth Avenue
    Stillwater, Oklahoma  74074

20. MIND Incorporated
    One Kings Highway, North
    Westport, Connecticut  06880

21. Minnesota Instructional Materials Center
    3300 Century Avenue, North
    White Bear Lake, Minnesota  55110

22. National Center on Educational Media and Materials for the Handicapped
    Ohio State University
    Columbus, Ohio  43210

23. National Center for Research in Vocational Education
    Ohio State University
    1960 Kenny Road
    Columbus, Ohio  43210

24. President's Committee on Employment of the Handicapped
    Washington, D.C.

25. Related Vocational Curriculum Supplements
    Vocational Education Materials Center
    Division of Vocational Education
    University of Georgia
    Athens, Georgia  30602

26. Research and Curriculum Unit for Vocational-Technical Education
    College of Education
    Mississippi State University
    Mississippi State, Mississippi

27. The Council for Exceptional Children
    1920 Association Drive
    Reston, Virginia  22091

28. Trade and Industries Instructional Materials Laboratory
    Ohio State University
    1885 Neil Avenue
    Columbus, Ohio  43210

29. Vocational Education Media Center
    109 Freeman Hall
    Clemson University
    Clemson, South Carolina  29631

30. Vocational Instructional Materials for Students with Special Needs
    Northwest Regional Laboratory
    710 S. W. Second Avenue
    Portland, Oregon  97204

31. Vocational Instructional Services
    FE Box 182
    Texas A & M University
    College Station, Texas  77843

32. Vocational Technical Curriculum Lab
    Rutgers University
    4103 Kilmer Campus
    New Brunswick, New Jersey  08903

disadvantaged student can be determined by communicating on a one-to-one basis with the individual and by planning cooperatively with support personnel.

There are several techniques that T & I teachers can use to modify behavior in the classroom or laboratory setting. Before a behavior can be modified it must first be identified as inappropriate. The teacher must first decide what the target behavior is. Then the target behavior should be observed to determine how fre-quently it occurs and how it affects the other students in the class. Finally, an incentive must be identified to create and reinforce the desired behavior.

The suggested techniques described below can be applied by the T & I teacher alone or by a cooperative effort with support personnel and other students.

1. *Time-out:* The time-out technique may be used when a student displays inappropriate behavior that is causing a problem in a classroom or laboratory

## Illustration 6.7

## TIPS TO REMEMBER WHEN SELECTING INSTRUCTIONAL MATERIALS

| Guideline/Tip | | Yes | No |
|---|---|---|---|
| 1. | The material is appropriate for the learning style or special needs of the learner(s) - (i.e., large print, braille, cassette, learning activity packet, film, records, slide/tape, video-tape, transparency, filmstrip) | | |
| 2. | The content of the material relates to the instructional program. | | |
| 3. | Pertinent vocational vocabulary terms are defined and used in the material. | | |
| 4. | The reading level of the material is appropriate for the learner(s). | | |
| 5. | The writing style of the material is clear and concise. | | |
| 6. | The material reinforces concepts covered in classroom instruction (supplementary aid). | | |
| 7. | The material provides a variety of periodic self-checks to reinforce the learner. | | |
| 8. | The material can be used for (a) individualized instruction, (b) small group instruction, and/or (c) large group instruction. | | |
| 9. | All directions can be clearly understood. | | |
| 10. | The material can easily be used by the teacher (i.e., preparation time). | | |
| 11. | The material provides for follow-up activities to reinforce concepts. | | |
| 12. | The cost of the material is compatible with the total budget. | | |
| 13. | The amount of time required to prepare, administer and evaluate pupil progress on the material is reasonable. | | |

\*  Decision: _____ purchase material for student use

            _____ purchase materials for reference

            _____ do not purchase material

Format adapted from Phelps and Lutz, Career exploration and preparation for the special needs learner. Boston: Allyn and Bacon, Inc., 1977.

154

**Illustration 6.8**

## TIPS TO REMEMBER WHEN REVISING INSTRUCTIONAL MATERIALS

| Guideline/Tip | Yes | No |
|---|---|---|
| Have you included: | | |
| 1. Related vocational vocabulary terms. | | |
| 2. Vocabulary meanings. | | |
| 3. Instructional objectives. | | |
| 4. Reading levels appropriate for the student(s). | | |
| 5. Student goals. | | |
| 6. Periodic self-assessment checks. | | |
| 7. Appropriate diagrams, illustrations and examples. | | |
| 8. Appropriate activities to reinforce learning concepts. | | |
| 9. System of feedback regarding student progress. | | |
| 10. Appropriate time periods for the student to use the material. | | |

activity. The time-out technique is frequently used with students who display aggressive or hostile behavior.

If such negative behavior is occurring more and more frequently, it could mean that the student is competing with the teacher for the attention of the class. This could interfere with the progress of the other students in the class.

In the time-out technique, the student is removed from the classroom or laboratory to an area in the hall or an isolated area of the classroom or laboratory. The teacher explains that the behavior is making it difficult for other students to complete their work. The student must realize that whenever the inappropriate behavior is displayed it will result in being removed from the class. It is imperative that the teacher be consistent in enforcing time-out for disruptive behavior.

Once the student has been removed from the classroom or the laboratory, the teacher can have an informal conversation on a one-to-one basis with the student. This is not a time to reprimand, threaten, or lecture the student. It is, however, a time to let the student know why the behavior is inappropriate. Once the student begins to display appropriate behavior, he/she may be allowed to join the class again.

By using time-out, the teacher can eliminate the disruptive behavior from the class environment while at the same time counseling the student to find out what might have caused the behavior. The one-to-one, teacher-student relationship should help the student to feel that the teacher cares. This can help the student to develop a positive self-concept.

2. Ignore negative behavior: When a student displays inappropriate or negative behavior, he/she is often looking for attention. When the teacher responds to this behavior by reprimanding or threat-

ening, the student has accomplished the objective of attracting attention both from the teacher and the entire class.

To avoid providing the student with this attention, one useful technique is to ignore the inappropriate or negative behavior when possible. This technique is most effective if the teacher also reinforces appropriate behavior with compliments and approval. Once this pattern has been established, the student begins to realize that he/she can gain attention when positive behavior is exhibited.

3. Reward appropriate behavior: Providing attention, praise, and approval when appropriate behavior is displayed can be very effective. In this manner, students receive positive reinforcement while at the same time improving their self-concept.

Providing the student with activities and experiences that will lead to success in the trade and industrial program can enhance this emphasis on appropriate behavior. As the student begins to feel competent and successful in the learning environment, positive behavior often replaces negative behavior. If the teacher provides attention when the appropriate behavior is displayed, it will usually occur more often.

4. Recording specific behavior—a progress profile: If specific negative behaviors occur frequently, the teacher should document the behavior. A progress profile can help to identify a pattern of behavior for the student. Then an appropriate technique can be identified to modify the behavior.

It is very important that the teacher document only objective statements in this record rather than opinions as to why the behavior occurred. The information recorded in the progress profile should include specific information about what happened and under what conditions the incident occurred. Information placed in student records should always be signed and dated. Teachers should remember that parents or guardians of the student have the right to inspect all records pertaining to the student and may challenge any information that they disagree with.

Teachers and support personnel can use the profile to review the behavior records of a particular student and to determine the most effective method of behavior modification. Support personnel, such as behavior disorder teachers, are trained in behavior modification techniques and can help the T & I teacher to design and implement the most appropriate techniques for modifying negative behaviors. Once the behavior modification program has been established in the trade and industrial classroom and/or laboratory, it can be reinforced by the support staff during the time the student is not in class.

The effects of the behavior modification program should be recorded. By recording the changes in behavior, the T & I teacher and the support personnel can determine whether or not the technique is successful.

Students can learn to record the frequency of their behavior. In keeping track of a specific behavior, the student becomes more aware of the behavior. A peer can also be selected to keep track of the number of times a behavior occurs within a certain amount of time. Teacher-student conferences should be scheduled regularly to discuss changes in behavior.

5. Student-teacher contract: Contracts can be an effective behavior modification technique. The contract individualizes the tasks or responsibilities according to the specific learning rate of the student.

The conditions of the contract should be clearly understood by the student. The behavior to be changed and/or tasks to be completed are identified. The terms of the contract are then stated, such as the behavior changes that are expected and/or the responsibilities that the student is to assume. The specific time allowed for behavior change or for completing the assigned responsibility is stated. Finally, the rewards or privileges are given. These should be granted to the student upon satisfactory completion of the contract requirements.

An initial conference should be held between the student, the T & I teacher, and any support personnel who work with the student to discuss possible tasks and responsibilities to be included. A second conference is then held to review the contract after it has been developed. The contract is reviewed and evaluated as the student completes the tasks.

6. Individual conference: Conferences provide an opportunity for the T & I teacher to meet with the student who is displaying inappropriate behavior. At this meeting there will be no audience so the student will probably not be disruptive.

At this conference the teacher should explain to the student that he/she is concerned about the negative behavior and would like to know if there are any problems that the student would like to discuss. The student may feel relieved that someone is interested enough to be concerned. Confidence and a sense of security will help to establish a positive relationship between the teacher and the student. At the same time the teacher can gain some helpful information that may be useful in discovering problems that cause the inappropriate behavior and identifying possible solutions.

Through individual conferences students learn that the teacher is concerned about them and their unique problems and that the teacher will not tolerate inappropriate behavior displayed in the classroom or laboratory environment. The teacher can follow up the conference by maintaining a positive relationship with the students in class and combining this with positive reinforcement of appropriate behavior.

## Facilitating Classroom or Laboratory Accessibility

Learning environments affect student behavior and performance, and some environments are more conducive to learning than others. The teacher's challenge is to provide and maintain an environment that suits the learning needs of individual students.

One of the age-old precepts of vocational education has been the provision of vocational training designed to meet the needs of the individual student. An often repeated goal of vocational education is "to provide realistic training for people who want it, need it, and can profit from it." However, in practice, these two precepts have often been ignored. Vocational educators, along with other educators, have often failed to remove physical and attitudinal barriers and have prevented some individuals from enrolling in educational and training programs that would have helped them to achieve dignified employment.

In recent years, however, educational opportunities for special needs students have multiplied. Stimulated by the provisions of federal legislation, vocational educators have accepted the challenge of providing an atmosphere in which all students can interact and learn together. However, handicapped students often have problems with physical barriers confronting them in existing programs.

Planning a learning environment that is suitable to the needs of all students is not just the responsibility of the vocational teacher. Rather it should be the task of a team of educators and resource persons available in the school and community. Environmental planning must take into consideration the types of handicaps students have, and it should be the product of input from a wide variety of school professionals and parents.

In assessing classroom and laboratory environment barriers, three questions will need to be answered: What are the barriers confronting a particular student? What measures can be taken to eliminate the barriers? Which measures will be the best to take in terms of cost, safety and effectiveness for enhancing learning?

Since each handicapped student has unique needs and capabilities, it is important to include the student and his/her parents in the assessment process. Barriers only exist when the demands of the learning environment are difficult for the student to meet. What might be a barrier for one student with a given handicap may not be a barrier for another student with a similar handicap.

When classroom and/or laboratory environment barriers are identified, they should be modified or eliminated to the greatest extent possible. In many instances the modifications required are not costly. This is particularly true for vocational education facilities, since many of these changes can become learning projects for students and can be handled internally by the school.

In identifying possible barriers for the handicapped it is useful to consider these factors: type of disability (mobility, vision, hearing, mental); site preparation (walks, parking); ramps; entrances to buildings, doors, and doorways; stairs and stairways; floors; rest room facilities; kneehold spaces under desks, tables and equipment; drinking fountains; public telephones; elevator and escalator usage; controls and switches; identification of rooms and doors; warning signals; and hazards. These topics can be included in a checklist to help the assessment team review facilities and identify possible barriers.

Module 7 will contain additional information about classroom and laboratory accessibility and the role of the teacher in providing a barrier-free learning environment for all students.

## Modifying Equipment for the Handicapped

Many of the tasks performed by workers in trade and industrial occupations require certain minimal levels of strength, sight, hearing, speech, or intellectual abilities. Workers often have to manipulate objects such as tools and equipment, make measurements, troubleshoot or solve problems, distinguish between sounds, exchange information with co-workers and perform many other activities related to a given occupational area. Each occupational area has its own unique set of job requirements and demands that must be met by workers if they are to function effectively in the work environment.

These job requirements and demands must also be met by students in the trade and industrial classroom and laboratories that are often designed to simulate the actual work environment. Some of these tasks are difficult to learn and accomplish because of special demands and requirements. Some tasks present special demands on students because of poor equipment design or the rigid way in which they are performed.

Most T & I teachers recognize tasks that will present special requirements and demands on students and which will be difficult to accomplish. Through the instructional program, teachers help students to learn ways to modify or alter procedures so as to complete tasks.

Students with certain handicapping conditions will experience more difficulty in performing some tasks of an occupational area than nonhandicapped students may encounter. These difficulties usually take the form of physical demands, visual demands, auditory demands, special and learning demands, and intellectual demands.

Many occupational tasks have certain physical demands such as grasping, holding, lifting, pulling, pushing, twisting, and coordinating eye, hand, finger, and foot movements. These demands may present some unique problems of manipulation for handicapped students.

Visually impaired students may experience difficulty in performing work tasks that require reading blueprints or instructions; taking readings from meters, gauges, indicators, and other measuring instruments, distinguishing between tools and supplies by sight; aligning tools and materials; and guiding materials through machines such as table saws and bandsaws.

Students with hearing impairments may experience difficulty with tasks that require detecting whether a machine, tool, or piece of equipment is functioning properly, listening for the sound of auditory signals such as timer bells or warning buzzers, and exchanging information with the instructor or fellow classmates.

Many occupational tasks require certain levels of intellectual ability such as understanding instructions; remembering the sequential order of operations; making measurements and calculations; reading and understanding schematics, diagrams, and blueprints; and solving problems by combining concepts and principles in unique ways. Such tasks may present some unique problems for retarded students and, in some instances, learning disabled students.

These demands of the work environment in a trade and industrial education program may present barriers for handicapped students. A barrier is created when a student encounters difficulty in performing a task because of the demands made by equipment or the process of performing the tasks.

The T & I teacher, working in cooperation with other school and community resource personnel, can identify the barriers of the work environment and develop strategies to help handicapped students overcome them. This may take the form of modifying the tools and equipment required to perform a given task or it may involve changing the process of performing the task. This area will be discussed further in Module 7.

## Evaluating Student Achievement

The grading and reporting system used by the T & I teacher should be reasonable and fair to all students and should be based on their capabilities rather than on a comparison of them with other students enrolled in the class. The teacher can discuss this policy openly when students first arrive in class. The evaluation system should be based on the amount of progress made by the student and the quality of work produced. This method will enhance the student's self-concept

and lower the anxiety level, contributing to a relaxed learning environment in which all students can accept more responsibility for achieving their own vocational goals.

Several methods can be used to record the progress and achievement of special needs learners in their instructional program. One method is to use a series of individualized units. Each unit should include the specific competencies required for successful completion of the content material. As the student demonstrates each competency, it is recorded on a proficiency profile. The profile can be used not only for evaluation purposes, but also as evidence of demonstrated competencies when it is time to talk to an employer concerning job opportunities (see Illustration 6.9).

Student-teacher contracts can also be an effective method to evaluate the progress of special needs students. The contract describes the specific nature of the work that the student is to complete, the minimum accepted criterion levels, and the amount of time allowed. The student and the teacher discuss the contract before signing it. At the completion of the task or project, the student participates in the evaluation session. In this manner, each student can be evaluated according to the quality of work produced rather than the amount of work everyone else produces.

An important guide in evaluating handicapped students in trade and industrial programs is the vocational component of the individualized education program (IEP). This educational plan is mandated by Public Law 94–142 (Education for All Handicapped Children Act of 1975) for all handicapped students to age 21.

The IEP must include a statement of annual goals as well as short-term objectives developed to meet the annual goals. When a student is enrolled in a trade and industrial program, the special education teacher, in a cooperative planning relationship with the T & I teacher, documents the present level of performance and

Illustration 6.9

## SAMPLE PROFICIENCY/COMPETENCY PROFILE

Student: Isabelle Anderson      Date: 9/81

Instructor: Cecilia Proper      Program/Course: Food Service

Module: Short Order Cooking - Breakfast Preparation

| Competency/Skill | Date Completed | Instructor Initial | Evaluation | | |
|---|---|---|---|---|---|
| | | | Needs Assistance | Adequate | Very Good |
| Prepares juices | | | | | |
| Prepares hot cereals | | | | | |
| Prepares cold cereals | | | | | |
| Prepares eggs | | | | | |
| Prepares omelets | | | | | |
| Prepares breakfast meats | | | | | |
| Prepares breakfast fruits | | | | | |
| Prepares breakfast breads/baked goods | | | | | |
| Prepares coffee | | | | | |
| Prepares tea | | | | | |
| Use of kitchen/ equipment | | | | | |
| Use of safety/ rules | | | | | |
| Quality of work | | | | | |
| Rate of work | | | | | |

Comments:

develops the goals for student performance in the trade and industrial program. These goals relate specifically to the needs and abilities of the student. Therefore, the successful completion of the goals and objectives developed in the IEP should be considered when evaluating student performance. This process is further demonstrated in Modules 4 and 9.

## PERSONAL-SOCIAL QUALITIES AND SPECIFIC COMPETENCIES NEEDED BY TRADE AND INDUSTRIAL TEACHERS

Trade and industrial teachers should manifest many personal-social qualities and competencies that are essential in working with special needs learners. Most

T & I teachers have unique combinations of occupational experience and college training that provide them with both practical and theoretical knowledge. Many of them have received instruction in working with special needs students either from college courses required to meet certification standards or from staff development activities sponsored by the State Department of Education or local educational agencies. A brief discussion of some of these teacher personal-social qualities and competencies follow.

## Personal-Social Qualities

Two personal-social qualities that T & I teachers should possess are patience and perseverance. Through occupational experience most T & I teachers probably have learned to exercise both patience and perseverence in getting a job done safely and correctly. Trade and industrial teachers will probably need to use these two personal-social qualities with special needs students who often require more time to learn a task and are easily discouraged from completing a job if they encounter difficulty.

Adaptability is another very important quality for a teacher of special needs students. Facilities, machinery and equipment, instructional techniques, and curriculum must sometimes be altered to meet the needs of these learners.

Trade and industrial teachers, as workers, have learned to make adjustments in standard procedures to satisfy or accommodate unique situations. They have learned to make the best of any situation when ideal tools or materials to complete a job were not available. Most T & I teachers should have little difficulty in making the necessary adaptions required to meet the special needs of their students. Trade and industrial teachers also need to exhibit the personal-social quality of open-mindedness.

Another personal-social quality needed by T & I teachers in working with special needs students is pride in craftsmanship.

Through occupational experience T & I teachers have learned to strive for the best possible work performance. They have learned that it is rewarding to produce a high quality product or provide high quality service. They should encourage special needs learners to have the same attitude by challenging them to try for excellence in the quality of their work.

Students often imitate the behavior of their teacher; thus the teacher serves as a role model. Trade and industrial teachers who exhibit the personal-social qualities of patience, perseverance, open-mindedness, adaptability, and pride in craftsmanship will be providing excellent patterns of behavior for special needs learners to imitate. Possessing good personal-social qualities is as important as having a good command of the knowledge and skills of an occupation.

## Specific Competencies

Trade and industrial teachers should demonstrate certain professional competencies that are beneficial in working with special needs learners. First, these teachers generally have developed a high level of knowledge and skills in their particular trades and occupations. Therefore, they should be able to identify the component parts that make up each work task. Special needs learners often need to receive instruction in smaller, more basic steps. Because of their concrete, cumulative nature, most trade and industrial tasks readily lend themselves to task analysis.

A second competency that T & I teachers should exhibit is the ability to provide ongoing reinforcement of student performance. The tangible nature of trade and industrial tasks allows teachers to design appropriate learning experiences programmed for special needs learners and to continuously observe student performance. Trade and industrial teachers can then provide immediate and continuous reinforcement to the special needs learner.

Another competency needed by T & I teachers is the ability to design, develop, and utilize individualized instructional experiences. Individualized instruction enables teachers to use their facilities and equipment to the maximum and to better meet the needs of their students. The tangible, cumulative nature of most T & I work tasks affords an excellent opportunity for teachers to design and utilize an individualized instruction delivery system.

A final important competency needed by T & I teachers in working with special needs learners is the ability to plan and work cooperatively with other school personnel. The education of special needs learners requires the cooperative efforts of school personnel, system-wide support personnel, parents, and the community. Most T & I teachers are committed to the goal of providing the best possible education for their students. Therefore, they welcome the opportunity to work with other educators and parents in helping students develop knowledge and skills required to become an independent worker and a contributing member of our society.

## SUMMARY

Trade and industrial and technical education programs offer different types of classes and instructional programs to meet the needs of various groups of people, including trade classes, cooperative education programs, apprenticeship classes, and adult education classes.

The major concerns of T & I teachers who work with special needs students involve (a) providing a safe environment, (b) motivating special needs learners, (c) developing peer relationships, (d) maintaining program standards, (e) selecting and/or developing appropriate instructional materials, (f) controlling student behavior, (g) facilitating classroom or laboratory accessibility, (h) modifying equipment for the handicapped, and (i) evaluating student achievement. Most of these concerns can be eliminated as teachers become more familiar with factual information and techniques appropriate for working with special needs students.

Trade and industrial teachers need a number of personal-social qualities that are beneficial in working with special needs learners, including patience, perseverance, adaptability, open-mindedness, and pride in craftsmanship.

Specific competencies that are useful in working with special needs students include a high level of knowledge and skill in an occupational area, which is essential if the teachable content of that area is to be identified; the ability to use the tangible nature of trade and industrial occupational tasks in reinforcing student performance; the ability to design, develop, and utilize individualized instructional experiences; and the ability to plan and work cooperatively with other school personnel. These competencies are essential if the T & I teacher, working with other school personnel, is to help these students develop the affective behaviors, knowledge, and skills required for employment.

## REFERENCES

Clarizo, H. *Toward positive classroom discipline.* New York: John Wiley and Sons, Inc., 1971.

Dahl, P., Appleby, J., and Lipe, D. *Mainstreaming guidebook for vocational educators.* Salt Lake City, Utah: Olympus Publishing Company, 1978.

Directing students in instruction of other students (Module C-4). Athens, Georgia: American Association for Vocational Instructional Materials (AAVIM), 1979.

Griggs, Mildred. Discipline: managing behavior in the classroom. *Illinois Teacher,* September/October 1977, 17–22.

Gugerty, J. Effective use of resources and materials in working with handicapped students. *Proceedings of the Conference on Mainstreaming Handicapped Students in Vocational Education Programs.* Blacksburg, Virginia: Virginia Polytechnic Institute and State University, Division of Vocational and Technical Education, February 16-18, 1978.

Jacobs, C. and Turner, J. *Developing shop safety skills.* Athens, Georgia: American Association for Vocational Industrial Materials (AAVIM), 1979.

Johnson, C. Curriculum customization for special needs learners. *Journal of Vocational Special Needs Education,* 1980, *2* (3), 3-6.

Litton, F. and Kay, R. Annotated bibliography of low cost vocationally oriented materials for adolescent and young adults mildly handicapped and disadvantaged individuals. *Journal of Vocational Special Needs Education,* 1980, *2* (2), 13-18.

McCarthy, R. and Stodden, R. Mainstreaming secondary students: A peer tutoring model. *Teaching Exceptional Children,* 1979, *11* (4), 162-163.

Otazo, K. and d'Oronzio, A. Helping vocational students improve reading skills. *Journal of Vocational Special Needs Education,* 1980, *2* (3), 7-12.

Phelps, L. and Lutz R. *Career exploration and preparation of the special needs learner.* Boston: Allyn and Bacon, Inc., 1977.

*Provide for student safety* (Module E-5). Athens, Georgia: American Association for Vocational Instructional Materials (AAVIM), 1977.

Razeghi, J. Analyzing, modifying and selecting vocational materials for research. *Journal of Vocational Special Needs Education,* 1980, *2* (3), 13-16.

Sanders, A. and Allen, H. *Safety education for modern living.* Wilkinsburg, Pennsylvania: Hayes School Publishing Company, Inc., 1971.

Strong, M. and Schaefer, C. *Introduction to trade, industrial and technical education.* Columbus, Ohio: Charles E. Merrill Publishing Company, 1975.

Towne, D. and Wallace, S. *Vocational instructional materials for students with special needs.* Portland, Oregon: Northwest Regional Educational Laboratory, 1972.

*Vocational-Technical Terminology.* Washington, D.C.: American Vocational Association, 1971.

Welsh, F. and Halfacre, J. Ten better ways to classroom management. *Teacher,* 1978, *96* (2), 86-87.

## SELF ASSESSMENT: CONCERNS AND ABILITIES OF TRADE AND INDUSTRIAL IN WORKING WITH SPECIAL NEEDS STUDENTS

1. Describe the nature of trade and industrial programs in relationship to working with special needs learners.

2. Identify the four types of instructional programs included in the trade and industrial area.

3. Describe the basic operating procedures for each of the four types of instructional programs.

4. Define technical education and describe the types of training that are developed in this area.

5. List the major concerns expressed by T & I teachers when asked to work with special needs learners in their regular programs.

6. Describe a procedure to assure that special needs students can use tools, equipment, and machinery safely.

7. Describe several methods that can be effective in motivating special needs learners.

8. Describe an orientation program that could be used to prepare students for the integration of special needs learners into trade and industrial programs.

9. Outline the procedure for appropriately mainstreaming special needs learners into trade and technical programs without "watering down" the curriculum.

10. Identify several sources of relevant information pertaining to working with special needs learners.

11. Describe modification procedures that can be applied to existing instructional materials so that they can be utilized by special needs learners.

12. Identify and describe some techniques that T & I teachers can use to control or modify classroom behavior.

13. Describe a strategy for evaluating the accessibility of your classroom and laboratory facility.

14. Outline a procedure for modifying a machine, tool, or piece of equipment for a given handicapped student.

15. Outline an evaluation procedure that allows individual differences in evaluating the progress made by special needs learners.

16. Identify the personal-social qualities that trade and industrial teachers need when working with special needs learners.

17. Identify the competencies that trade and industrial teachers need when working with special needs learners.

## ASSOCIATED ACTIVITIES

1. Develop a safety check sheet to be used with all students in your trade and industrial program. Include a list of all safety rules, tools, machinery, and equipment that must be mastered by students before they can work safely and independently.

2. If your program is not developed in units, take a section of material that is in your curriculum and develop a unit. Be sure to list all proficiencies needed for successful completion of the unit.

3. Plan and implement an initial cooperative planning session with the special education personnel in your building. This will give you an opportunity to discover first-hand how they may help the special needs student enrolled in your program. Identify the resources and supplementary services that they are able to provide.

4. Discuss with an administrator and a vocational counselor the possibilities of flexible scheduling for special needs students. Note the problem areas and identify several solutions to overcome these obstacles.

5. Prepare a short orientation discussion for your program prior to the integration of special needs learners. Outline the basic points that you would cover so that an open-minded and accepting attitude can be established.

6. Discuss with your vocational director or supervisor the possibility of developing an in-service program regarding special needs learners for trade and industrial personnel. Develop a tentative outline for the program. Include pertinent topics, possible speakers and follow-up plans, activities and projects.

7. Conduct an informal needs assessment with the trade and industrial teachers in your school to identify their concerns and needs in working with special needs learners.

8. With the help of special education personnel in your building, complete a readability test of your textbooks and/or instructional materials. Determine the functional reading level of the special needs learners in your program. Compare the readability level of the materials with the reading level of each student. Consult with the special education personnel to develop appropriate plans to modify these materials if necessary.

9. Arrange visits to different types of schools where trade and industrial and technical education programs are offered. Observe the nature of the different types of classes and instructional programs offered. Following the visit, prepare your own definition and description of trade and industrial and technical education programs.

10. After talking with knowledgeable people in trade and industrial and technical education, compare and contrast these two types of programs. Point out their similarities and differences.

11. Interview several T & I and technical education teachers. Ask them what personal-social qualities and specific competencies they believe are beneficial in working with special needs learners. Prepare a short paper as a result of these interviews.

12. Interview several special needs learners enrolled in a trade and industrial or technical education program. Ask them what qualities and competencies they feel their teachers possess that makes it easier for them to achieve their goals in the programs. Prepare a paper summarizing the results of these interviews.

13. Form an architectural barrier examination group composed of special needs students, regular T & I students, T & I teachers and administrators, and special needs support personnel. Arrange for this group to check the vocational facilities to identify any barriers for handicapped students.

14. Imagine that you have a handicapped student who is confined to a wheelchair in your occupational area. This student has excellent strength in his shoulders, arms, and fingers but is paralyzed from the waist down. Identify the tasks in your program that this student may have trouble accomplishing successfully and recommend a solution for each problem.

## CASE HISTORY: EDWARD'S STORY

Edward is a learning disabled student enrolled in a carpentry and cabinet-making program. Edward is also enrolled in a special education program. He has above average intelligence as indicated on his current psychological examination results. However, because of a visual perception problem he has trouble in reading and math.

Edward begins every task or assignment with enthusiasm but easily becomes frustrated and gives up. This habit is probably due to the many failures he has experienced in the past. He has made several close friends in the carpentry and cabinet-making program and works very well with this small group of students. He is still a bit shy and insecure with other members of the class.

The program instructor has been working closely with the special education teacher. They have both actively participated on the IEP planning team. Edward's career goal is to work either in a custom cabinet shop or in a furniture manufacturing factory. With the combined assistance of both teachers, Edward has successfully completed units in blueprint reading, proper use of hand and power tools, machine tool operation, and frame and form construction. He has required additional assistance in several areas that have taken him longer to complete, including related mathematics, door hanging, and window setting.

The special education program has helped to modify these sections of the curriculum. The written materials have been reinforced verbally and a variety of hands-on activities have been developed to allow for direct application of skills demonstrated in class. The program instructor has allowed for modification of assignments and activities to allow Edward to learn through his strongest learning style. The special education teacher also gives all tests to Edward by reading test questions out loud and taping the responses. The program instructor then listens to the tape and evaluates the answers.

## CASE HISTORY ACTIVITY

Katherine is a learning disabled student who has enrolled in your program. She is also enrolled in the special education program in your school. You have already met with the special education teacher and have learned that Katherine is very bright but, despite her potential, her grades in school have not been good. She has problems with reading, writing, spelling and math. Katherine is an auditory learner and can perform best when she can listen rather than having to read and write. She becomes frustrated easily and doubts her ability to succeed at most tasks. When she is frustrated she becomes very withdrawn and will not communicate with anyone around her.

Based on this information, complete the case history profile worksheet for Katherine's participation in your program.

# CASE HISTORY PROFILE WORKSHEET

Student: _____ Page: _____

Handicapping Condition(s): _____

T & I Program: _____ Academic Levels: _____

Career Goal/Occupational Interest: _____

Considerations (e.g., medication, behavior): _____

_____

| Adaptation | Specific Services Needed | Where to Obtain Service |
|---|---|---|
| Cooperative Planning (School Personnel) | | |
| Support Services | | |
| Architectural Changes | | |
| Adaptive Equipment | | |
| Curriculum Modification | | |
| Instructional Materials/ Supplies | | |
| Teaching Techniques | | |
| Agency Involvement | | |
| Possible Job Placement | | |

# MODULE 7

## Vocational Facility and Equipment Modification

Without barrier-free access to vocational buildings and grounds, handicapped persons are denied their right to participate in vocational education programs. Similarly, unless appropriate modifications are made to tools, machines, equipment, and work station apparatus, handicapped persons will be unable to develop work skills that will help them become a part of the work force.

Module 6 introduced the topics of facility and equipment modification as a major concern of T & I teachers. This module covers two major areas: (1) modifying vocational facilities for the handicapped, and (2) modifying the laboratory and work environment. Specific sections include: (a) laws requiring program accessibility, (b) identifying architectural barriers, (c) suggestions for vocational facility accessibility, (d) identifying laboratory and work task barriers, and (e) suggestions for work environment modifications.

## MODULE OBJECTIVES

After you have read and reviewed this module, studied the case history, reviewed the self assessment questions, and completed the associated activities, you should be able to:

1. Explain the rationale for identifying and eliminating facility and equipment barriers in T & I programs.

2. List the basic architectural requirements that assure physically handicapped individuals access to vocational grounds and buildings.

3. Describe a procedure for identifying architectural and equipment barriers that

may need to be eliminated or modified to accommodate physically handicapped students.

4. Explain the requirements of federal legislation that require program accessibility for the handicapped learner.

5. List some strategies that T & I teachers could use to modify tools, machines, equipment, and work station apparatus to accommodate handicapped persons.

## MODIFYING VOCATIONAL FACILITIES FOR THE HANDICAPPED

This section of the module describes some of the areas of vocational grounds and buildings that often present barriers to handicapped persons. Vocational facilities having architectural barriers that prevent access by handicapped individuals are a direct form of discrimination. Therefore, they must be appropriately modified. Architectural accessibility is not a privilege for the handicapped, but a right. Congress essentially guaranteed this right when it passed the Architectural Barriers Act of 1968 and the Rehabilitation Act of 1973.

### Laws Requiring Program Accessibility

The Architectural Barriers Act of 1968, Public Law 90–480, requires essentially that any public facility built or substantially renovated since 1968 that receives federal support must be accessible to handicapped persons. The law was replaced in 1976 by Public Law 94–541, which strengthened existing federal laws mandating architectural accessibility. Public Law 94–541 requires federal agencies to assume responsibility for assuring that all public buildings are made accessible and that a system of continuing surveys be established to insure compliance.

The 1973 Rehabilitation Act, Public Law 93–112, contains regulations in Section 504 that specify requirements to insure program accessibility for the handicapped. Broadly defined, the law stipulates that handicapped persons cannot be excluded from participating in any program or activity receiving federal support because its facilities are inaccessible. The law does not require that all facilities be accessible, but that each program or activity in which a handicapped person can enroll and profit be made accessible.

The regulations of Public Law 93–112 also include strategies and methods for achieving program accessibility, time periods for implementing change, the formulation of transition plans, and regulations for new construction.

*Responding to Accessibility Laws.* The implications of federal laws and regulations are clear: vocational educators must find ways of modifying facilities and equipment so that handicapped persons will have equal access to programs, services, and activities.

Vocational planners and administrators should contact their respective State Architectural Barriers Board or State Department of Education regarding guidelines and standards that have been developed to comply with federal mandates. The federal government has adopted the American National Standards Institute (ANSI) accessibility standards as its mandatory guidelines for removal of architectural barriers.

Several states have developed their own facility standards for insuring barrier-free schools and other public buildings. (See bibliography for resources on eliminating architectural barriers.)

## Identifying Architectural Barriers

In a sense, no facility can be completely free of architectural barriers. This is because of the wide range of handicapping conditions and the modifications needed to accommodate persons with physical disabilities. For example, a solution or modification to eliminate a barrier for one person with a specific type of physical disability might actually create a barrier for another person with a different disability or for a nonhandicapped person. It is essential that thought be given to meeting the needs of all persons who will be using a facility before choosing a facility design or making modifications.

The major concern in providing architectural accessibility for the handicapped is safety, although there is a concern for efficiency and convenience. Vocational educators must keep these concerns in mind when identifying and eliminating or modifying barriers.

A barrier for a handicapped person occurs when the physical demands of a situation are extremely difficult to cope with or cannot be overcome at all. For example, it may be extremely difficult for a handicapped person with weak arms and hands to open a door with a heavy closer unit. For this person, a barrier exists in getting into a vocational building with a door of this type.

The solution to the barrier caused by a heavy door closer is simple: reduce the tension on the door closer or remove the closer altogether. This modification would cost very little. Frequently, however, removing or modifying a barrier caused by poor facility design or equipment design can be expensive. The cost of making modifications to vocational facilities and equipment can often be significantly reduced by making the modifications part of a "live work" learning situation and by using the technical expertise of T & I instructors.

*Barrier Areas.* Architectural barriers can exist in every area of a vocational facility. Barriers are present in getting to vocational buildings as well as moving about inside them. Illustration 7.1 shows some of the areas of a vocational facility that should be considered in the barrier identification process.

There are three major areas present in

**Illustration 7.1**

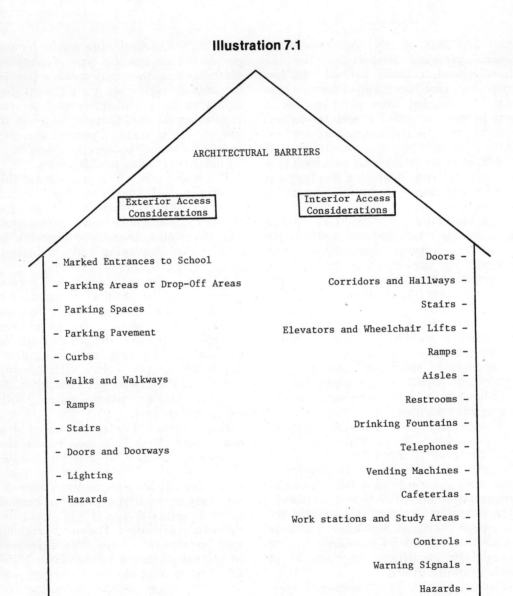

ARCHITECTURAL BARRIERS

| Exterior Access Considerations | Interior Access Considerations |

- Marked Entrances to School

- Parking Areas or Drop-Off Areas

- Parking Spaces

- Parking Pavement

- Curbs

- Walks and Walkways

- Ramps

- Stairs

- Doors and Doorways

- Lighting

- Hazards

Doors -

Corridors and Hallways -

Stairs -

Elevators and Wheelchair Lifts -

Ramps -

Aisles -

Restrooms -

Drinking Fountains -

Telephones -

Vending Machines -

Cafeterias -

Work stations and Study Areas -

Controls -

Warning Signals -

Hazards -

most vocational facilities that may present barriers to handicapped persons. These are:

1. *Getting to and entering the building* —getting to the grounds from public or private transportation; parking; negotiating parking lot pavement, curbs, walkways, ramps, and stairways; and entering exterior doors.

2. *Moving about inside a building*— moving through corridors and hallways, moving from floor to floor, identifying and entering classrooms, laboratories, and auxiliary areas; moving through aisles and traffic lanes inside classrooms and laboratories.

3. *Using school fixtures, appliances, and study/work station area equipment*—

using restrooms, drinking fountains, audiovisual machines, vending machines, telephones, controls, tools, machines, equipment, and work station apparatus.

*Identifying Barriers.* The identification of barriers in vocational school facilities that may place unreasonable demands on disabled persons is a difficult task to undertake. Several factors contribute to this problem. For example, the ways in which handicapped persons respond to their disabilities vary greatly. What is a barrier for one person with a specific disability may not be a barrier for another person with a similar handicapping condition. Many handicapped persons have learned to cope with facilities that were not designed with them in mind. Usually, therefore, they will be able to use a facility even if some architectural barriers exist within it.

In identifying possible architectural and equipment barriers, vocational administrators, planners, and teachers would do well to use the inventiveness, coping skills, and experiences of handicapped persons.

*Team Approach to Barrier Identification Process.* In order to insure an architecturally accessible facility, a team of individuals should be involved in conducting a facility assessment. The assessment team should include the following members:

1. A person familiar with the types of architectural barriers that pose problems for the handicapped. This may be an individual with special training in a local system, a state department of education consultant, or a representative from vocational rehabilitation.

2. Trade and industrial teachers and other vocational teachers whose facilities may be affected by possible modifications.

3. Handicapped individuals who may actually face the barriers inherent in a facility.

4. One who is able to handle the logistics of the needed changes such as recording and costing-out the modifications

required. This could be an architect or contractor for vocational schools under construction, or it could be school's physical plant manager or a construction trades teacher for existing vocational facilities.

*Conducting the Assessment.* Conducting a vocational facility assessment involves a number of steps ranging from publicizing the assessment to formulating a barrier identification plan. Generally, the following steps are involved in conducting barrier identification assessments:

1. Meet with the faculty and staff of a vocational facility and explain the nature and purpose of the assessment. This step should result in identifying teacher concerns and gaining teacher cooperation.

2. Develop an assessment plan. This plan should include (a) the development of facility checklists (Appendix C) that can be used to identify and record barriers, (b) a description of the assessment team members and their duties and responsibilities, and (c) the planning of time lines for making the assessment.

3. Conduct the assessment according to the plan. This step should result in the identification and description of barriers that are recorded on the checklists, which can be used in the barrier elimination or modification process.

4. Obtain recommendations from members of the assessment team and other appropriate individuals for the elimination or modification of each identified barrier.

5. The final step in the process is to prepare barrier elimination or modification plans based upon recommendations made in step two. These plans should include (a) a description of barriers, (b) plans for eliminating or modifying them, (c) a cost analysis for each modification, and (d) a suggested priority or time line for making the modification. It should be noted that handicapped persons can often cope with some moderate barriers that should eventually be eliminated or modified but may be placed in a lower priority.

## Suggestions for Vocational Facility Accessibility

Earlier in this module the major areas of a vocational facility that present barriers to handicapped persons were identified. These areas include (a) getting to and entering the building, (b) moving about inside a building, and (c) using school fixtures, appliances, learning areas, tools, machines, equipment, and work station apparatus.

This section of ther module presents information about barriers common to each major area except those that are caused by tool, machine, equipment, and work station design and organization, which will be discussed later in this module.

*Approaching and Entering the Building.* There are a number of possible barriers for handicapped persons to negotiate in getting to vocational buildings and entering them. These include the following:

1. Parking areas that are inconvenient or not clearly marked.

2. Parking spaces too few in number or located too far from the building entrances, or not wide enough to allow wheelchair-confined persons to load and unload.

3. Curbs that are difficult to cross because they contain no marked breaks or are unramped.

4. Parking lots with loose gravel or rough pavement.

5. Parking areas with storm drain covers that permit wheelchairs or crutch tips to sink.

6. Walks that are too steep, too narrow, or lack appropriate curbs or guardrails.

7. Doors and doorways that are either too narrow, contain raised thresholds, or have door closers too heavy to open.

8. Inadequately lighted parking areas, walkways, and building entrances.

9. Stairways that lack guardrails or have projecting tread noses.

10. Entrance ways that lack protection against the weather.

The following guidelines should be considered in eliminating these barriers:

1. *Parking areas or drop-off areas—* Parking areas or drop-off areas should be provided as close to the building entrances as possible. They should be well lighted and clearly marked with the international symbol of access: ♿ Parking lot surfaces should be relatively smooth (not slippery) and free of storm drain covers that permit crutch tips or wheelchairs to sink. The slope of parking areas should be almost level near building entrances and have a gradient not greater than 5 percent.

2. *Parking spaces—* A sufficient number of parking spaces (at least two per building) should be provided for the handicapped. These spaces should be located so that handicapped persons do not have to travel behind parked cars. They should be at least 12 feet wide, open on one side, and positioned so that handicapped persons can move onto a level surface from their vehicles.

3. *Curb cuts—* At least one clearly marked curb cut or curb ramp with a maximum gradient of 8.3 percent should be provided near designated parking spaces and located so that it cannot be obstructed by cars or other barriers. Curb cuts or ramps should have some type of tactile warning devices such as railings, or grooves in the surfaces of entry approaches, to assist visually impaired persons.

4. *Walks—* Walks should be at least 5 feet wide and contain a maximum slope of 5 percent, or 1 foot to 20 feet. They should have nonslip surfaces such as a broom finish and should blend to a common level at all intersections such as parking lots, driveways, or other walks. Walks should terminate at building entrances with a level platform at least 5 feet by 5 feet with 1 foot extension beyond each side of the doorway. Entrances to walkways, like curb cuts, should have tactile warning devices to aid visually impaired persons. Walkways should be adequately lighted and protected from the elements if possible.

5. *Exterior stairs—* Stairs leading to

building entrances should contain handrails mounted 32 inches above tread nosings that extend 18 inches beyond the bottom and top of the stairways unless they project into a walkway. Step treads should be at least 11 inches wide and have nonslip surfaces. Step risers should not be more than 7 inches high and should be free of projecting tread nosings. Stairways should be well lighted and step treads and step risers should be pointed in sharply contrasting colors to aid the visually impaired. Raised or engraved numbers or letters should be located on the top guard rails directly above the top step tread to designate floor levels if the stairway continues.

6. *Ramps*—Ramps at least 4 feet wide should be provided for physically disabled persons who cannot enter buildings by negotiating stairs. Ramps should have slopes with a gradient no greater than 8.3 percent, or a 1-foot rise in 12 feet. Ramps should have a nonslip surface such as a broom finish. Ramps that are open on both sides should have guardrails that are 32 inches high, extending 18 inches beyond the bottom and top of each ramp. Ramps that terminate at building entrances, like walks, should join onto level platforms that are at least 5 feet by 5 feet and extend at least 1 foot beyond each side of the doorway. Ramps should have a 6-foot straight clearance at the bottom and should have level platforms at least 6 feet long every 30 feet on a rampway or wherever they turn. Protective curbs are desirable on rampway sides that end in a dropoff.

7. *Door and doorways*—Doors should be at least 32 inches wide, with lever handles, 12-inch high kick plates located on the door bottoms, and closers that are adjusted so that not more than eight pounds of pressure is required to open doors. In new or renovated facilities automatic doors are preferable. There should be a minimum of 6 feet–6 inches separation between inner and outer doors. Exterior doorways should contain enlarged, raised, or engraved numbers or letters

placed 5 feet high on the wall adjacent to the opening side of the doorway to aid visually impaired persons.

*Moving about Inside Buildings.* Handicapped persons frequently encounter a number of barriers in the following areas inside vocational buildings:

1. Moving between floor levels.

2. Traveling between classrooms, laboratories, and auxiliary areas such as restrooms, lounge areas, cafeterias, snack bars, and the like.

3. Identifying room entrances and negotiating them.

4. Traveling inside classrooms and laboratories.

5. Using fixtures such as toilets, lavatories, drinking fountains, vending machines, study carrels, work stations, telephones, and emergency controls and fixtures.

The following general guidelines should be considered in eliminating barriers that confront handicapped persons who move about inside vocational buildings:

1. *Floors*—Floors should be at a common level throughout the building or be connected by ramps that meet the criteria presented for exterior ramps. All changes in floor level should be clearly marked by visual as well as tactile devices. Plush and shag type carpeting should be avoided.

2. *Corridors and hallways*—Corridors and hallways should be at least 5 feet wide to allow two wheelchairs to pass. Travel routes for the handicapped should be clearly marked. For example, signs should be posted to indicate accessibility routes to various parts of the building and to indicate emergency exits. Entrances to classrooms, laboratories and auxiliary areas should be marked with raised or engraved letters, numbers, or symbols at least 2 inches high, mounted 5 feet high on the wall adjacent to the opening side of doorways. Protruding fixtures such as fire extinguishers, telephones, drinking fountains and the like should be removed or placed in accessible recess areas in corridors.

3. *Interior stairs and ramps*—Interior stairs and ramps should meet the same guidelines as those for exterior stairs and ramps.

4. *Movement between floor levels*—Moving between floor levels in multi-level buildings for individuals who cannot use stairways can be done by elevators, ramps, or wheelchair lifts. Elevators and wheelchair lifts should be strategically located close to the main entrances to buildings. These devices should be clearly marked with raised or engraved signs and have controls located between 2 feet–11 inches and 4 feet–6 inches above the floor level. Elevator cabs should be at least 5 feet by 5 feet and contain a rear-view mirror to assist wheelchair-confined persons in backing out. Photoelectric eye locations on elevator entrance ways should be marked with OSHA yellow stripes. Floor levels should be placed as high as possible and auditory signals should differentiate between up and down elevator movements. Wheelchair lifts can be used when the drop between floors is less than 4 feet–6 inches and where insufficient space is available to install ramps. Wheelchair lifts can be installed on either the exterior or interior of the building and occupy as little space as 5 feet–5 inches.

5. *Movement inside classrooms and laboratories*—Aisles and traffic lanes inside classrooms and laboratories should be at least 3 feet wide (4 feet preferably) and wider where obstructions frequently occur such as near work benches which have vises. These traffic areas should be marked according to OSHA guidelines.

6. *Restrooms*—At least one barrier-free toilet should be available in each separate vocational building or wing. Toilet stalls should have swing out doors and should be no less than 5 feet–6 inches by 6 feet in dimension. Grab bars should be installed on both sides of the stall 33 inches off the floor. Toilets should be the type with narrow understructures and should be 19 inches to 20 inches high. Lavatories should be mounted high enough to allow 27½ inches of knee clearance. Hot water pipes should be protected with insulation or other barriers to prevent possible burns to the lower limbs of handicapped persons. Restrooms should be marked for the visually impaired similar to the markings described for other room entrances.

7. *Drinking fountains*—A minimum of one barrier-free fountain should be available in each separate vocational wing or building. It should be placed in a recessed area of a corridor or hallway about 30 inches from the floor unless cups are provided. Fountains should be equipped with push-button type hand controls and foot pedals. They should display the symbol of access.

8. *Telephones*—At least one barrier-free telephone should be provided in each separate vocational wing or building. Telephones should be placed in a recessed area and installed so they are accessible to wheelchair-confined persons (no higher than 4 feet–4 inches). Telephones for the handicapped should be the button type and should be equipped with adjustable receiver volume.

9. *Vending machines*—Vending machines of the push-button, solenoid type should be used whenever possible and should have coin slots no higher than 4 feet–8 inches off the floor.

10. *Cafeterias*—Cafeterias should be made accessible to handicapped persons. They should contain doorways at least 34 inches in width, employ tray slides mounted 34 inches off the floor, have food or service lines at least 36 inches in width, and have tables spaced 6 feet apart with clearance of at least 27½ inches.

11. *Work stations and study areas*—Student work stations in laboratories or study areas in classrooms should be at least 32 inches in width and have knee space of 22 inches depth and 27½ inches in height. In lecture halls or classrooms a space of at least 36 inches wide and 4 feet–4 inches in length should be provided for wheelchair-confined persons. Typical work station furniture in vocational laboratories and classrooms includes: study

carrels, work benches, and tables. Modifications to work station furniture are often needed to accommodate the handicapped.

12. *Controls*—Controls and switches for such essentials as light, heat, ventilation, windows, draperies, fire alarms and the like should be placed so that wheelchair-confined persons can use them. These controls should be no higher than 5 feet off the floor.

13. *Warning devices*—Warning devices that use auditory signals, such as fire alarms and class change devices, should also be equipped with simultaneous visual signals to serve individuals with both hearing and visual impairments.

14. *Hazards*—Most buildings have some type of hazard, and when these cannot be eliminated they should be clearly marked and have some type of obstruction to protect individuals from injury. Typical hazards include uneven walks; manhole covers raised above the pavement or sunken below it; open access panels, open excavations; low-mounted door closers; telephone or electric cords crossing the floors; telephones, drinking fountains, fire extinguishers and fire alarms protruding into hallways or corridors, ramps and stairs without guardrails; materials protruding into traffic lanes, and many other obvious hazards.

*Orienting Students to Vocational Facilities.* Making vocational facilities accessible to the handicapped involves more than eliminating physical barriers; it also involves orienting students to the school environment. Students with disabilities often feel anxious upon arriving at a vocational facility. In addition to the transition problems facing all students, such as adjusting to the instructional program and meeting new friends and the like, handicapped individuals must make adjustments to the physical environment. Making the transition to the physical environment can be made easier by a good orientation program.

A successful orientation program for physically handicapped persons often involves more than a one-shot approach. Perhaps the first day of orientation should be devoted to a preview of the physical facility with special attention given to architectural accommodations (e.g., location of elevators, ramps, stairs, building entrances, parking spaces, accessible restrooms and drinking fountains, etc.) Special needs students with more severe handicaps may need a specialized orientation that may require several days to cover ways of adjusting to facilities. Typically these adjustments involve choosing the best route from one location to another and building confidence in their ability to move about inside the vocational facility. The orientation may be conducted by the vocational counselor, an administrator, or a faculty member. For students with severe disabilities, it is advisable to use the services of a specialist in conducting the orientation process.

## MODIFYING THE LABORATORY WORK ENVIRONMENT

The presence of architectural barriers in school facilities is a major reason why handicapped students do not participate in T & I programs. Linked closely to architectural barriers, however, are the barriers that exist in using the tools, machines, equipment, and work station apparatus involved in most T & I programs.

Performing the learning tasks in T & I programs requires the safe manipulation of a wide variety of materials, tools, machines, equipment, and work station apparatus. Likewise, a wide variety of basic behaviors are involved in performing these work tasks.

Examples of basic behaviors involved in performing T & I work tasks include:

1. Crawling.
2. Lifting.
3. Grasping.
4. Reaching.
5. Sitting.

6. Standing.
7. Maintaining balance.
8. Kneeling or crouching.
9. Carrying objects.
10. Pulling objects.
11. Pushing objects.
12. Turning objects.
13. Depressing and releasing.
14. Using limbs quickly.
15. Coordinating limbs.
16. Detecting size, shape, texture, and position.
17. Detecting temperature and pressure.
18. Reading diagrams, schematics, blueprints, and instructions.
19. Exchanging information.
20. Making judgments.
21. Solving problems.

While these basic work-related behaviors are easily accomplished by students without disabilities, handicapped students with certain impairments may experience barriers in performing them.

Trade and industrial teachers often recognize tasks that are difficult for students to accomplish and find ways to help their students overcome whatever problems these tasks present. Frequently, changes in task procedures will enable students to perform them more easily. Sometimes an aid will need to be provided or a modification made to a tool or piece of equipment to help students overcome barriers to successful task performance.

The number of possible barriers that handicapped students may encounter in T & I programs seems almost unlimited. Realization of this has caused some T & I teachers to express the belief that extensive modifications would be needed to their laboratory work environment in order to accommodate such students.

Typically, however, the extent to which modifications are needed to overcome barriers in T & I laboratories is less than teachers expect. Many handicapped students have learned how to adjust to their disabilities, and they experience barriers only when their handicapping condition makes it difficult or impossible for them to manipulate the materials, tools, machines, and equipment required to perform a T & I work task successfully. Often these barriers can be overcome by making low-cost modifications to a tool or a piece of machinery or equipment or to the work site. Illustration 7.2 shows a modification to a drill press that permits it to be operated by an amputee.

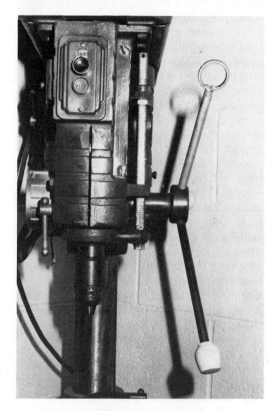

**Illustration 7.2**

Modified drill press for use by disabled persons.

While modifications to the tools, machines, equipment, and work stations used in a T & I laboratory may be needed to accommodate certain handicapped students, unnecessary modification should be avoided. Students who are surrounded with many special devices to assist them in performing work tasks may never learn to cope with the actual work environment in industry. The principle of helping students develop and use their capabilities to adjust to the T & I work environment should be followed in determining the modifications or aids that may be needed to help them perform work tasks.

## Identifying Laboratory Work Task Barriers

There are four major demands that may present barriers to T & I handicapped students in the T & I laboratory environment (Dahl, Appleby, White, 1978). These are: physical, visual, hearing and speech, and intellectual. Examples of physical demands include the many basic behaviors involved in manipulating objects, such as grasping and twisting tools, picking up and moving objects, and feeding materials through machines. Visual demands include: reading instructions, blueprints, and schematics; taking measurements; and positioning and aligning tools and materials.

Examples of hearing and speech demands include: receiving information from teachers, determining whether a machine is operating properly, detecting warning signals, and communicating with peers and the teacher.

Intellectual demands include understanding instructions, recalling operational steps in performing tasks, taking accurate measurements and performing calculations, making decisions, and solving problems associated with work tasks.

Whether these demands result in barriers for T & I handicapped students depends upon the nature and severity of their disabilities, the adjustments they have made to their disabilities, the type of prosthetic devices or aids used as well as their skill in using them, and the nature of T & I laboratory work tasks.

Although T & I teachers can often recognize which work tasks will present barriers for certain handicapped students, it is good practice to use the assessment team approach described in the architec-

tural barrier identification section of this module. The team approach provides the T & I teacher with important information about the nature of the barrier as well as ideas from experienced professionals that can be used to help students overcome a particular work environment barrier. The goal of the team approach should be to arrive at a strategy that capitalizes upon the student's ability to get the job done, even if it requires providing a special tool, an aid, or an equipment modification.

*Teacher Responses to Identified Barriers.* There are three general responses that T & I teachers can make when they identify equipment or work environment barriers. The first is to select tools, machines, equipment, furniture, and other devices that are as barrier-free as possible. For example, T & I teachers can select digital readout engine analyzers, which are easier to read than conventional meter faces. (Illustration 7.3)

A second general response is to assist students in obtaining commercially available aids or devices that will help them manipulate tools, machines, and equipment required to perform work tasks. For example, a handicapped student preparing to be an auto parts clerk can type orders using a template to improve hand and finger control. (Illustration 7.4)

The third general teacher response to overcoming barriers is to alter or modify tools, machines, and equipment so they are usable by handicapped students. (Illustration 7.5)

The type of response that T & I teachers can make when they identify work task related barriers depends upon the options available to them. Because of cost, it is often difficult to obtain new tools, machines, and equipment that are barrier-free. Sometimes aids can be purchased for handicapped students and paid for by vocational rehabilitation funds or by some other out-of-school funding source. The option of devising aids or modifying the T & I work environment may be the

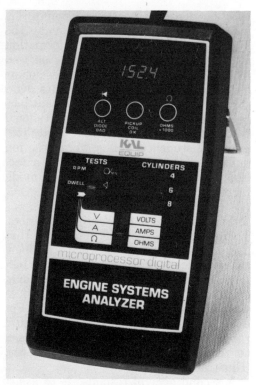

**Illustration 7.3**

Digital read-out engine analyzer, courtesy of Kal-Equip Co., Ostego, Michigan.

**Illustration 7.5**

A parallel bar drafting table modified so it is counter-balanced to stay in position.

**Illustration 7.4**

A typewriter template used to improve hand and finger control for a handicapped student.

most feasible, and appropriate option.

Trade and industrial teachers can obtain ideas for modifying tools, equipment, and work environment from their handicapped students, from special education personnel available in most school systems, and from vocational rehabilitation counselors. The materials and machines required to make aids and modifications are normally available in the vocational school. All that is normally needed are T & I teachers who have the desire and ingenuity to construct aids or modify their laboratory environment and equipment to accommodate handicapped students. Illustration 7.6 shows a simple teacher-made aid that helps a student with limited arm and hand strength to turn dial controls in a cosmotology laboratory.

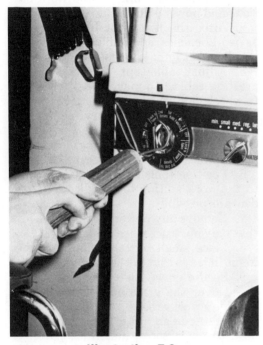

**Illustration 7.6**

Teacher-constructed aid used to improve leverage for manipulating equipment controls. *Top:* Close-up of aid. *Bottom:* Aid in use.

*Available Aids, Tools, Machines, and Equipment.* Increasing amounts of specially designed aids, tools, machines, equipment, and furniture are becoming available for purchase to accommodate handicapped students. These items can be found in school supply catalogs, as well as in catalogs published by special

institutes, agencies, and foundations for the handicapped, such as the American Foundation for the Blind.

Examples of commercially available devices include telephone aids that cover a wide variety of communication problems, electronic calculators and computers that convert keyboard signals into tape and video displays that can be read, reading devices that permit visually impaired persons to read the printed word, sonic guides to aid the blind in mobility, and a wide range of tools and instruments that use tactile markings and auditory sounds to make measurement such as combination squares with raised dots and audible multimeters.

Information about commercially available devices is available from special education personnel in school systems, vocational rehabilitation counselors, or from State Department of Education consultants. These sources usually maintain libraries of materials from which T & I teachers can draw to assist them in identifying possible devices for their handicapped students.

In addition to these specially designed devices, there is a wide variety of standard tools, appliances, equipment, and devices available to make work tasks easier for all students. Examples of these items include electric pencil sharpeners and erasers for use by drafting students, and a lawnmower lift for use in a small engine repair program. (Illustration 7.7)

## Suggestions for Work Environment Modifications

The remaining section of this module will present a number of suggestions for eliminating or reducing work environment barriers by modifying tools, machines, equipment, furniture, and work stations to meet the specific needs of handicapped students.

In addition to the suggestions found in

179

**Illustration 7.7**

A commercially available lawn mower lift for use in a small engine repair program.

this module, an excellent source of information about aids and modifications is the Wisconsin Vocational Studies Center (see list of references at the end of this module). This organization provides a 600-page catalog containing listings of commercially available equipment as well as a wide variety of aids and modifications to tools, equipment, and machinery in relation to twenty-five skill areas and seven disability areas. This catalog can be a very useful tool for T & I teachers who need ideas about aids and modification required in their laboratories in order to accommodate handicapped students.

*Modifying the Work Environment for Wheelchair-Confined Persons.* The major barriers for wheelchair-confined students are those that prevent them from getting to the work site; reaching tools, materials, and equipment controls; and keeping work materials at an appropriate level. Suggestions for helping students overcome these barriers are as follows:

1. Rearrange machines and work station furniture so that adequate space is provided for aisles and around work stations and power equipment.

2. Alter the height of furniture such as workbenches and tables and remove barriers that limit knee space.

3. Adjust table tops (such as those on drafting tables) to make them accessible to wheelchair-confined students.

4. Mount semi-stationary equipment (such as grinders) on adjustable bases.

5. Rearrange storage areas for tools and supplies into low cabinets or shelves.

6. Position tools and materials as near to the work station for handicapped students as possible.

7. Remove any power cords from floors that may obstruct wheelchair mobility.

8. Place small parts, tools, and other items in trays that are accessible.

9. Secure or devise a tray that can be fitted over the arms of a wheelchair to provide a work area.

10. Provide an aid or tool that can be used to reach tools, materials, parts, or work apparatus such as reachers, giant tongs, grocer's hooks, and other devices (Illustration 7.8).

11. Provide ramps where it is difficult to adjust furniture, machine, or equipment height. Illustration 7.9 shows a ramp that raises the wheelchair several inches off the floor to provide access to the recessed area for wheelchair foot rests.

12. Convert controls or switches on machines and equipment that use foot pedals or hand or arm operated devices (Illustration 7.10).

13. Relocate rear-mounted switches and controls on machines and equipment, placing them near the front for easier access.

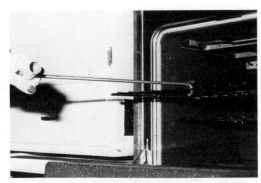

**Illustration 7.8**

Teacher-made hook to enable a wheelchair confined food service student to move oven racks.

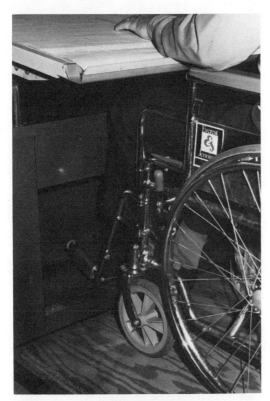

**Illustration 7.9**

Teacher-constructed ramp used to elevate wheelchair to allow foot rest to enter recessed area of a drafting table base.

14. Secure or devise an adjustable work-holding device such as the mower lift shown in Illustration 7.7.

15. Lower adjustable stationary power tools or machines such as a standard floor-mounted drill press.

16. Position bench-mounted power tools on the ends of benches to provide access on at least two sides.

**Illustration 7.10**

Commercial sewing machine modified for arm control to allow operation by an individual in a wheelchair.

*Modifying the Work Environment for the Student with Upper Extremity Disabilities.* Trade and industrial teachers may work with students who have any number of disabilities to their upper extremities. These disabilities include unsteadiness of upper limbs; lack of finger and hand dexterity; lack of arm, hand, and finger strength; and amputations of limbs. These disabilities often result in barriers to reaching, grasping, holding, and manipulating objects such as tools, materials, machine controls, and equipment handles.

The following suggestions may help T & I teachers overcome barriers for students with upper-extremity disabilities:

1. Modify machine controls so they can be operated with prostheses such as an arm hook (Illustration 7.2).

2. Replace door knobs and other knob controls with handles or levers when possible.

3. Convert hard-to-turn machine and equipment controls to levers.

4. Convert electric or electronic equipment using knob-type, on-off, or adjusting controls to toggle switches, levers, or slide-adjustment mechanisms.

5. Provide the student with an aid that increases mechanical advantage in manipulating controls (Illustration 7.11).

**Illustration 7.11**

Teacher-made lever used to convert a knob on a table saw fence to increase the ability to manipulate controls.

**Illustration 7.12**

A foam pad aid used to help handicapped individuals in picking up small parts.

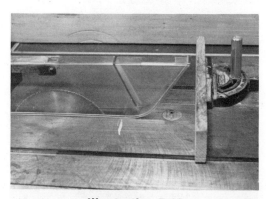

**Illustration 7.13**

A table saw with guard in place to prevent injury to operators.

6. Place small parts or instruments on a foam pad that aids students in picking them up (Illustration 7.12).

7. Place guards on all power machines needing them (Illustration 7.13).

8. Select tools that require only one hand to operate, such as split screwdrivers, which hold screws and bolts for starting.

9. Convert machines and equipment that have hand controls to the foot pedal type when possible.

10. Secure or devise holding devices such as vacuum-vices, stationary vises, clamps, nonslip pads, and jigs and fixtures that permit one-hand operation (Illustration 7.14).

11. Provide the student with tools that supply more mechanical advantage to loosen or tighten screws or bolts, such as a lever-type socket set or an offset screwdriver.

12. Select power tools that reduce the level of pressure or force required to perform a work task—for example, a circular saw greatly reduces the need for hand and arm strength.

13. Increase the size of tool handles or pencils by replacing them with larger diameter handles or by enlarging them with tubing or tape wrappings.

14. Attach straps to appliance handles

**Illustration 7.14**

A teacher-made aid to enable a handicapped food service student to grate vegetables with one hand.

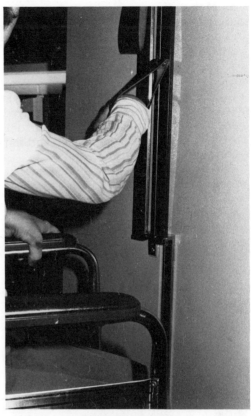

**Illustration 7.15**

Straps attached to a freezer door to enable a handicapped food service student to open it more easily.

and other objects to allow them to be opened more easily (Illustration 7.15).

15. Attach handles to or drill holes in flat objects such as steel rulers, flat steel squares, T-squares, and parallel bars to make them easier to grasp and manipulate.

16. Select machines that do not require two-hand operation, such as a radial arm saw instead of a table saw.

17. Provide templates to aid drafting students who have trouble manipulating standard drafting instruments.

18. Obtain or construct required braces, straps, or other supports for students who have problems controlling their limbs.

*Modifying the Work Environment for Students with Visual Impairments.* Students who have visual impairments may encounter a number of barriers in performing work tasks that require reading instruction, schematics, blueprints, and drawings; taking measurements; positioning and aligning tools and materials; guiding materials through machines, or hand tools through materials; and other tasks requiring good eyesight.

The following suggestions may be helpful to T & I teachers who are looking for ways to help students overcome barriers caused by impaired or lost vision.

1. Make transparencies of reading materials required to perform work tasks and project them with the overhead projector.

2. Employ a videotape system with large screen monitors if available.

3. Purchase commercially available measuring tools with raised or engraved markings that can be read by touch, such as steel tapes, rules, combination and flat steel squares, and micrometers.

4. Purchase measuring devices that provide auditory signals, such as audible multimeters and audible therometers.

5. Select digital readout measuring devices such as tack/drill meters, multimeters, and timing devices (Illustration 7.3).

6. Enlarge markings on tools, tool holders, or machine controls that normally require only a few markings (Illustration 7.16).

**Illustration 7.16**

Teacher-made drill holder with enlarged markings to assist the partially sighted in tool selection.

7. Provide jigs, guides, and templates to aid students in positioning and guiding tools (Illustration 7.17).

8. Purchase regular magnifiers or illuminated magnifiers to assist the partially sighted students (Illustration 7.18).

9. Provide relief markings on tools by scratching lines at appropriate locations.

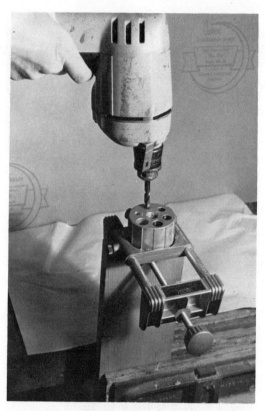

**Illustration 7.17**

A dowel jig used to help a visually impaired cabinet-making student in preparing a dowel joint.

**Illustration 7.18**

A magnifier which can assist a partially sighted student in reading small print.

10. Identify controls by changing their size, shape, or texture.

11. Modify a standard tape recorder by using labeling tape or other tape markings to designate the different controls.

12. Assist the student in obtaining appropriate communication aids and devices such as the Optacon, talking calculators, and other electronic equipment.

*Modifying the Work Environment for Students with Hearing and Speech Impairments.* Students who have hearing and speech impairments may encounter a number of barriers to understanding the communication of others, detecting warning signals, determining proper machine and equipment operation, and sharing information with teachers and fellow classmates. On the other hand, students with these two types of disabilities usually experience fewer work environment barriers than those who have physical or visual disabilities. Many T & I work tasks can be performed successfully without good hearing or speaking abilities, although it is often much safer to be able to hear sounds emitted by tools and machines as they perform operations on materials.

The following suggestions may be helpful to T & I teachers who have students with hearing and speech impairments:

1. Assist the student in obtaining aids and devices that can improve partial hearing, such as personal sound systems. T & I teachers can find many of these devices in catalogs and brochures normally kept on file by special needs professionals.

2. Install visual warning lights on machines and equipment to signal when they are in operation.

3. Install amplification devices on auditory warning signals so that they can be heard by those with partial hearing.

4. Employ visual timers in place of those that emit sounds.

5. When speaking to deaf students or those with partial hearing, get their attention and face them.

6. Convert information that is available only on cassettes and films to scripts that can be read.

7. Provide written instruction through handouts, information sheets, and chalkboard displays.

8. Assist students who have speech disabilities in obtaining aids and devices such as the talking calculator, the artificial larynx, or any of a variety of other devices that either support available speech skills or substitute for speech communication altogether.

9. Exercise patience in communicating with students who must talk slowly.

10. Obtain the services of a sign language translator if necessary or learn basic sign language.

*Modifying the Work Environment for Students with Mental Disabilities.* Students who have mental disabilities (such as the mildly retarded) may experience barriers to completing complex tasks because of the memory and understanding factor. Normally these students can learn to use tools, machines, and equipment without modification, but often the procedures to accomplish work tasks must be altered. For example, breaking work tasks into smaller steps as discussed in Module 8 is one technique proven to be successful in helping these students to accomplish tasks.

The suggestions that follow may be helpful to T & I teachers who have students that encounter work task barriers due to mental disabilities:

1. Analyze work tasks and break them into smaller steps.

2. Provide operation sheets or work sheets that have step-by-step instructions for accomplishing tasks.

3. Devise jigs, fixtures, templates, and guides to simplify work task operations.

4. Color code your machine and equipment controls according to function for easy identification.

5. Teach students to obtain and organize their tools and materials before beginning work tasks.

6. Place small parts that must be assembled into divided trays in operational order.

7. Construct or provide completed objects or models so that students can see what their work task results should look like.

8. Employ peer tutoring or the "buddy system" technique to help students accomplish complex work tasks.

## SUMMARY

Without question, handicapped students have been denied their right to participate in T & I programs because of architectural and work environment barriers. Today, however, this situation is changing. Vocational educators, with the added incentive of federal legislation, are identifying architectural barriers in their facilities and taking measures to eliminate them.

Trade and industrial teachers, working in cooperation with special education personnel in their schools and communities, are identifying barriers caused by the physical, visual, hearing and speech, and intellectual demands of the work environment. Using the assessment team approach, these teachers also are making appropriate responses to the work environment barriers that they identify.

Sometimes these responses involve purchasing special tools, equipment, and devices for use by handicapped students. Typically, however, the most appropriate responses are to provide or construct simple aids that allow students to accomplish work tasks with standard equipment, or to make simple, low-cost modifications to their laboratory work environment.

Provided with accessible vocational facilities and modified work environments when necessary, handicapped students can learn to perform most laboratory work tasks successfully and thereby prepare themselves for employment in T & I occupations.

## REFERENCES

*American national standards specifications for making building and facilities accessible to and useable by the physically handicapped.* New York: American National Standards Institute, 1961.

Cotler, S. and Deqratt, A. *Architectural accessibility for the disabled of college campuses.* Albany, New York: State University Construction Fund, 1976.

Dahl, P., Appleby, J., and Lipe, D. *Mainstreaming guidebook for vocational educators.* Salt Lake City, Utah: Olympus Publishing Company, 1978.

Gugerty, J., Roshal, F., Tradewell, M., and Anthony, L. *Tools, equipment and machinery adapted for the vocational education and employment of handicapped people.* Madison, Wisconsin: Wisconsin Vocational Studies Center, 1980.

*Into a mainstream: a syllabus for a barrier-free environment.* (Superintendent of Documents, CPD No.: 1796–210 82615043). Washington, D.C.: U.S. Government Printing Office, 1976.

Mace, R., and Laslett, B. (Eds.) *An illustrated handbook of the handicapped section of the North Carolina state building code.* Raleigh, North Carolina, 1976.

Steinfeld, E., Schroeder, S., and Bishop, M. *Adaptable dwellings.* (U.S. Department of Housing and Urban Development Service Publication). Washington, D.C.: U.S. Government Printing Office, 1974.

Weisgerber, R., Dahl, P., and Appleby, J. *Training the handicapped for production employment.* Rockville, Maryland: Aspen Systems Corporation, 1980.

## SELF ASSESSMENT: VOCATIONAL FACILITY AND EQUIPMENT MODIFICATION

1. Describe what architectural barriers are and give several examples of them.
2. Describe what laboratory work environment barriers are and give several examples of them.
3. Describe the laws that guarantee handicapped persons access to vocational school facilities.
4. List some common barriers in getting to vocational buildings and entering them.
5. List some common barriers in moving about inside vocational buildings.
6. Describe the assessment team approach to identifying barriers.
7. Describe the three responses T & I teachers can make when they have identified laboratory work environment barriers.
8. Give some examples of flexible, barrier-free tools, machines, and equipment that could be used for students with physical disabilities.
9. Give some examples of things you could do to modify your laboratory work environment for persons with visual and auditory impairments.

## ASSOCIATED ACTIVITIES

1. Using the Facilities Accessibility Checklist included in Appendix C, perform an assessment of your school's facilities to identify possible architectural barriers.
2. Participate as a member of an assessment team in studying barriers and recommending possible solutions to eliminate or reduce them.
3. If you have handicapped students with certain disabilities, analyze your work tasks and work environment to identify possible barriers that may confront them.

4. Secure catalogs of special equipment and devices from the libraries of special education personnel in your school or community and familiarize yourself with what is available to help handicapped students.
5. Construct a simple aid to help a handicapped person perform a work task in your laboratory.
6. Make appropriate modifications to your work environment—including tools, machines, and equipment—to accommodate handicapped students.
7. Talk with other T & I teachers in your instructional area to discover what responses they have made to accommodate handicapped students.

## CASE HISTORY: KEITH'S STORY

Keith is a speech impaired learner enrolled in a machine shop. He has a strong lisp and frequently stutters. When he becomes nervous he often experiences periods of delayed speech when the words will not come out no matter how hard he tries. His school records reveal that he has average intelligence and has received good grades in all his academic classes. Keith is very insecure and shy around other people. He seldom speaks unless he is spoken to. He has been working with a speech therapist on a regular basis for the past several years.

Keith wants to be a tool and die maker. He has demonstrated proficiency in the use and function of all the basic machine tools in the laboratory such as the lathe, shaper, grinder, milling machine, and drill press. He can also demonstrate the proper use of the micrometers, calipers, dial indicators, and other devices.

Keith's greatest problem lies in establishing appropriate working relationships with others. He ignores others when they try to communicate with him during group laboratory activities. The program instructor is concerned about this. If Keith can't get along with co-workers, his chances of finding and holding a job are not good.

The district communications specialist has recently been working closely with the program instructor and has suggested some methods and techniques that could be used in the classroom to make Keith feel more comfortable and able to relate to others. The instructor has discussed the problem with the class, and the students have been very cooperative about involving Keith in group activities. They are all patient when Keith attempts to speak, being careful to maintain eye contact.

These combined efforts have helped Keith to feel more confident. As a result, he is beginning to respond in small group situations. Keith continues to meet with the communication specialist for his scheduled speech therapy sessions. In addition, the program instructor has spoken to a member of his advisory committee who has expressed an interest in hiring Keith once he completes the program requirements.

## CASE HISTORY ACTIVITY

Erica has recently enrolled in your program. She has a stuttering problem. Although she has normal intelligence, her grades in academic classes have only been fair. Her reading level is also several grade levels below her peers. She is shy and insecure and does not participate in classroom discussions. She is also very reluctant to participate in group laboratory activities; instead she prefers to work alone.

Based on this information, complete the case history profile worksheet for Erica's participation in your program.

## CASE HISTORY PROFILE WORKSHEET

Student: _____ Page: _____

Handicapping Condition(s): _____

T & I Program: _____ Academic Levels: _____

Career Goal/Occupational Interest: _____

Considerations (e.g., medication, behavior): _____

| Adaptation | Specific Services Needed | Where to Obtain Service |
|---|---|---|
| Cooperative Planning (School Personnel) | | |
| Support Services | | |
| Architectural Changes | | |
| Adaptive Equipment | | |
| Curriculum Modification | | |
| Instructional Materials/ Supplies | | |
| Teaching Techniques | | |
| Agency Involvement | | |
| Possible Job Placement | | |

# MODULE 8*

## Modifying the Curriculum for Special Needs Learners in Trade and Industrial Education

Modifying or adapting the regular T & I education curriculum is probably one of the most pressing tasks facing the T & I instructor. Its difficulty lies not so much in knowing what needs to be done as in scheduling and accomplishing what needs to be done. Yet, it should be pointed out that modifying the curriculum for the special needs learner also enhances the usability of the curriculum for all students who enroll in the program.

If the term *curriculum*, in relationship to vocational education, is defined as the sum total of all the experiences and activities encountered by the student in pursuit of occupational preparation under the direction of the school, then *curriculum modification* can be defined as tailoring those experiences and activities to meet the unique needs of the individual student. Although this module will outline a process whereby the existing T & I curriculum can be adapted to "zero in" on the special needs target population, it will not replace the significant amount of labor that must accompany the steps outlined in the process. The purpose of this module is to help the T & I educator to channel that labor and, subsequently, to tailor individual experiences and activities that maximize occupational preparation.

Genuine curriculum modification flows

directly from within the confines and context of the regular T & I curriculum. There are four basic steps for modifying the curriculum for special needs learners. These steps are sequential in nature. They are both interdependent and interrelated —interdependent in the sense that each stands alone, and interrelated in the sense that each step serves as the foundation for the following step. The overall curriculum modification process presented in this module is graphically illustrated in Illustration 8.1. The flowchart may help to place the entire process in perspective. The remainder of the module will be aimed at discussing each of the four major steps in some detail. Examples of specific programs of T & I education will be used extensively. It should be noted that the examples are used merely to illustrate a point. The process is obviously more important than the examples, because the process has application to any program of T & I education.

## MODULE OBJECTIVES

After you have read and reviewed this module, studied the case history, and reviewed the self-assessment questions, you should be able to:

1. Establish a composite curriculum framework for your area of T & I education.

2. Develop an instructional task analysis for your area of T & I education.

3. Develop a curriculum supplement for your area of T & I education with the help of special needs instructional support personnel.

4. Develop a student module from a single learning-and-supplemental-learning-plan set from your curriculum supplement.

5. Describe the process of curriculum modification as presented in this module.

6. Increase your instructional effectiveness with special needs learners en-

*This module was written by Douglas H. Gill, Vocational Special Needs, University of Georgia, Athens, Georgia.

rolled in your program of T & I education through the use of the curriculum modification process described in this module.

## ESTABLISHING THE CURRICULUM FRAMEWORK

The initial phase in modifying the curriculum to meet the goals of the special needs learner in T & I education is, first, to establish the existing program's curriculum framework. This entails outlining, in detail, the curriculum sequence that *any* student would follow relative to the particular program in question. As previously mentioned, effective curriculum modification flows from within the confines and context of the regular curriculum. Therefore, establishing the curriculum framework is merely an effort to organize the curriculum in such a way that it can be modified.

Organizing the curriculum in this manner involves three basic steps. The first step is to identify and list the overall long-range objectives or goals of the program. The long-range objective is a statement of desired student performance at the conclusion of his/her experience in the given T & I program. The second step is to identify and list the intermediate or short-term objectives that sequentially comprise the long-range objective. The third step is to identify and list the instructional units that sequentially comprise each short-term objective. Establishing the curriculum framework is the foundation of the curriculum modification process described in this module. Failure to adequately prepare the curriculum framework usually results in all other phases of the process being "out of synch."

### The Long-range Objective.

The long-range objective is intended to focus the program and answer two key questions: What is the student preparing to do, and what is the purpose of the program? An appropriate long-range objective will identify the scope of the student's involvement in a given program of T & I education.

Usually, program goals or long-range objectives are readily available to instructors. These goals or long-range objectives generally stem from the existing school or program philosophy. Three examples of long-range objectives that reflect a philosophy of job entry level skill development are as follows:

1. Given proper tools, equipment, and materials, the student will be able to successfully demonstrate job entry level skills in the carpentry area of residential construction.

2. Given proper tools, equipment, and materials, the student will be able to demonstrate the skills necessary for entry into the residential construction area of plumbing.

3. Given proper tools, equipment, and materials, the student will be able to demonstrate instructor-specified job entry level skills in the masonry area of construction trades at the acceptable rate of time and accuracy.

### The Short-term Objective.

The short-term objectives are designed to establish a sequence of attainment for the long-range objective. In that sense, a series of short-term objectives will collectively form a long-range objective. This makes it possible to begin a systematic arrangement of the curriculum. Using a sample long-range objective previously provided, the addition of sequenced short-term objectives will show how the curriculum can be systematically arranged.

*Long-range objective:* Given appropriate tools, equipment, and materials, the student will be able to demonstrate instructor-specified job entry level skills in the masonry area construction trades at an acceptable rate of time and accuracy.

*Short-term objective #1:* Student will be able to demonstrate the basic skills of bricklaying.

## Illustration 8.1

## CURRICULUM MODIFICATION PROCESS

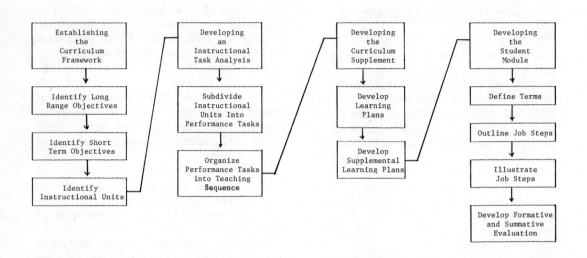

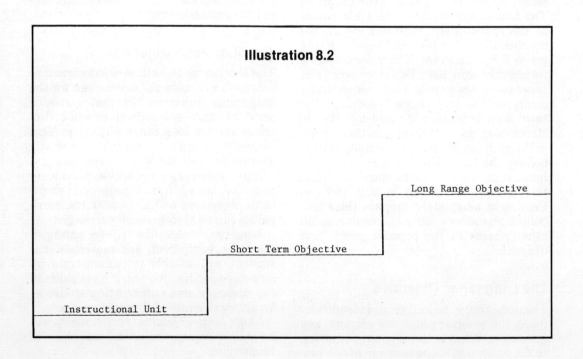

## Illustration 8.2

Long Range Objective

Short Term Objective

Instructional Unit

*Short-term objective #2:* Student will be able to demonstrate use of the brick-spacing rule.

*Short-term objective #3:* Student will be able to demonstrate construction of double brick walls.

*Short-term objective #4:* Student will be able to demonstrate construction of concrete block corners.

*Short-term objective #5:* Student will be able to lay a variety of brick bonds.

*Short-term objective #6:* student will be able to demonstrate knowledge of concrete masonry.*

### The Instructional Unit.

Just as short-term objectives are designed to establish a sequence for attainment of the long-range objective, instructional units are designed to establish a sequence for attainment of the short-term objective. The inclusion of the instructional unit completes the establishment of the curriculum framework. Once this has been done, the actual modification of the curriculum for special needs learners can occur. Again, the curriculum framework is an outline of the teaching structure as it already exists. This outline serves to organize instruction in a systematic and sequential manner. Illustration 8.3 provides a completed sample of the curriculum framework.

# DEVELOPING AN INSTRUCTIONAL TASK ANALYSIS

Once the curriculum framework has been established, the process of developing an instructional task analysis begins. The instructional task analysis is a listing of the tasks that, when sequenced, make up the instructional unit. Therefore, what the instructor is actually doing at this point is designing an instructional "road map." This "road map" will pinpoint des-

tination (long-range objective), intermediate stops (short-term objective), major routes (instructional units), and now, points along the way (instructional tasks).

Regarding the special needs learner in the T & I program, it is important that both the curriculum framework and the instructional task analysis be performance-based. The focus should be on what the student is actually *required to do* as opposed to what the student is asked to read about or write about doing. Reading and writing are activities that supplement or enhance performance in most instances. The point of the instructional task analysis is to identify the required performance. Academically oriented activities will surface later in this module.

Instructional task analysis in relationship to vocational education is certainly nothing new. Vocational education in general and T & I education in particular have long been proponents of a task analysis approach to curriculum development. The establishment of the curriculum framework and the subsequent development of an instructional task analysis is intended simply to organize the instructional process. It requires more re-structuring than invention on the instructor's part. An example of an instructional task analysis in regard to the first short-term objective in masonry follows. Illustration 8.4 is used merely to be consistent with previous examples so that the reader is exposed to a program from start to finish.

# DEVELOPING THE CURRICULUM SUPPLEMENT

Developing the curriculum supplement for use by teachers with special needs students in T & I programs requires that the established curriculum framework and corresponding instructional task listing be transformed from a state of organization to a state of implementation. This transformation results in the construc-

---

*These goals and short term objectives were obtained from a state curriculum guide in the area of masonry.

# Illustration 8.3

## CURRICULUM FRAMEWORK FOR MASONRY PROGRAM

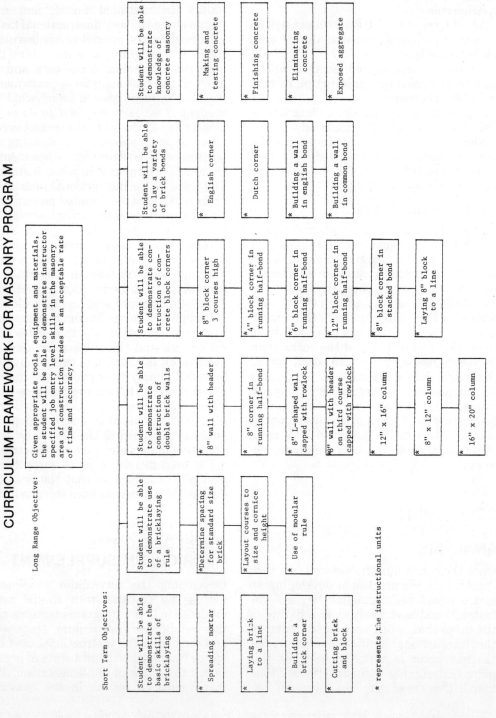

**Long Range Objective:**

Given appropriate tools, equipment and materials, the student will be able to demonstrate instructor specified job entry level skills in the masonry area of construction trades at an acceptable rate of time and accuracy.

**Short Term Objectives:**

| Student will be able to demonstrate the basic skills of bricklaying | Student will be able to demonstrate use of a bricklaying rule | Student will be able to demonstrate construction of double brick walls | Student will be able to demonstrate construction of concrete block corners | Student will be able to lay a variety of brick bonds | Student will be able to demonstrate knowledge of concrete masonry |
|---|---|---|---|---|---|
| * Spreading mortar | *Determine spacing for standard size brick | * 8" wall with header | * 8" block corner 3 courses high | * English corner | * Making and testing concrete |
| * Laying brick to a line | *Layout courses to size and cornice height | * 8" corner in running half-bond | * 4" block corner in running half-bond | * Dutch corner | * Finishing concrete |
| * Building a brick corner | * Use of modular rule | * 8" L-shaped wall capped with rowlock | * 6" block corner in running half-bond | * Building a wall in english bond | * Eliminating concrete |
| * Cutting brick and block | | *8" wall with header on third course capped with rowlock | * 12" block corner in running half-bond | * Building a wall in common bond | * Exposed aggregate |
| | | * 12" x 16" column | * 8" block corner in stacked bond | | |
| | | * 8" x 12" column | * Laying 8" block to a line | | |
| | | * 16" x 20" column | | | |

* represents the instructional units

194

tion of usable supplements for the existing curriculum. The curriculum supplement is designed to be used by the regular T & I instructor and the instructional support teacher for the special needs student. Without a dual developmental effort on the part of both of these segments of the instructional community, successful occupational preparation of the special needs student is less likely to occur.

As a direct outgrowth of the curriculum framework and instructional task analysis, the curriculum supplement is composed of two major parts: the learning plan and the supplemental learning plan. Each part can be used separately by the appropriate instructor as well as jointly by both.

The learning plan is utilized primarily by the T & I instructor and consists of four basic components. The four basic components are: (1) the instructional unit, (2) the instructional task, (3) performance-based task activities, and (4) the performanced-based task check. While the instructional unit and instructional task are simply taken from the curriculum framework and instructional task listing, the performance-based task activities indicate for the instructor what the student will be asked to do in relationship to a given task. The performance-based task check is a measurement of whether or not the student has mastered the task at hand.

The supplemental learning plan is developed for use with the special needs instructional support personnel. It is composed of six basic components: (1) the instructional unit, (2) the instructional task, (3) task terminology, (4) essential math operations, (5) coordinated movements, and (6) related concepts. Just as in the learning plan, the supplemental learning plan incorporates the instructional unit and instructional task from the curriculum framework and instructional task analysis. However, the additional four areas of the supplemental learning plan distinguish it from the learning plan in terms of instructional

support. The task terminology consists of those terms that are necessary for the student to recognize and understand in the accomplishment of a given task. The same is true of the math operations—those math operations that are necessary to student performance. The coordinated movements section indicates the physical activities unique to the task. The related concepts section is an attempt to help identify the stated instructional task with an analogous activity. Examples of a learning plan and supplemental learning plan are presented in Illustrations 8.5 and 8.6. In order for the curriculum supplement to be complete, a learning plan and supplemental learning plan must be developed for each identified instructional task.

The learning and supplemental learning plan concept provide the mechanism to establish the parallel teaching thrust that is necessary for the special needs learner to become sufficiently prepared to enter the world of work. Parallel teaching is mirroring or simulating in the instructional support environment that which takes place in the T & I classroom or laboratory. Parallel teaching allows the learners to become "double insulated," and it is the essence of the cooperative relationship, because it matches the learning technology expertise of the special needs support staff with the occupational content expertise of the T & I staff.

The joint development of the curriculum supplement also provides T & I and special needs instructional support personnel with the opportunity to become familiar with each other's instructional content and methodology. It is obvious that one way in which instructional support personnel can be effectively functional is for them to understand what the T & I instructor is trying to accomplish. By the same token, T & I instructors can become familiar with what instructional support personnel are trying to accomplish. Consequently, the results of this joint development activity can provide curriculum supplements that are

## Illustration 8.4

## INSTRUCTIONAL TASK ANALYSIS FOR INITIAL SHORT
## TERM OBJECTIVE IN MASONRY

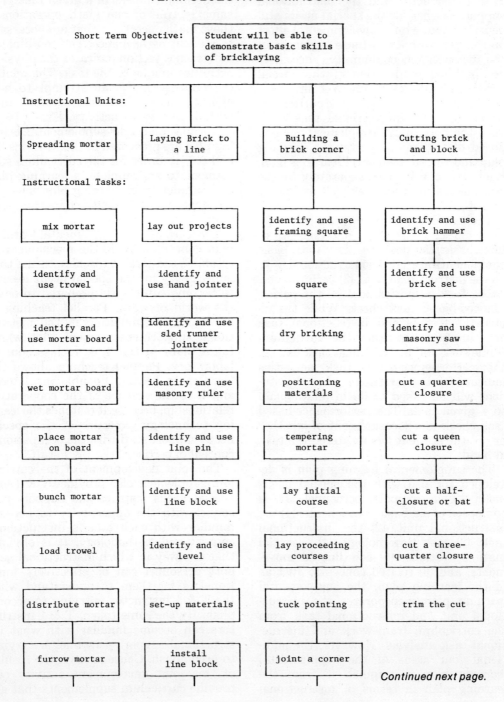

Short Term Objective: | Student will be able to demonstrate basic skills of bricklaying

Instructional Units:

| Spreading mortar | Laying Brick to a line | Building a brick corner | Cutting brick and block |

Instructional Tasks:

| mix mortar | lay out projects | identify and use framing square | identify and use brick hammer |
| identify and use trowel | identify and use hand jointer | square | identify and use brick set |
| identify and use mortar board | identify and use sled runner jointer | dry bricking | identify and use masonry saw |
| wet mortar board | identify and use masonry ruler | positioning materials | cut a quarter closure |
| place mortar on board | identify and use line pin | tempering mortar | cut a queen closure |
| bunch mortar | identify and use line block | lay initial course | cut a half-closure or bat |
| load trowel | identify and use level | lay proceeding courses | cut a three-quarter closure |
| distribute mortar | set-up materials | tuck pointing | trim the cut |
| furrow mortar | install line block | joint a corner | |

*Continued next page.*

**Illustration 8.4 (continued)**

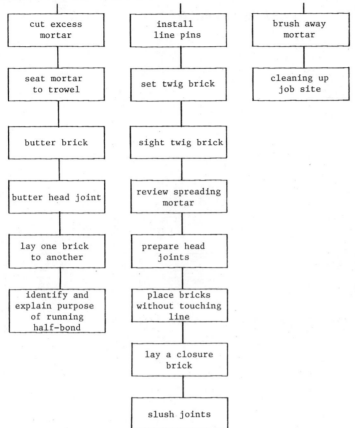

the backbone of the parallel teaching effort, moving curriculum modification from a state of organization to a state of implementation.

Once compiled, the curriculum supplements are used to fortify the occupational preparation process for special needs learners. When a student has difficulty mastering a particular operation, the curriculum supplements can be used to help resolve that difficulty. It is important to realize that curriculum supplements are used to support or supplement the regular instructional process, not supplant it.

## DEVELOPING THE STUDENT MODULE

The final step in the curriculum modification process is the development of the student module. The student module flows directly from the learning and supplementary learning plan and is the culmination of the curriculum framework, instructional task analysis, and curriculum supplement. Utilization of the student module allows the vocational instructor time to work with individual students as needed. It also allows for reinforcement of learning in the instructional support setting. An example of a student module that has been developed in concert with the other examples used in this module is presented in Illustration 8.7.

Although the student module is self-explanatory by way of example, some considerations relative to development need to be mentioned. The student module format consists of four areas.

The first area to be developed is task terminology or what is referred to in the

**Illustration 8.5**

# LEARNING PLAN

Instructional Unit:

| |
|---|
| *Spreading mortar* |

Task No. ___#1___

---

**Instructional Task**

*Mixing mortar*

---

**Performance-Based Task Activities**

*The student will:*

1. *add appropriate ingredients to mortar box;*

2. *mix ingredients together.*

---

**Performance-Based Task Check**

*Given appropriate materials, the student will be able to mix mortar to the proper consistency.*

## Illustration 8.6

## SUPPLEMENTAL LEARNING PLAN

Instructional Unit:

| |
|---|
| *Spreading mortar* |

Task No. _____ *#1* _____

---

**Instructional Task**

    *Mixing mortar*

---

**Task Terminology**

| | |
|---|---|
| *sand* | *mortar box* |
| *shovel* | *wheel barrow* |
| *hoe* | *water* |
| *mortar mix* | *mixture* |
| *mortar* | *ingredients* |
| *carotex* | *masonry cement* |
| *consistency* | *mixer* |
| *temper* | |

---

**Essential Math Operations**

    *counting*
    *proportions*
    *liquid and solid measures*

---

**Essential Coordinated Movements and Related Concepts**

| | | | |
|---|---|---|---|
| *precision working* | *standing* | *pulling* | <u>*Related Concepts*</u>: |
| *manipulating* | *turning* | *lifting* | 1.   *icing on a cake* |
| *handling* | *stooping* | *carrying* | 2.   *mud pies* |
| *walking* | *reaching* | | |
| *balancing* | *pushing* | | |

**Illustration 8.7**

# STUDENT MODULE

VOCATIONAL AREA:  <u>Trade and Industrial Education</u>

PROGRAM:  <u>Construction Trades</u>

OCCUPATION:  <u>Masonry</u>

INSTRUCTIONAL UNIT:  <u>Spreading Mortar</u>

PERFORMANCE TASK:  <u>Mixing Mortar</u>

PERFORMANCE-BASED TASK ACTIVITIES:

You will:

1.  Add correct ingredients to mortar box.

2.  Mix ingredients together.

## WORDS

| HOW TO SPELL | WHAT IT MEANS |
| --- | --- |
| Mixture | Made of many parts |
| Ingredients | Parts of a mixture |
| Mortar | A mud like mixture |
| Mortar Box | What mortar is mixed in |
| Sand | Part of the mortar mixture |
| Water | Part of the mortar mixture |
| Masonry Cement | Part of the mortar mixture |
| Coratex | Can be used instead of mortar mix |
| Temper | Mixing all ingredients together |
| Consistency | When all the parts are well mixed |
| Shovel | A tool to pick up sand or other ingredients |

| | |
|---|---|
| Wheel Barrow | An object used to carry ingredients like sand or masonry cement |
| Hoe | A hand tool used to mix mortar |
| Mixer | A machine used to mix mortar |

YOU WILL LEARN TO:

1. Put sand in a mortar box.

2. Put masonry cement into a mortar box.

3. Mix sand and masonry cement.

4. Add water.

5. Mix sand, masonry cement and water.

YOU WILL BE GIVEN:

Shovel

Wheel Barrow

Mortar Box

Sand

Masonry Cement

Hoe

Water

YOU CAN DO THIS WHEN:

You can mix mortar to a correct consistency.

WHAT YOU DO:

1. Put sand in mortar box.

Here is a picture of a wheel barrow.

The wheel barrow is used to carry sand and masonry cement
to the mortar box.

This is a shovel used to put sand or masonry cement in the
wheelbarrow.

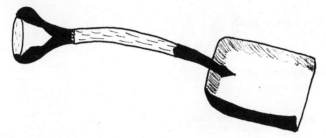

Here is a picture of a mortar box.

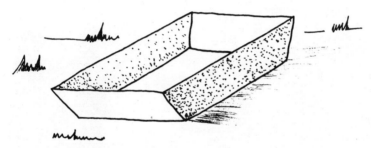

The sand, masonry cement and water are mixed in the
mortar box.

Mortar is a mixture of 3 parts sand,

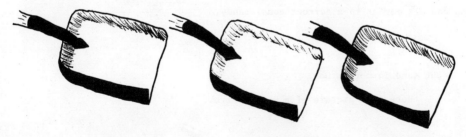

2 parts of masonry cement,

and water.

Now put 3 shovels of sand into the mortar box.

WHAT YOU KNOW:

1. Mortar is made of _____

   _____

   _____

2. Mortar has 2 parts of _____

   Mortar has 3 parts of _____

   Mortar also uses _____

WHAT YOU DO:

2. Put 2 shovels of masonry cement into the mortar box.

3. Mix sand and masonry cement in mortar box.

   This is a hoe.

   The hoe is used to mix the sand and masonry cement

   completely, in this way, until no sand can be seen

   in the mixture.

Pull hoe to you.

Make short chops.

Hit bottom of mortar box with the hoe.

Lift as you pull mixture toward you.

The man in the picture makes short chopping strokes and pulls the sand and masonry cement mixture to him. You will soon have all the mixture at your end of the mortar box. Then go to the other end of the box and begin mixing again.

WHAT YOU KNOW:

1. Number these steps in the right order:

_____ Hit bottom of mortar box with hoe

_____ Make short chops

_____ Lift as you pull

_____ Pull hoe to you

2. (True or False) The sand and masonry cement are completely mixed when no sand can be seen.

Answers

1. 3

   2

   4

   1

2. True

WHAT YOU DO:

4. Pour a little water into the mortar box.

Now completely mix the water, sand and masonry cement again.

5. Now add more water and mix again. Until the mixture looks like thick mud or icing for a cake. (Check with the teacher for correct consistency of mortar.)

WHAT YOU HAVE LEARNED:

1. Mortar is made of _____

_____

_____

2. Mortar has 2 parts of _____

Mortar has 3 parts of _____

Mortar also uses _____

3. Number these steps for mixing the mortar:

_____ Make short chops

_____ Lift as you pull

_____ Pull hoe to you

_____ Hit bottom of mortar box with hoe

4. (True or False)  The sand and masonry cement are completely mixed when no sand can be seen.

5. (True or False)  Water is added to the sand and masonry cement in small amounts.

6. Mortar mixed correctly should look like

   a. Thick mud

   b. Soup

7. Number the steps below in the order that you do them.

   _____ Put sand in mortar box

   _____ Add water

   _____ Add masonry cement to the mortar box

   _____ Mix sand, masonry cement and water

   _____ Mix sand and masonry cement


M I X I N G    M O R T A R

sample student module as "words." The "words" section includes the terms identified on the supplemental learning plan. However, the student module goes one step further and defines each term. The definition of terms relative to the student module are functional in nature. Unless absolutely necessary, specific technical definitions are avoided. This is done to avoid potential vocabulary problems that may arise for some special needs learners.

Defining the actual job steps is the second area of development for the student module. The definition of job steps requires that each performance-based task activity listed on the learning plan be "spelled out" in considerable detail. The job steps also rely heavily upon the math operations, coordinated movements, and related concepts sections of the supplemental learning plan.

As the job steps are being delineated in the student module, they must also be clearly illustrated. The illustrations serve to clarify the job steps in the mastery of an instructional task. The illustrations may be either original or borrowed from another source. Whichever route is taken, the illustrations should be clear and concise. Complex illustrations may serve to confuse rather than clarify.

The fourth and final area of student module development involves an evaluation of the student's progress. The student module incorporates two types of evaluation: formative and summative. Formative evaluation is an enroute assessment or indication of how well the student is faring up to a specific point. Summative evaluation is an indication of how well the student did on the complete module. In addition to measuring progress, use of both the formative and summative evaluation techniques can help prevent minor difficulties from developing into major deficiencies.

## SUMMARY

The curriculum modification process described in this module consists of four major steps. These steps range from establishing the curriculum framework to developing a student module. *Curriculum* in relationship to vocational education has been defined as the sum total of all the experiences and activities encountered by the student in pursuit of occupational preparation under the direction of the school. *Curriculum modification* has been defined as the tailoring of those experiences and activities to meet the unique needs of the individual student.

The four-step model that has been described flows directly from within the confines and context of the regular T & I education curriculum. If curriculum modification does not exhibit this characteristic, it is not curriculum modification; it is curriculum development. Obviously, these are two separate endeavors. The module presented here describes each of the four proposed steps to curriculum modification in detail and utilizes examples for each step. Although the four-step model is presented very simplistically, it does not attempt to disguise the fact that its implementation requires a significant amount of labor on the part of both the T & I instructor and special needs instructional support personnel over an extended period of time.

Modifying or adapting the regular T & I program curriculum is probably one of the most pressing tasks facing the T & I instructor at this point in time. Its difficulty lies not so much in what needs to be done as in the actual process of doing it. However, it should be pointed out that modifying the curriculum for the special needs learner enhances the usability of the curriculum for all students who enroll in the program.

# REFERENCES

Gill, D. Mainstreaming in the vocational setting. *Technical Education News,* September-October, 1980.

Gill, D. and Scott, C. A practical model for mainstreaming handicapped learners in vocational education. *The Journal for Vocational Special Needs Education,* April, 1979.

O'Kelley, G. Approaches to curriculum planning in law, Gordon, F. (Ed.), *Contemporary Concepts in Vocational Education,* The American Vocational Association, 1971.

*RVI Curriculum Supplements for Construction Trades,* Vocational Education Materials Center, The University of Georgia, 1978.

Sullivan, P. Career related instruction offers a head start. *School Shop,* 1978, *37*(8).

## SELF ASSESSMENT: MODIFYING THE CURRICULUM FOR SPECIAL NEEDS LEARNERS IN TRADE AND INDUSTRIAL EDUCATION PROGRAMS

1. What is a curriculum?
2. What is curriculum modification?
3. What are the three major components of establishing a curriculum framework?
4. What are two considerations in developing an instructional task analysis?
5. Who is responsible for developing the curriculum supplement?
6. What are the two major parts of the curriculum supplement?
7. How does one part of the curriculum supplement relate to the other?
8. What are four considerations in the development of the student module?
9. Explain the overall process for modifying the T & I curriculum to meet the needs of the special student.

## CASE HISTORY: GARY'S STORY

Gary is a health impaired learner enrolled in an electrical technology program. Gary has had a serious case of asthma since childhood. Luckily, he was diagnosed early and received help from a respiratory clinic for a number of years. He is now able to lead a normal life with the help of medication. During his grade school years, he missed quite a bit of school and had to rely on the school's homebound instruction in order to keep up with his peers.

Gary's introduction to vocational education was far from successful. Expressing a desire to become a barber, he enrolled in a four-quarter course which he hoped would adequately prepare him to pass the State Barbering Board examination for a barber's license. Unfortunately, the shampooing, haircutting, and hair styling phases of the program severely affected his asthma and he was forced to withdraw from the program.

After a brief period of aimlessness, Gary sought vocational counseling and, after a series of aptitude and interest tests and a number of counseling sessions, he was able to select a realistic vocational program goal that would not conflict with or jeopardize his asthmatic condition. Therefore, several possible interest areas —cabinetmaking and chemical technology—were ruled out because of the possible negative effects of the dust and chemicals on his impaired health.

Gary is well adjusted to his health impairment. He has learned how to anticipate the first symptoms of an attack, which makes it possible for him to take control of the attack instead of permitting it to control him. He has also learned relaxation techniques to help him during the attacks and has learned to drink warm coater to help control the attacks. He knows how to administer his own medication.

Gary is succeeding very well in the electrical technology program. He remains at the top of the class in the areas of technical mathematics, electrical installation and planning, and industrial electronics. His occupational goal is to become an engineering design operator. His instructor feels that Gary will have no problems achieving his goal and already has several prospective employers in mind for when Gary completes the program.

## CASE HISTORY ACTIVITY

Natalie has recently enrolled in your program. She has a moderate case of arthritis in her left hand and in her knees. She has missed some school the past year and a half due to medical appointments. Natalie is very bright. She scored high on standardized tests in reading and math. She also has a very positive attitude and a strong desire to succeed in your program.

Based on this information, complete the case history profile worksheet for Natalie's participation in your program.

# CASE HISTORY PROFILE WORKSHEET

Student: _____ Page: _____

Handicapping Condition(s): _____

T & I Program: _____ Academic Levels: _____

Career Goal/Occupational Interest: _____

Considerations (e.g., medication, behavior): _____

_____

| Adaptation | Specific Services Needed | Where to Obtain Service |
|---|---|---|
| Cooperative Planning (School Personnel) | | |
| Support Services | | |
| Architectural Changes | | |
| Adaptive Equipment | | |
| Curriculum Modification | | |
| Instructional Materials/ Supplies | | |
| Teaching Techniques | | |
| Agency Involvement | | |
| Possible Job Placement | | |

# MODULE 9

## Instructional Techniques and Evaluation Methods

The methods T & I teachers use to present program information to special needs learners may make the difference between success and failure. One instructional technique will not meet the unique needs of every handicapped and disadvantaged learner enrolled in a T & I program. Therefore, a variety of techniques should be used to address the individual differences of these students.

Each special needs learner will have individual abilities, needs, learning styles, and occupational goals. These should be considered in designing the instructional program and identifying the ways in which instruction will be delivered. It is often helpful for T & I teachers to work cooperatively with other personnel who may be familiar with appropriate instructional techniques for specific special needs students.

The evaluation system for measuring and reporting the progress of special needs students should be based on their needs and capabilities rather than on how well these students perform as compared with other students. The IEP serves as the basic guide for establishing an evaluation system, and the cooperative effort of IEP team members can result in a system that is fair and reasonable to all students.

This module will present information concerning two major areas: (1) instructional techniques and (2) evaluation methods. These areas will address instructional techniques that can be used to meet the abilities, learning styles, and specific needs of handicapped and disadvantaged

learners enrolled in T & I programs. In addition, information on establishing an evaluation and grading system to measure and report the progress of special needs students will be discussed.

Sections in this module include: (a) demonstrations, (b) field trips and job site visitations, (c) grouping, (d) individualized instruction activities, (e) media aids, (f) projects, (g) simulation and role-playing activities, (h) student-teacher contracts, (i) task analysis, (j) team teaching, (k) tutors, (l) the IEP as a guide to evaluation, (m) evaluation topics, (n) establishing the evaluation system, (o) evaluation methods and techniques, and (p) grading and marking systems.

## MODULE OBJECTIVES

After you have read and reviewed this module, studied the case history, reviewed the self assessment questions, and completed the associated activities, you should be able to:

1. Discuss the nature of individual differences among students and explain why a variety of instructional techniques should be utilized with special needs learners.

2. List a number of different instructional techniques that can be used to meet the needs of handicapped and disadvantaged learners enrolled in T & I programs.

3. Describe how these various instructional techniques can be incorporated into your T & I program.

4. Describe why the evaluation and grading system for special needs students should be based upon their needs and abilities rather than on how they perform as compared with other students.

5. Develop an evaluation and grading system for special needs students based upon the IEP.

Special needs learners represent a diverse population of learners who possess a variety of different learning styles. They cannot all learn at the same rate or through the same instructional techniques.

The characteristics, abilities, interests, learning styles, and the needs of each student must be taken into consideration.

## INSTRUCTIONAL TECHNIQUES

Trade and industrial teachers are beginning to experience success with special needs learners by utilizing a variety of approaches to delivering program instruction. A number of different techniques are described in this module. The point should be made that not every instructional technique presented here can be used successfully with every special needs learner. It will require a degree of flexibility and experimentation on the part of T & I teachers to determine which techniques best meet the needs of each handicapped or disadvantaged learner. Cooperative planning with other personnel who are familiar with the student can be very helpful in selecting and utilizing appropriate instructional techniques.

Some initial considerations should be addressed by T & I personnel when selecting instructional techniques to be used with special needs learners. These considerations include such important concerns as: (a) individual differences among students, (b) ability levels of the students (e.g., reading level, math level, vocational assessment results, present level of educational performance information on the IEP), (c) preferred learning style of the student, and (d) difficulty of subject matter to be covered (e.g., readability levels of books and materials, related terminology, level of related math involved).

Trade and industrial teachers should be willing to exercise flexibility in selecting and utilizing instructional techniques. They should also be willing to modify their teaching style to meet the specific needs of students in the class. Cooperative planning, instructional resources, and support services can be beneficial in the instructional planning, implementation, and evaluation stages. Many of the initial considerations mentioned above are discussed further in Module 6.

## Demonstrations

The demonstration method is a very effective technique to use in introducing a new skill to special needs learners. By showing students how to perform a task while explaining the procedure, the teacher enables special needs students to use more than one sense and learning mode at the same time. They can listen to the instructor while observing the proper performance steps of the task or skill being demonstrated. Usually an activity or laboratory assignment will follow which allows students to practice what they have seen and heard.

In preparing a demonstration, the T & I teacher should identify the sequence of steps that will be necessary to display fully the specific skill, task, or procedure. Tasks should be broken down into small steps to avoid confusing or frustrating students. Sufficient time should be set aside for the demonstration without attempting to present too much new material at one time. A demonstration can be organized into several sessions if necessary.

Tips which may be useful to T & I teachers in preparing a demonstration include the following:

1. Arrange all supplies, materials, tools, and equipment that will be needed during the demonstration.

2. Introduce the demonstration by reviewing previously taught information and/or skills that are relevant to the demonstration.

3. Introduce and discuss any technical terms that are relevant to the demonstration.

4. Emphasize relevant safety practices during the demonstration.

5. Demonstrate the manipulative skill or task in a way that closely resembles the actual work environment where the skill or task will be performed.

6. Use visual materials (e.g., charts and diagrams) whenever possible to reinforce the performance steps being demonstrated.

7. Question students periodically during the demonstration to be certain that

they are able to follow and understand the performance steps being demonstrated.

8. The demonstration may have to be repeated for students who did not grasp fully all of the details and, in some cases, broken down into smaller steps and presented more slowly.

9. Assign a related activity following the demonstration (The Center for Vocational Education, 1977).

Some specific considerations to keep in mind regarding special needs learners when preparing a demonstration include the following:

1. Visually handicapped learners may need to stand close to the teacher while the demonstration is taking place and/or be allowed to "feel" the various performance steps as the teacher demonstrates them.

2. Hearing impaired students may need to stand close to the teacher while the demonstration is taking place and/or be provided with the services of an interpreter.

3. Some special needs learners (e.g., mentally handicapped, learning disabled, emotionally disturbed/behavior disordered, and disadvantaged) may profit from hearing the demonstration more than once if the teacher will tape-record the session.

4. Special considerations may have to be made for specific physical disabilities during the demonstration and/or the related follow-up activity.

### Field Trips and Job Site Visitations

Many special needs learners have had little or no first-hand exposure to specific occupations that are available in the community. Field trips or job site visitations can provide students with an opportunity to observe workers on the job, allow them to become familiar with the specific duties involved in jobs related to the T & I program, and provide information about possible exit points available through the program.

Field trips and job site visitations can be arranged for the entire class, small groups of students, or on an individual basis. They can be used as (a) career exploration activities, (b) incentives or rewards for completion of program assignments and units, (c) individual, group or class projects, (d) class reports, and/or (e) preplacement exposure experiences. Observations made during these visitations can be valuable in relating classroom and laboratory activities to the world of work.

One particular method that allows students to experience field trips and job site observations is called *shadowing*. This method involves making arrangements for a student or small group of students to spend time on the job with a worker in a particular occupational area. By acting as a "shadow," students gain an insight into the actual work environment and work tasks associated with the job. For students who have never before observed workers on the job this experience offers them a realistic look into the world of work and can assist them in making appropriate career decisions. Sources of workers to be used in this technique include employers who have hired former graduates and advisory committee contacts.

Trade and industrial teachers can use this teaching technique to develop leadership skills and a sense of responsibility for special needs learners by including them in the various stages of planning field trips, job site visitations, and shadowing experiences. They can be given responsibility for contacting the business or industry, making arrangements with the employer and/or co-workers, planning for appropriate transportation services, obtaining permission from school officials, and taking leadership responsibility for preparing class reports, group discussions and follow-up activities.

### Grouping

Grouping can be an effective way for T & I teachers to individualize classroom instruction and laboratory activities for special needs students. This method consists of organizing students into various size groups according to the objective of the lesson or the nature of the activity. Grouping allows the program instructor to arrange classroom and laboratory experiences so that special needs learners are integrated and participating with their peers. It can also be used as a technique to provide remedial assistance by forming small groups of students in need of academic or technical assistance. Special activities students can also be grouped according to ability level or the level that they have achieved on a certain unit, module, or assignment. Another grouping arrangement option is to organize students according to interests. Perhaps the most useful grouping approach is called flexible grouping. Teachers using this technique use different types of grouping arrangements in different situations so that all students in the class learn to work together in a variety of situations.

Grouping has several advantages for both the T & I teacher and the special needs learners:

1. It allows the T & I teacher more time to work among students in the class rather than having to spend a great deal of time with one or two students.

2. It allows the T & I teacher to individualize instruction, tasks, and assignments to meet the needs of students in a specific group.

3. It provides special needs learners with an opportunity to work with peers and establish positive interpersonal and working relationships with them.

4. It serves as a motivating factor for special needs learners because the individualized nature of the group work does not threaten or frustrate them and allows them to work at their own pace through their strongest learning style.

5. It allows another effective instructional technique, peer tutoring, to develop between special needs learners and their peers.

6. It allows T & I teachers to arrange for instruction for the entire class, small group discussions, project groups, and small remedial sessions so that instruction will be diversified and more meaningful for all students enrolled in the program.

7. It allows the T & I teacher to meet the learning needs of specific special needs learners in a small group through the use of media, supplementary services, and instructional resources.

8. It allows the T & I teacher to modify the task or assignment for a small group of students with specific needs, as in the case of learners who have a physical disability.

## Individualized Instruction Activities

Individualized instruction is a method of instruction that is tailored to meet the particular needs of each student and that allows the T & I teacher a variety of alternatives in delivering program instruction. This method is particularly useful in working with special needs learners because it allows them to work at their own pace using resources, media, and materials that will assist them in learning.

This approach does not require that T & I teachers water down course objectives or compromise on proficiency skills necessary for program completion. It does, however, mean that T & I teachers should work closely with other school personnel to find out as much relevant information about each special needs learner as possible so that an appropriate individualized instruction program can be established and implemented. This information should include such details as the student's reading level, math level, other relevant abilities, interests, occupational goals, and preferred learning style. In other words, individual differences among students must be taken into consideration in planning instruction. For handicapped students, much of this information should be available in the individualized education program (IEP).

There are various techniques involved

in the individualized instruction approach. Examples of these techniques include:

1. Units.
2. Modules.
3. Learning activity packets.
4. Learning center activities.
5. Self-paced and programmed instruction materials.
6. Independent and supervised study activities.

Individualized instruction experiences can motivate special needs learners and increase their attention span. They are able to assume responsibility for completing program assignments while being able to progress at their own learning rate in a manner that does not threaten or frustrate them. In addition, they are evaluated according to their own progress and the quality of work produced rather than being compared to the progress of other students in the class.

Individualized instruction can assist the T & I teacher in helping more students in the class rather than spending a great deal of time with one or two special needs learners. By working at their own pace and ability level, special needs students can successfully progress through the task or assignment with a minimum amount of help from the teacher. Many of the reading and writing assignments can be self-checked by the student. This releases the T & I teacher to work with other students. Spot checks, pre-tests, and post-tests can be administered by the T & I teacher and/or support staff to help assess student progress.

In designing a program of individualized instruction for use with special needs learners, the following considerations should be addressed by T & I teachers:

1. Individualized instruction experiences can be developed specifically for one special needs learner or for a small group who have similar abilities and interests.

2. Even if it takes special needs learners longer to complete required tasks or assignments, they should be given the same credit as other students who com-plete the work in less time as long as the quality of the completed work meets the standards of the teacher.

3. Specific objectives should be developed and carefully explained to special needs learners before they begin the activity or assignment and should be stated in behavioral or performance terms so that students clearly understand exactly what they are to do.

4. T & I teachers should determine what previous knowledge and/or skills are necessary for completion of the individualized assignment and make certain that students possess the prerequisite information, terminology, and skills.

5. Special needs students should be aware of the tools, equipment, materials, resources, media, and aids that will be provided to assist them in completing the activity or assignment.

6. Routine and periodic supervision should be provided by T & I instructors while students are working on individualized instruction activities.

7. Criteria for evaluation should be clearly defined and understood before the activity or assignment is started.

8. The learning environment where individualized instruction is to take place should be flexible and allow for a variety of activities and experiences according to the specific needs of the students.

9. Individualized instruction materials, modules, units, or packets have been developed for many T & I programs, and teachers should contact the State Department of Education, other teachers, local vocational administrators, companies producing commercial materials, and other sources to obtain readily available materials that can meet the specific needs of special needs learners as well as of the T & I program.

## Media Aids

Educational media aids can make an important contribution to the teaching of concepts in T & I programs. They can (a) assist the T & I teacher in presenting the proficiency or skill requirements for a specific job, (b) reinforce concepts presented in a classroom, laboratory, or demonstration activity, (c) provide a vehicle for special needs learners to show what they have learned, (d) provide a valuable source of remedial assistance, (e) provide simulated learning experiences, (f) provide individualized learning experiences, (g) allow special needs learners to learn through their strongest style, and (h) add variety to the instructional program.

Specific media aids that can be used to accommodate the individual needs of handicapped and disadvantaged learners include the following:

1. Audiotapes (cassette, reel-to-reel).
2. Films (sound, silent, and/or captioned).
3. Filmstrips/filmloops (sound or silent).
4. Flip charts.
5. Models.
6. Charts.
7. Diagrams.
8. Tape recorders.
9. Slides (regular and captioned) and projectors.
10. Overhead transparencies.
11. Educational television (sound and/or captioned).
12. Radio programs.
13. Videotapes.
14. Opaque projections.
15. Graphs.
16. Maps.
17. Photographs (student-made, teacher-made, and commercial).
18. Exhibits.
19. Bulletin boards.
20. Posters.
21. Records.
22. Videotapes (reel-to-reel, cassette).
23. Audiovisual teaching machines.
24. Learning centers equipped with an activity format.
25. Computer/television and computer/radio.
26. Slide tape presentations.
27. Magazines and newspapers.

## Projects

Projects can be a useful technique in providing special needs learners with an opportunity to develop independent and interpersonal skills. It can also provide T & I teachers with a method of observing and evaluating student progress.

Projects can be done individually or in small groups. Specific projects can be assigned, or they can be selected or developed by the students. Work on the project can take place in the classroom, in the laboratory, in other areas of the school, at home, in a community environment, or in a combination of these settings. When assigning a project, T & I teachers should make certain that the objectives are clearly stated and understood, as well as the general tasks involved in the project and the specific criteria for evaluation.

Advantages of using such projects to assist special needs learners include the following:

1. They can act as motivating experiences for special needs students to demonstrate the competencies and skills they have learned in the T & I program.
2. They can help special needs students to relate the knowledge and skills of the T & I instructional program to practical experiences.
3. They can help special needs students to develop responsibility in selecting an appropriate project area and/or in actively participating in the planning and completion stages.
4. They allow special needs students to practice the proper use of machinery, tools, equipment, and raw materials associated with the T & I program.
5. They allow supervision of special needs students as they progress at their own pace.
6. They allow T & I teachers to evaluate the level and degree of proficiency that special needs students demonstrate while working on the project as well as the quality of the finished product.

Examples of projects that can be assigned by T & I teachers or developed by special needs students follow:

1. Projects designed for the classroom and/or laboratory:
   a. memo pads (graphic arts)
   b. knurled center punch (machine trades)
   c. tool box (sheet metal fabrication)
   d. battery tester (electronics)
   e. saw horses (construction trades)
2. Projects designed for other areas of the school:
   a. magazine racks (construction trades)
   b. brick or stone planters (masonry)
   c. letter heads (graphic arts)
   d. construction plans (drafting)
3. Projects designed for completion at home:
   a. brick steps or patio (masonry)
   b. replace lamp cords (electrical trades)
   c. replace faucet washer (plumbing)
   d. change oil in car (auto mechanics)
4. Projects designed for completion in the community:
   a. build and install picnic tables at local parks (construction trades)
   b. repair sidewalks for a public building (masonry)
   c. replace light switch for public building (electrical trades)
   d. print posters for community fund raising activities (graphic arts)
5. Projects designed for completion in a combination of settings:
   a. build storage cabinets (cabinet making)
   b. install a wall receptacle outlet (electrical trades)
   c. prepare and serve refreshments (food service)
   d. prepare plans for a project (drafting).

### Simulation and Role-playing Activities

Simulation and role-playing activities can help T & I teachers provide realistic experiences that lend themselves to a specific occupational area and to the world of work in general. This technique is especially relevant to those special needs learners who have never been exposed to job training or employment situations.

Simulation and role-playing experiences have several advantages for special needs learners, including:

1. Allowing them to learn and practice appropriate occupational behaviors and skills in a nonthreatening environment without fearing failure.
2. Allowing them to develop interpersonal relationships with their peers.
3. Helping them to relate the concepts and skills being taught in the T & I program to the world of work.
4. Assisting them to develop appropriate decision-making skills.
5. Providing them with experiences that will enable them to analyze their own behaviors and reactions and develop appropriate alternatives.
6. Allowing special needs learners to exercise their abilities and skills in a situation other than a reading or writing exercise.
7. Providing for constructive criticism and relevant feedback from T & I teachers and peers concerning appropriate reactions to a specific simulation or role-playing situation.

Examples of topical areas that could be used to develop simulation and role-playing activities include (a) preparing for a job interview, (b) getting along with co-workers, (c) reacting to criticism from a supervisor, (d) dealing with customers, (e) reacting to job-related pressure, and (f) displaying appropriate skills in completing a product in the laboratory.

In developing simulation and role-playing activities for use with special needs learners, T & I teachers should make certain that learners clearly understand the purpose of the activity and their roles as participants and reactors. Sufficient time should be provided for feedback and discussion following the completion of the activity.

Examples of specific simulation and role-playing activities that can be developed and assigned by T & I teachers to assist special needs learners follow:

1. Greeting a customer in a cosmetology shop.

2. Taking food orders from a customer in a restaurant.

3. Listening to an irate customer complain about service work done on his/her car.

4. Introducing a friend or visitor to the class or to fellow workers.

5. Demonstrating how to organize tools and materials for work.

6. Demonstrating how to sell oneself in a job interview.

7. Demonstrating how to take constructive criticism from a job supervisor.

8. Demonstrating the work habits that show initiative and industriousness.

9. Carrying on a conversation with a patron in a cosmetology shop.

10. Demonstrating safe work habits in performing a work task.

## Student-Teacher Contracts

Student-teacher contracts developed between T & I teachers and special needs learners can be an effective method in assisting them to succeed in meeting program requirements. The contract should be honest, fair, and positive. The terms of the contract should be developed cooperatively. It should contain terms and conditions that are clearly understood by all parties involved. The contract payoff or reward should be identified as well as the consequences to be accepted by the learner if contract terms are not met.

Some guidelines for developing student-teacher contracts follow:

1. Decide on the specific project, task, or assignment—requirements should be stated specifically.

2. Determine the minimum acceptable accuracy.

3. Set a time limit.

4. Decide on rewards and other consequences relating to the contract.

5. Both the special needs learner and the T & I teacher should review the con-

tract, reach an agreement, and sign it.

6. The special needs learner should work toward completion of the contract.

7. Both the T & I teacher and the special needs learner should periodically evaluate progress on the contract as well as the completed product.

8. The student should accept either the reward or consequence agreed upon. (Young, 1976)

Trade and industrial teachers should address the following concerns to effectively evaluate student-teacher contracts:

1. Did the special needs learner begin the contract within a reasonable amount of time?

2. Did the special needs learner organize essential materials, supplies, tools, and equipment in a way that makes the best use of study or project time?

3. Did the special needs learner organize overall project time wisely?

4. Did the T & I teacher provide positive reinforcement during the time the special needs learner was working to complete the contract requirements?

5. Was the specified time period too short for completion of the contract?

6. Would a system of self-checks have been beneficial to the special needs learner (e.g., self-correcting exercises or programmed instruction materials)? (Young, 1976)

Further information concerning student-teacher contracts is provided in Module 6.

## Task Analysis

Task analysis is a technique that can be extremely effective with special needs learners. It involves analyzing a job task and the competencies required to successfully complete the task. In the process, the task is broken into its component parts. The task should have a major goal or objective associated with it. The goal or objective should be clearly described at the beginning of the task analysis so that the T & I teacher, the special needs student, and/or support personnel will have a clear understanding of what is expected at the completion of the task analysis activity.

Skills and competencies associated with the task should then be identified. This includes prerequisite skills that are necessary to perform the task as well as skills that will be necessary to complete the specific steps of the task analysis. Identification of skills and competencies can be facilitated by consulting curriculum guides, other T & I personnel, and specific program requirements.

The job task should then be broken down into a series of small steps. The number of steps into which the task is broken depends upon the abilities and needs of the student. In other words, in the case of special needs students who learn more slowly than other students, the job task should be broken down into more specific steps.

The steps of the task analysis should be written in performance terms so that the learners know exactly what has to be done to complete each step. The directions for completing each step should be short, clear, and specific. The steps should be listed in order so that when all of the sequential steps have been successfully completed, the task will be mastered.

The task analysis procedure is an effective technique to use with most special needs learners because only one step of the task is introduced at a time. Students work at their own pace and can practice each step as many times as necessary until success is experienced. A new step is not introduced until success is experienced. A new step is not introduced until all previous steps in the task analysis have been mastered. Therefore, this procedure is effective in allowing these learners to master the task at their own pace while at the same time motivating them from one step to another.

When developing task analysis activities, T & I teachers should identify criteria for completion of the task. It is important that both the teacher and the student be aware of the evaluation requirements for completion of the task.

An example of a task analysis developed for use with special needs learners enrolled in a specific T & I program follows:

## Sample Task Analysis

*Program:* Cosmetology*
*Duty:* Setting and combing hair into styles
*Task:* Make pin curls
*Steps of Procedure:*
1. Sanitize hands.
2. Seat patron (draped and shampooed).
3. Discuss desired hair style with patron.
4. Select and arrange needed materials.
5. Comb through hair to remove tangles.
6. Apply setting lotion (unless patron requests otherwise).
7. Comb setting lotion through hair, ending with hair combed in the direction of desired style.
8. Slice out small section of hair.
9. Ribbon section through comb to smooth hair.
10. Roll pin curl according to style desired.
11. Secure curl with clip in a position that will not interfere with next curl.
12. Repeat steps 8 through 11, overlapping each additional pin curl.
13. Continue procedure described in step 12 until desired style has been achieved.
*Criterion:*
1. Selected correct tools and materials.
2. Followed correct procedure.
3. Curls were wound smoothly.
4. Curls were appropriate for desired hair style.
5. Spot pin curls were installed in 15 minutes.
6. All pin curls were completed in 30 minutes.
7. Patron was satisfied.

*Adapted from V-TECH catalog for Cosmetology, available from V-TECH Consortium of States.

## Team Teaching

Team teaching, as in the case of cooperative planning, is an excellent way to combine the knowledge and expertise of several professionals in a common effort to help special needs learners succeed in T & I programs. The team can be composed of two or more individuals who will use various skills to meet the specific needs of these students. Team membership can include representation from (a) other T & I teachers, (b) other vocational education personnel, (c) special education personnel, (d) disadvantaged specialists, (e) teacher aides, and (f) support personnel.

Team teaching requires planning and coordination among the team members in order to clarify goals, objectives, content, instructional techniques, and evaluation methods for a specific unit, module, lesson, or activity. This method works particularly well when combined with flexible grouping. In this manner, team members can work with a small group of special needs learners and use a variety of teaching methods, media, and remedial techniques to meet the unique needs of individuals in the group.

Members of the team should contribute and lead in those areas where their strength and expertise lie. Cooperative team teaching arrangements for special needs learners should incorporate a schedule and a list of responsibilities so that individuals can prepare their contributions to the team effort. Planning should also take into consideration the following concerns: (a) use of media aids, (b) amount of time required for each session or activity, (c) necessary facilities, supplies, equipment, and tools, and (d) appropriate assessment methods.

Planning can be organized for large group sessions, small group sessions and/or individualized sessions. This will allow for one team member to work with special needs learners who may need remedial assistance in program terminology, reading assignments, related math, preparing for a test or quiz, or practicing hands-on skills.

## Tutors

Tutors can be extremely effective in working with handicapped and disadvantaged learners. This method of instruction can be beneficial in a number of ways. The special needs learner is given an opportunity to develop interpersonal relations with others. It also relieves the T & I teacher from having to spend an unrealistic amount of time with one or two students. Tutoring enables students who may be progressing slower than others to develop the proficiencies that are necessary for success in the program.

Tutors can be used to teach content area instruction, reinforce classroom instruction, assist in teaching remedial academics (e.g., reading and math), perform presentations and demonstrations, work in one-to-one or small group activities in the laboratory, aid in completing classroom assignments and projects, and help review for tests.

There are a variety of sources from which tutors can be recruited. Examples of the types of tutors available to T & I teachers are:

1. Instructor tutoring can be done by the T & I teacher, special needs staff, or a team approach by both. Tutoring can be done on a one-to-one or a small group basis, depending on the number of special needs learners who require assistance.

2. The *buddy system* employs what is commonly referred to as peer tutoring. This method pairs a special needs learner with another student in the class. In many cases both the peer tutor and the special needs learner improve through reinforcement of program content. The peer tutor feels competent and useful by being selected to tutor. The special needs learner can progress at an individualized pace without pressure from others in the class. Peer tutoring relationships frequently foster enthusiasm, motivation, confidence, increased attendance, improved performance, and positive attitudes toward school.

Peer tutors can be recruited from students in the same class, students enrolled in advanced courses, and student volunteers interested in pursuing a career in teaching (e.g., members of the Future Teachers of America organization). Extra credit can be offered as an incentive. Schedules will have to be arranged cooperatively with students and other teachers.

3. Senior citizens can be an excellent source of volunteer tutors. This valuable resource should not be overlooked. Retirees have many years of occupational experience from which to draw. They have a need to feel useful and contributing. They can share their experience and expertise with special needs learners. In return, they receive a sense of dignity and respect, a chance for social interaction, and a sense of commitment to share their knowledge with others. In addition to tutoring students in skills development and remedial academics, senior citizens can offer career guidance and job-seeking information to handicapped and disadvantaged learners. Retirees have an understanding of the requirements, performance skills, and social skills necessary for employment in a specific occupational area. They may also have contacts in the community who would be willing to hire special needs learners.

4. College students can also be a potential source of volunteer tutors. If these individuals are in teacher preparation programs, they may welcome an opportunity to work with students and gain some practical teaching experience.

5. Part-time workers in the community can often be encouraged to volunteer their services to tutor special needs learners. The schedules of the students will have to be modified in some cases to meet the schedules of the tutors.

6. Parents of students can also serve as volunteer tutors. The T & I teacher can enlist the services of parents regarding program objectives and specific services they can provide special needs learners through tutoring.

## EVALUATION METHODS

One of the concerns frequently expressed by T & I teachers is how to make evaluation fair to both special needs students and other students without lowering program standards. This topic was presented briefly in Module 6 and will be discussed in more detail here.

The evaluation and grading system used by T & I teachers should be reasonable and fair to all students and should be based on their capabilities and needs rather than on a system that compares students with other students. In other words, the evaluation system should be based on the amount of progress made by students and the quality of work produced as compared to the assessed abilities, interests, and needs of each student.

This does not mean that T & I teachers should lower program standards for special needs students so they can earn passing grades. If special needs students are to be employable upon completion of the program, they must meet employability standards set by industry. Rather than lowering program standards, T & I teachers need to design flexibility into their program and provide training for a variety of jobs that requrie different sets of competencies and different levels of achievement.

Multiple exit points leading to a variety of jobs in trades and industry can be identified for each trade and industrial program. This approach, involving multiple exit points, can provide T & I teachers with a way to match the abilities and proficiencies of students with realistic employment opportunities and improve the chances for students to successfully complete portions of the total program leading to productive employment.

Flexibility in planning T & I programs involves more than providing multiple exit points. It also provides students with extended time when necessary to successfully complete individual education programs. If the final goal is for students to master a specified set of competencies at set industrial standards, then it makes sense to allow special needs learners more time to develop these competencies if necessary. This procedure is certainly better than failing these students because they cannot keep up with the predetermined pace.

Flexibility in planning programs in which special needs students can experience success should also involve special needs support personnel. Special education teachers and other support personnel can offer remedial instruction to students who are not able to keep up with other students in assigned work activities. This additional instruction can often mean the difference between success and failure for special needs students enrolled in T & I programs.

## The IEP as a Guide for Evaluation

The overall guide for evaluating handicapped students enrolled in T & I programs should be the vocational component of the IEP. The IEP contains a listing of goals and short-term objectives that relate to the needs and abilities of students in relation to a predetermined job or career. Evaluation should be based on the progress or achievement that these students have demonstrated in successfully accomplishing the content contained in the IEP.

The rules and regulations of Public Law 94–142 specify that the short-term objectives of the IEP be evaluated at least annually. This is a minimal standard, however, for it is inconceivable that T & I teachers would allow a year to pass before evaluating student progress toward accomplishing the objectives specified in the IEP. If T & I teachers only evaluated student progress on the IEP annually, they would not be able to recognize problem areas and make appropriate adjustments in the objectives of the IEP, teaching techniques, instructional materials, classroom and laboratory environment, and support services, which are often required to help special needs students achieve

their maximum potential. Evaluation must become an integral part of the daily teaching-learning progress and not simply an exercise that occurs at the end of a specified grading period.

## Evaluation Topics

There are many factors that should be considered when evaluating student progress in T & I programs. Some of these major factors are as follows:

1. Task or competency performance.
2. Work habit development.
3. Attendance.
4. Attitude and personal growth.
5. Daily class effort.
6. Quality of homework and outside assignments.
7. Performance on quizzes and tests measuring cognitive achievement.
8. Safety practices.
9. Completed project or product.

Many T & I teachers make use of multiple factors in their evaluation and grading systems. They have found that including a variety of factors in the evaluation and grading system provides incentive for students to develop proficiencies in the three major areas that concern employers: skill performance, theory or understanding as required to perform work tasks effectively, and work attitude and work habits as required to become a good employee.

The practice of using multiple factors in the evaluation and grading system provides several advantages for special needs students. First, it provides students with a guide to the type of behaviors expected in the program. If students are aware that their grades will be based on daily work performance, demonstration of good work habits and a positive attitude, quizzes and written tests, and performance of required tasks or competencies, they will normally exert more attention to these areas. The second advantage is that it provides some components that can be covered through remedial instruction by special education teachers to improve student performance. A third advantage is that it provides a way of earning a passing grade in a class even though a student may do poorly on one factor, such as quizzes or tests. Finally, using a variety of evaluation factors makes it possible to provide more specific feedback to the student about areas of strength and weakness in preparing for employment. It also provides direction to the teacher for altering the instructional approach or learning environment. Additional information on using multiple evaluative factors will be presented in the grading system segment of this module.

## Establishing the Evaluation System

Trade and industrial education teachers will need to plan which factors they will consider in evaluating each special needs student. The IEP can be a useful tool for planning and implementing the evaluation system. During the preparation of the IEP, the T & I teachers should discuss evaluation and grading practices used in the instructional program with other IEP team members or support staff. This discussion should include (a) the factors to be evaluated, (b) the criteria for each factor, (c) the methods that will be used to evaluate each factor, and (d) the way that grades will be determined. The special education teachers and other IEP team members can provide information about how they believe the student will respond to the tentative evaluation system and what problems might occur in assessing each evaluation factor.

There are a number of advantages in using the IEP cooperative planning team approach to establish an evaluation and grading system. First, T & I teachers can receive input from others in determining which factors should be included and which standards of performance should be required for the student to earn a passing grade. Secondly, T & I teachers can receive some idea of what assistance or support services they can receive from special education teachers in preparing

students for evaluation. Thirdly, special education teachers can provide valuable tips on evaluation methods and techniques that may be needed to enable the student to more accurately demonstrate achievement. For example, it may be necessary to print tests in large type to aid visually impaired persons or it may be necessary to allow more time for certain individuals to take a test or demonstrate a competency because of certain disabilities. Finally, the team approach provides an extra stimulus to base evaluation and grading practices on specified proficiencies specified in the IEP, which assures that the evaluation system will assess each student's performance against predetermined standards rather than upon how well that student performs as compared with other students.

## Evaluation Methods and Techniques

Several methods that can be used to evaluate and record the progress of special needs learners in the T & I programs were discussed briefly in Module 6. The first method involves the use of a sequenced series of individualized units that contain specific competencies. As the student demonstrates each competency, the T & I teacher evaluates performance and records it on a proficiency profile (see Illustration 6.9 in Module 6).

Another evaluation method involves developing and using student-teacher contracts for a specified grading period. The contract is developed by the T & I teacher with input from the student and resource personnel. It describes the tasks to be performed, the minimum accepted performance levels, and the amount of time required to complete the contract. The student and teacher discuss the contract before signing it. As the student completes each component of the contract, his/her performance is evaluated according to specified criteria included in the contract. At the end of the contract period the teacher and student jointly evaluate progress and arrive at a fair grade. Performances that have not been completed successfully can be included in the contract for the next grading period.

There are many techniques that can be used to evaluate the different types of behaviors demonstrated in T & I programs. Illustration 9.1 shows a number of different behaviors with accompanying evaluation techniques.

Several good textbooks for measuring student achievement in vocational education are listed in the references of this module, along with a number of professional vocational education textbooks that contain chapters on evaluation. These sources contain adequate information for developing pencil-paper tests, performance tests, rating devices, and other measuring instruments as well as information on how to measure and evaluate achievement in vocational education.

The only major behavior technique that will be discussed further in this module is that of developing tests to measure task or competency performance. The student achievement factor that usually carries the most weight in T & I programs is performance on required tasks or competencies. Most of these tasks or competencies involve considerable manipulative performance, although other types of learning are involved as well. The student must be able to recall and apply knowledge of tools, materials, and processes in order to complete tasks. Students must also be able to demonstrate good work habits and safety practices such as following directions, organizing their work, and observing safety rules in order to complete tasks in a safe manner according to predetermined standards. It is easy to see why student performance on required tasks and competencies usually carries the most weight in determining grades in T & I programs since such performance involves the three major types of learning behaviors.

In evaluating the performance of special needs students on required tasks and competencies, T & I teachers must develop performance rating devices if they are not already available. Illustration 9.2 shows an example rating device for the task of charging an automobile battery.

In order to develop a performance rating sheet for each of the tasks and competencies the T & I teacher should use the following procedures:

1. Select the task or competency to be evaluated.

2. Select the criteria to be used to determine successful performance of the task. These criteria should truly reflect industry standards. They consist of task steps, points, items, and concepts representing successful performance of the task according to industry standards. For example, Illustration 9.2 contains the criteria of "followed all safety practices" for the task of charging the battery. Notice that the criteria in Illustration 9.2 address both the *process* of charging the battery and the end *product* of a fully charged battery. The eventual success of T & I graduates will depend upon how tasks are performed as well as the quality of the end product or service.

As a starting point, it is helpful to review the steps involved in performing the task or competency. This should be followed by listing all the criteria that are appropriate for a particular task. The final step is to choose the criteria that will be included and place them in correct order and written form.

3. Validate the criteria for each task or competency. Although T & I teachers are qualified experts in their occupational field and are knowledgeable about industry standards for task performance, it is good practice to have task criteria validated by appropriate members of a craft advisory committee, practitioners in the field, or by other T & I teachers in a similar program.

4. Establish a level of performance for each task or competency. A system should be selected that provides a way of determining how well special needs students meet each criteria. The example shown in Illustration 9.2 shows the levels of performance for the criterion to be *none,*

## Illustration 9.1

## BEHAVIORS TO BE EVALUATED AND
## EVALUATION TECHNIQUES

| Behaviors to be Evaluated | Evaluation Technique |
|---|---|
| Cognitive Achievement | Oral or written test containing a variety of test items such as True-False, Completion, Essay, Multiple Choice, and Matching. |
| Manipulative Performance | Observation of task performance using a checklist or rating device. |
| Safety Procedures | A number of techniques can be used to evaluate this behavior including written test, performance test and observation. |
| Work Habit Development (i.e., initiative, industriousness, concentration, organizes work, etc.) | Observation of work habit skills using a rating device. |
| Attitude | Pencil-paper inventory tests or through observation and the use of checklists and rating devices. |
| Completed Project or Product | Measured by student and teacher using a rating sheet which describes criteria and performance levels. |
| Reports, Homework and Outside Assignments | Measured by teacher and student according to some stated criteria. |
| Classroom and Laboratory Work Behavior | Measured by the teacher using a progress sheet containing behavior indicators. |

*poor, fair, good,* and *excellent.* These levels can be assigned a number that can be later converted into a letter grade, if desired.

The level of performance must also consider the total number of criteria as an indicator of successful performance of the task. The example shown in Illustration 9.2 indicates that all criteria must receive a response of *good* or *excellent* and gives direction to the student if this level is not met.

5. Construct the task performance rating instrument. In constructing the rating instrument, the T & I teacher simply writes the directions and includes the criteria and level of performance devel-

oped in steps 2 through 4 of this procedure. If desired, the T & I teacher can include an additional step in the rating instrument—a conversion table for translating numbered criteria into letters for the grading system.

The use of this type of task performance assessment instrument makes it possible to implement a competency-based instructional program. Either (1) the special needs learner develops the competency and performs the task at the established level of performance and is allowed to continue on to the next task or (2) the learner cannot perform at the acceptable level of performance and must engage in additional activities in order to meet the

225

## Illustration 9.2

## PERFORMANCE RATING SHEET

Charge a Battery

Assessment: Rate the student's level of performance on each of the
following performance components involved in charging
an automobile storage battery. Indicate the student's
level of accomplishment by placing an "X" in the appropriate column under the Level of Performance.

The Student:

| | Level of Performance | | | | |
|---|---|---|---|---|---|
| | None | Poor | Fair | Good | Excellent |
| | 0 | 1 | 2 | 3 | 4 |
| 1. Test the battery . . . | | | | | |
| 2. Cleaned the battery . . . | | | | | |
| 3. Followed the correct procedure . . . | | | | | |
| 4. Followed the safety practices . . . | | | | | |
| 5. Cleaned and returned all tools . . . | | | | | |

The Battery:

6. Showed a full state of charge . . .    _____

Level of Performance

All items must receive Good or Excellent responses. If any item
received a None, Poor or Fair response, the learning experience, or part
of it, must be repeated. Discuss this with your teacher.

| 0 | 1 | 2 | 3 | 4 |
|---|---|---|---|---|
| U | D | C | B | A |

predetermined standard. This technique can be easily and effectively coordinated with the vocational segment of the IEP for handicapped students.

## Grading and Marking Systems

The grading and marking system for special needs students should be based upon progress made on specified objectives for a given grading period. It should be fair and should reflect the competencies developed by each student rather than how well the student did compared to other students. It should be based on multiple factors and take into consideration student effort as well as achievement. The grading system should provide for student involvement in determining achievement and should be planned by the T & I teacher with input from the support personnel whenever possible. The grading system must be manageable, must be easily understood by students and parents, and must have the support of school administrators.

Grades are often dreaded by students and teachers alike. However, they do serve an important role in the instructional process. They can serve as a source of motivation for students and can keep them informed about their progress in learning or lack of it. Grades can serve as a guidance function in that they can be used to decide whether a student is interested in or prepared for a chosen job or career. Grades also provide a means of communicating the level of student achievement to other teachers, parents, school administrators, and eventually to employers. Grades must be determined carefully so that they provide an accurate picture of student progress in relation to specified objectives that lead to preparation for productive employment.

Trade and industrial teachers must develop a fair and impartial system for arriving at grades for special needs students. In few stituations can the teacher simply award a grade of "pass" or "fail," and even if this is the case, there must ultimately be a way to arrive at the decision. In most schools T & I teachers are expected to grade students on a five-factor scale. This scale may be communicated either as grades or points that stand for levels of performance. The translation of such a reporting system is usually as follows:

| Letter | Points | Status |
|--------|--------|--------|
| A | 4 | Excellent |
| B | 3 | Good |
| C | 2 | Fair |
| D | 1 | Poor |
| F | 0 | Failure |

## Marking Systems

There are many marking systems in use today, but they generally fall into two categories: the point system and the averaging system. These two systems will be discussed in the remaining section of this module.

In the point system, each evaluation factor and its behaviors, such as written tests, safety tests, and classroom behavior, is awarded a certain number of points. These point values represent the total number of points that a student can earn in a given marking period. Illustration 9.3 shows a typical summary of a point system for determining grades in a T & I program.

Points earned for different evaluation factors can also be weighted to reflect the value and importance of each type of performance. For example, performance on tasks or competencies is usually given more weight in the grading system than other factors. Illustration 9.4 shows a weighted point system for determining grades in a T & I education program.

In establishing a point system, T & I teachers with input from the special education teacher, should review each special needs student's IEP and decide what evaluation factors should be included in a new marking period. They should assign point values to each evaluative factor after determining which factors are most important. They should also determine the point limits for letter grades.

The T & I teacher can use past experiences with other students in determining the upper and lower limits of the point system as a general guideline. However, it is important to consider the abilities of the special needs student as well as the student's IEP in establishing the point value system.

There are several methods that can be used to determine the point limits for letter grades. One way is to determine the lower limit of the "A" level and the lower limit of the "D" level for a special needs student. For example, Illustration

## Illustration 9.3

## POINT SYSTEM FOR DETERMINING GRADES

| Evaluation Factor | Points |
|---|---|
| Task Performance (10 tests @ 30 points each) | 300 |
| Written Exams (3 exams @ 100 points each) | 300 |
| Work Habit Development (10 observations @ 20 points each) | 200 |
| Attitude and Effort (10 observations @ 10 points each) | 100 |
| Outside Assignments (5 evaluations @ 20 points each) | 100 |
| TOTAL | 1000 |

Point Conversion Chart

| Points | Grade |
|---|---|
| 800 - 1000 | A |
| 600 - 799 | B |
| 400 - 599 | C |
| 200 - 399 | D |
| 0 - 199 | F |

9.4 shows the lower limit of the "A" level to be 90 weighted points and the lower level of the "D" level to be 60 weighted points. The next step is to set the lower limits of the "C" and "B" grade levels. Experience has shown that a good distribution of marks usually results by subtracting the lower limits of the "D" mark from the lower limits for the "A" mark and dividing this value by three to determine the points for each grade level. Using the values shown in Illustration 9.4, an example would be: 90 − 60 = 30, and 30 divided by 3 = 10. To determine the lower limits of the "C" grade level, add 10 to the lower limit of the "D" mark, which gives a value of 70. To determine the lower limit of the "B" grade level, simply add 10 to the lower limit of the

"C" mark. The completed table is shown in Illustration 9.4.

The second method for determining point limits for letter grades is similar to the first but uses a different mathematical procedure. Illustration 9.3 contains an example of a point conversion chart calculated by this method. The first step is to use the maximum number of points that can be earned as a starting point. In the example, this value was 1,000 points for the upper limits of the "A" grade level. In order to establish the lower limits for each grade level, divide the upper limit of the "A" level or the maximum point value of 1,000 in the example by 5, which yields a value of 200 points. The resulting table is shown in Illustration 9.3.

## Illustration 9.4

## WEIGHTED POINT SYSTEM FOR DETERMINING GRADES

| Evaluation Factor | Points | Weight | Weighted Points | Percentage of Total Weighted Points |
|---|---|---|---|---|
| Task Performance (10 tests @ 30 points each) | 300 | .20 | 60 | 60% |
| Written Exams (3 exams @ 100 points each) | 300 | .05 | 15 | 15% |
| Work Habit Development (10 observations @ 20 points each) | 200 | .05 | 10 | 10% |
| Attitude and Effort (10 observations @ 10 points each) | 100 | .05 | 5 | 5% |
| Outside Assignments (5 evaluations @ 20 points each) | 100 | .10 | 10 | 10% |
| TOTAL | 1000 | | 100 | 100% |

NOTE: Weights can be arbitrarily assigned or they can be assigned on the basis of percentage of total weighted points. This can be calculated by converting weighted points on a 100 point scale which reflects the desired percentage value. The weights can then be determined by dividing the weighted points by the total points assigned to each factor. For example, task performance was given a percentage weight of 60 percent in the chart above or a weighted point value of 60. The weight value was calculated by dividing 60 by 300 which gives a weight of .20. To determine a given students weighted point value for any factor, simply multiply the total points earned by the assigned weight. To avoid small numbers, one could simply multiply by a value of 2 to convert the 100 point scale to 200.

### POINT CONVERSION CHART

| Points | Grade |
|---|---|
| 90 - 100 | A |
| 80 - 90 | B |
| 70 - 80 | C |
| 60 - 70 | D |
| Below 60 | F |

The second major system that can be used to determine grades for special needs students in a given marking period is the averaging system. Each evaluation factor and activity, such as task performance and performance test, is evaluated against a common base (highest achievement as 100 percent) and given a relative weight in relation to other activities and factors. The total is averaged and the final grade determined by comparing it against the school's marking system. For example, the school may follow the limits of 90–100 percent equals an "A" grade. Illustration 9.5 shows an example of a marking system using the averaging system.

The T & I teacher, in cooperation with the support personnel, will need to decide which grading system is the most appropriate for meeting school requirements as well as the abilities and needs of the student. Regardless of which system is used, a clear understanding of it should be communicated to the student and supplementary personnel at the beginning of the grading period.

## SUMMARY

Special needs learners possess a variety of different abilities, needs, learning styles, and occupational goals. These considerations should be addressed in designing T & I instructional programs and identifying the instructional techniques that will best accommodate these students. One instructional technique will not meet the needs of every handicapped and disadvantaged learner. Therefore, a variety of techniques should be used.

Specific instructional techniques that have proven to be successful with this population include (a) demonstrations, (b) field trips and job site visitations, (c) grouping, (d) individualized instruction activities, (e) media aids, (f) projects, (g) simulation and role-playing activities, (h) student-teacher contracts, (i) task analysis, (j) team teaching and (k) tutors. Each of these instructional techniques is discussed in this module.

The evaluation and grading system for reporting the achievement of special needs students should consider the needs and abilities of the student rather than how the student compares to other students. The T & I teacher and support personnel should cooperatively plan and implement an evaluation program for each special needs student. This evaluation program should contain a number of evaluation factors designed to provide feedback on student progress in relation to behaviors required in a specific job or occupation. Such factors as task or competency performance, work habit development, attitude and effort, and cognitive achievement should be included in the evaluation system.

When working with handicapped learners in T & I programs, teachers should use the IEP as a management tool in evaluating student progress in the program. An evaluation system based on the student's IEP—which includes many evaluation factors, methods, and techniques and which is fair and impartial—can provide a number of advantages to both the student and the teacher. The student is given the incentive to succeed as well as important feedback about performance. The T & I teacher is provided with feedback information about the appropriateness of IEP content, the instructional method, and instructional materials. Evaluation should be an integral part of the instructional process and not an added component designed solely for the purpose of assigning a grade at the end of an instructional period.

The evaluation system should be established for each grading period and should make use of a number of evaluation methods and techniques. One of the most important evaluation techniques is to develop a performance test for each task or competency, since typically this evaluation factor is given more weight than other factors in most T & I programs.

**Illustration 9.5**

# AVERAGING SYSTEM FOR DETERMINING GRADES

| Evaluation Factor | Relative Weight | Maximum Points |
|---|---|---|
| Task Performance<br>(10 tests @ 30 points each) | 50% | 300 |
| Written Exams<br>(3 exams @ 100 points each) | 20% | 300 |
| Work Habits<br>(10 observations @ 20 points each) | 15% | 200 |
| Attitude and Effort<br>(10 observations @ 10 points each) | 5% | 100 |
| Outside Assignments<br>(5 evaluations @ 20 points each) | 10% | 100 |

STUDENT EXAMPLE

Example of How to Calculate a Factor

Three Unit Written Exams

Exam 1 – 24 out of 30 points converted to 100% scale (24 X 3.33 = 79.92)

Exam 2 – 45 out of 50 points converted to 100% scale (45 X 2.00 = 90.00)

Exam 3 – 38 out of 40 points converted to 100% scale (38 X 2.50 = 95.00)

$$\overline{265.00}$$

Total = 265      265 ÷ 3 = 88

To arrive at final weighted grade for exams simply multiply 88 X 22 (assigned weight) = 176.

Summary of Other Student Factors

| Factor | Weighted Values |
|---|---|
| Performance Tests | 282 |
| Written Exams | 176 |
| Work Habits | 192 |
| Attitude and Effort | 97 |
| Outside Assignments | 88 |
| TOTAL | 835 |

| Grading Scale | Example Grade |
|---|---|
| 880 – 1000 points = A | Individual earned 835 points resulting in a grade of "B" |
| 780 – 879 points = B | |
| 680 – 779 points = C | |
| 600 – 679 points = D | |
| Below 600 points = F | |

Trade and industrial teachers and support personnel should establish the point values or weights for each evaluation factor and develop a plan to summarize and report grades to the student and outside audiences. Good grades are just as important to special needs students as they are to other students.

## REFERENCES

Ervin, E. Peer teaching. *Journal of Vocational Special Needs Education*, January, 1980, pp. 18–20.

Gronlund, N. *Measurement and evaluation in teaching.* New York: The MacMillan Company, 1971.

Hull, M. and Eddy, A. Some considerations for grading and evaluating special needs students. *Journal of Vocational Special Needs Education*, 1980, pp. 18–20.

McCarthy, R. and Stodden, R. Mainstreaming secondary students: a peer tutoring model. *Teaching Exceptional Children*, 1979, *11* (4), 162–63.

Miller, W., and Rose, H. *Instructors and their jobs.* Chicago, Illinois: American Technical Publishers, 1975, pp. 218–243.

Schroeder, P. (Ed.). *Proceedings of a symposium on task analysis/task inventories.* Columbus, Ohio: The Ohio State University, The Center for Vocational Education, 1975.

Shepard, N. What the "gray revolution" means to you. *Vocational Education*, 1979, *54* (4), 44–47.

Stern-Otazo, K. Curriculum modification and instructional practices. In Gary D. Meers (Ed.) *Handbook of special vocational needs education.* Rockville, Maryland: Asper Systems Corporation, 1980.

The Center for Vocational Education. *Demonstrate a manipulative skill.* Columbus, Ohio: The Ohio State University, 1977.

The Center for Vocational Education. *Determine student grades.* Columbus, Ohio: The Ohio State University, 1977.

Wargo, W. Individualizing instruction. *Industrial Education.* November, 1977, *66*, 20, 24.

Wentling, T. *Evaluating occupational and training programs, second edition.* Rockleigh, New Jersey: Longwood Division, Allyn and Bacon, Incorporated, 1980.

## SELF ASSESSMENT: INSTRUCTIONAL TECHNIQUES AND EVALUATION OF SPECIAL NEEDS LEARNERS

1. Why should a number of instructional techniques be used in providing instruction to special needs learners?

2. How can the demonstration method be used to help special needs learners succeed in T & I programs?

3. What considerations should be addressed by T & I teachers when planning demonstrations?

4. How can field trips and job site visitations be used to help special needs learners succeed in T & I programs?

5. How can special needs learners participate in planning for field trips and job site visitations?

6. How can grouping special needs learners be used to help them succeed in T & I programs?

7. Name several different types of grouping patterns that T & I teachers could use in planning the instructional program.

8. List several advantages for T & I teachers when they use the grouping technique to plan for special needs learners.

9. How can individualized instruction activities be used to help special needs learners succeed in the T & I programs?

10. Name several techniques involved in the individualized instruction approach.

11. What considerations should be addressed by T & I teachers when planning individualized instruction activities?

12. How can educational media aids be used to help special needs learners succeed in T & I programs?

13. List some specific media aids that can be used to accommodate the individual needs of handicapped and disadvantaged learners.

14. How can projects be used to help special needs learners succeed in T & I programs?

15. How can simulation and role-playing activities be used to help special needs learners succeed in T & I programs?

16. How can student-teacher contracts be used to help special needs learners succeed in T & I programs?

17. What are some guidelines to remember when developing student-teacher contracts?

18. How can the task analysis technique be used to help special needs learners succeed in T & I programs?

19. How can the team teaching approach be used to help special needs learners succeed in T & I programs?

20. How can tutors be used to help special needs learners succeed in T & I programs?

21. Name several types of tutors.

22. Why is it important not to compromise task performance standards in order to help special needs students improve their grades in a trade and industrial program?

23. Explain why the evaluation system for assessing the achievement of special needs students should be based on the IEP rather than on a comparison of the student's achievement with the achievement of others.

24. Identify and describe some evaluation factors that should be considered in an evaluation system for special needs students.

25. Describe the individualized units method and the contract method of evaluating achievement of special needs students.

26. Describe the steps involved in developing performance tests to measure student performance on tasks and competencies.

27. Describe the point system for determining a student's grade.

28. Describe the averaging system for determining a student's grade.

29. List some of the advantages an effective evaluation and reporting system can provide to the student and T & I teacher.

## ASSOCIATED ACTIVITIES

1. Make a list of all special needs learners enrolled in your program. Contact support personnel to discuss their ability levels, strong learning style, and specific needs. Discuss which instructional techniques would probably be effective in planning for each student. Use cooperative planning techniques with other personnel in planning your instructional program to meet the needs of these handicapped and disadvantaged learners.

2. Plan a demonstration to be incorporated into a lesson or unit that you will be teaching soon. Be sure to keep in mind the considerations mentioned in this module.

3. Plan a field trip or a job site visita-

tion for the entire class or a small group of special needs learners. Allow these students to participate in planning and implementing the activity.

4. Study your class list and develop some flexible grouping patterns that would help special needs learners to succeed in classroom or laboratory activities, projects and program assignments.

5. Talk to other T & I teachers, special needs personnel, vocational administrators, and state department contacts to determine whether there are commercial or teacher-prepared individualized instruction materials available for use by special needs learners in your program.

6. If there are no individualized instruction materials readily available to you, inquire about the existence of special needs funds to purchase some of these materials. If you still receive a negative response, work cooperatively with other personnel to develop individualized materials and activities for your program.

7. Locate educational media aids in your building that can accommodate the individual needs of special needs learners enrolled in your program.

8. Develop some project guidelines for use with special needs learners in your program. Plan these projects in coordination with students and support staff.

9. Develop some simulation and role-playing activities for use with special needs learners in your program.

10. Develop a format for student-teacher contracts to be used with special needs learners in your program. Plan the contract format, guidelines, and evaluation criteria in coordination with students and support staff.

11. Analyze proficiency and skill requirements necessary for successful completion of your program. For specific special needs learners, develop task analysis activities for each of the tasks involved in the required skills and proficiency. Seek assistance from support personnel.

12. Develop team teaching arrangements with other T & I personnel, special needs personnel, and/or support staff.

These arrangements should include appropriate planning to meet the needs of special needs learners in your program.

13. Identify sources of possible tutoring services in your school and community. Contact these sources to find some volunteers willing to participate in a tutoring program.

14. Develop an orientation program for potential tutors to introduce them to the objectives of your program, their specific duties in working with special needs learners, and resources available to assist them.

15. Secure a textbook that contains information about evaluating achievement in vocational education and review it.

16. Talk to T & I teachers in your school, in your field, and in other schools to determine how they evaluate and grade special needs students.

17. Begin a reading program on measurement and evaluation in vocational education.

18. Establish and maintain a file on measurement and evaluation and seek materials on these topics such as tests, rating instruments, evaluation systems, and the like.

19. Participate with the special education teacher in planning and implementing the evaluation and grading system for a special needs student enrolled in your program.

20. Develop a performance test for each task or competency in your trade and industrial program and required rating instruments and tests to assess other evaluation factors.

## CASE HISTORY: JESSIE'S STORY

Jessie is enrolled in a drafting program. She has a physical disability in the form of a steel bar in her right leg due to an auto accident. She uses a cane for mobility, but her doctor feels that it may merely be a psychological crutch. She is also a slow learner and works in the resource room with the special education teacher who works with the educable mentally retarded students.

Jessie's reading, comprehension, and math levels are at the fifth grade level. Her lack of self-confidence makes her reluctant to use the machinery, equipment, and tools in the laboratory by herself. However, she works very well in group situations.

The program instructor has done some cooperative planning with Jessie's special education teacher. She receives instruction in the regular drafting program while the special education teacher provides remedial help in remedial academics and by reinforcing what is covered in the drafting class. In addition, several peer tutors are used in helping Jessie keep up with the rest of the class.

These methods are proving very successful. As Jessie is beginning to succeed in developing the required competencies for the program, her self-confidence is increasing. As a result, she is beginning to walk without the aid of her cane for greater periods of time. Although extra time is required for her to perform the required skills for success in the program, the quality of her work remains consistently above average.

Jessie is currently involved in a work-study program during her last year in school. She is working part-time in the drafting area, and her employer is so pleased with her job performance that he has expressed an interest in hiring her full-time when she graduates. The special education teacher has contacted the local office of vocational rehabilitation. The rehabilitation counselor has agreed to interview Jessie and have her evaluated for eligibility as a client. If she is eligible for rehabilitation services, she will be provided with transportation to and from work and will be given any adaptive devices or special tools that might be necessary to help her succeed on the job.

## CASE HISTORY ACTIVITY

Joshua has recently enrolled in your program. He is a paraplegic. He has above average intelligence. Joshua is very outgoing and determined to succeed in your program. He gets along very well with others in the class. He has a vocational rehabilitation counselor who has assured him that the agency will provide any equipment modifications and adaptive equipment that will be necessary for him to succeed in your program.

Based on this information, complete the case history profile worksheet for Joshua's participation in your program.

## CASE HISTORY PROFILE WORKSHEET

Student: _____ Page: _____

Handicapping Condition(s): _____

T & I Program: _____ Academic Levels: _____

Career Goal/Occupational Interest: _____

Considerations (e.g., medication, behavior): _____

_____

| Adaptation | Specific Services Needed | Where to Obtain Service |
|---|---|---|
| Cooperative Planning (School Personnel) | | |
| Support Services | | |
| Architectural Changes | | |
| Adaptive Equipment | | |
| Curriculum Modification | | |
| Instructional Materials/ Supplies | | |
| Teaching Techniques | | |
| Agency Involvement | | |
| Possible Job Placement | | |

236

# MODULE 10

## Job Placement and Follow-up

Job placement, to special needs persons, may well be the most important step of their lives. The ability to obtain and hold a job indicates the capacity to participate fully in society. To special needs persons, like other individuals, a job brings status and respect. The years of education that they have experienced are of little value unless they can become vocationally productive and partially or completely self-sufficient.

The need for effective job placement services for all vocational students and especially for those with special needs is critical. Consider some of the major concerns addressed by Congress in recent legislation regarding vocational education and employment of special needs persons: an unacceptably high rate of unemployment, underutilization of the special needs workforce, discriminatory practices in employing and promoting special needs persons, and occupational stereotyping that brands them as second-class citizens.

Special needs persons can become productive employees if given appropriate vocational education matched with the employment needs of industry and the guidance and support services that lead to placement. For example, many employers who have hired handicapped persons, like DuPont, testify that hiring these workers is a safe and beneficial practice for any employer.

One of the great challenges for vocational educators in this decade is to make job placement and follow-up services a vital part of vocational preparation for all students. Job placement and follow-up services must begin when students enter training programs and end with successful placement upon completion of the program. Job placement services that aspire to be successful in serving special needs students must be more than a job referral service; they must become an integral part of the vocational preparation of students. Job placement team members must become actively involved in analyzing, modifying, and creating new jobs in the industrial community.

This module describes the type of job placement and follow-up services needed to adequately serve special needs students. More specifically, the following topics are covered: (a) the need for placement and follow-up services, (b) barriers to placement, (c) placement options, (d) placement as a team effort, (e) the placement process, and (f) follow-up services.

## MODULE OBJECTIVES

After you have read and reviewed this module, studied the case history, reviewed the self assessment questions and completed some of the associated activities, you should be able to:

1. Describe why job placement and follow-up services are needed to assist T & I special needs students and graduates in obtaining appropriate jobs.

2. Identify and describe some of the placement options available for special needs students.

3. Identify and describe the three major categories of barriers to employment for special needs students.

4. Describe the placement team approach to providing job placement and follow-up services.

5. Identify some of the placement team members and describe some of their major duties.

6. Describe the placement progress, including the components of building a market for placements, conducting the preplacement program, and matching students with jobs.

7. Describe the follow-up process to job placement.

## THE NEED FOR PLACEMENT AND FOLLOW-UP SERVICES

The transition from school to work is one of the most difficult adjustments a person must make. It is also one of the most critical adjustments, for how it is made can mean the difference between a lifetime of dependency and frustration or a satisfying and productive career. The transition to employment is even more difficult for special needs persons because of real or imagined employment barriers.

School placement and follow-up services that are integrated into the total vocational program can help to smooth this transition for all students. Through these services, special needs students can receive appropriate vocational education, work adjustment skills, and assistance in finding a job and keeping it.

The formidable barriers that once kept special needs students from entering vocational education programs and employment are beginning to break down. Federal legislation has played an important part in this change process. For example, recent legislation has made it unlawful to discriminate against handicapped persons in employment. The Rehabilitation Act of 1973, as amended in 1974, made it possible for the handicapped to enroll in regular vocational programs and to receive the necessary support services to overcome barriers caused by disabilities. In addition, under Section 503 of the Act, any federal contractor doing $2,500 of business annually with the federal government must take affirmative steps to recruit, hire, and promote qualified handicapped persons. Affirmative action by employers includes removing any discriminatory practices in the hiring process.

Employees who fall under the regulations of the Rehabilitation Act must make reasonable accommodations for qualified handicapped persons. Examples of these accommodations include modifications to the worksite and the provision of necessary aids or devices that enable these persons to perform work tasks successfully.

The regulations of the Rehabilitation Act of 1973, as amended, essentially guarantee special needs persons the same rights and benefits as other job applicants and employees. The act, coupled with the targeted jobs and Work Incentive (WIN) credits program of the Revenue Act of 1978, has provided employers with added incentives to recruit and hire qualified handicapped persons. The targeted jobs credit program, by providing tax write-offs, is designed to provide an incentive for employers to hire vocational rehabilitation referrals, economically disadvantaged youth, and Vietnam-era veterans.

As a result of mainstreaming, an increasing number of special needs persons are entering vocational programs such as T & I. They are declaring career objectives and working hard to become employable. At the same time, business and industry are beginning to recruit and hire more special needs persons. More than ever, job placement services are needed to match the capabilities and interests of special needs persons with the job requirements of employers.

Job placement personnel need to do more than simply choose capable students for existing jobs. They need to work with employees in analyzing existing jobs to determine training requirements, to assist employers in job redesign, and to work with other school personnel in implementing programs to help special needs students make the transition from school to work.

Placement and follow-up services can provide the vital link between T & I education programs and productive employment. Trade and industrial teachers who have special needs students will be able to realize the goal of seeing their graduates succeed in jobs for which they were prepared. Similarly, business and industry will be provided with a source of potential employees that in the past has been virtually untapped.

Consider the alternatives to successful

placement of special needs persons. Most of them who do not enter the labor market will be under protective custody of their families. If they are not employed, they will receive welfare. They may become institutionalized in hospitals or rehabilitation centers for life.

# BARRIERS TO PLACEMENT

The employment outlook for special needs students continues to brighten. Major industries such as DuPont are hiring qualified special needs individuals and are telling other employers that they make capable, productive workers. The U.S. Employment Service, an agency in the Department of Labor, has made the placement of handicapped persons who appear at local offices a top priority. Many agencies, such as the Office of Personnel Management and labor unions, are also promoting equal employment opportunities for the handicapped.

Even with the encouraging employment outlook, special needs individuals face many barriers when seeking employment. There is still widespread prejudice against people who look and act differently from the norm. There is still discrimination against handicapped people. Fear of the unknown causes an irrational fear of people who shake and who have epilepsy. Also, employers want to avoid a hiring mistake that may slow down production or raise their insurance rates, and they often perceive the hiring of handicapped people as a gamble. And then there is a fear on the part of handicapped persons themselves of competing for jobs with the nonhandicapped, whom they believe have the advantage.

Barriers to placement and employment can be classified into three major types: barriers among handicapped persons, their families, and advocates; barriers within the helping system; and barriers within society (Barriers and Bridges, 1977).

## Barriers Among Handicapped Persons

Handicapped persons often have low self-esteem and a negative impression of themselves and their abilities. This barrier presents problems for them in job interviews and in developing positive interpersonal relationships. Many of them who have tried to obtain employment have been rejected so frequently that they eventually begin to doubt their own abilities. This situation strengthens their already strong sense of hopeless dependency. Family and friends often contribute to the problem of low self-esteem by communicating low expectations which further impairs their self-concept.

Other barriers to employment for handicapped individuals may include inadequate preparation for the job interview, poor grooming habits, and a lack of understanding of the resources available to them.

These barriers to placement and employment that exist among special needs persons can be reduced or eliminated by appropriate work adjustment training and the desire to become independent. As society's attitudes change toward accepting special needs persons as individuals capable of productive employment and independence, this population will develop a different picture of themselves as reflected by society's acceptance mirror. As this occurs, barriers among special needs persons caused by low self-esteem should begin to dissolve.

## Barriers in the Helping System

There are many agencies and groups that compete for the right to serve special needs persons. These groups and agencies are sometimes labeled as the *helping system*. In practice, however, the helping system itself can generate barriers to placement and employment. The system is made up of many groups and agencies that have one purpose—namely, to help special needs persons. The problem lies in the different procedures they follow in providing services to them. Often one group or agency is unaware of what others do or why they do it. Sometimes these agencies actually contradict themselves. This situation subjects special needs persons to inconsistent expectations as they move from one agency to another.

There are two major barriers caused by the helping system. One of these is a lack of interagency communication. The other barrier is the lack of enough trained personnel to make the helping system work effectively. The first barrier is being substantially reduced in schools through cooperative planning with school personnel. For example, helping agency representatives are now frequently included in the IEP process for handicapped persons. The problem of an insufficient number of trained personnel is also being reduced by preservice and inservice education programs designed to make helping system personnel more effective in serving special needs persons. For example, T & I teachers are receiving training in working with special needs learners while special needs teachers are receiving training in the principles and practices of vocational education.

The job placement program can be instrumental in helping to overcome both barriers by promoting open communication and cooperation among helping agencies and by working with teachers and other school personnel to ensure that special needs persons are adequately prepared for employment.

## Barriers within Society

Special needs persons applying for employment, like other job applicants, experience feelings of insecurity as they enter personnel offices for an interview. This feeling is generated by an awareness that they will be competing for jobs with other applicants and that they will be subjected to the employer's assessment. This uneasy feeling is magnified by the fear of rejection.

While many able job applicants experience these feelings generated by fear, special needs persons may suffer more acutely because of employment barriers. For example, special needs persons applying for a job are concerned about architectural and physical accessibility, whether they will be able to pass a required physical examination, and how they will be able to present themselves in an interview because of their disability. In addition, they are aware that they must pass screening tests and complete application forms that usually require previous job experience. They are also fearful of traditional employer views toward hiring them.

Special needs persons encounter many employment barriers that result from employer ignorance about their capabilities. Frequently, employers focus on what special needs persons cannot do, instead of what they can. They may be so convinced that special needs students cannot become good employees that they may not give them a chance to prove otherwise. Such employer attitudes are an example of the many barriers that exist within our society toward this population.

Some of the common misconceptions that employers hold that become employment barriers for special needs persons are as follows:

1. Insurance rates will skyrocket.
2. Considerable expense will be involved in making architectural modifications and modifications to the work environment for the handicapped person.
3. Safety records will be jeopardized.
4. Special privileges will have to be granted.
5. Other employees will not accept special needs employees.
6. Production will suffer because of poor job performance and high absenteeism on the part of the special needs person.

Every one of these reasons that employers give for not hiring special needs persons have been proven through experience to be groundless. Some of America's largest firms, such as DuPont, IBM, and Xerox, have hired special needs persons for years and have conducted studies that reveal their productivity to be comparable with that of nonhandicapped workers.

Societal barriers to employment of special needs persons have decreased somewhat since the passage of the Rehabilitation Act of 1973 and will continue to decrease as more employers hire special needs persons through their affirmative action programs.

Job placement services will likely play an important part in helping to remove these barriers.

## PLACEMENT OPTIONS

Typically, vocational school job placement services are viewed narrowly as those services provided to help program graduates locate and obtain full-time jobs. In actual practice, however, most vocational placement programs provide services leading to a number of different placement options for special needs students. Illustration 10.1 presents seven different placement options.

### Placement in Rehabilitation Sponsored Centers

Handicapped individuals can be placed in work activity centers, work adjustment centers, and transition centers (Jacobs, Larsen and Smith, 1979). While the major purpose of these centers is to provide diagnostic vocational evaluation and training, they may become a type of terminal placement for the severely handicapped.

Work activity centers provide sequenced work activities and personal-social activities designed to help trainees improve their normal living skills. The emphasis in these centers is not on productivity, but rather it is on providing remedial instruction for performing basic behaviors required for daily living activities.

Work adjustment centers provide prevocational skill training as well as training in worker adjustment skills such as

work attitudes, work habits, and personal-social habits. Like work activity centers, the emphasis is not on productivity, but rather it is on preparing the trainee to enter the competitive employment market.

Transition centers are different from the two previously discussed centers in that they do emphasize productivity. These centers use "live work" experiences as the primary method of developing job skills that can help them compete in the job market. Transition centers usually contract with local business and industries to produce certain products or to provide specific services for which they receive pay. These centers attempt to provide an environment similar to the ones that may be found in industry. Trainees receive pay for their productivity and are introduced to certain standards of productivity. An example of a transition center is Goodwill Industries of America. Sometimes these centers are called sheltered workshops.

Trainees may also be placed into special rehabilitation facilities that are able to provide more specialized services than can be provided in centers. Each state has a number of rehabilitation centers, such as the Warm Springs Rehabilitation Center located in Warm Springs, Georgia. The purpose of these facilities is not to provide a lifetime home for their trainees, but rather to provide a wide variety of services, including vocational training, that can give them the best possible chance of being productive in a sheltered, semi-sheltered or competitive employment environment.

### Placement in School System Jobs

Another placement option available for special needs students is employment in various jobs within the school system. Usually students are placed as helpers under the direct supervision of school staff and do not receive pay. The purpose of this placement option is to provide additional training through actual job experience.

## Illustration 10.1

## TRADE AND INDUSTRIAL STUDENTS PLACEMENT OPTIONS

Placement Options:  Special needs students who complete trade and industrial programs may receive placement
services for the following kinds of placement options.

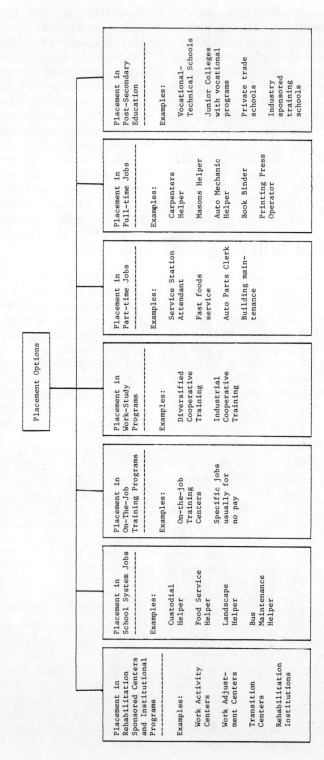

Examples of T & I job areas in which students could be placed within the school system include: (a) custodial helper, (b) janitorial helper, (c) food service helper, (d) landscape helper, and (e) bus maintenance mechanics helper.

### Placement in On-the-job Training Program

Special needs students may also be placed in on-the-job training (OJT) centers or sites that are actual work situations. The purpose of these OJT programs is to provide specific job preparation. While trainees work under direct supervision of a job supervisor, they are usually assisted in making the adjustment to OJT jobs by follow-up staff from the vocational school. They may continue to receive support training back at their local schools after work hours. Vocational rehabilitation and CETA agencies may support this type of placement by providing some monetary incentives to employers who provide OJT experiences for special needs persons.

### Placement in Work-Study Programs

Many vocational schools offer students a chance to obtain actual job experience while they continue their educational programs at school through cooperative vocational education or work-study programs. Special needs students can be trained initially in T & I cooperative programs or they can be placed in these programs during the latter part of their job preparation program. Students work under close supervision of a training supervisor on the job and are visited by the teacher-coordinator on a periodic basis. Students spend a part of their day at school completing course requirements and part of the day working on the job for which they receive pay. Examples of such programs are diversified cooperative training and industrial cooperative training.

### Placement in Part-time Jobs

Special needs students can be placed in part-time jobs until they become more prepared for full-time employment or until full-time employment can be obtained. In some cases they need to begin employment on a part-time basis until they build up their stamina for full-time employment. In addition, it is often easier to make adjustments to the work environment during part-time work. Trainees who are employed part-time also have the advantage of being able to return to the school or to some other agency for remedial and support services if necessary.

### Placement in Full-Time Employment

Obviously the most desired type of placement is full-time employment that is in line with the special needs person's interests and capabilities. Special needs persons who have completed T & I programs need employment that provides them with job satisfaction, an opportunity to earn a living wage, and an opportunity to advance in their chosen occupations. For some full-time employed persons, additional training will be needed so that they may continue to make progress in their jobs.

### Placement in Post-Secondary Education

Jobs continue to become more complex each year and prospective job seekers will need to obtain higher levels of education and training to secure employment. Special needs students can be placed in a variety of post-secondary education institutions ranging from vocational-technical schools to colleges and universities. Often they can obtain financial support and other support services to help them prepare for higher employment levels. Most schools have been emphasizing this type of placement option for a long time and are very successful in helping graduates choose and enter higher education institutions.

## PLACEMENT: A TEAM EFFORT

Placement and follow-up services begin the day that students enter a T & I program and conclude only after a student is successfully employed. The placement and follow-up process must be a team effort composed of the entire school staff, supplemented with outside assistance from agencies and organizations such as employment services, vocational rehabilitation agencies, local vocational advisory committees, and other advocacy groups. An essential part of this team effort is the special needs individual who is trying to obtain education and support services necessary to enter employment in a specific occupational area.

Like a football team, the placement team must have an organizational structure with a few leaders and a number of players who work together cooperatively. There must be a game plan. For handicapped students this plan is the IEP discussed in Module 4. The team must huddle together occasionally to change the game plan or call new plays. And for the team to be successful they must have support from everybody involved in the game. This analogy seems fitting, for if special needs persons are going to obtain productive employment they will need the support of the placement team to push them across the goal line.

The following section presents information about team members and their responsibilities.

1. *Vocational administrators:* The success or failure of the placement and follow-up process depends greatly upon the efforts and cooperation of the vocational school administrators. In addition to supporting the placement and follow-up process by supplying staff, suppliers, and an operation budget, administrators should perform the following duties:

a. Keep all teachers and school staff informed and involved concerning the purpose, goals, and activities of the program.

b. Assist in establishing a placement and follow-up advisory committee and insure that placement is addressed by the various T & I craft committees.

c. Provide release time for school staff who engage in placement program public relations (PR) activities and become involved in PR activities when appropriate.

d. Initiate and maintain contact with employers who have special needs students.

e. Promote support for the placement/follow-up program with other school administrators, community leaders, and special needs advocacy groups.

f. Work with the State Department of Education, vocational rehabilitation, and other state and federal agencies in administering the program.

g. Inform all school staff of their responsibilities and duties in the placement/follow-up process.

h. Utilize placement and follow-up data to make appropriate changes in the school's total program.

2. *Student Personnel Specialists and Counselors:* It is essential that guidance counselors and other student personnel specialists work closely with other placement team members in providing services for special needs persons who are preparing for placement. Counselors and school personnel specialists should perform the following duties:

a. Obtain current information about the local job market and the types of jobs that T & I students may enter after training.

b. Provide current, factual job placement information to T & I teachers and to T & I students so they can examine job possibilities.

c. Provide information to special needs students regarding the assistance they can receive from the school and community agencies to help them prepare for and obtain jobs.

d. Assist special needs students in making decisions about job alternatives related to their interests, values, and capabilities.

e. Counsel students regarding their work adjustment development in such areas as work attitudes, work habits, grooming and dress, and job performance.

f. Assist T & I teachers in making any modifications to their laboratory environment by serving on the assessment team.

g. Assist the job placement staff in preparing job placement profiles.

3. *Work Sample/Evaluation Center Personnel:* Some vocational schools employ specially trained staff to operate a work sample/evaluation center that is designed to help prospective vocational students and regular students identify their areas of interest and their capabilities. (Module 3 presents a more detailed discussion of work sample/evaluation services.) Work sample/evaluation staff should perform the following duties as members of the placement team:

a. Assist counselors and student personnel specialist in determining the interests and capabilities of special needs students.

b. Provide the job placement staff with information about new employer contacts and leads about possible job openings.

c. Assist T & I teachers, special needs teachers, and cooperative education coordinators in providing work adjustment training.

d. Assist T & I teachers in identifying work environment barriers as members of the barrier assessment team.

4. *Trade and Industrial Teachers:* Trade and industrial teachers must be actively involved in the job placement and follow-up process for special needs students. These teachers, along with special needs personnel, interact daily with special needs students and usually know their interests, capabilities, and limitations. Trade and industrial teachers maintain continuous contact with employers and are often called when job openings become available. They are familiar with job requirements in their technical area and can determine if special needs student capabilities are compatible.

Trade and industrial teachers are in the placement business daily as they prepare their students for employment. Through cooperative planning and joint effort with other placement team members, T & I teachers can help special needs students complete their desired program and improve their chances for successful job placement. Trade and industrial teachers should perform the following placement and follow-up duties:

a. Develop and maintain a good working relationship with all members of the placement follow-up team.

b. Assist the placement and follow-up staff in identifying potential employers.

c. Assist the placement and follow-up specialist in analyzing identified jobs and developing job profiles.

d. Maintain continuous contact with local employers and provide meaningful feedback to the placement team.

e. Provide an orientation for all students, stressing job placement as the ultimate goal of the instructional program and of the placement services that are available to help them prepare for and obtain employment.

f. Maintain an active craft advisory committee and involve them in the placement and follow-up program.

g. Provide worker-adjustment skills as well as technical skills in instructional programs.

h. Maintain a laboratory environment similar to that found in industry.

i. Encourage all students to visit employers and observe what workers do as they perform their daily work activities.

j. Arrange field trips to various industries and businesses to provide students with first-hand information about jobs and job opportunities.

k. Refer special needs students to other school staff for special guidance and instruction.

l. Participate in trade, technical, and professional organizations to keep abreast of the changing nature of work in your teaching area.

m. Refer students to the placement and follow-up staff for part-time and full-time placement assistance.

n. Work with special needs teachers, students, and parents in developing the IEP for handicapped students.

5. *Cooperative-Education/Work-Study Coordinators:* Cooperative T & I education coordinators can make important contributions to their job placement and follow-up program. Coordinators spend about one-half of their day working with employers and student-employees at the place of employment. They are able to provide valuable information regarding employer contacts, job leads, and information about the nature of jobs in the community. In addition, these coordinators are experienced job placement specialists, for they are continually trying to develop jobs for their students and match their students with available jobs. Trade and industrial cooperative education coordinators should perform the following duties:

a. Assist special needs persons enrolled in their programs in finding work-study placement.

b. Provide information to job placement staff regarding employer contacts, job leads, and specific information about the nature of jobs in the community.

c. Assist job placement staff in analyzing jobs and preparing job profiles.

d. Assist job placement staff in promoting public relations for the placement program.

6. *Special Needs Personnel:* Special needs teachers and specialists also play a key role in the job placement and follow-up effort of a vocational program. They provide instruction and support services for special needs students. They also work closely with T & I teachers to provide remedial instruction in a given technical area. For example, special needs persons may need additional help in performing mathematical computations or in understanding trade terms. Special needs teach-

ers can provide appropriate remedial instruction to help these students make progress in their T & I program.

Special needs personnel should perform the following placement duties:

a. Work with handicapped students, their parents, and T & I teachers in planning the IEP.

b. Assist T & I teachers and other placement team members in understanding the nature and needs of special needs learners.

c. Assist T & I teachers in providing appropriate instruction.

d. Provide work adjustment skill training to special needs students.

e. Assist T & I teachers in assessing the laboratory work environment for a specific handicapped student and in making suggestions for appropriate modifications.

f. Assist T & I teachers in obtaining appropriate aids and devices to eliminate identified barriers.

7. *Job Placement and Follow-up Staff:* Placement and follow-up specialists also have specific duties to perform as placement team members, but their chief responsibility is to coordinate the entire placement and follow-up effort and to gain the assistance of all involved. These professionals "hit the streets" and talk placement wherever they go. They serve as the liaison between the school and the community and are directly involved with employers in matching the vocational competencies of special needs students with the personnel qualification needs of employers.

Job placement and follow-up staff should perform the following duties:

a. Develop and maintain a team-oriented job placement and follow-up program.

b. Prepare for and conduct a continuous public relations program to promote the placement effort.

c. Develop and maintain current information on employers, employer contacts, and placements.

d. Visit potential employers to initiate and promote student placement.

e. Work with employers in developing job profiles and, if possible, in redesigning jobs for special needs students.
f. Establish and maintain a placement and follow-up advisory committee.
g. Work with out-of-school agencies that provide special services such as vocational rehabilitation and employment security to enhance the job placement and follow-up effort.
h. Obtain data on special needs students and work with other placement team members in preparing student job placement profiles.
i. Provide T & I teachers and other placement team members with information related to the placement and follow-up of program completers.
j. Coordinate pre-placement training for those students who have been referred.
k. Provide placement and referral services to special needs students who are deemed ready for placement.
l. Follow up former special needs students who have been placed to smooth the transition between school and employment.
m. Maintain records of all activities of the placement and follow-up program.

8. *Special Needs Students:* Special needs students are the very heart of the placement and follow-up process. Every activity that is carried on is directly or indirectly related to student placement upon program completion. Since job placement is unique for each individual, each student must be involved as a team member. Successful placement is not simply putting special needs students to work, but rather it is placing students in employment according to their capabilities and interests. Placement is successful only when individuals stay employed and not simply during the follow-up period.

Special needs students can perform the following duties:
a. Participate in the development of the IEP (handicapped students).

b. Become as informed as possible about entrance requirements and job requirements in the chosen area of interest.
c. Visit employers and observe firsthand what workers do.
d. Take advantage of all the services offered by the helping system to prepare for and enter employment.

9. *Advisory Committees:* Placement and follow-up advisory committees and T & I craft advisory committees can provide service to the placement and follow-up effort. Advisory committee members should perform the following duties:
a. Provide information about job leads and employer contacts.
b. Identify employers who have previously hired handicapped individuals.
c. Promote job placement among colleagues, employers, and business associates.
d. Assist in helping to remove attitudinal and physical barriers confronting special needs job applicants.

10. *Rehabilitation Agencies and Special Needs Advocacy Groups:* There are a number of agencies, foundations, institutes, and special groups that can provide services for the placement effort. Examples of these include vocational rehabilitation offices, the American Foundation for the Blind, the National Association for Retarded Citizens, and the President's Committee on Employment of the Handicapped. These agencies should be contacted to determine what services they can provide. They can often perform the following duties:
a. Provide suggestions for helping special needs students make the transition from school to work.
b. Provide direct job placement services when appropriate.
c. Provide specific helping services in line with their respective programs.
d. Assist in overcoming barriers to the employment of special needs persons.

## THE PLACEMENT PROCESS

The existence of a placement and follow-up program at a local school depends upon personnel being available to serve as team members. Large vocational schools may have all of the types of team members described in the previous section of this module and more. Smaller vocational schools and vocational programs in comprehensive high schools may be able to involve only T & I teachers, special needs personnel, work-study coordinators, and guidance counselors in the placement effort. In any case, the local program of job placement and follow up will need to be organized around the staff available to serve as team members.

Regardless of the organization of the placement and follow-up program at the local school level, there are a number of functions that must be performed by the placement and follow-up team. These functions include (a) building a market for job placement, (b) conducting the pre-placement program, (c) placing students in jobs, and (d) performing follow-up activities.

### Building a Market for Job Placements

Perhaps the first step in job placement is to assess the local employment situation and to identify jobs for which special needs students can be prepared and placed. This can be done by conducting a job information search from a variety of sources. Some of these sources are: the local Employment Security Office, the Chamber of Commerce, Area Planning and Development Commissions, sheltered workshops and rehabilitation centers, the yellow pages of the phone directory, newspaper classified ads, vocational rehabilitation offices, labor unions, service clubs, civic groups, vocational advisory committees, local management and employer organizations, city directories, and census data.

The results of the job information search can be used to compile a listing of potential employers. A recommended way to organize information obtained in the job search is to place it on file cards. Such information will include the name, address, and telephone number of the employer; the person to contact; the type of job; the job performance requirements; the hiring requirements and procedures; the contract requirements (hours of work and wages paid, and referral instruction) and whom to see and when to apply. Illustration 10.2 shows a typical job information card. Job information cards can be placed into a master file and used for job placement and as a source of mail-outs and follow up. The master job file must be periodically reviewed and kept up to date.

Once the exhaustive job search has been completed, the next step is to conduct a selected employer survey to determine more detailed information about jobs in which special needs students may be placed. The employer survey should be designed to obtain detailed information about the type of jobs, the availability of on-the-job training, the job turnover rate, and other information needed to prepare job profiles and an overview of job tasks and requirements. It is usually necessary to follow up the employer survey with a prearranged visit to the company. There is no better way to facilitate job development than to meet the potential employer and to observe firsthand the actual work environment.

In preparation for visits to companies, the placement staff should learn as much as possible about the company and the products or services it provides. Conversation should focus on the possibility of hiring qualified special needs students when job vacancies occur. Positive factors such as the pre-placement training and screening that students receive before they are referred for placement should be emphasized.

Employers should be informed that a major goal of the placement program is to help them find qualified job applicants to meet their personal needs. During the visit or a subsequent visit, placement

**Illustration 10.2**

## TYPICAL JOB INFORMATION CARD

Side 1

Name of Company:

Address:

Telephone:

Person to Contact:

Types of Jobs (What-How-Why):

Side 2

Worker Performance Requirements:

Working Conditions:

Hiring Requirements (age, training, experience, screening test):

Contract Requirements (wages, work hours, full or part-time):

Referral Instructions (whom to see, where to apply):

team members can gather information about jobs that may be appropriate for special needs persons. This information, combined with the information obtained in the employer survey, can be used to prepare job profiles.

## Job Profiles

In order to match the capabilities of special needs persons with appropriate jobs, it is necessary to obtain as much detailed information about each job as possible. This information should be organized into job profiles. Job profiles should contain the following types of information: (a) job title and number from the Dictionary of Occupational Titles (DOT), (b) general job description, (c) listing of job tasks, (d) listing of specific job requirements, and (e) listing of related jobs. Illustration 10.3 shows a sample of a job profile for a bindery worker.

## Illustration 10.3

## JOB PROFILE FOR A BOOK BINDERY WORKER

```
Book Binder:   (D.O.T. 977.781)

General Duties:  Book Bindery workers operate automatic and manual machines
                 and equipment to fold, sew, staple, drill and bind many
                 printed items such as books and magazines.

Job Tasks:

1.    Measure copy and graphics
2.    File art work and maintain records
3.    Lubricate and clean bindery equipment
4.    Set-up and operate cutting and trimming machines
5.    Set-up and operate folding machines
6.    Set-up and operate stitching machines
7.    Set-up and operate paper drill machines
8.    Set-up and operate jogging machines
9.    Set-up and operate collating machines and equipment
10.   Set-up and operate stapling machines
11.   Set-up and operate bindery machines and equipment
12.   Bind printed materials with various plastic fasteners such as rings and
      strips
13.   Bind printed materials with glue and presses
14.   Place paper jackets on finished books
15.   Wrap and package finished products
16.   Store delivered supplies and materials
17.   Maintain a clean and organized work area

Specific Job Requirements:

1.    Safely operate machines and equipment
2.    Lift, carry and move heavy loads by hand or by hand truck or dolly
3.    Knowledge of bindery process
4.    Knowledge of the various materials and supplies used in bindery
5.    Ability to work in a noisy environment

Related Jobs:

      Book Repairer (D.O.T. 997.684-610)
      Hand-Sticker, Printing and Publishing (D.O.T. 977.684-022)
      Hand Collator, Printing and Publishing (D.O.T. 977.687-010)
```

The profile should be headed by the title of the job and accompanied by the DOT number. In some cases it will be difficult to find the actual DOT number for a given job title and the placement specialists will need to choose the most relevant one listed.

The general job description should contain a brief summary of major job duties.

The task listing should contain essential job activities expressed as commands to perform work. For example, one task performed daily by a book binder is to stack and jog paper. Tasks are those independent work activities that an employee gets paid to do.

The job requirement section of the profile should contain a listing of specific knowledge and abilities that a worker should have in order to function effectively on the job. The listed abilities should not be limited to manipulative performance behaviors but should also include the communication and personal-social skills that are essential for the job.

A listing of related jobs should be included in the profile so that the placement team can identify other possible job opportunities for future placement. It is also necessary to obtain this information so that the job applicant can be adequately prepared for the actual work environment. This preparation usually requires a team effort.

## Other Ways of Locating Jobs

In addition to locating jobs through employer surveys, followed by personal visits, the placement team should actively seek the services of out-of-school agencies. The local office of the Employment Service, an agency of the Department of Labor, should be contacted. This agency has given priority to the placement of special needs persons. It can often provide job leads as well as special guidance and assistance to special needs persons.

The job bank system in each state should also be used to identify local job opportunities. This is a system for locating jobs through the use of a scanner and microfilmed listing of available jobs throughout the state. Special needs individuals can scan these listings until they find a potential job for which they qualify. They then can be sent to the local Labor Department Office and through them be referred to the job.

Another excellent source for obtaining information about job opportunities is the civil service agencies that are available within most school communities. Contact should be made with these agencies to determine current job listings as well as testing procedures to help prepare students for the various civil service examinations.

In order to help special needs students find jobs, placement team members must use their contacts in the community to obtain job orders or information about available jobs. For example, T & I teach-

ers should maintain close contact with the employer in their specific field and frequently contact them to keep informed of job openings. This information should be forwarded to the placement staff for further action.

Additional information about specific job development activities will be discussed later in this module under the heading, Placing Special Needs Persons in Jobs.

## The Pre-placement Program

The pre-placement program begins the day that special needs students enter the school. As a result of the vocational assessment process discussed in Module 5, students are placed into a specific T & I program according to their interests and capabilities. Through cooperative planning and joint effort, the T & I teacher, the special needs teacher, and other school and community professionals can assist the special needs student in identifying and preparing for an appropriate occupational goal.

There are two additional parts of the pre-placement program that deserve more attention. These are the work adjustment training program and the preparation of job placement profiles.

## Work Adjustment Training

Frequently, special needs students fail to obtain placement or lose their jobs shortly after placement because of poorly developed work habits or other work adjustment attitudes and behaviors. Although most T & I teachers and special needs teachers give students some instruction in work adjustment skills in their programs, many special needs students need to receive additional instruction in work adjustment behaviors prior to placement.

The work adjustment training program for special needs students is usually conducted by the special needs teacher with input from T & I teachers, job placement staff, and other members of the placement team to make it as relevant to the employment environment as possible. The program may be offered to a group of special needs students who are ready for placement at the same time or provided on an individualized basis.

Some of the topics that should be included in the work adjustment training program are as follows:

1. Finding jobs.
2. Preparing resumes.
3. Presenting yourself in an interview.
4. Preparing for entrance exams, health exams, and special screening tests.
5. Developing good work habits.
6. Developing positive attitudes toward work.
7. Solving transportation problems.
8. Interacting successfully with others.
9. Promoting yourself on the job.
10. Building self-esteem.

## Preparing Placement Profiles

Another important part of the pre-placement program is the collection of descriptive and evaluative information on each special needs student and the organization of this information into a job placement profile. Job placement profiles showing the interests and capabilities of each student can then be matched with the job profiles described earlier in this module and used to make placement decisions.

There are at least two types of job placement profiles currently being used by job placement specialists. The first is a simple placement profile containing the following types of information: (a) a listing of tasks that students have mastered, (b) a listing of demonstrated basic skills and abilities, and (c) a rating of personal-social behaviors exhibited (Illustration 10.4).

The second type of placement profile is much more comprehensive and resembles an updated version of the special needs student profile discussed in Module 5 involving vocational assessment. The comprehensive placement profile contains information in the following areas: (a) educational academic/psychological, (b) physical/medical, (c) social/interpersonal relations, and (d) prevocational/vocational (Illustration 10.5).

Regardless of the type of placement option selected, the placement staff will need to collect student background information and evaluative information from T & I teachers, special needs teachers, and other appropriate placement team members. This information should be compiled into a placement profile that presents an accurate picture of the student's interests and proficiencies.

While the primary purpose of the job placement profile is to provide a basic source of information for the job placement staff to use in matching special needs students to job profiles, it has several other uses. It can be used to determine whether or not special needs students are ready for placement or if they should be given additional training in an identified area of weakness. Job placement profiles are also useful in the follow-up period immediately after initial placement in determining areas that may cause problems. Measures can then be taken to prevent these problems from surfacing.

## Placing Special Needs Persons in Jobs

There are two major approaches that can be used to place special needs persons. The first and most common approach is to find a job first and then select the best qualified candidates to apply for it. The second approach is to find a job that is suitable for a given special needs student (Jacobs, Larsen, Smith, 1979). Both approaches make use of placement profiles and job profiles in the matching process, but placement procedures are different for the two approaches.

## Matching Students with Identified Job Openings

Most school placement personnel use the placement approach that involves selecting from among several placement candi-

# Illustration 10.4

# SAMPLE PLACEMENT PROFILE

PROGRAM: *Graphic Arts*                    STUDENT: *Jack Scott*

JOB AREA: *Book Bindery*

MASTERED TASKS:

1. *Measure copy and graphics*
2. *Maintain bindery machines, equipment and work areas*
3. *Operate cutting and trimming machines*
4. *Operate folding machines*
5. *Operate paper drills*
6. *Operate stitching machines*
7. *Operate collating machines*
8. *Operate jogging machines*
9. *Operate stapling machines*
10. *Operate bindery machines and equipment*
11. *Bind printed materials with plastic fasteners*
12. *Bind books*
13. *Wrap and package finished products*

BASIC SKILLS AND ABILITIES:

1. *Knowledge of bindery processes*
2. *Ability to operate machinery and equipment safely*
3. *Knowledge of materials and supplies used in bindery*
4. *Ability to lift, carry and move materials and products*
5. *Ability to work with or without supervision*
6. *Desire and ability to learn and improve job skills*

PERSONAL/SOCIAL BEHAVIORS:                                    RATINGS

|  | Excellent | Good | Fair |
|---|---|---|---|
| Attitude Toward Work | X | | |
| Work Habits | | X | |
| Interpersonal Skills | X | | |
| Self-Esteem | | X | |
| Motivation | X | | |
| Character | X | | |
| Personality | | X | |

**Illustration 10.5**

## SAMPLE COMPREHENSIVE PLACEMENT PROFILE

PROGRAM: *Construction Trades*          STUDENT: *Harvey Miller*

JOB AREA: *Carpentry Helper*

MASTERED COMPETENCIES:

1. *Gather and transport tools and materials from company storage to the work site*
2. *Load, unload and stack lumber and building materials*
3. *Measure lumber and other building materials*
4. *Select appropriate tools and materials for a given work task*
5. *Maintain tools and machines (clean and lubricate)*
6. *Operate radial arm saw*
7. *Operate portable sabre saw*
8. *Operate portable power saw*
9. *Operate portable electric drill*
10. *Cut materials with hand saw*
11. *Nail materials*
12. *Assist in building forms and scaffolding*
13. *Assist with simple carpentry tasks*

SPECIFIC SKILLS AND ABILITIES:

1. *Knowledge of tools, machines, materials and supplies used in carpentry*
2. *Knowledge of basic carpentry tasks and processes*
3. *Ability to lift, carry and move heavy objects*
4. *Ability to follow directions and work under supervision*
5. *Ability to drive a pick-up truck or other work vehicle*
6. *Ability to take and make measurements*
7. *Ability to operate basic hand and power tools used in carpentry*
8. *Ability to climb ladders and work above ground level on scaffolds, building structors or roofs*
9. *Ability to read and communicate the written word*

PERSONAL/SOCIAL BEHAVIORS:

|     |                                          | RATING    |      |      |
| --- | ---------------------------------------- | --------- | ---- | ---- |
|     |                                          | Excellent | Good | Fair |
| 1.  | Attitude Toward Work                     | X         |      |      |
| 2.  | Work Habits (punctual, initiative, etc.) | X         |      |      |
| 3.  | Character                                |           | X    |      |
| 4.  | Self-Esteem                              |           | X    |      |
| 5.  | Personality                              |           | X    |      |
| 6.  | Honesty and Loyalty                      | X         |      |      |
| 7.  | Motivation                               |           | X    |      |
| 8.  | Self-Control                             |           | X    |      |
| 9.  | Assumes Responsibility                   | X         |      |      |
| 10. | Ability to Adjust                        |           | X    |      |
| 11. | Personal Hygiene and Grooming            |           |      | X    |

PREVOCATIONAL/VOCATIONAL:

1. *Completed two years building trades program (see competencies and abilities)*
2. *Worked for his uncle as a carpentry assistant three summers while in high school*
3. *Interested in a career as a carpenter*
4. *Likes to build things out of wood as a hobby*
5. *Work habits are consistent with those required in carpentry*

PHYSICAL/MEDICAL FACTORS:

1. *Good general health*
2. *Good strength and stamina*
3. *Good eye-hand coordination*
4. *Good manual and finger dexterity on right hand only*
5. *Good hearing and vision ability*
6. *Individual is fitted with mechanical hand*

*individual has become very proficient with artificial hand*

EDUCATIONAL/PSYCHOLOGICAL:

1. *Reads at 9th grade level*
2. *Has good mathematic ability*
3. *Average learner (C average)*
4. *Possesses good listening and communication skills*
5. *Above average school attendance*
6. *Interest is in working out-of-doors and with mechanical devices*
7. *Well-adjusted psychologically*
8. *Has good mechanical aptitude*

dates for a specific job opening. Illustration 10.6 shows the procedural steps involved in placing students through this approach.

The first step in this placement approach is to contact the prospective employer immediately after receiving a job order and obtain information about the hiring practices, the type of job, specific job requirements, and other information to use in preparing a job profile. The initial contact is usually made by phone but should be followed up by an actual visit to the company if possible. During the company visit, the placement specialist should obtain as much detailed information as possible about entrance requirement, job requirements, and the work environment to supplement the information that was obtained through the phone contact. If time does not permit a visit to the company or detailed information cannot be obtained to prepare a job profile, existing profiles of similar or related jobs can be used in the placement process.

Records should be prepared concerning the proceedings involved in this step and filed for future reference.

The second step is to publicize the job opening so that placement team members and potential placement candidates will know about it. Notices of the job opening should be given to appropriate T & I teachers who may have students who can qualify for the job. Job placement profiles should be reviewed to determine if any persons who have left the school have the essential qualifications and, if so, these students should be notified about the job opening.

The third step in this placement approach is for the placement staff to compare the placement profiles of interested and qualified candidates with the job profile. This procedure should result in identifying several potential placement candidates, but it may turn out that no special needs persons have the qualifications required in the job profile. Place-

## Illustration 10.6

### STEPS IN MATCHING STUDENTS TO IDENTIFIED JOBS

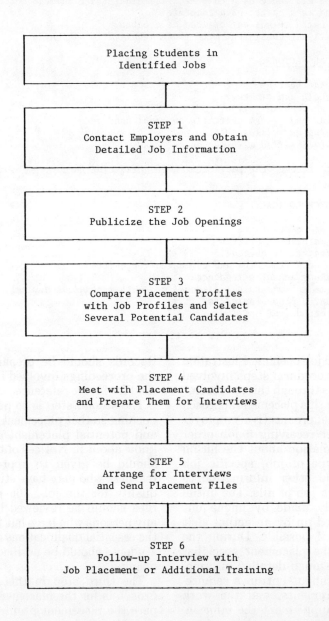

```
┌─────────────────────────────────┐
│      Placing Students in         │
│       Identified Jobs            │
└─────────────────────────────────┘
┌─────────────────────────────────┐
│            STEP 1                │
│   Contact Employers and Obtain   │
│      Detailed Job Information     │
└─────────────────────────────────┘
┌─────────────────────────────────┐
│            STEP 2                │
│     Publicize the Job Openings   │
└─────────────────────────────────┘
┌─────────────────────────────────┐
│            STEP 3                │
│   Compare Placement Profiles     │
│     with Job Profiles and Select │
│    Several Potential Candidates   │
└─────────────────────────────────┘
┌─────────────────────────────────┐
│            STEP 4                │
│   Meet with Placement Candidates │
│    and Prepare Them for Interviews│
└─────────────────────────────────┘
┌─────────────────────────────────┐
│            STEP 5                │
│      Arrange for Interviews      │
│     and Send Placement Files     │
└─────────────────────────────────┘
┌─────────────────────────────────┐
│            STEP 6                │
│     Follow-up Interview with     │
│  Job Placement or Additional Training │
└─────────────────────────────────┘
```

ment specialists should consider recommending students who have potential, even though they do not meet all of the required qualifications to match the job profile. With proper orientation, pre-

placement training, and follow-up services, some of these marginally qualified candidates can become productive employees.

The fourth step is to obtain placement commitments from selected special needs students and to assist them in applying for the job and preparing for the job interview. At this time, a records release form should be obtained from students who wish to have their placement profiles and other appropriate records sent to the employer for review. In this step, placement candidates should be briefed about the company and should be checked to see if they are ready for placement. If time permits, a brief simulated interview should be conducted with those who are to be referred for employer assessment.

The fifth step is to contact the employer and obtain a commitment from the personnel department to interview placement candidates. In obtaining this commitment, placement staff should discuss the candidates' capabilities in reference to the announced job requirements and indicate that candidates are carefully evaluated and screened before they are recommended for placement.

Once the employer agrees to interview the candidates, the special needs persons' records should be sent to the employer for review and a date and time should be arranged for the interviews. The candidate who has the best qualifications in relation to the job profile should be sent first.

The sixth and final step in this placement approach is to follow up the interviews regardless of the outcome. If one of the candidates is hired, the placement team should provide instruction to the individual regarding the transition from school to work. If one or more of the candidates are rejected, the placement staff should determine why they were not hired and provide appropriate instruction that will improve their chances for placement in the future.

All of the steps involved in this placement approach must be performed immediately upon receipt of a job order. Employers want to fill a job vacancy as soon as possible. If there is any delay, the job may be filled by some other means. This fact points out the need for a well-organized, efficient job placement program.

# FINDING A JOB FOR A SPECIFIC SPECIAL NEEDS PERSON

The placement approach for finding a specific job or creating one for special needs students may be the most effective one. The approach provides the placement team with sufficient time to develop and assess the potential of students while they are in the T & I program as well as time to locate appropriate jobs for them when they are ready for placement. This approach also provides time for the placement staff to identify a number of potential employers who would be willing to redesign their jobs to accommodate qualified special needs persons.

The job redesign technique can be used to provide jobs for special needs students who have difficulty obtaining jobs in their area of training. In redesigning jobs, employers must be willing to analyze their present job categories and reorganize them. Few employers will be willing to try this venture unless they can see how job redesign will improve productivity. They must be shown how job redesign will release their more experienced and skilled workers to perform job activities that require higher skill levels, thereby increasing worker effectiveness and productivity.

In assisting a willing employer with job redesign, the placement staff should analyze the employer's job structure and use the results of this analysis to zero in on a group of similar jobs that can be redesigned. Each of the jobs in this cluster must be analyzed or broken down into tasks and worker requirements and then sequenced according to ability levels. The final step is to assist the employer in making the necessary physical accommodations and in retraining the displaced workers for their new job activities.

The job redesign process described above is an example of what could be done under ideal conditions. Job redesign does not need to be this elaborate. Often it must be done under less than ideal conditions, and in this case it may consist of only slightly reorganizing the duties and activities of several jobs, involving minimal time and expense. Simple job redesign can be an attractive alternative for employers who are willing to hire qualified special needs persons but feel they have no suitable jobs available.

Another job redesign alternative that may appeal to employers is to create a homebound job for a qualified special needs person. Sometimes job activities that do not involve the use of heavy machinery and equipment can be performed efficiently at the employee's home. This alternative is attractive to employers who would have to make costly modifications to their facilities to make them accessible or to those who are concerned about what their employees' reactions would be if special needs persons were hired. The homebound employment alternative is also attractive to special needs persons who have limited mobility because of physical handicaps.

Job placement staff can be instrumental in helping the employer set up the job site in a special needs person's home and in designing a system for scheduling the pickup of work orders and materials from the company and returning the completed work. Placement and follow-up staff can also provide supervision to help homebound employees adjust to a regular work schedule.

The placement approach of finding or creating jobs for special needs persons involves a number of steps that differ from those which are used in matching candidates to an identified job. These placement steps are shown in Illustration 10.7.

The first step in this placement approach is to review the file of placement candidates and select a specific special needs person who is ready for placement. Step two is to review the file of potential employers who may have suitable jobs for the placement candidate and identify those who should be contacted. The third step is to contact prospective employers to see if they have any job openings for which the placement candidate may qualify. The job redesign process should be discussed with them as well as the possibility of hiring a special needs person on a trial basis without pay. The fourth step is to arrange for a company visit to those employers who express an interest and discuss with them the candidate's capabilities and the services that the placement and follow-up team can provide if the employer should be receptive to the candidate. Prior to the interview, the employer should receive the candidate's staff in redesigning similar jobs leading to a possible job opening. The fifth step is to arrange for an interview between the potential employer and the placement candidate. Prior to the interview, the employers should receive the candidate's placement profile and other appropriate records. The placement staff should prepare the candidate for the job interview by providing information about the job entrance requirements and other appropriate information about the job and the company. The sixth and final step is to follow up the job interview by providing appropriate placement services to the new employee or to provide additional instruction to the rejected candidate.

## Criteria for Effective Job Placement

Regardless of the type of placement approach employed, job placement staff should provide services in the following areas:

1. Conduct a continuous program of job development—the process of seeking out existing work opportunities or developing them through job creation or job redesign.

2. Develop good rapport with potential employers so that they will make contact with the school when jobs become available.

3. Collect and synthesize accurate information about each placement candidate and each prospective job—so that the placement profiles and job profiles can be prepared.

**Illustration 10.7**

## STEPS IN FINDING A SPECIFIC JOB FOR A SPECIAL NEEDS PERSON

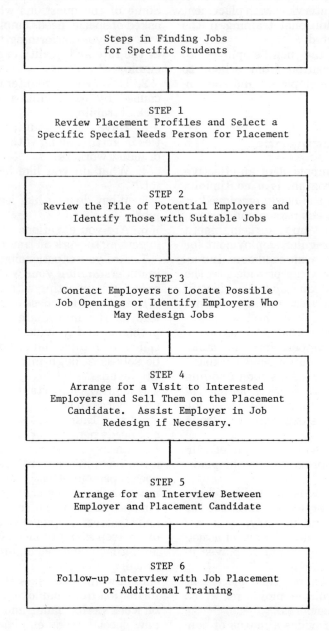

```
┌─────────────────────────────────────┐
│        Steps in Finding Jobs         │
│          for Specific Students       │
└─────────────────────────────────────┘
                   │
┌─────────────────────────────────────┐
│                STEP 1                │
│   Review Placement Profiles and Select a  │
│ Specific Special Needs Person for Placement │
└─────────────────────────────────────┘
                   │
┌─────────────────────────────────────┐
│                STEP 2                │
│ Review the File of Potential Employers and │
│     Identify Those with Suitable Jobs      │
└─────────────────────────────────────┘
                   │
┌─────────────────────────────────────┐
│                STEP 3                │
│    Contact Employers to Locate Possible    │
│ Job Openings or Identify Employers Who     │
│            May Redesign Jobs               │
└─────────────────────────────────────┘
                   │
┌─────────────────────────────────────┐
│                STEP 4                │
│     Arrange for a Visit to Interested      │
│ Employers and Sell Them on the Placement   │
│     Candidate.  Assist Employer in Job     │
│         Redesign if Necessary.             │
└─────────────────────────────────────┘
                   │
┌─────────────────────────────────────┐
│                STEP 5                │
│    Arrange for an Interview Between        │
│   Employer and Placement Candidate         │
└─────────────────────────────────────┘
                   │
┌─────────────────────────────────────┐
│                STEP 6                │
│  Follow-up Interview with Job Placement    │
│        or Additional Training              │
└─────────────────────────────────────┘
```

4. Prepare the placement candidate and the prospective employer—the process of informing the candidate about entrance requirements and job requirements and informing the employer about the preparation and capabilities of the prospective employee.

5. Provide support services to the em-

ployer and the placement candidate—the process of arranging for the placement interview, sending the candidate's records, following up the interview with placement assistance or additional training if the candidate is rejected.

6. Follow up the new employee to smooth the transition from school to work for both the employee and the employer.

## FOLLOW-UP SERVICES

An important component of an effective job placement program is a continuous follow up of both the newly employed or rejected special needs person and the employer. Initial follow-up visits help smooth the transition to regular employment for the successful placement candidate. Immediate follow-up services provided to the rejected candidate can lead to the identification of problem areas and appropriate action to overcome them. Follow-up services help to assure that program completers do not disappear into the ranks of the labor market or unemployment rolls.

There are many reasons for providing continuous follow-up services as part of the placement program. Some of the following reasons were expressed by Brolin (1976):

1. Follow up provides a means of validating the T & I program and the placement program.

2. Follow up provides feedback to keep the T & I training program relevant to the needs of students and industry.

3. Follow up provides a means of assisting both the employer and employee in the event problems arise.

4. Follow up assures that placement results in continuous employment, which leads to other placements.

5. Follow up provides a means of continuous support during the difficult, early stages of employment.

Follow-up services must be provided simultaneously to both the newly placed special needs person and to the employer.

Information must be obtained from special needs employees to determine their adjustment to the work environment. Some of the questions which should be asked of special needs employees follow:

1. Are you performing the work tasks at the rate and quality expected by your employer?

2. Have you encountered any barriers caused by the facilities, equipment, or lack of training?

3. Have you encountered any difficulties in getting along with your supervisor or fellow workers?

4. What do you like best about your job?

5. What do you like least about your job?

6. Are you experiencing any problems in getting to work on time?

7. Are you experiencing any problems in understanding your work assignments or in communicating with others?

Responses to these questions should lead to the immediate identification of problems and provide the follow-up specialist with direction as to how they can be solved through intervention with the employer.

It is just as important to provide follow-up services to the employer as to the new employee. Employers who have hired special needs persons for the first time often feel uneasy in supervising them. They often have misconceptions about special needs persons that influence their behavior toward them in an adverse way. An open discussion of any identified problems between employee and employer will often keep such problems from reaching a level that could result in early termination of employment.

Follow-up specialists should obtain information from employers about the level of work performance and adjustment of new special needs employees. In collecting information from employers, the follow-up specialist should seek responses to the following questions:

1. Is the new employee performing job tasks at the rate and quality level that

you expect of other employees?

2. Is the employee punctual in getting to work and returning from breaks?

3. Do you feel the employee understands the job requirements?

4. Can you communicate clearly with the new employee?

5. Is the employee having any trouble using the machinery or equipment or moving about in the work environment?

6. Does the employee interact successfully with his direct supervisor and with fellow workers?

7. Have you assigned a fellow worker to help the new employee make the transition to work?

8. What do you like best about the employee?

9. What do you like least about the employee?

10. Have any problems surfaced that you think the placement and follow-up team can help overcome?

11. Have you noticed any area(s) in which the employee seems to lack training? If so, please describe the situation.

Each follow-up program has a set of procedures that it follows in providing services to special needs placements and employers. Typically, follow-up services are provided at the end of the first day of employment and weekly for the first month. After this critical period of employment, follow-up services are provided monthly for six months and annually thereafter.

The following procedures are an example of what should be included in a follow-up plan:

1. Near the end of the first day of employment, visit with the new employee and his/her employer. Emphasize the positive achievements during the first workday but also try to identify any problem areas and take measures to resolve them.

2. At the end of the first week, contact the new special needs employee and his/her employer by phone or personal visit to obtain responses from both parties to questions presented earlier in this module.

Counsel with the employee and employer if necessary to work out any problems that have occurred.

3. During the latter part of the second week of employment, visit the company and talk with both the new placement and employer. Observe firsthand the employee's job performance and recommend any required modifications. Obtain additional information about job satisfaction and worker adjustment from both parties.

4. At the end of the third week, repeat the procedures described in step three.

5. Visit the employer at the end of the first month of employment to assess the special needs employee's progress on the job. Try to determine if the employer is satisfied with the new employee's work performance and adjustment to work. Following the visit to the employer, meet with the special needs employee and obtain similar information. Counsel with the employee on the basis of information received from both parties.

6. At the end of the second month, visit the company again to observe job performance and to obtain information from the employee and the employer about job satisfaction and work adjustment.

7. At the end of the third through the sixth month of employment, make contact with the employee and employer by phone or visit the job site to monitor progress on the job and to recommend any required modifications.

8. At the end of one year and annually thereafter, make contact with the employee and employer by phone, mail-in postcard or survey form, or by personal visit to obtain summary information about the placement.

Once a follow-up plan has been developed, it is essential that this plan be discussed with both the special needs employee and the employer. Special needs employees need to know that follow-up services are available to help them make adjustments to the work environment. Maintaining contacts with employers assures them that services are available to help resolve any potential problems that may arise during the early stages of employment.

When the first follow-up contact is made with employers, it is important to discuss the follow-up plan and to determine when phone contacts and visits should be made. It is equally important to stress the positive aspects of placement and to indicate that failure is not expected. Advise employers that continuing follow-up services are available and that they may call at any time for further assistance.

Effective follow-up programs begin by providing services to special needs students when they enter the T & I program and continue providing these services long after the student is placed. Special needs students should be informed about the follow-up program during orientation. The orientation to the follow-up program should include information about the purpose of the program, services provided, and operational procedures. Records should be kept on each student, beginning with orientation and continuing throughout the educational program.

An exit interview should be conducted with all students who complete the program or leave the program before completing it to remind them that placement and follow-up services are available and to remind them to respond to the follow-up questionnaires when they receive them.

Immediate follow-up services should be provided to both new special needs employees and their employers during the first week of employment and on a regular basis throughout the first year of employment. Follow-up services should be provided to former special needs students as needed after the first year of employment to help them advance in their jobs or to obtain new ones.

Follow-up questionnaires should be used at least annually to collect information from both former students and their employers regarding job performance, job placement, and the effectiveness of the T & I preparation program. Responses to these questionnaires should provide important feedback that can be used to iden-

tify weaknesses in the training program and the placement and follow-up program and give direction for change.

## SUMMARY

Without effective job placement and follow-up services, many qualified special needs students will experience great difficulty in obtaining and holding a job. The transition from T & I programs to the work environment is troublesome for most students and particularly for special needs students despite federal legislation which essentially guarantees these persons the same rights and benefits as other job applicants and employees.

Special needs students can become productive employees if given appropriate T & I education, matched with the needs of business and industry, and the kind of guidance and support services that lead to successful placement. The employment outlook for special needs students is getting brighter. More and more employers who have hired special needs persons are testifying that hiring these persons is a good investment for any employer.

There are a number of placement options open for special needs students. These include placement in (a) rehabilitation sponsored centers and institutions, (b) school system jobs, (c) on-the-job training programs, (d) work-study programs, (e) part-time jobs, (f) full-time jobs, and (g) post-secondary education programs. Of course, the most desirable placement option is in full-time employment. Full-time employment brings status and respect to special needs students and reinforces their ability to fully participate in our society.

The placement and follow-up program of a school depends upon the personnel available to serve as team members. The placement team should include (a) vocational administrators, (b) student personnel specialists and counselors, (c) work sample/evaluation center personnel, (d) T & I teachers, (e) cooperative educational/

work-study coordinators, (f) special needs personnel, (g) job placement and follow-up staff, (h) special needs students, (i) advisory committees and (j) rehabilitation agencies and special needs advocacy groups.

Regardless of the organizational structure of a job placement and follow-up program, the following major services are usually provided: (a) building a market for placement, (b) conducting the pre-placement program (c) placing special needs students in jobs, and (d) providing follow-up services.

## SELF ASSESSMENT: JOB PLACEMENT AND FOLLOW-UP

1. Explain why job placement and follow-up services are needed to assist special needs students and graduates in obtaining appropriate jobs.

2. List and describe some of the placement options available for special needs students and graduates.

3. Explain some of the major provisions of the Rehabilitation Act of 1973 that should help handicapped individuals obtain employment.

4. Describe barriers to employment that exist among special needs students.

5. Describe barriers to the employment of special needs students that are caused by the "helping system."

6. Describe barriers to the employment of special needs students that exist in our society.

7. List some of the common misconceptions that employers hold about special needs persons which become employment barriers.

8. Explain why job placement and follow-up services should be provided by a cooperative team approach.

9. Describe the role that T & I teachers should play in providing job placement and follow-up services.

10. Describe some of the activities involved in building a market for job placement.

11. Describe some of the activities involved in conducting the pre-placement program.

12. Describe the placement process of matching students with identified job openings.

13. Describe the placement process of finding a job for a specific special needs person.

14. List the criteria for effective job placement services.

15. List reasons for providing continuous follow-up services as part of the placement and follow-up program.

16. Describe a plan for providing follow-up services to special needs persons, beginning on the first day of employment and continuing on an annual basis.

## ASSOCIATED ACTIVITIES

1. Visit the local office of employment security and obtain information about services they can provide in placing special needs persons.

2. Identify employers who have hired special needs persons and contact them to obtain information about placement.

3. Contact the nearest local office of vocational rehabilitation and obtain information from them about job placement and follow-up services that they provide.

4. If there is a sheltered workshop or rehabilitation institution nearby, visit it to obtain firsthand information about this placement option.

5. If the placement team approach is not being used in your school, meet with your administrators and discuss the possibility of establishing this system of placement.

6. Obtain all the information you can about job placement and follow up for special needs persons.

7. Discuss job placement and follow up with your craft advisory committee.

8. Contact your job placement and follow-up specialists and offer your services in the placement process.

# REFERENCES

*Barriers and bridges: An overview of vocational services available for handicapped Californians.* Sacramento, California: California Advisory Council on Vocational Education, 1977.

Brolin, D. *Vocational preparation of retarded citizens.* Columbus, Ohio: Charles E. Merrill Publishing Company, 1976.

Dahl, P., Appleby, J. and Lipe, D. *Mainstreaming guidebook for vocational educators.* Salt Lake City, Utah: Olympus Publishing Company, 1978.

*Dear employer.* Washington, D.C.: The President's Committee on Employment of the Handicapped, U.S. Government Printing Office, 1979.

Fair, G. Employment opportunities in the 80's for special needs students. *Journal for Vocational Special Needs Education,* 1980, 3, 18–20.

Finney, J. *A resource manual for job placement for handicapped youth and adults.* Pittsburg, Kansas: Vocational Curriculum Center at Pittsburg State University, 1979.

Jacobs, A., Larson, J., and Smith, C. *Handbook for job placement of mentally retarded workers.* New York: Garland STPM Press, 1979.

O'Keefe, A. *Barriers to employment for the handicapped.* College Station, Texas: Center for Career Development and Occupational Preparation, Texas A & M University, 1978.

*Placement services: A training manual.* Ann Arbor, Michigan: National Association for Industry Education Cooperation, Prakken Publications, Inc., 1977.

Sheppard, N., and Pacs, N. *Workshop on the development of educational personnel to meet the employment and job placement needs of handicapped persons.* Blacksburg, Virginia: Virginia Polytechnic Institution and State University, 1977 (Eric Document Reproduction Service, No. ED 141 642).

*Targeted jobs and WIN credits.* Washington, D.C.: The Department of Treasury, Internal Revenue Service (Publication No. 906), U.S. Government Printing Office, 1979.

*Ten good reasons to hire the handicapped.* Albany, New York: Governors Office, (Publication No. 764), 1977.

Weisgerberg, R., Dahl, P. and Appleby, J. *Training the handicapped for productive employment.* Rockville, Maryland: Aspen Systems Corporation, 1980.

*Your rights as a disabled person.* Washington, D.C.: U.S. Department of Health, Education and Welfare, U.S. Government Printing Office, 1978.

## CASE HISTORY: MANUEL'S STORY

Manuel is an academically and economically disadvantaged learner enrolled in a masonry program. He is a bilingual student whose family came from Puerto Rico seven years ago. There are ten children in the family. Manuel's father sometimes finds employment doing odd jobs. Most of the time, however, he is unemployed. The family is on public assistance. Spanish is spoken in the home.

When Manuel first entered public schools in this country, he was given a psychological test. His difficulty in understanding

English resulted in a low score, which automatically placed him in a special education class for the mentally retarded. When it came time for his periodic reevaluation, he had developed a sufficient proficiency in English to test out of the special education class. The psychologist was also bilingual and was able to administer the test questions in either Spanish or English.

Currently Manuel is registered in regular classes in the school. He works with a bilingual teacher several times a week and attends a class in a resource room each day for assistance in remedial academics. His reading and math levels are three levels below his peers. The district social worker also has Manuel on her caseload and visits the home periodically in order to keep an open channel of communication between the school and the family. She is also looking into the possibility of enrolling Manuel in a summer youth employment program run by a local CETA prime sponsor.

Manuel is succeeding very well in the skills development phase of the masonry program. He has demonstrated proficiency in laying brick, making bonds and ties, building footings and arches, and working with a variety of materials such as glass, cork, cement, and artificial stone.

He has been having difficulties in keeping up with the classroom lectures and reading assignments as well as the areas of construction theory and blueprint reading. The resource room teacher and the bilingual teacher are both working cooperatively with the program instructor to help him in these areas.

## CASE HISTORY ACTIVITY

Rosa has recently enrolled in your program. She comes from a broken home where her mother must rely on public assistance to raise her seven children. Rosa is frequently absent and her poor grades reflect this. Rosa is very shy and does not have any friends in the class. She also has some personal hygiene problems. Her reading and math levels are below her peers. Rosa does not often complete required written assignments and has scored poorly on the two tests she has taken so far. Yet records show that she has normal intelligence.

Based on this information, complete the case history profile worksheet for Rosa's participation in your program.

CASE HISTORY PROFILE WORKSHEET

Student: _____ Page: _____

Handicapping Condition(s): _____

T & I Program: _____ Academic Levels: _____

Career Goal/Occupational Interest: _____

Considerations (e.g., medication, behavior): _____

_____

| Adaptation | Specific Services Needed | Where to Obtain Service |
|---|---|---|
| Cooperative Planning (School Personnel) | | |
| Support Services | | |
| Architectural Changes | | |
| Adaptive Equipment | | |
| Curriculum Modification | | |
| Instructional Materials/ Supplies | | |
| Teaching Techniques | | |
| Agency Involvement | | |
| Possible Job Placement | | |

266

# APPENDIX A

## Agencies and Organizations That Provide Assistance for Special Needs Individuals.

In our quest to provide appropriate program opportunities for handicapped and disadvantaged individuals, we must realize that one of the keys lies in cooperation with other disciplines, agencies and organizations. Various sources can be beneficial in providing such services as vocational counseling, personal adjustment training, prevocational training, vocational training, post-school work adjustment training, work-study program opportunities, and job placement assistance. A list of agencies and organizations is organized on the following pages.

## GENERAL SOURCES OF ASSISTANCE

### National

Accent on Information
P.O. Box 700
Bloomington, Illinois 61701

American Coalition of Citizens with Disabilities
1200 15th Street, N.W.
Washington, D.C. 20005

American Psychological Association
1200 17th Street, N.W.
Washington, D.C. 20036

American Rehabilitation
Rehabilitation Services Administration
330 C Street, S.W.
Washington, D.C. 20201

Bureau of Education for the Handicapped
Department of Education
Washington, D.C.

Bureau of Occupational and Adult Education
Department of Education
Washington, D.C.

Center on Human Policy
216 Ostrom Avenue
Syracuse, New York 13210

Closer Look—National Information Center for
  the Handicapped
Box 1492
Washington, D.C. 20013

Council of State Administrators of Vocational
  Rehabilitation
1522 K Street, N.W.
Suite 1110
Washington, D.C. 20007

Eric Clearinghouse on Handicapped and Gifted
  Children
1920 Association Drive
Reston, Virginia 22091

Goodwill Industries of America
9200 Wisconsin Avenue
Washington, D.C. 20014

Mainstream, Inc.
1200 15th Street, N.W.
Washington, D.C. 20005

National Center for a Barrier Free Environment
7315 Wisconsin Avenue, N.W.
Washington, D.C. 20014

National Easter Seal Society for Crippled Children
  and Adults
2023 West Ogden Avenue
Chicago, Illinois 60612

People-to-People
Commitee for the Handicapped
1522 K Street, N.W. #1130
Washington, D.C. 20005

Project PAVE
Parents Advocating for Vocational Education
1201 16th Street, N.W.
Washington, D.C. 20036

The Council for Exceptional Children
1920 Association Drive
Reston, Virginia 22091

The National Foundation—March of Dimes
P.O. Box 2000
White Plains, New York 10602

The President's Committee on Employment of the
Handicapped
1111 20th Street, N.W.
Washington, D.C. 20210

## State

Department of Family and Children Services

Department of Labor (CETA programs)

Department of Mental Health

Department of Welfare

Family Service Agency

Federal Job Information Center

Governor's Committee for Employment of the
Handicapped

Governor's Office (CETA programs)

Public Health Agency

Recording for the Blind, Inc.

State Agency for the Blind

State Agency for the Deaf

State Association for Retarded Children

State Division of Vocational Rehabilitation

State Employment Office

State Employment Security Office

State Vocational Rehabilitation Office

Talking Books

## Local

Church Groups

Community Medical Center

Community Mental Health Center

County Public Health Agencies

County Welfare Departments

Easter Seal Society

Family County Detention Department

Local CETA Prime Sponsors

Local Civic Groups (Civitan, Elk, Kiwanis,
Lions, Moose)

Local/County Health Department

Local/Regional Association for Retarded Children

Local/Regional Blind Association

Local/Regional Goodwill Industries

Local Vocational Rehabilitation Office

Mayor's Committee for Employment of the
Handicapped

Mental Retardation Center

Parents Organization for Specific Handicapped
Groups

Speech and Hearing Clinic

Veteran's Administration

# PROFESSIONAL ORGANIZATIONS AND ASSOCIATIONS

American Association for the Education of the
Severely and Profoundly Handicapped (AAESPH)
Council for Exceptional Children
1920 Association Drive
Reston, Virginia 22091

American Vocational Association
2020 North 14th Street
Arlington, Virginia 22201

Council for Children with Behavioral
Disorders (CCBD)
Council for Exceptional Children
1920 Association Drive
Reston, Virginia 22091

Division for Children with Communication
Disorders (DCCD)
Council for Exceptional Children
1920 Association Drive
Reston, Virginia 22091

Division for Children with Learning
Disabilities (DCLD)
Council for Exceptional Children
1920 Association Drive
Reston, Virginia 22091

Division for the Visually Handicapped (DVH)
Council for Exceptional Children
1920 Association Drive
Reston, Virginia 22091

Division of the Physically Handicapped (DPH)
Council for Exceptional Children
1920 Association Drive
Reston, Virginia 22091

Division on Career Development (DCD)
The Council for Exceptional Children
1920 Association Drive
Reston, Virginia 22091
(Journal: *Career Development for Exceptional
   Individuals)*

Division on Mental Retardation (CEC-MR)
Council for Exceptional Children
1920 Association Drive
Reston, Virginia 22091

National Association of Vocational Education
   Special Needs Personnel (NAVESNP)
105 Bancroft Hall
University of Nebraska–Lincoln
Lincoln, Nebraska 68588
(Journal: *Journal of Vocational Special Needs)*

National Rehabilitation Association
1522 K Street, N.W.
Washington, D.C. 20005
(Journal: *Journal of Rehabilitation)*

The Council for Exceptional Children
1920 Association Drive
Reston, Virginia 22091
(Journal: *Teaching Exceptional Children)*

Vocational Evaluation and Work Adjustment
   Association (VEWAA)
National Rehabilitation Association
1522 K Street, N.W.
Washington, D.C. 20005

## SOURCES OF ASSISTANCE FOR DISADVANTAGED INDIVIDUALS

Adult Basic Education Programs

Association of Mexican-American Educators

Bureau of Indian Affairs (federal)

CETA Prime Sponsors (state/local)

Department of Welfare (state)

Governor's Committee (CETA programs)

Job Corps

JOBS—National Alliance of Businessmen (local)

National Council on Crime and Delinquency
44 East 23rd Street
New York, New York 10010

State Employment Office

Urban League (state/local)

## SOURCES OF ASSISTANCE FOR EMOTIONALLY DISTURBED AND BEHAVIOR DISORDERED INDIVIDUALS

American Psychiatric Association
1700 18 Street, N.W.
Washington, D.C. 20009

Mental Health Association
1800 North Kent Street
Arlington, Virginia 22209

National Association for Mental Health, Inc.
Suite 1300
10 Columbus Circle
New York, New York 10019

National Association of State Mental Health
   Program Directors
1001 Third Street, S.W.
Suite 115
Washington, D.C. 20024

## SOURCES OF ASSISTANCE FOR HEALTH IMPAIRED INDIVIDUALS

American Allergy Academy
225 East Michigan Street
Milwaukee, Wisconsin 53202

American Cancer Society
219 East 42nd Street
New York, New York 10017

American Diabetes Association, Inc.
1 West 48th Street
New York, New York 10020

American Heart Association, Inc.
44 East 23rd Street
New York, New York 10010

American Lung Association
1740 Broadway
New York, New York 10019

Epilepsy Foundation of America
1828 L Street, N.W.
Washington, D.C. 20036

National Cystic Fibrosis Research
3379 Peachtree Road, N.E.
Atlanta, Georgia 30326

National Health Council, Inc.
1740 Broadway
New York, New York 10019

National Hemophilia Foundation
25 West 39th Street
New York, New York 10018

National Tuberculosis and Respiratory Disease
   Association
1740 Broadway
New York, New York 10019

The Arthritis Foundation
1212 Avenue of the Americas
New York, New York 10036

# SOURCES OF ASSISTANCE FOR HEARING IMPAIRED INDIVIDUALS

Alexander Graham Bell Association for the Deaf
3417 Volta Place, N.W.
Washington, D.C. 20007

Council of Organizations Serving the Deaf
P.O. Box 894
Columbia, Maryland 21044

Gallaudet College
School for the Deaf
Florida Avenue at Seventh Street, N.E.
Washington, D.C. 20002

National Association of the Deaf
814 Thayer Avenue
Silver Springs, Maryland

National Association of Hearing and Speech
   Agencies
814 Thayer Avenue
Silver Springs, Maryland

National Technical Institute for the Deaf
One Lomb Memorial Drive
Rochester, New York 15623

# SOURCES OF ASSISTANCE FOR LEARNING DISABLED INDIVIDUALS

Association for Children with Learning
   Disabilities
4156 Library Road
Pittsburgh, Pennsylvania 19234

# SOURCES OF ASSISTANCE FOR THE MENTALLY HANDICAPPED INDIVIDUAL

American Association on Mental Deficiency
5201 Connecticut Avenue, N.W.
Washington, D.C. 20015

Association for Retarded Citizens
2709 Avenue E East
Arlington, Texas 76011

National Association of Coordinators of State
   Programs for the Mentally Retarded
2001 Jefferson Davis Highway
Suite 802
Arlington, Virginia 22202

President's Committee on Mental Retardation
Seventh and D Streets, N.W.
Washington, D.C. 20201

# SOURCES OF ASSISTANCE FOR MULTI-HANDICAPPED INDIVIDUALS

National Committee for Multi-Handicapped
   Children
239 14th Street
Niagra Falls, New York 14303

# SOURCES OF ASSISTANCE FOR PHYSICALLY HANDICAPPED INDIVIDUALS

American Occupational Therapy Association
6000 Executive Boulevard
Rockville, Maryland 20852

American Orthotic and Prosthetic Association
1440 N Street, N.W.
Washington, D.C. 20005

American Physical Therapy Association
1156 15th Street, N.W.
Washington, D.C. 20005

Arthritis Foundation
1212 Avenues of the Americas
New York, New York 10036

Disabled in Action, Ltd.
175 Willoughby Street
Brooklyn, New York 11201

Disabled Americans
807 Maine Avenue, S.W.
Washington, D.C. 20024

Epilepsy Foundation of America
1828 L Street, N.W.
Washington, D.C. 20036

Library of Congress
Division for the Blind and Physically
   Handicapped
Washington, D.C. 20542

Muscular Dystrophy Associations of America
810 Seventh Avenue
New York, New York 10019

National Amputation Foundation
12–45 150th Street
Whitestone, New York 11357

National Association for the Physically
   Handicapped, Inc.
6473 Grandville Avenue
Detroit, Michigan 48228

National Congress of Organizations of the
   Physically Handicapped, Inc.
7611 Oakland Avenue
Minneapolis, Minnesota 55423

National Epilepsy League, Inc.
203 North Wabash Avenue
Room 2200
Chicago, Illinois 60601

National Foundation—March of Dimes
800 2nd Avenue
New York, New York 10017

National Multiple Sclerosis Society
257 Park Avenue, South
New York, New York 10010

National Paraplegia Foundation
333 North Michigan Avenue
Chicago, Illinois 60601

National Rehabilitation Association
1522 K Street, N.W.
Washington, D.C. 20005

Paralyzed Veterans of America
7315 Wisconsin Avenue
Suite 301-W
Washington, D.C. 20014

Spina Bifida Association of America
343 South Dearborn
Suite 319
Chicago, Illinois 60604

United Cerebral Palsy Association, Inc.
66 East 34th Street
New York, New York 10016

## SOURCES OF ASSISTANCE FOR SPEECH IMPAIRED INDIVIDUALS

The American Speech and Hearing Association
9030 Old Georgetown Road
Washington, D.C. 20014

## SOURCES OF ASSISTANCE FOR VISUALLY HANDICAPPED INDIVIDUALS

American Association of Workers for the
   Blind, Inc.
1511 K Street, N.W.
Washington, D.C. 20005

American Foundation for the Blind, Inc.
15 West 16th Street
New York, New York 10011

American Printing House for the Blind, Inc.
1839 Frankfort Avenue
Louisville, Kentucky 40206

Association for Education of the Visually
   Handicapped
711 14th Street, N.W.
Washington, D.C. 20005

Library of Congress
Division for the Blind and Physically
   Handicapped
1291 Taylor Street, N.W.
Washington, D.C. 20540

Lions International
300 22nd Street
Oak Brook, Illinois 60521

Recording for the Blind
P.O. Box 1339
Washington, D.C. 20013

National Association for Visually Handicapped
3201 Balboa Street
San Francisco, California 94121

National Braille Association
85 Godwin Avenue
Midland Park, New Jersey 07432

National Federation of the Blind
218 Randolph Hotel Building
Des Moines, Iowa 50309

National Industries for the Blind
1455 Broad Street
Bloomfield, New Jersey 07003

# APPENDIX B

## Readability Formulas

### READABILITY FORMULA A

SMOG Grading, a readability formula by G. Harry McLaughlin, Associate Professor of Communications, School of Journalism, Syracuse University, follows.

1. Count 10 consecutive sentences near the beginning of the text to be assessed, 10 in the middle and 10 near the end. Count as a sentence any string of words ending with a period, question mark or exclamation point.

2. In the 30 selected sentences count every word of three or more syllables. Any string of letters or numerals beginning and ending with a space or punctuation mark should be counted if you can distinguish at least three syllables when you read it aloud in context. If a polysyllabic word is repeated, count each repetition.

3. Estimate the square root of the number of polysyllabic words counted. This is done by taking the square root of the nearest perfect square. For example, if the count is 95, the nearest perfect square is 100, which yields a square root of 10. If the count lies roughly between two perfect squares, choose the lower number. For instance if the count is 110, take the square root of 100 rather than that of 121.

4. Add 3 to the approximate square root. This gives the SMOG Grade, which is the reading grade that a person must have reached if he is to understand fully the text assessed.*

*Reprinted from *Journal of Reading* (8) 12: May, 1969, by G. Harry McLaughlin by permission of G. Harry McLaughlin and the International Reading Association. Copyright 1969 by the International Reading Association, Inc.

Edward Fry of Rutgers University Reading Center, Rutgers University, New Brunswick, New Jersey.

### READABILITY FORMULA B

Expanded directions follow for working the readability graph developed by Edward Fry of Rutgers University Reading Center, Rutgers University, New Brunswick, New Jersey.

1. Randomly select three (3) sample passages and count out exactly 100 words each, beginning with the beginning of a sentence. Do count proper nouns, initializations, and numerals.

2. Count the number of sentences in the hundred words, estimating length of the fraction of the last sentence to the nearest one-tenth.

3. Count the total number of syllables in the 100-word passage. If you don't have a hand counter available, an easy way is to simply put a mark above every syllable over one in each word, then when you get to the end of the passage, count the number of marks and add 100. Small calculators can also be used as counters by pushing numeral 1, then push the + sign for each word or syllable when counting.

## Figure 2

### GRAPH FOR ESTIMATING READABILITY —EXTENDED

by Edward Fry, Rutgers University Reading Center, New Brunswick, N.J. 08904

Average number of syllables per 100 words

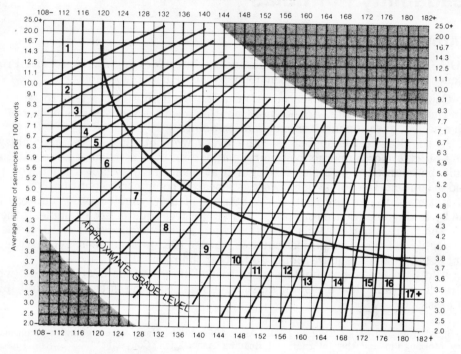

4. Enter graph with *average* sentence length and *average* number of syllables; plot dot where the two lines intersect. Area where dot is plotted will give you the approximate grade level.

5. If a great deal of variability is found in syllable count or sentence count, putting more samples into the average is desirable.

6. A word is defined as a group of symbols with a space on either side; thus, *Joe, IRA, 1945,* and & are each one word.

7. A syllable is defined as a phonetic syllable. Generally, there are as many syllables as vowel sounds. For example, *stopped* is one syllable and *wanted* is two syllables. When counting syllables for numerals and initializations, count one syllable for each symbol. For example, *1945* is four syllables, *IRA* is three syllables, and & is one syllable.*

Note: This "extended graph" does not outmode or render the earlier (1968) version inoperative or inaccurate; it is an extension. (REPRODUCTION PERMITTED—NO COPYRIGHT)

*Reproduced from *Journal of Reading,* December 1977, p. 249.

# READABILITY FORMULA C

To estimate the reading ease of a book or material by the Flesch formula (Flesch table is on following page) follow these steps:

1. Choose your samples
   a. Pick a series of random samples from the book or material.
   b. Select enough samples to make a fair judgment of the reading ease.
   c. Each sample should start at the beginning of a paragraph.
2. Count the number of words
   a. Count the number of words in each sample until you reach 100 words.
   b. Contractions count as one word (e.g., didn't, shouldn't, can't).
   c. Words with hyphens count as one word (e.g., role-play).
   d. Numbers and letters count as one word (e.g., 1979, P.O.).
3. Count the number of sentences
   a. Count the total number of complete sentences.
   b. Colons (:) or semi-colon (;) are used to separate two sentences or complete units of thought (e.g., The saw is a tool; it is often used in a carpentry class.).
4. Determine the average sentence length
   a. Figure the average sentence length for all the samples combined.
   b. Take the total numbers of words in all the samples (e.g., 7 samples would have 100 words each for a total of 700 words).*
   c. Divide the total number of words (step 2) by the number of sentences in all the samples combined.
5. Count all words with only one syllable
   a. Determine the total number of words in all of the samples which have only one syllable.
   b. Divide this total by the number of samples you have selected.
6. Finding the reading ease score
   a. Take the average sentence length in words and the average number of one-syllable words per sample and apply them to the Flesch Reading Ease Index Table.
   b. This will give you the reading ease index number.
   c. Now use the Flesch Conversion Table to determine the approximate reading level of the book or material.*

---

*Adapted from Farr, J., Jenkins, J. and Patterson, D., Simplification of Flesch reading ease formula. *Journal of Applied Psychology,* (35), October, 1951, pp. 333–37. Copyright, 1951 by the American Psychological Association. Reprinted by permission.

# FLESCH READING EASE INDEX TABLE

| Number of Sentences per Hundred Words | Number of One-Syllable Words per Hundred Words | | | | | | | | | | | | | | | | | | | | | | |
|---|---|---|---|---|---|---|---|---|---|---|---|---|---|---|---|---|---|---|---|---|---|---|---|
|  | 84 | 82 | 80 | 78 | 76 | 74 | 72 | 70 | 68 | 66 | 64 | 62 | 60 | 58 | 56 | 54 | 52 | 50 | 48 | 46 | 44 | 42 | 40 |
| 9 | 94 | 90 | 87 | 84 | 81 | 78 | 74 | 72 | 68 | 65 | 61 | 58 | 56 | 52 | 49 | 45 | 42 | 40 | 36 | 33 | 29 | 27 | 23 |
| 10 | 93 | 89 | 86 | 83 | 80 | 77 | 73 | 71 | 67 | 64 | 60 | 57 | 55 | 51 | 48 | 44 | 41 | 39 | 35 | 32 | 28 | 26 | 22 |
| 11 | 92 | 88 | 85 | 82 | 79 | 76 | 72 | 70 | 66 | 63 | 59 | 56 | 54 | 50 | 47 | 43 | 40 | 38 | 34 | 31 | 27 | 25 | 21 |
| 12 | 91 | 87 | 84 | 81 | 78 | 75 | 71 | 69 | 65 | 62 | 58 | 55 | 53 | 49 | 46 | 42 | 39 | 37 | 33 | 30 | 26 | 24 | 20 |
| 13 | 90 | 86 | 83 | 80 | 77 | 74 | 70 | 68 | 64 | 61 | 57 | 54 | 52 | 48 | 45 | 41 | 38 | 35 | 32 | 29 | 25 | 23 | 19 |
| 14 | 89 | 85 | 82 | 79 | 76 | 72 | 69 | 67 | 63 | 60 | 56 | 53 | 50 | 47 | 44 | 40 | 37 | 34 | 31 | 28 | 24 | 22 | 18 |
| 15 | 88 | 84 | 81 | 78 | 75 | 71 | 68 | 66 | 62 | 59 | 55 | 52 | 49 | 46 | 43 | 39 | 36 | 33 | 30 | 27 | 23 | 21 | 17 |
| 16 | 87 | 83 | 80 | 77 | 74 | 70 | 67 | 65 | 61 | 58 | 54 | 51 | 48 | 45 | 42 | 38 | 35 | 32 | 29 | 26 | 22 | 20 | 16 |
| 17 | 86 | 82 | 79 | 76 | 73 | 69 | 66 | 64 | 60 | 57 | 53 | 50 | 47 | 44 | 41 | 37 | 34 | 31 | 28 | 25 | 21 | 19 | 15 |
| 18 | 85 | 81 | 78 | 75 | 72 | 68 | 65 | 63 | 59 | 56 | 52 | 49 | 46 | 43 | 40 | 36 | 33 | 30 | 27 | 24 | 20 | 18 | 14 |
| 19 | 83 | 80 | 77 | 74 | 71 | 67 | 64 | 61 | 58 | 55 | 51 | 48 | 45 | 42 | 39 | 35 | 32 | 29 | 26 | 23 | 19 | 17 | 13 |
| 20 | 82 | 79 | 76 | 73 | 70 | 66 | 63 | 60 | 57 | 54 | 50 | 47 | 44 | 41 | 38 | 34 | 31 | 28 | 25 | 22 | 18 | 16 | 12 |
| 21 | 81 | 78 | 75 | 72 | 69 | 65 | 62 | 59 | 56 | 53 | 49 | 46 | 43 | 40 | 37 | 33 | 30 | 27 | 24 | 21 | 17 | 15 | 11 |
| 22 | 80 | 77 | 74 | 71 | 68 | 64 | 61 | 58 | 55 | 52 | 48 | 45 | 42 | 39 | 36 | 32 | 29 | 26 | 23 | 20 | 16 | 14 | 10 |
| 23 | 79 | 76 | 73 | 70 | 67 | 63 | 60 | 57 | 54 | 51 | 47 | 44 | 41 | 38 | 35 | 31 | 28 | 25 | 22 | 19 | 15 | 13 | 9 |
| 24 | 78 | 75 | 72 | 69 | 66 | 62 | 59 | 56 | 53 | 50 | 46 | 43 | 40 | 37 | 34 | 30 | 27 | 24 | 21 | 18 | 14 | 12 | 8 |
| 25 | 77 | 74 | 71 | 68 | 65 | 61 | 58 | 55 | 52 | 49 | 45 | 42 | 39 | 36 | 33 | 29 | 26 | 23 | 20 | 17 | 13 | 11 | 7 |
| 26 | 76 | 73 | 70 | 67 | 64 | 60 | 57 | 54 | 51 | 48 | 44 | 41 | 38 | 35 | 32 | 28 | 25 | 22 | 19 | 16 | 12 | 10 | 6 |
| 27 | 75 | 72 | 69 | 66 | 63 | 59 | 56 | 53 | 50 | 47 | 43 | 40 | 37 | 34 | 31 | 27 | 24 | 21 | 18 | 15 | 11 | 9 | 5 |
| 28 | 74 | 71 | 68 | 65 | 62 | 58 | 55 | 52 | 49 | 46 | 42 | 39 | 36 | 33 | 30 | 26 | 23 | 20 | 17 | 13 | 10 | 8 | 4 |
| 29 | 73 | 70 | 67 | 64 | 61 | 57 | 54 | 51 | 48 | 45 | 41 | 38 | 35 | 32 | 29 | 25 | 22 | 19 | 16 | 12 | 9 | 7 | 3 |
| 30 | 72 | 69 | 66 | 63 | 60 | 56 | 53 | 50 | 47 | 44 | 40 | 37 | 34 | 31 | 27 | 24 | 21 | 18 | 15 | 11 | 8 | 6 | 2 |
| 31 | 71 | 68 | 65 | 62 | 59 | 55 | 52 | 49 | 46 | 43 | 39 | 36 | 33 | 30 | 26 | 23 | 20 | 17 | 14 | 10 | 7 | 5 | 1 |
| 32 | 70 | 67 | 64 | 61 | 58 | 54 | 51 | 48 | 45 | 42 | 38 | 35 | 32 | 29 | 25 | 22 | 19 | 16 | 13 | 9 | 6 | 4 |  |
| 33 | 69 | 66 | 63 | 60 | 57 | 53 | 50 | 47 | 44 | 41 | 37 | 34 | 31 | 28 | 24 | 21 | 18 | 15 | 12 | 8 | 5 | 2 |  |
| 34 | 68 | 65 | 61 | 59 | 56 | 52 | 49 | 46 | 43 | 40 | 36 | 33 | 30 | 27 | 23 | 20 | 17 | 14 | 11 | 7 | 4 | 1 |  |
| 35 | 67 | 64 | 60 | 58 | 55 | 51 | 48 | 45 | 42 | 38 | 35 | 32 | 29 | 26 | 22 | 19 | 16 | 13 | 10 | 6 | 3 |  |  |
| 36 | 66 | 63 | 59 | 57 | 54 | 50 | 47 | 44 | 41 | 37 | 34 | 31 | 28 | 25 | 21 | 18 | 15 | 12 | 9 | 5 | 2 |  |  |
| 37 | 65 | 62 | 58 | 56 | 53 | 49 | 46 | 43 | 40 | 36 | 33 | 30 | 27 | 24 | 20 | 17 | 14 | 11 | 8 | 4 | 1 |  |  |
| 38 | 64 | 61 | 57 | 55 | 52 | 48 | 45 | 42 | 39 | 35 | 32 | 29 | 26 | 23 | 19 | 16 | 13 | 10 | 7 | 3 |  |  |  |

# FLESCH CONVERSION TABLE

| READING EASE SCORE | ESTIMATED READING GRADE |
|---|---|
| 90 to 100 | 5th Grade |
| 80 to 90 | 6th Grade |
| 70 to 80 | 7th Grade |
| 60 to 70 | 8th to 9th Grade |
| 50 to 60 | 10th to 12th Grade |
| 30 to 50 | 13th to 16th Grade |
| 0 to 30 | College Graduate |

# APPENDIX C

## Architectural Accessibility Checklist

### GETTING TO VOCATIONAL BUILDINGS AND ENTERING

A. Entrances to Vocational Grounds

1. Are entrances to parking areas for handicapped persons clearly marked?     Yes    No

2. Are entrances to vocational grounds adequately lighted?     Yes    No

3. Are there drive-up phone installations for use by disabled persons?     Yes    No

NOTES: _____

_____

B. Passenger Unloading and Parking Areas

1. Are passenger unloading and parking areas for disabled persons close to the building entrance?     Yes    No

2. Are there sufficient parking spaces (at least two per building) for handicapped persons to use?     Yes    No

3. Are parking spaces at least 12 feet wide?     Yes    No

4. Do parking spaces allow disabled persons to get in and out on a level surface?     Yes    No

5. Are parking areas positioned so handicapped persons do not need to move behind parked cars?     Yes    No

6. Is the pavement surface free of loose gravel, debris, and drain covers in which wheel chairs and crutches may sink?     Yes    No

7. Are parking areas adequately lighted?     Yes    No

NOTES: _____

_____

C. Curb Cuts or Curb Ramps

1. Is there at least one curb cut with no more than 8.3% gradient per parking lot?     Yes    No

2. Do curb cuts have a non-slip surface such as a broom finish?     Yes    No

3. Are curb cuts located near to designated handicapped parking spaces and where it is impossible for them to be blocked by cars or other obstructions? Yes No

NOTES: _____

_____

D. Walks

1. Are walks at least 4 feet wide? Yes No
2. Do walks have a slope no greater than 5% (1" to 20')? Yes No
3. Do walk surfaces blend to a common level at intersections? Yes No
4. Do walk surfaces have a non-slip surface? Yes No

NOTES: _____

_____

E. Ramps

1. Do ramps have a slope no greater than 8.33% or 1 foot rise in 12 feet? Yes No
2. Do ramps have smooth hand rails located 32" high on both sides if they are not located along the wall? Yes No
3. Do handrails extend 1' beyond the bottom and top of ramps? Yes No
4. Do ramps have a non-slip surface? Yes No
5. Do ramps have level platforms 6 feet long on 30" intervals? Yes No
6. Do ramps end on the bottom with at least 6" level platforms or walks? Yes No

NOTES: _____

_____

F. Exterior Stairs or Steps

1. Do exterior steps have risers no greater than 7" with non-slip treads at least 10" deep? Yes No
2. Do stairs have handrails 32" high as measured from the front of step treads? Yes No
3. Do handrails extend 18" beyond the top and bottom of stairs unless they present an obstruction? Yes No
4. Are steps free of projecting noses? Yes No

5. Do stairs end on a level platform at the top which is at least 5' by 5' and which extends at least 1' beyond each side of the doorway?      Yes   No

NOTES: _____

_____

G. Exterior Doors and Doorways

1. Is there at least one 3' wide door provided at the main entrance to each building?      Yes   No

2. Can doors be opened with no more than 8 pounds of pressure?      Yes   No

3. Is there at least 6'6" maximum separation between outer and inner doors?      Yes   No

4. Do doors have flush thresholds?      Yes   No

5. Do doors have lever type handles mounted no higher than 42" inches?      Yes   No

6. Do doors have kick plates mounted at least 12" high as measured from the bottom of the door?      Yes   No

NOTES: _____

_____

## MOVING ABOUT INSIDE BUILDING

A. Floors

1. Are floors at a common level or connected by a ramp?      Yes   No

2. Are changes in floor levels marked by visual as well as tactile devices?      Yes   No

NOTES: _____

_____

B. Corridors and Hallways

1. Are corridors and hallways at least 5' wide?      Yes   No

2. Are travel routes for the handicapped clearly marked?      Yes   No

3. Are there protruding fixtures in corridors and hallways such as fire extinguishers, telephones and drinking fountains?      Yes   No

4. Are classrooms, laboratories and auxiliary areas clearly and appropriately marked?                                            Yes     No

NOTES: _____

_____


C.  Interior Stairs and Steps

1. Do interior steps have risers no greater than 7" with non-slip treads at least 10" deep?                                    Yes     No

2. Do stairs have handrails 32" high as measured from the front of step treads?                                                  Yes     No

3. Do handrails extend 18" beyond the top and bottom of stairs unless they present an obstruction?                          Yes     No

4. Are steps free of projecting noses?                         Yes     No

5. Do stairs end on a level platform at the top which is at least 5' by 5' and which extends at least 1' beyond each side of the doorway?                                                       Yes     No

NOTES: _____

_____


D.  Ramps

1. Do ramps have a slope no greater than 8.33% or 1 foot rise in 12 feet?                                                          Yes     No

2. Do ramps have smooth handrails located 32" high on both sides if they are not located along the wall?                      Yes     No

3. Do handrails extend 1' beyond the bottom and top of ramps?  Yes     No

4. Do ramps have a non-slip surface?                          Yes     No

NOTES: _____

_____


E.  Movement between Floor Levels

1. Are elevators provided in multi-story buildings?           Yes     No

2. Are wheelchair lifts provided for areas that have drops of 4'6" or less and where there is insufficient space for ramps?     Yes     No

3. Is the elevator cab at least 5 feet by 5 feet?            Yes     No

4. Are elevator controls mounted between 2'11" and 4'6" off the floor?                                                          Yes     No

5. Are elevator controls and signals clearly marked and do they employ both visual and auditory signals?　　　　　　　Yes　　No

6. Do elevator cabs contain a rear-view mirror?　　　　　Yes　　No

NOTES: _____

_____

F. Movement Inside Classrooms and Laboratories

1. Are aisles and traffic lanes at least 3' wide (preferably 4')?　　Yes　　No

2. Are aisles and traffic lanes marked according to OSHA guidelines?　　Yes　　No

3. Are work stations and operator zones around machines and equipment clearly marked?　　　　　　　　　　Yes　　No

NOTES: _____

_____

G. Restrooms

1. Is there at least one barrier-free toilet available for each sex in each vocational building?　　　　　　　　　　Yes　　No

2. Are toilet stalls at least 5'6" x 6' in dimension?　　　Yes　　No

3. Do toilet stalls have grab bars and swing out doors?　　Yes　　No

4. Are there lavoratories mounted high enough to provide 27 1/2" of knee clearance?　　　　　　　　　　Yes　　No

5. Do laboratories have controls mounted no more than 18" from the front?　　　　　　　　　　Yes　　No

6. Are drain pipes and hot water pipes under laboratories insulated or covered?　　　　　　　　　　Yes　　No

7. Are there urinals for men that have basins mounted 19" from the floor?　　　　　　　　　　Yes　　No

8. Are towel racks, towel dispensers and disposal units available and mounted no higher than 40" from the floor?　　Yes　　No

NOTES: _____

_____

H. Drinking Fountains

1. Is there at least one barrier-free fountain available in each building or vocational wing?　　　　　　　　　Yes　　No

2. Are fountains contained in a recessed area of the corridor?    Yes    No

3. Do fountains or water coolers have push-button type hand controls as well as foot controls?    Yes    No

4. Are coolers and fountains mounted so that spouts are no higher than 30" off the floor?    Yes    No

5. Are fountains accessible to people in wheelchairs?    Yes    No

NOTES: _____

_____

I. Telephones

1. Is there at least one barrier-free telephone available in each building?    Yes    No

2. Are telephones mounted no higher than 4'4" in a recessed area of a corridor?    Yes    No

3. Do accessible telephones have adjustable receiver volume devices?    Yes    No

4. Do telephones have push-button controls?    Yes    No

NOTES: _____

_____

J. Vending Machines

1. Are vending machines available which have push-button type controls?    Yes    No

2. Are the coin slots no higher than 4'8" off the floor?    Yes    No

NOTES: _____

_____

K. Cafeterias

1. Do cafeterias have doors at least 34" wide?    Yes    No

2. Do cafeterias have service lanes which are at least 36" wide?    Yes    No

3. Do cafeterias have tray slides mounted 34" off the floor?    Yes    No

4. Are cafeteria tables mounted at least 6' apart?    Yes    No

5. Do cafeteria tables provide at least 27 1/2" of knee space as measured from the floor?    Yes    No

NOTES: _____

_____

L. Work Stations and Study Areas

    1. Are work stations and study areas at least 32" wide?      Yes    No

    2. Do study carrels provide knee space at least 22" in depth and 27 1/2" in height?      Yes    No

NOTES: _____

_____

M. Controls

    1. Are controls and switches for such essentials as light, heat, ventilation, windows, draperies, and fire alarms mounted within reach of student in wheelchairs? (no higher than 5')      Yes    No

NOTES: _____

_____

N. Warning Devices

    1. Do warning devices such as fire alarms and class change systems employ both visual and auditory signals?      Yes    No

NOTES: _____

_____

O. Identification (letters, numerals and symbols)

    1. Are raised or recessed letters, numerals and symbols used to identify rooms and offices?      Yes    No

    2. Are raised or recessed identifiers placed on the wall next to the opening side of the door?      Yes    No

    3. Are door knobs to dangerous areas not designed for normal entry marked with knolls or other warning markings?      Yes    No

    4. Are identifiers mounted between 4'6" and 5'6" off the floor?      Yes    No

NOTES: _____

_____

P. Hazards

    1. Are there low hanging objects such as door closers, ceiling light fixtures, and low-hanging signs that protrude into corridors, doorways and traffic lanes?      Yes    No

    2. Are areas under construction barricaded to prevent entry?      Yes    No

    3. Are emergency exit routes and procedures advertised?      Yes    No

NOTES: _____

_____

# Glossary of Terms

The following terms are operationally defined as they are used in the text of this book.

**Academic disadvantagement:** means that a person (a) lacks reading and writing skills, (b) lacks mathematical skills, or (c) performs below grade level (Public Law 94–482).

**Accessibility:** means that individuals are able to arrive at a vocational facility, enter it, and move about inside the building with little or no assistance.

**Adaptive equipment and aids:** specially designed equipment, jigs, fixtures and other devices that help disabled students function effectively in performing learning and work tasks.

**Advisory or craft committees:** a group of selected persons from a community or area who represent various job groups in an occupational area. For example, a construction trades craft committee is made up of workers, employers, suppliers, etc.

**Advocacy organizations and groups:** individuals who represent and fully support the interests and causes of a specific individual or group of people, as in the case of advocacy groups in support of the rights of the handicapped.

**Affirmative action:** providing the same opportunities and policies for hiring, promoting, and training handicapped job applicants as are available to nonhandicapped applicants.

**Annual goals:** a mandated component of the individualized education program (IEP), annual goals indicate the general direction the handicapped student will follow during the year and describe the performance to be demonstrated at the end of the year.

**Architectural barriers:** obstructions caused by building design and construction that cause a handicapped person extreme difficulty.

**Audiologist:** a trained professional who diagnoses and evaluates hearing losses and fits individuals for hearing aids. Another term often used for this individual is a "hearing clinician."

**Behavior modification:** the shaping of an individual's behavior to eliminate negative behaviors and to reward or emphasize positive behaviors. This shaping occurs as a result of a system of planned and coordinated activities that are developed according to the principles of learning.

**Blind individuals:** people who have a visual disability so severe that they must depend to a great extent on the sense of hearing and touch in the learning process rather than on the sense of sight. There are laws in each state defining the guidelines for legal blindness.

**CETA:** the Comprehensive Employment and Training Act of 1973, Public Law 93–23, as amended in 1978.

**Community manpower survey:** a method of collecting job analysis information by surveying local industries to determine the types and numbers of available jobs, specific skills required for each job, and working conditions.

**Competitive employment:** the state of being employed in an environment in which workers must be able to function as effectively as other workers.

**Cooperative planning process:** coordinated effort by various individuals and agencies to provide a comprehensive and realistic instructional plan for a specific learner.

**Craft committee:** see advisory committee.

**Curb cut:** a break in a continuous curb, providing a sloped walkway or ramp from a parking area to a sidewalk.

**Curriculum modification:** the tailoring of all the experiences and activities encountered in pursuit of occupational preparation under the direction of a school to meet the unique needs of the individual student.

**Deaf:** means a hearing impairment so severe that the individual is impaired in processing linguistic information through hearing, with or without amplification, which adversely affects educational performance (Public Law 94-142, 121 a. 5).

**Dictionary of Occupational Titles (DOT):** an inventory of occupations within our economy prepared by the United States Department of Labor. This resource provides information about the physical demands, working conditions, and aptitudes for a specific job as well as identifying the relationships to people, data and things. The information is collected through observation of workers and job sites by occupational analysts.

**Disadvantaged:** means persons (other than handicapped persons) who: (a) have academic or economic disadvantages and (b) require special services, assistance, or programs in order to enable them to succeed in vocational education programs (Public Law 94-482).

**Due process:** guarantees that a specific procedure be followed in thoroughly evaluating a student thought to be handicapped so that the decision regarding the proper educational placement is in the best interest of the student. Parents are involved at all steps of this evaluation and decision-making process.

**Economic disadvantage:** means (a) family income is at or below national poverty level, (b) participant or parent(s) or guardian of the participant is unemployed, (c) participant or parent of participant is a recipient of public assistance, or (d) participant is institutionalized or under state guardianship (Public Law 94-482).

**Evaluation:** a process that determines the worth of something. It is a judgment arrived at after considering a number of measures of student achievement.

**Extremity:** a limb of the body such as a hand or foot.

**Follow-up:** the process of visiting a special needs employee and employer to provide services and to obtain information upon which to base change.

**Free, appropriate public education:** assures that a special education program with appropriate related services will be developed for each identified handicapped student. The same educational opportunities must be provided for the handicapped as are available to all other students, including access to vocational education programs.

**Gradient:** the rate of regular or graded ascent or descent.

**Grading:** the process of assigning values to student achievement.

**Handicapped individuals:** persons who are mentally retarded, hard-of-hearing, deaf, speech impaired, visually handicapped, seriously emotionally disturbed, crippled, or other health impaired persons who require special education and related services and who, because of their handicapping condition, cannot succeed in the regular vocational education program without special education assistance or who require a modified vocational education program (Public Law 94-482, Section 195).

**Hard-of-hearing:** means a hearing impairment, whether permanent or fluctuating, that adversely affects (an individual's) educational performance but is not included under the definition of "deaf" in this section (Public Law 94-142, 121 a. 5).

**Helping system:** those agencies and advocacy groups that offer services to special needs individuals to help them prepare for productive employment or to function in everyday life activities.

**Homebound job:** a job performed in a special needs individual's home.

**Impairments:** a lack of strength or capability due to damage caused at birth or through injury or disease.

**Individual education program (IEP):** mandated by Public Law 94-142, the Education for All Handicapped Children Act of 1975, this component requires that a written plan of instruction for each handicapped student receiving special education services be developed. The IEP must include a statement of the student's present level of educational performance, annual goals, short-term objectives, specific service needed by the student, dates when these services will begin and end, and specific criteria for evaluation.

A team composed of a representative of the local school system, the student's teacher(s), the parent/guardian and, if appropriate, the student, meets to plan and approve the IEP at least once annually.

**Intelligence quotient (IQ):** the number used to represent an individual's level of mental development. The numerical figure is determined by dividing the mental age (MA) of an individual (e.g., performance on an intelligence test) by the chronological age (CA) and multiplying by 100.

**Interpreter:** a support person, usually for the deaf, who uses finger-spelling and/or sign language to translate what is being said for the deaf individual.

**Itinerant teacher:** a trained professional who travels among schools and/or homes to work with special needs learners who require specific assistance. The role of the itinerant teacher is usually to supply students with appropriate educational materials and equipment and to act as a consultant to teachers who have these learners enrolled in their programs and classes.

**Job analysis:** a procedure providing information on what a worker does, how the job is done, and why it is necessary.

**Labeling:** the practice of attaching a name to a handicapped person that may carry with it a stigma or stereotyped impression of the individual's abilities and limitations (e.g., "mentally retarded," "behavior disordered").

**Learner profile:** information gathered and organized to provide relevant background information pertaining to a particular student. Components usually include information in the following areas: (a) educational/academic/psychological, (b) physical/medical, (c) social/interpersonal relations, and (d) prevocational/vocational.

**Least restrictive environment:** mandated by Public Law 94–142, the Education for All Handicapped Children Act of 1975, this concept gives handicapped students the right to be placed in regular education programs whenever possible so that their abilities are not restricted. Necessary support services and resources must be provided to help them succeed.

**Limited English-speaking ability:** means individuals who were not born in the United States or whose native tongue is a language other than English and/or individuals who came from environments where a language other than English is dominant, and by reasons thereof, have difficulties speaking and understanding instruction in the English language (Public Law 94–482).

**Live work:** an instructional technique that uses real-life materials in the learning process. An example would be the act of repairing television sets for the faculty and student body in a radio-television program.

**Mainstreaming:** the process of serving special needs students within regular school programs with as much support, help and resources as are needed for them to succeed. When referring to handicapped learners this term relates to the concept of "least restrictive environment," which promotes educating handicapped students in regular programs with their peers to the greatest extent possible rather than placing them in segregated classes and/or schools.

**Mentally retarded:** means significantly subaverage general intellectual functioning that exists concurrently with deficits in adaptive behavior, is manifested during the developmental period, and adversely affects (an individual's) education performance (Public Law 94–142, 121 a. 5).

**Modification:** a change in a part of a vocational school facility or some type of equipment, furniture or tool used in an instructional program in order to eliminate a barrier for a handicapped person.

**Multi-handicapped:** means concomitant impairments (such as mentally retarded-blind, mentally retarded-orthopedically impaired, etc.), the combination of which causes such severe educational problems that the individual cannot be accommodated in a special education program designed for just one of the impairments. The term does not include deaf-blind (individuals). (Public Law 94–142, 121 a. 5).

**Negotiate:** the process of being able to move about in a vocational facility.

**Nondiscriminatory testing:** tests used to evaluate special needs learners cannot be racially or culturally biased and must be administered in the language spoken in the student's home.

**Occupational Outlook Handbook:** a publication of the United States Department of Labor that provides information concerning more than 850 occupations in a variety of major industries. Specific information provided for each major job includes: (a) what the job is like, (b) places of employment, (c) personal qualifications, (d) training qualifications, (e) educational qualifications, (f) working conditions, (g) earnings, (h) opportunities for advancement and (i) sources of additional information.

**Occupational therapist:** a trained professional who provides therapy designed to improve, develop or restore functions lost or impaired through illness, injury or deprivation; to improve the ability of the individual to perform tasks for independent functioning when functions are impaired or lost; and to prevent, through early intervention, initial or further impairment or loss of function. (Public Law 94–142, 121 a. 13).

**On-the-job training:** educational and training experiences provided at a job site. For example, a cooperative education student learns work skill behaviors in an actual employment environment.

**Orthopedically impaired:** means a severe orthopedic impairment which adversely affects (an individual's) educational performance. The term includes impairments caused by congenital anomaly (e.g., clubfoot, absence of some member), impairments caused by disease (e.g., poliomyelitis, bone tuberculosis), and impairments from other causes (e.g., cerebral palsy, amputations, and fractures or burns which cause contractures). (Public Law 94–142, 121 a. 5).

**OSHA:** Occupational Safety and Health Administration (an agency that has published safety standards that govern industry.)

**Other health impaired:** means limited strength, vitality or alertness resulting from chronic or acute health problems (such as heart condition, tuberculosis, rheumatic fever, nephritis, asthma, sickle cell anemia, hemophilia, epilepsy, lead poisoning, leukemia, or diabetes) adversely affecting (an individual's) educational performance (Public Law 94–142, 121 a. 5).

**Partially sighted individuals:** people who have limited vision even with corrections such as heavy lenses or surgery.

**Performance testing:** the process of measuring student performance on manipulative tasks or competencies.

**Placement:** the act of being assigned or employed in a specific place.

**Present level of educational performance:** a mandated component of the individualized education program (IEP), this statement includes performance levels in a variety of education content areas including (a) academic achievement, (b) personal-social skills, (c) psychomotor skills, (d) self-help skills, and (e) pre-vocational and vocational skills.

**Prosthesis:** an artificial device to replace a missing part of the body.

**Psychologist:** a trained professional who administers psychological and educational tests, interprets the assessment results, collects pertinent information regarding the individual's behavior and conditions related to learning, consults with other staff members to plan an appropriate educational plan, and provides psychological counseling for students and their parents (Public Law 94–142, 121 a. 13).

**Readability level:** a measure of the reading difficulty level of a specific book or material.

**Reasonable accommodation:** Section 504 of the Rehabilitation Act of 1978 mandates that specific changes be made to the work environment to meet the needs of handicapped workers. These changes must be reasonable and realistic in light of employer capabilities.

**Resource room teacher:** a specialist who works with students having difficulty learning in a regular program environment. This professional also acts as a consultant for regular classroom teachers working with these students, secures appropriate materials, and provides students who come to the resource room at designated times with specialized instruction.

**Self-care skills:** developing an individual's ability to carry out daily living tasks with a minimum amount of assistance. Self-care skills are often called "independent living skills."

**Self-esteem:** picturing oneself as being a good individual.

**Seriously emotionally disturbed:** means a condition exhibiting one or more of the following characteristics over a long period of time and to a marked degree, which adversely affects education performance: (a) an inability to learn that cannot be explained by intellectual, sensory, or health factors; (b) an inability to build or maintain satisfactory interpersonal relationships with peers and teachers; (c) inappropriate types of behavior or feelings under normal circumstances; (d) a general, pervasive mood of unhappiness or depression; or (e) a tendency to develop physical symptoms or fears associated with personal or school problems. The term includes (individuals) who are schizophrenic or autistic. The term does not include (individuals) who are socially maladjusted, unless it is determined that they are seriously emotionally disturbed (Public Law 94–142, 121 a. 5).

**Short-term instructional objectives:** a mandated component of the individualized education program (IEP), short-term instructional objectives are written in behavioral terms and act as specific guidelines for accomplishing the annual goals. These objectives represent intermediate steps between the handicapped learner's present level of educational performance and the annual goals.

**Situational assessment:** a technique that uses observation skills to record the vocational behaviors and work habits that learners exhibit while performing specific work tasks in a simulated or actual job situation. Learners are observed and evaluated while working in a group setting rather than on an individual basis.

**Social worker:** an individual who usually works closely with handicapped and disadvantaged individuals by acting as a liaison between the school and the home. This person collects pertinent information and helps to coordinate the needs of the learner and family with necessary services available from the school and the community.

**Special education teacher:** a trained professional who develops, implements and evaluates programs and services for physically, mentally or emotionally handicapped learners. These programs and services usually include specific learning experiences, instructional techniques and materials that meet the needs of individual students.

**Special needs individuals:** those individuals who need special assistance or services in order to enter a regular vocational education program and successfully complete the requirements. This population includes both handicapped and disadvantaged individuals as well as other groups such as racial group members, persons with limited English-speaking ability, persons in correctional institutes, migrant workers, and persons who are gifted and talented. (The National Center for Research in Vocational Education). These individuals will have difficulty succeeding in vocational education programs without assistance in the form of support services, different teaching techniques and/or specific modifications in vocational programs and facilities.

**Specialist:** a person who is an expert in a specific field.

**Specific learning disability:** means a disorder in one or more of the basic psychological processes involved in understanding or in using language, spoken or written, which may manifest itself in an imperfect ability to listen, think, speak, read, write, spell, or to do mathematical calculations. The term includes such conditions as perceptual handicaps, brain injury, minimal brain disfunction, dyslexia, and developmental aphasia. The term does not include (individuals) who have learning problems that are primarily the result of visual, hearing, or motor handicaps, of mental retardation, or of environmental, cultural, or economic disadvantage (Public Law 94–142, 121 a. 5).

**Speech clinician:** a trained professional who works with individuals who have a speech or language handicap. Specific services provided include speech therapy and speech adjustment.

**Speech impaired:** means a communication disorder, such as stuttering, impaired articulation, a language impairment, or a voice impairment, adversely affecting (an individual's) educational performance (Public Law 94–142, 121 a. 5).

**Support personnel:** individuals who provide specific support for special needs individuals and regular class teachers to enable these learners to succeed in their educational development. Another term that is often used to describe the services provided by support personnel is "related services."

**Tactile:** something that can be read or determined by touch.

**Transition:** moving from one stage or environment to another.

**Visually handicapped:** means a visual impairment that, even with correction, adversely affects (an individual's) educational performance. The term includes both partially sighted and blind (individuals). (Public Law 94–142, 121 a. 5).

**Vocational assessment:** a process that provides information relating to an individual's vocational potential through real work situations and/or simulated work activities.

**Vocational evaluator:** a trained individual who administers and interprets vocational assessment tests and other varieties of vocational evaluation activities and procedures.

**Vocational rehabilitation:** located in every state, this government agency provides services such as assessment and diagnosis, guidance, training, physical restoration and placement to handicapped individuals. The general objective of these services is to prepare this population for employment and independent living.

**Work adjustment:** behaviors that must be learned in order to function effectively with fellow workers and job supervisors.

**Work habits:** behaviors related to work that are demonstrated without conscious thought, such as dependability, initiative, and loyalty.

**Work samples:** activities that simulate real work tasks and are closely associated with actual jobs in the labor market. They emphasize performance skills rather than verbal or written skills and incorporate the tools and standards associated with the actual job.

**Work-study coordinator:** an individual who supervises students working on a job part-time and attending classes at school for the remainder of the time. This person becomes the liaison between the school and the world of work.

## References

Kelly, L. and Vergason, G. *Dictionary of special education and rehabilitation.* Denver, Colorado: Love Publishing Company, 1978.

# INDEX